Tuning and Customizing a Linux System

DANIEL L. MORRILL

Apress™

Tuning and Customizing a Linux System

ISBN 978-1-893115-27-9

Technical Reviewer: Douglas Kilpatrick

Editorial Directors: Dan Appleman, Peter Blackburn, Gary Cornell, Jason Gilmore, Simon Hayes, Karen Watterson, John Zukowski

Managing Editor: Grace Wong

Development Editor and Indexer: Valerie Perry

Copy Editors: Kim Goodfriend, Ami Knox, Nicole LeClerc

Production Editor: Kari Brooks

Compositor: Diana Van Winkle, Van Winkle Design Group

Artist: Cara Brunk, Blue Mud Productions

Cover Designer: Kurt Krames

Manufacturing Manager: Tom Debolski

Marketing Manager: Stephanie Rodriguez

Distributed to the book trade in the United States by Springer-Verlag New York, Inc., 175 Fifth Avenue, New York, NY, 10010 and outside the United States by Springer-Verlag GmbH & Co. KG, Tiergartenstr. 17, 69112 Heidelberg, Germany.

In the United States, phone 1-800-SPRINGER, email orders@springer-ny.com, or visit http://www.springer-ny.com.

Outside the United States, fax +49 6221 345229, email orders@springer.de, or visit http://www.springer.de.

For information on translations, please contact Apress directly at 2560 9th Street, Suite 219, Berkeley, CA 94710. Phone 510-549-5930, fax: 510-549-5939, email info@apress.com, or visit http://www.apress.com.

The source code for this book is available to readers at http://www.apress.com in the Downloads section. You will need to answer questions pertaining to this book in order to successfully download the code.

To Aimee Morgan, who has always wanted to see her name in a bookstore.
This will have to do . . . for now.

Contents at a Glance

Contents

Part Three
Installing Software...171

Chapter 7   *Installing and Configuring Software* *173*

Chapter 8   *OpenSSH Secure Shell* *195*

Chapter 15 A Corporate Software Development Environment 327

Appendix *414*

Index *419*

About the Author

Dan Morrill holds a master's degree in computer science and currently works as a researcher at GE's Global Research Center in upstate New York. He is skilled in a wide variety of software development areas, from real-time and embedded systems development, to desktop applications, to web infrastructure and applications. He has been using Unix systems since 1994 and has used Linux systems exclusively since 1998. Before being Enlightened, he used other operating systems, including IBM's OS/2, Microsoft's Windows, and various Unix platforms.

Dan lives in a modest house filled with far too many toys for his own good and delights in tinkering with them all. Sometimes they even survive.

About the
Technical Reviewer

Douglas Kilpatrick has been working with Unix systems since 1992 and Linux systems since 1993. While he does have a beard, he offically denies rumors that he wears suspenders. Douglas has been working in the field of computer security for the last 4 years and has taken to random fits of maniacal laughter when the subject is raised.

Acknowledgments

First, I must thank the staff at Apress, especially the editors, whose patience and professionalism are like unto angels. If true quality takes time, this had better be the best book ever written, because they certainly waited long enough.

I am also indebted to my parents, Kevin and Carolyn Morrill, who set the stage for that fateful day when the busy glow of my own computer monitor first lit upon my face. Thanks for the support, then and since.

Sometimes it seems as if much of my success was inspired by others whose talent so vastly surpassed mine. Without these people and the professional milestones to which they drove me, this book would not exist, and so I must thank: Vincent Kane, for shaming me into learning programming; Chris "Hocy" Ho, for shaming me into learning Slackware; Douglas Kilpatrick, for shaming me into learning C; Richard Arthur, for shaming me into learning software engineering; David Czarnecki, for shaming me into starting a book; and Aimee Morgan, for shaming me into completing it.

And finally, to my colleagues at GE—both current and former—I can say only this: YLB. YPM.

Preface

Back in 1991, a Finnish computer science student named Linus Torvalds needed a Unix-like operating system for his studies. As an interesting intellectual exercise (and because he was a bit strapped for cash!) he decided to write his own Unix system, rather than buy one of the commercial versions. Linus began working with other developers, and in short order, they had the core of an operating system and the beginnings of the Linux phenomenon.

Since then, and especially in the past couple of years, Linux's fame (and indeed, its notoriety) has grown tremendously. Some might even say that Linux's ascent has reached the level of "buzzword." It's become a common topic in many technology companies' boardrooms: "Do we have a Java strategy?" "Forget that—do we have a *Linux* strategy?!" Ultimately, though, Linux's success began—and in a real sense, ends—with its users. With no "market strategy" or corporate backing, the advent of Linux was fueled solely by its millions of satisfied users.

What This Book Covers

Whether or not you're a current user of a Linux system, chances are you've still heard a lot about what such systems can do for you. From the server to the desktop, and from corporate applications to home uses, the diversity of software that Linux supports is exciting, but it can also be bewildering, especially for new and intermediate users.

So, when it comes to Linux systems, the most common question I hear is, "I just installed Linux on my computer! What do I do now?" Makers of Linux distributions have streamlined the installation and management chores enough so that pretty much anyone can install a Linux system. These days, the real trick is learning how to bend the system to your will. Linux systems offer a huge amount of flexibility and power, but they also offer a huge amount of complexity that can be tricky to master.

If you're an expert Linux user, you can make the system do pretty much whatever you want to, if you're persistent enough. This mastery comes through understanding how Linux (and in general, Unix) systems are laid out, and the most common patterns and techniques for accomplishing things. This book has two goals: to convey an understanding of these techniques and patterns, and to provide enough working knowledge so that you'll be able to tackle any task you want to complete, even if it's not covered directly in this book. In essence, this book aims to teach you how Linux systems are built, and how they "think" and operate.

Now, this book isn't a reference. There's just so much you can do with a Linux system that any comprehensive reference would be encyclopedic in length, which this book most certainly is not. This book is also not a tutorial. Many excellent books have been written that can guide you through the process of installing a Linux system, configuring it, and getting around in it. This book will teach you the next step beyond that: how to live and work in a Linux system.

This book will generally not explain every step of a task; it assumes you already know how to complete the most basic tasks. For example, this book doesn't describe how to extract tarballs (.tar.gz archive files); it assumes that you already know how to do this. If you're a power user with some experience with a Unix-like system, or even with another system such as Microsoft's Windows, this shouldn't be a problem for you at all. If you're a beginner or are completely new to Unix-like systems, though, you might need a second reference to augment this book that, dealing with how to install your system and perform basic tasks.

It's also worth stressing that this book focuses on providing you with general skills and tools that can be applied to any distribution. That is, while this book absolutely strives to cover the most current versions of all the software it discusses, the object isn't really to discuss any particular version of software. You'll hopefully find the knowledge you gain from this book to be applicable to any version of any distribution—even versions that come out after this book was published. For example, this book covers Slackware Linux 8.0; however, Slackware Linux 8.1 was released just before the publication process was completed. Despite this, you'll find the material on Slackware 8.0 very relevant anyway, and applicable to later versions of Slackware Linux, including version 8.1 and beyond.

What You Will Learn

This book is divided into four parts. Part One, "Background," covers some of the basic issues related to Linux systems, such as the nature of free and open source software, and some general aspects of what goes into a Linux distribution. Part One will give you a healthy introduction to the "Zen" of the Linux world.

Part Two, "Linux Distributions," introduces the notion of a "Linux distribution." After outlining the nuts and bolts of a distribution, I discuss three actual sample distributions in detail. These chapters in Part Two illustrate different approaches, techniques, and solutions to the problem of constructing a Linux system. Part Two will help you break through the surface of a Linux system and sink your teeth into the meat below. If you read it all the way through, you will be substantially familiar with the details of some of the most popular Linux distributions, and you will be well equipped to deal with any other Linux (or even any

Unix-like!) system you encounter in the future. You'll also be able to quickly understand any changes made to the existing distributions down the road as new versions are released.

Part Three, "Installing Software," builds on the material in Part Two to teach you how to install software on your system. That is, while Part Two teaches you the nuts and bolts of the system, Part Three teaches you how to tweak and customize the system, within the constraints of the distribution. The examples in these chapters in Part Three demonstrate most of the common techniques for installing software, so if you read and internalize them all you should be ready to start bending your system to your will, so that you can get real work done with the software you need.

Part Four, "Case Studies," in turn builds on the material in Part Three and demonstrates several different case studies of Linux systems. Each chapter in Part Four discusses an actual, real-world usage of a Linux system. These chapters really illustrate where the rubber meets the road, by showing how the same stock system can be customized to fit a wide variety of needs. If you read or skim these chapters, you will have gone a long way indeed toward mastering Linux systems.

So, what will you learn? Well, if you really think about it, you're building a house of knowledge. Part One surveys the lay of the land, Part Two builds the foundation, Part Three frames in the walls and ceiling, and Part Four installs the details and makes the house into a home. At least, that is the intent. I hope you'll agree!

What You Will Not Learn

After you've been using your Linux-based system for a while, you'll inevitably encounter something that this book doesn't prepare you for. (For example, you may want to install TrueType fonts on a Slackware Linux system, which is not explicitly discussed in this book.) There is, of course, no way for a single book to cover every possible scenario; however, we all know that up-front. For that reason, this book doesn't focus on being an encyclopedic reference (which I've already said), but instead tries to provide you with the basic skills you need to be self-sufficient. So, when you encounter your next thorny obstacle, draw on the *general* techniques and approaches in this book, rather than specific examples. With this knowledge and a little experience, you'll master your system in no time!

Here's a bit of advice, though. Some people say that it's better to know what every tool in your toolbox is used for, rather than mastering just a few; you can learn what you need to know about each tool as you need to know it. Each Linux system has its own toolbox of software, patterns, and techniques for doing things, and so it helps to know this toolbox well. (For example, Red Hat's chkconfig and service tools, which are discussed in Chapter 4, are very convenient, but if you don't know about them you'll never use them.)

In other words, it pays to know your distribution; know what tools are provided and what they do. That's really the guiding philosophy of this book: Know your toolbox. The most important thing you can do is have is the courage to explore your tools and your Linux system!

What You Will Need

To use this book and benefit from its examples, you'll need a computer with a Linux distribution installed on it. You'll be able to use this book no matter which distribution you have, but you will have to handle the installation yourself. See the chapters in Part Two for information on several common, popular distributions.

As for the computer hardware itself, almost any configuration will suffice; one of the beauties of Linux is that it will run on relatively modest hardware configurations. With one exception, every distribution, software package, and case study discussed in this book was installed and run on a system consisting of a middle-of-the-road processor, 128MB of memory, and a 30GB hard drive; this entire system (including a high-quality monitor!) was purchased for less than $1,000. While you wouldn't want to use this configuration for a production-level, enterprise-class server, it more than suffices for most uses—and it was even used exclusively to write this book. Oh, and the exception? Well, that was the firewall case study in Chapter 16, which was run on even more modest hardware.

Linux systems can unchain you from your PC and let you focus on actually making your computer solve your problems. Like all freedoms, though, this one is sometimes easy and sometimes challenging, but it's always exciting. This book will help you along that path. Congratulations on taking the Linux plunge; good luck, good reading, and happy computing! Try not to have *too* much fun along the way . . . .

Part One

Background

Part One of this book provides some background information on Linux, free software, and open source software. You'll learn about where Linux comes from, both historically and ideologically. While this is important material, it isn't really crucial to the true purpose of this book, which is tuning and customizing a Linux System. So, if you are already familiar with this material, or if you're just not interested, feel free to skip ahead to Part Two.

CHAPTER 1

The Physiology
of Linux

Linux is an operating system, but it's also representative of a lot more. In some ways, Linux is the champion of a set of ideals. Whether you buy into these ideals is a separate issue from whether you use the technology, of course, but nonetheless a complete understanding of Linux and Linux-based systems requires at least an awareness of the legacy. So, this chapter will slow down a bit and start things off right by describing a bit of the history that led to Linux.

When you spend enough time in the technical trenches, you tend to forget where you came from. That is, you spend so much of your time using your knowledge, that you lose some of the wonder you felt when you first picked it up. However, if you're even reading this book at all, you're probably pretty excited, or at least curious, about Linux. You've still got that sense of adventure, and you want to know everything there is to know about this "Linux thing." In the end, this book fails if it doesn't leave the reader filled with the sense of power and coolness that Linux systems provide.

A large part of that coolness derives from Linux's colorful and rather prestigious pedigree; any true Linux guru understands the history and culture of Linux just as implicitly as she understands init levels, C libraries, and package managers. So, this chapter will cover some of the history and culture of Linux. If you're already familiar with the background of Linux (or if you're still just not interested) feel free to skim or skip the remainder of Part One.

The Origins of Linux

If you go back far enough, you find that the history of Linux is closely tied to the history of Unix, and even to the history of computing. The history of Unix is an interesting one, as Unix has had a subtle yet mind-bogglingly large impact on computing in general. All roads lead to Unix, so to speak. Around 1971, AT&T's Bell Labs group developed the first incarnation of Unix (which was originally known as Unics or Uniplexed Information and Computing System) Unix' name was a pun on Multics, a more complex forerunner of Unix. For a while, Unix had very limited exposure. It was used primarily within AT&T, for internal purposes.

Eventually, it was released as a product to the world at large, and started to build momentum. AT&T's Unix reached its pinnacle in the version dubbed System V (as in "System Five," and sometimes abbreviated as SysV). Perhaps inevitably, though, offshoots and derivatives started appearing.

In 1978, the University of California at Berkeley released an operating system known as the Berkeley Systems Distribution, or BSD, which was very much like Unix. The reasons for this divergence varied. There were issues with the license for the source code that AT&T required for Unix; some people argued that AT&T was not being proactive enough in enhancing and improving key aspects of System V Unix. But whatever the reasons, BSD became tremendously popular, and became the basis for many other offshoots.

When the dust settled (if it can truly be said to have settled, even today), most of the offshoot Unix "flavors" provided by various vendors were derived from either SysV Unix, BSD, or a hybrid of both. Additionally, a specification known as POSIX was created by the IEEE (Institute of Electrical and Electronics Engineers, Inc.) to attempt to codify the common features of these various offshoots into a single standard.

Today, there are a great many flavors of Unix competing with one another. Each major hardware vendor generally has it's own flavor, and there are several free flavors as well. Among commercial vendors, IBM has AIX, Hewlett-Packard has HP-UX, Compaq has Tru64 Unix, SGI has Irix, Sun Microsystems has Solaris, and this list is not even comprehensive. Even Microsoft had a flavor, called Xenix, and there are tools to provide a Unix-like environment on top of Microsoft's Windows operating systems.

The free versions of Unix include several offshoots of BSD (FreeBSD, NetBSD, and OpenBSD) and, of course, Linux. Linux and the free BSD systems are similar in origin and intent, but vary widely in focus and ideology. Linux systems appear to have the greater industry momentum, but otherwise they are fairly similar (until you get under the hood, at least). Just to add even more confusion, there is a commercial cousin of the free BSD operating systems called BSDi. You can make a few interesting observations about these offshoots. Perhaps most noteworthy is that the commercial vendors' flavors generally run exclusively on the vendors' own hardware architectures. (Even Sun, which had an Intel version of their Solaris flavor, has not had great success with it, by most accounts.) The free flavors, in contrast, have each been ported to several different platforms. Linux, for example, has been ported to the Intel, Alpha, PowerPC, SPARC, MIPS, ARM, Motorola m68k, IBM S/390 architectures, and even other more exotic platforms. NetBSD, meanwhile, runs on even more architectures than Linux!

Many pundits have described this colorful bag of flavors as the fragmentation of Unix. It is hard to decide which of these "fragments" is the best—which operating system is best for a given application is pretty subjective and variable. Some platforms win at database applications, others win at web server performance, and still others win at numerical scientific computing.

However, the free operating systems are really starting to shake things up. Initially dismissed as irrelevant, or cited by the pundits as simply further examples of the fragmentation of Unix, these operating systems (and Linux in particular) have actually shown signs of reversing the fragmentation of Unix. That is, almost every major vendor of Unix flavors has begun to embrace Linux to a greater or lesser degree. At the time of this writing, the only holdout appears to be Sun Microsystems, which is perhaps not surprising, since Sun's Solaris is arguably the most successful commercial Unix flavor available.

Of course, it's by no means a foregone conclusion that Linux will "defragment" the Unix landscape. However, the rate at which traditional Unix vendors are adopting Linux strategies is striking. Curious readers may justifiably ask why. Well, the primary reason is, of course, the same reason this book exists: because Linux represents quality, flexible, powerful, and free software, and businesses are just as interested in these things as are readers of this book. However, it's also possible that the Unix vendors have begun to realize that developing and maintaining a Unix-like operating system is a very expensive proposition, and is usually not profitable. (Most hardware vendors make their profits on the systems and services they sell, not the operating systems they sell with them.) Rather than compete with each other in a sort of computing arms race, many businesses are choosing to reduce their development costs by adopting Linux, and focusing their competition where it matters: on the hardware. In the end, though, it's hard to generalize the market strategies of large corporations as we just have, so you can find as many opinions on the matter as there are pundits.

The Unix Trademark

The term "Unix" is actually a trademarked name. Only the original, AT&T version of Unix can properly be called "Unix"; the offshoots (including BSD) are "Unix-like." The actual owner of the "Unix" trademark is the Open Group (at www.opengroup.org). Among other things, they attempt to promote and certify compliance of standard Unix systems. However, the most direct descendant of the original AT&T Unix is probably Caldera's UnixWare product.

The Nature of an Operating System

All this talk of flavors and the Unix alphabet soup is probably making you wonder what the difference is between all of them. If you've heard anything at all about

Linux in the media, you've probably heard it described in a number of (sometimes inaccurate) ways: "Alternative Operating System," "Upstart OS," or "Competitor to Microsoft Operating Software." These are true to a degree, but like so many other things, it unfortunately depends on how you define an operating system, and on how you define Linux itself.

The technical definition of an *operating system* is generally accepted to be a piece of software that performs resource and process management tasks for application software. Now, that's a pretty dry definition, so let's break it down a bit into the following categories:

- Resources

- Kernel

- System libraries

Resources

A *resource* is anything that an application might want to make use of. System memory, hard disk drives, serial ports, video cards, display adapters, and network cards are all examples of resources that need to be managed—essentially, any hardware in the computer. The operating system must manage these resources—and protect them! On multiuser systems you don't want hostile users to be able to access your resources and data, and even on single-user systems you don't want one program's mistake to crash an innocent "byte-stander." To this list of resources, you can actually add the CPU (or CPUs, if you have a multi-processor computer). A CPU can only execute one instruction at a time, so if multiple programs need to run at the same time, they have to be managed. This management of the CPU and the related tasks of managing which program gets to run on the CPU in what order (and how to start new programs) is called *process management.*

So, in a nutshell, an operating system generally only has to provide a framework that a user's application software can run within. This definition doesn't say anything at all about a graphical user interface (GUI), or even any user interface at all. However, since a computer system isn't really usable without these features, many people extend the definition of an operating system to include some kind of user interface. Generally, then, an operating system is usually split into two parts: the kernel (sometimes called the monitor, among other things) and the system libraries.

The Kernel

The *kernel* is the part of the operating system that fulfills the core parts of the definition. The kernel manages I/O, system memory, the disk drives, and any other hardware that's been put into the system, and also performs process management (i.e., starting and multitasking programs). The kernel can be thought of as the bare-bones framework that everything else depends on and runs within. Since the kernel (by definition) does not include a user interface, users never see or interact with it directly; in a very real sense, kernels are indistinguishable from the perspective of end users, except insofar as one kernel may appear to perform better than another. (Kernels are, of course, very different from the perspective of software developers.)

System Libraries

The *system libraries* are what truly distinguish operating systems from each other. These are the tools and programs that actually implement the basic system services, such as a GUI, or a text interface. These are the libraries that actually make the system usable. However, these libraries do not provide any actual programs; for example, an email client or web browser would not be part of the system libraries, but would instead be considered a user application.

Confused?

If you're a bit (or a lot!) confused by this mincing of words, you're not alone. This is just one author's way of describing these concepts. In practice, different operating systems actually draw these boundaries in different places. Where kernel space ends and user space begins varies by product, and sometimes even by product version. In other words, the definition of an operating system can vary by operating system vendor. Different operating systems have equally different architectures, and you generally don't need to care about the architecture of any system other than your own. So, the next question is, "What about Linux?"

Is Linux an Operating System?

Strictly speaking, Linux is "merely" a kernel. That is, Linux is a piece of software that manages resources and processes, but provides no system libraries or user interface. Since Linux is just a kernel, it requires a set of system libraries to become a useful environment.

If Linux is just a kernel, where do these system libraries come from? Who writes them? Who maintains them? Obviously, whoever maintains these libraries makes a huge contribution to Linux systems in general. In the vast majority of Linux installations, the system libraries are the GNU utilities, written and maintained by the Free Software Foundation.

Linux and GNU

The Free Software Foundation (FSF) is an organization founded by Richard Stallman of MIT's Media Lab. The Free Software Foundation has had a huge impact on the Internet and the world of computing, but perhaps their two greatest contributions are GNU and the GNU General Public License. (GNU stands for "GNU's Not Unix!" Watch out for that recursive acronym, it's a mind-bender.) In their own words from their web site:

"The Free Software Foundation (FSF) is dedicated to eliminating restrictions on copying, redistribution, understanding, and modification of computer programs. We do this by promoting the development and use of free software in all areas of computing—but most particularly, by helping to develop the GNU operating system."

The GNU project was founded in 1983 and is intended to be nothing less than a full-fledged operating system, including a kernel, system libraries, and a comprehensive set of useful user applications. However, back in the late '80s and early '90s, GNU lacked a kernel. The kernel is like the keystone of an arch, and without it, the ideal of GNU as a full-fledged operating system was incomplete.

In 1991, Linus Torvalds (then a college student) began writing a Unix-like operating system kernel, because he was dissatisfied with the existing free options, and, like so many of us in our college days, too cash-strapped to buy a commercial system. Linus' kernel (eventually called Linux) began evolving quickly. When Linus chose to release his kernel under the GNU General Public License, it filled the gap left in the GNU project; while GNU provided the system libraries and user applications, it was not a complete operating system without a kernel. With Linux's "mere finishing stroke," GNU became a reality. Of course, in recent years the GNU projects own kernel (called the HURD) has matured immensely, and is close to the point where it can be used to replace Linux in actual systems.

When this occurred, it caused quite a stir in the academic community. Perhaps unfortunately, Linus and his Linux kernel garnered the lion's share of the accolades at the expense of the GNU software that made the overall system a reality, and people began speaking of "Linux systems." Now, a decade later, we have reached the point where people speak of the "Linux phenomenon" and the "Linux operating system."

Other Possibilities

If Linux is just a kernel, and GNU is just a set of libraries, then they should be interchangeable, right? Perhaps you could replace Linux with a different kernel, and have a GNU system based on something else. Or, perhaps you could use the Linux kernel with a different set of system libraries, and have some other environment running on the Linux kernel. This section will describe some of the cooler things you can do with Linux.

In fact, interchanging both kernel and system libraries is possible, in theory and sometimes in practice. For example, it might be possible to replace the GNU libraries with the system libraries developed for, say, FreeBSD. In that case, you might have a BSD/Linux system. Or, you could compile the GNU libraries for the Solaris kernel, and have a GNU/Solaris system. Meanwhile, the GNU project is continuing work on its HURD kernel, and already has a functional distribution based on Debian (see Chapter 6) that runs on the HURD instead of Linux.

This can get even more exotic, if you branch outside the realm of Unix-like system libraries. For example, Apple recently released their OS X version of their operating system for the Macintosh. The core of this project is known as Darwin, and is based on BSD. There is a group working to port Darwin to the Linux kernel. Meanwhile, Transvirtual Technologies, Inc. produces an open-source Java virtual machine known as Kaffe. They have a related effort called PocketLinux to produce a Java operating environment by using Kaffe as essentially the system library running on a Linux kernel, for embedded devices such as PDAs.

The possibilities are endless, and in fact there are a lot of efforts out there for merging various products and running Linux in many unique ways, with many types of environments and system libraries. Some of these are more theoretical than others (for example, Linux/BSD would probably be extremely difficult in practice), but it's definitely one of the cooler aspects of Linux and free software.

GNU and Linux: The Operating System of Champions

Moving back into more concrete territory, perhaps you're still not sure what all the Linux hoopla is really about. You probably already believe that Linux systems are pretty useful and becoming extremely popular, or you wouldn't be reading this right now. But, you may not really understand why this is true. What is it about Linux systems that are so much better than other Unix flavors? Well, this entire book is really the answer to that question; once you're done reading it, you'll understand all the exciting and useful things Linux lets you do. However, this section will take a first stab at answering this question, and describe some of Linux's most positive attributes in broad strokes.

As a child, Linux was taught the virtue of practicality. Now, as Linux reaches adulthood, those values are what make Linux systems so remarkably versatile and effective. All metaphors aside, Linux systems are really the most practical operating systems money can buy (and the best things in life are free!) Linux systems let you do anything you can do with any other Unix-like system, and frequently offer more features in doing so.

The popular phrase describing how open source projects get started is that developers are "scratching an itch." That is, a software developer finds she needs a tool, and that there either isn't an existing tool that fills the need, the existing tools are inadequate, or perhaps the tools are simply too expensive. There can be any number of reasons for why a developer would want to write a particular piece of software, but in most cases a developer starts or joins a project because she needs the software she's writing, or the feature she's adding.

So, nearly every piece of software commonly found installed on Linux systems was written from the ground up to fulfill a particular need. The features and quality of this software reflect these origins; in general, the tools you find on a Linux system are usually very robust and feature-complete, especially when compared to the equivalent tools on commercial systems.

The ls Program

As a very simple example this notion of "scratching an itch," consider the ubiquitous ls program. Every commercial Unix flavor has a version of the directory listing program ls; it's a fundamental part of the user interface. However, ls is an extremely straightforward program to write, and so once Unix vendors have a working version, most don't bother to improve on it. After all, software development is an expensive activity, and Unix vendors can get a better return on their investment by focusing on adding features that they can charge a premium for, instead of improving small programs in minor ways.

However, most Linux systems use the GNU color-ls program as their version of ls. color-ls is just a typical version of ls that adds the capability to display color-coded directory listings. This is eye candy; pretty colors don't add a whole lot of value to the totality of an operating system. However, in its niche, it is a very useful feature to have; after you use it for a while, you'll probably get attached enough to it that when you have to use another commercial Unix that doesn't have it installed, you'll actually notice the lack.

gzip, bzip2, tar, and vim

Of course, the ls program is not the only example of a Linux program that "scratches an itch." In fact, the examples are literally too numerous to list. The GNU gzip and bzip2 file compression utilities have better compression rates than most commercial equivalents. GNU tar has built-in support for handling Unix compress and gzip archives, so users don't need to use zcat. GNU's version of the make utility has extended syntax that makes software development easier. Many Linux systems ship with vim (VI iMproved), which is compatible with standard vi programs but offers many useful extensions. GNU provides a set of tools known as autoconf that make porting and installing software on disparate Unix systems much easier. The GNOME and KDE desktop environments are orders of magnitude more sophisticated and usable than the desktops used on most Unix systems.

The Secret of Success

Are you beginning to see the pattern? People usually hear that Linux is "a flavor of Unix" and immediately lump it in with all the other flavors. Pundits sometimes dismiss it as a fad, since, as everyone knows, "Unix" is not user-friendly. Yet the reality is that Linux systems, almost literally point-for-point, are equally robust and have more features than other Unix systems.

What this all boils down to is that these little features add up to make Linux one of the top Unix-like user environments. Many companies use Linux as their base development platform when writing Unix software, since the tools are so much better; other Unix flavors are "ports." Many individual professionals, when confronted with a non-Linux system that they must use, start out by installing the GNU tools on the system, to improve their work environment. (There are even ports of the GNU tools to Microsoft Windows systems!) This is quite an impressive accomplishment for developers who are "scratching itches."

This itch scratching business isn't a silver bullet, of course, and a good user environment does not automatically provide for performance and scalability.

The lack of the guiding mandate that corporations have (not to mention lack of funding!) means that Linux has historically lagged behind commercial Unix flavors in terms of high-end "enterprise" computing support. Since precious few individual developers have 32-processor systems with 8GB of memory, precious few developers are itching to get Linux running on such systems. This is changing, however, as the smarter Unix companies out there are noticing that their employees are using Linux systems at home, and sometimes at work. Smart management is to leverage what is good, even if it's better than your own product, and businesses have itches too.

The Zen of the Platform

Linux vendors produce different operating systems based on the Linux kernel and various other software, such as the GNU tools and libraries. Frequently, however, you hear people in the IT industry refer to "platforms" in various ways. Occasionally, sometimes you can even hear someone refer to the different Linux distributions as platforms. Before we delve into the remainder of the book, it's worthwhile to take a moment to talk about platforms.

The term *platform* is an overloaded buzzword, but in the end it's just a word people use to refer to an overall system that allows them to get their work done. So, the term platform encompasses both hardware and software. Microsoft Windows running on an Intel processor is a platform (sometimes called "Wintel"), and a Linux system running on an Intel is another, different platform, even though it could be the same hardware.

An interesting thing to note is that a platform is both the operating system, as well as the hardware running the operating system. For many platforms (and most Unix platforms), the hardware manufacturer also makes the software. For example, the typical Solaris platform consists of Sun Microsystems' Solaris running on a SPARC processor, also manufactured by Sun.

However, Linux is an exception to this rule. Recall that the Linux kernel has been ported to an amazing number of hardware architectures. The first version was for the Intel architecture, and that's still where Linux is strongest. However, it also runs extremely well on Compaq's Alpha, IBM/Motorola's PowerPC, and Sun's SPARC processors, as well as many others.

So what, you ask? Well, you may have noticed by now that one of our recurring themes is that your computer should do what you need it to; if it doesn't, it's just a waste of time and material. If you just need it to work, do you really care how it works? Does it matter if you have the latest MHz processor, or the best video card, or the biggest hard drive, if all you want to do is check your email and browse the web while running a web server in the background? Do you need to upgrade to the latest hardware every time it changes?

Well, maybe the answer is yes; only you can decide that for yourself. However, for many—perhaps even most—of us, the answer is a resounding "No!" For these people, it doesn't matter what the computer is actually made up of—it could be Windows running on an Intel chip, or it could be Linux running on a SPARC. As long as the email client and web server run when you need them to, most people won't even notice the difference.

Again, you ask, so what? How is this relevant? It's relevant because it illustrates one of the important, almost Zen-like qualities of Linux systems: that as long as the system works, it doesn't matter how. Once you've mastered an operating system, it doesn't really matter what the "platform" is. The author's primary workstation is Red Hat Linux running on a 533MHz Compaq Alpha 21164PCA. With only two exceptions, every single topic covered in this book works on that system, as well as the Intel-based testbed system used to develop the content. The reason is because a Linux system is a Linux system no matter where it runs.

Once you've mastered the material in this book, you'll be self-sufficient on Linux systems. Moreover, you'll be self-sufficient on any Linux *platform*, and it just won't make any difference to you anymore. It's quite refreshing to be able to step out of the rat race in the mainstream PC world, and be able to make your system work, the way you want it to, with a minimum of fuss.

The GNU/Linux vs. Linux Debate

In strict terms of total lines of code, the Linux kernel is only a fraction of the code that makes up a full-fledged system; code from the GNU project is a crucially important part of the Linux-based operating systems that people use every day. So, it might be more accurate to describe such systems as GNU systems, or GNU/Linux systems as a compromise. Such terms reflect the major contribution that the GNU project has made to the success of Linux.

Unfortunately, the damage is done. A decade of momentum is hard to reverse, and the common name for such systems has become, simply, Linux. Once the media begins using a term, however inaccurately, it enters the public discourse, and the act of insisting on a more accurate name itself becomes an oddity. This phenomenon presents books such as this one with a thorny dilemma. The goal of a book is to be accurate and detailed, yet it must be accurate in both meaning and usage. Is it more accurate to refer to a Linux-based system as Linux as in common usage, or to use the more correct but less widely recognized term GNU/Linux?

The GNU/Linux vs. Linux debate has been a heated one in the community, and is the source of a lot of hard feelings. And rightfully so: no one likes to have the magnitude of their contributions diluted by a single, small part of the whole, just as no one likes to have their integral contributions smothered by the whole.

All that we can do is attempt to be as accurate as possible, given the constraints. So, this book refers to GNU/Linux systems as Linux-based systems, or Linux systems for brevity. Hopefully this strikes a balance between accuracy and approachability.

References

If you're interested in the history of Unix, start with the Unix FAQ for the newsgroups `comp.unix.questions` and `comp.unix.shell`. Chapter 6 of that document provides a fairly comprehensive summary of the lineages of various Unix flavors, as well as additional references.

The best source for information on the Free Software Foundation and the GNU project (including the HURD) is their web site at `www.fsf.org`.

More information about Darwin on Linux can be found at `www.darwinlinux.org`; similarly, information on Transvirtual's PocketLinux is at `www.pocketlinux.com`.

An amusing insight into the motivations and goals of Linux can be found in an online Usenet exchange between Andy Tanenbaum (the creator of Minix) and Linus Torvalds. This discussion can be found on various web sites; simply search for "Linus vs. Tanenbaum" or "Linux is Obsolete" at your favorite web search engine. This discussion thread, when read today, is an amazing look back at the beginning of the whole "Linux revolution."

CHAPTER 2

An Open
Source Primer

Linux systems are generally *open source* software, meaning that their source code is readily available and freely redistributable. However, many people don't understand what it actually means to be open source; even more, many people don't understand just how fundamental the open source ethos is to the evolution of Linux. This chapter will discuss open source and free software, and explore what these concepts mean to GNU and Linux. Readers who are already well versed in open source and free software may wish to skim or skip this chapter, and move on to Chapter 3.

The Nature of Software

There is a great deal of passion and rhetoric surrounding open source and free software. There are several basic arguments that appear in various forms, which establish the foundations for open source and free software. The philosophical issue of free software remains largely subjective, and an argument that one person considers valid may not work for someone else. In other words, it's a touchy issue. This section will attempt to outline the basic tenets of the various following arguments, as objectively as possible. However, readers should take this section with a grain of salt, and remember that it's just one humble author's perspective.

Software development isn't easy. It takes knowledge and skill, and most of all, time. For these reasons, software development has a cost. For commercial organizations, it's expensive financially; even for free software developers, it's expensive in terms of effort. For these reasons, it makes a lot of sense to share as much as possible. In that respect, software development is just like any other scientific or technical discipline. Scientists share information about their work with one another, and work together as a community to advance the state of the art, building on each others' work.

In contrast, companies have a profit motive, and strive to make as much profit as they can. Companies that sell products must, of course, perform the research and development that creates these products. However, companies have no motive to share this information with anyone else; after all, if they did, another organization might be able to profit from it as well, which is profit that the company could have had for themselves.

Normally, this two-faceted model works fine: scientists in academia (and sometimes in industry) produce theories and discoveries, perform experiments, and share their findings. Engineers, meanwhile, take this information and use it to build actual products that companies sell. The companies exist in order to marshal and manage the resources required to bring those products to market— a task which is usually beyond the capability of a single person.

However, like so many others, this model breaks down when applied to software. The primary difficulty is that software itself has no intrinsic value. A tangible piece of equipment such as a car has value, essentially because it cost something to build. That is, even if you have the full schematics for a car, you still must have the raw materials to build it, and those raw materials are not free. Thus, the car has an intrinsic value, separate from the cost it took to design it.

A software program, however, costs nothing to build. Once you have it written, you can replicate it endlessly, effortlessly, and exactly (with never any errors). A car, on the other hand, has costs in raw materials and fabrication. Cars and software programs both cost money to develop, of course; however, once the R&D is done, the actual cars must still be manufactured, while the software is simply copied. Since software has no cost of replication, its only cost is the effort spent to develop it. Thus, unlike a car, software has no intrinsic value. Because of this, the concept of a "software company" that actually sells software is incredibly bizarre, if you stop to think about it. It's like selling air.

Now, it's still true that software developers have to recoup their R&D costs. However, this kind of R&D is really just an overhead cost of the main product. For vendors of hardware that includes software (such as web servers, cellular phones, or personal digital assistants) the software is viewed as simply a necessary cost of developing the product. For service-oriented companies such as web site developers and network support companies, the software is simply an overhead cost of providing the service. In neither case is software being sold for its own value. When you think of things this way, the notion of selling software seems more and more odd the longer you think about it.

 NOTE   *Of course, this whole argument is a generalization and isn't always true. Specifically, it's only true of **horizontal software**. The concept of a horizontal software product is described in its own section a little later in this chapter.*

The upshot of all this is that since the only cost of many types of software is the cost to develop it, there is no rational reason for a company to exist for the purpose of marshalling and managing the resources required to manufacture it. This argument—or at least similar notions—form the foundation for activists who believe in a very different philosophy for software development.

Richard Stallman is an activist and computer scientist who founded the Free Software Foundation and the GNU project in order to foster a sharing culture for software development. The FSF fosters sharing and collaboration—the scientific ethic—for software development. All of the FSF's software is released along with its source code and a license that ensures its continued openness.

Stallman describes software developed in this way as *free software*. In what has become an old saw in the open source community, the "free" in "free software" is "free" as in "free speech," not "free" as in "free beer." That is an important distinction. Software that is given away without source code (such as some web browsers), is not free software, but is merely "no-cost" software.

The arguments presented in this chapter are largely based on vaguely economic, philosophical, and political notions. While this book strives for objectivity, readers should realize that there are many different perspectives on these issues, and are highly encouraged to read Stallman's (and this FSF's) own arguments and documentation on the subject. One of the best sources of such information is obviously the Free Software Foundation's web site, at www.fsf.org. At that site, you can find the official positions of the FSF, and all their arguments on these issues.

Open Source vs. Free Software

All these abstract ethical and economic issues are well and good, but the idea of free software is, to many people, a bit radical, since it seems to espouse ideals that are at odds with the normal course of industry. Some people are even vehemently opposed to the idea; one particularly notable opponent is a man named Bill Gates, who built a software monopoly on extremely proprietary software.

To soften the radical impressions, the concept of open source enters here, as an alternative to the term "free software." The distinction between open source and free software is mostly a matter of semantics and focus, rather than a difference in ideology.

Essentially, free software is about accessibility; to be successful, free software must be accessible to as many parties as possible. In light of this, some people believe that free software can only succeed if it is practiced by the most prolific software producers; since the most prolific software producers are commercial businesses, the idea of free software must be marketed or sold to them.

However, businesses are generally reluctant to get involved in political issues, and some people believe that the ideological connotations of the term "free software" are likely to discourage businesses from participating in the process. Moreover, there is confusion in the term itself—the old free beer vs. freedom issue.

To help resolve these difficulties, some people began using the term "open source" instead of "free software." However, the term "open source" does not really capture the sense of liberty that "free software" does, and so some people (including Stallman) object to open source. The argument here is essentially that the idea is *supposed* to be radical, so softening the delivery is abandoning the actual ideal.

This is an especially thorny issue, and not one that is likely to go away any time soon. Stallman has published an excellent article on the FSF web site, entitled, "Why 'Free Software' is Better Than 'Open-Source.'" Interested readers should read Stallman's and the FSF's own words on the subject at `www.fsf.org`.

My own opinion on the subject is that "open source" is the more realistic, and less emotionally charged term, and so this book will use the term "open source," simply to escape the debate and focus on the technology.

Open Source Software in Action

Let's get serious. We're all geeks here, right? Let's put all this talk of cars and software and freedom aside for a while, and cut to the chase. This section will discuss how open source software development works, and describes its biggest asset: sheer numbers.

It's all about the software. When you sit down in front of your computer, you just want it to do what you need it to do. Sure, you want your computer to do it in the coolest, most elegant way possible, but in general, you're after functionality. That's really what open source software is all about. Free software is our conscience, but in practice, open source is simply about writing quality software.

Ultimately, software is written by people: computer scientists, programmers, software engineers, or whatever they call themselves. The more people you have contributing to a piece of software, the better off that software is. If you have five full-time developers, and each can fix ten bugs per month, you're still not as well off as if you had 100 occasional developers who each fix one bug per month.

In a series of influential articles, Eric Raymond described the benefits that the open source methodology can provide. In "The Cathedral and the Bazaar," he popularized the phrase, "Given enough eyes, all bugs are shallow." This phrase is a concise summary of the actual mechanics of open source development, and is a good jumping-off point to understanding how open source software actually works.

Open source software development succeeds by getting as many people as possible working on a given piece of software. However, since open source development is fundamentally voluntary, an open source project can only attract a large number of volunteers when it is appealing to a large number of users. So, open source works best in two cases: extremely horizontal applications and formal collaborations between organizations pooling their resources.

Horizontal Applications

The arguments on "The Nature of Software" discussed earlier in this chapter included a disclaimer, in that they only apply to horizontal software applications. A *horizontal application* is one that fills a need shared by many problem domains. (A vertical application fills only a very narrow, specific need, and some of the arguments given earlier don't apply to vertical applications.) These are some common horizontal application domains:

- Operating systems (which everyone needs to do anything at all on a computer)

- Programming language compilers (which everyone who wants to develop software needs)

- Web servers (which anyone who wants to be on the web needs)

Since many people need the application, an open source version has a wide base from which to attract contributors.

The most successful traditional open source applications are therefore generally in horizontal domains: Linux and the GNU system make up an operating system; the Apache web server runs more web sites than any other web server on the face of the planet; the K Desktop Environment (KDE) is a user interface, which is almost as general as an operating system; the GNU Compiler Collection is a staple of software developers, and there are more. Each of these applications is an example of software that "everyone" who meets a particular profile needs; when "everyone" needs something, a lot of them are willing to contribute to its development.

Once you have a lot of developers contributing to a project, it starts to become more than the sum of its code. Joe may not need a particular feature, and so might not care if Andrea does. However, if Andrea goes ahead and implements that feature, she might have to add some architectural changes that Joe may benefit from later. A concrete example of this is Linux's *virtual filesystem* (VFS) functionality, which defines a common API across all filesystem types. This feature was added to make it easier to write device drivers for filesystems, but it also allowed developers to implement advanced "false" filesystems, such as for device drivers, USB devices, user login terminals, and process information. These useful features would have been more difficult or even impossible to implement, if the developers had not first added the VFS architecture.

Collaborative Software Development

The other major way in which the open source model can be successful occurs when organizations pool their resources. In this case, multiple organizations collaborate on some particular piece of software, sharing the source code and results.

Through collaboration, potentially competing companies produce software that benefits all involved. For example, for a rather long time, the Linux kernel lacked good enterprise features, such as support for multiple processors, large amounts of memory, and journaling filesystems. Once major corporations such as SGI, IBM, and Compaq started collaborating with Linus Torvalds and the other core kernel developers, these features began to improve quickly, and in fact, in some cases there are now competing solutions; there are now at least three options for a journaling filesystem for Linux, for example.

The reason that open source provides a benefit to companies is that in the end, all participants are equal. The license for open source code prevents any one entity from dominating the project; each of the participants has essentially equal right to all the source code (along with any other individual or new organization that wishes to participate or use the software). One company can get miffed and go home, but it can't take its ball with it.

So, open source software is making inroads into companies where the software being developed can be used by all the participants. For example, the primary reason that most of the big hardware companies (such as IBM, Compaq, and HP) are backing Linux is because they make most of their profit on their hardware and service offerings; their operating systems are really just there to sell hardware. It's been speculated that some companies even lose money on developing their operating systems.

To such companies, the cost of developing an operating system is actually a liability, and by pooling their resources, they can collectively produce a better operating system than any could individually, allowing them to focus on their core hardware and service offerings. For example, if five companies each spend $5,000,000 per year on operating system development, then with the open source model they could pool their development funds, and collectively produce a system of equal or better quality, with less cost to each participating company.

Meanwhile, of course, individual private users gain the same benefits from the enhancements. It is this synergy that makes the free software model beneficial to individual users, and the open source model so compelling to businesses.

Licensing Open Source

So far, we've seen how open source software works, and how it benefits the parties involved. But what, exactly, makes it tick? How does open source work its magic? The answer is in the license. Open source software takes advantage of existing copyright laws to enact a licensing framework in which users of the software are essentially required to play fair. Because everyone is on a level playing field, there is no risk that one contributor can poison the pot and usurp everyone else's hard work; this makes open source software safe for everyone involved, and encourages people to contribute. This section will discuss open source licensing, and describe some of the most common examples.

Contrary to an all-too-common belief, open source software is not the same as being in the public domain. Some people use the terms "public domain" and "open source" (or "free software") interchangeably, but they are not. *Public domain software* is exactly that: owned by the public. The person or group that wrote the software has chosen to abdicate ownership, and released it to the public domain. Any other person or group may take a piece of public domain software and do whatever they choose with it. That is, nothing protects public domain software from being reused in proprietary software.

Free software, in contrast, does not relinquish ownership. The prevalent model in software sales today is licensing. When you purchase (or are given) a piece of software, what you actually own is permission to use the software, not the software itself. The entity that provided you with the software still owns it, and what you can and cannot do with the software is determined by the terms of the license you agreed to when you received the software.

Typically, companies sell software to users, and the license is used to prevent the user from giving the copy to anyone else. (In this way, other users who wish to use the software must themselves purchase it from the company that owns it.) Free software, however, simply makes use of the license to ensure that the software and its source code are unencumbered by restrictions on use or modification. This essentially boils down to one key fact: any time someone modifies the software and distributes the modified version, they must also distribute the source code to their modifications, without additional licensing restrictions.

Of course, sometimes it's not quite as simple as that. For instance, some licenses do not require that users submitting modifications to the software assign their copyright on their contributions to the owner of the original license. This means that if Joe releases software under a free license and Jane submits a change, Jane still owns the copyright on her submission. Even though it falls under the same license as the original software, Joe cannot choose to license the software to Mike under a different license without Jane's approval, because now Jane owns part of it, and Joe can't ignore that. Joe can, of course, choose to not include Jane's contribution in the version he licenses to Mike, but then Jane can always simply redistribute her own derived version of Joe's software to Mike, too. To avoid this problem, some projects and licenses take steps to ensure that such mixed copyright issues are avoided.

The upshot is that free software and open source software have real, legitimate copyrights and licenses, which can be as simple and as complex as copyright law allows them to be. As of this writing, none of the common open source or free software licenses have been challenged in a court of law, so no one really knows for certain whether they'll hold up.

Generally, free software and open source software describe the same thing. However, they vary slightly in their definitions, and sometimes a license that qualifies as open source by the definition specified by the Open Source Initiative (OSI) doesn't quite qualify as free software by the definition specified by the Free Software Foundation. Such licenses, however, are relatively uncommon.

 NOTE *The Open Source Initiative (OSI) at* www.opensource.org *is a non-profit organization that promotes open source software and also provides certification services for open source licenses.*

Here are a few examples of actual open source licenses, with quick comparisons and summaries. These examples will illustrate some of the major variances among open source licenses; most licenses can be compared to one of these examples, or will pick and choose features from them.

The GNU General Public License

The General Public License (GPL) is the license that most of the GNU project is released under. Sometimes referred to as a "copyleft" (to emphasize its distinction from copyright), the GPL was really the first free software license, and, true to its heritage, is still one of the strongest licenses around.

The full text of the GPL can be found at `www.gnu.org/copyleft/gpl.html`, but in brief it says this:

- There are no restrictions on the use or redistribution of the software (though a fee may be charged for distribution costs and handling).

- If the user redistributes the software, the source code must be available.

- The user may modify the software for private use.

- If the user modifies the software and distributes the changed version, the source code must be available.

- If the user modifies the software and distributes the changed version, it must be available under the same terms.

- If the user incorporates the software into a larger work, the larger work must also be under the license or a stronger license.

You should, of course, read the GPL yourself rather than taking this book's word for it before making any important decisions.

The last point about larger works means that if Jane incorporates Joe's Software into her own SuperSoftware—even if she doesn't change Joe's Software at all but is merely using it—her own SuperSoftware must also be available under the GPL or a stronger license. This is sometimes referred to as a "viral" license, since it "infects" Jane's software, requiring that she also use the GPL.

On the one hand, this encourages developers who are building on free software to make their software free. However, this restricts the range of use; for example, a business may wish to use GPL software as part of their product, but can't because they wish to sell their product. This makes the GPL probably the strongest (that is, most free) license around, but its hostility to commercial use is a large part of why other licenses were created.

The BSD License

The Berkeley Software Distribution (BSD) license is a stark contrast to the GPL. Where the GPL requires free use, demands that the source code be distributed with the software, and "infects" derived works, the BSD license does not.

The BSD license is very simple: it simply says that if the software is redistributed in source form, or if a modified or derived version is distributed in source form, then the original authors' names and their copyright notice must be displayed in the redistributed code. If the software (or a modified or derived version) is distributed in binary form, then the authors must be given due credit either in the documentation or software itself.

The BSD license is extremely and deliberately friendly to commercial use. It permits a developer to incorporate the software into another larger work, with the sole requirement being that the original authors be given due credit. The philosophy of the BSD license is a bit more academically pure than the GPL; BSD developers are simply interested in producing the best possible code that can be produced, without regard to where it is used.

Since it allows licensees to incorporate the software into proprietary works (even though due credit must be given), the BSD license is much farther away from the free software ideal than the GPL. However, it is still an open source license, and it's friendlier to businesses.

The GNU Lesser General Public License

The GNU Lesser General Public License (LGPL) is a slightly relaxed version of the GPL and lies somewhere in between the two extremes just presented. The LGPL was created in response to the issues involved with *statically linking libraries* released under the GPL. A statically linked library is one whose code is physically embedded in a program. The other possibility is a *dynamically linked library*, in which a given program only refers to the library, of which there is only one copy shared among all programs that use it. There are plusses and minuses for each approach.

Since a statically linked library (such as the system C libraries or a graphics API) is physically copied into the binary object code and is required for programs to run, any program making use of these libraries is implicitly merging with the library and becoming a "larger work." Since the GPL is a viral license, as mentioned earlier in this chapter, any program statically linking against a GPL-covered library must also be released under the GPL (or a stronger license)—even if the library was used completely unchanged!

This effect was judged too extreme, so a new license, called the Lesser or Library General Public License was created. This license is identical to the GPL, except that it is not viral; it relaxes the clause requiring that larger works including the software also be licensed under the same terms.

Since it's not viral, the LGPL has a little bit more in common with the BSD license than the GPL. However, since this is a slight weakening of the free software ideal, the Free Software Foundation generally advocates the use of the GPL over the LGPL, except where the LGPL is strictly required.

The Mozilla Public License

When Netscape Communications Corporation decided to release their Communicator product as open source, they looked at the existing open source licenses. However, the GPL was too strong (since they wanted their code to be usable in larger works), and the BSD License was too weak (since they wanted to preserve the requirement that derived and modified versions include the source code).The license that Netscape produced was named the Mozilla Public License (MPL), and is a lot like the LGPL, except that it's a bit more liberal in what constitutes a larger work. The MPL includes additional clauses establishing further protections against rogue contributors; for example, one clause prevents anyone from contributing patented code, and then attempting to enforce the patent against users of the software or other contributors or licensees. (The GPL has similar clauses protecting against rogue contributors, but is less explicit in the details.)

Other Licenses

Most other licenses are more or less similar to at least one of these licenses. The Apache license, for example, is much like the BSD license, except that it also restricts any licensees from using the name "Apache" in the name of their product. (The BSD license only restricts the use of the name in promotions or endorsements.) There are numerous licenses out there—too many to keep track of. Generally, though, most are either variants of or fairly similar to one of the licenses discussed here. If the OSI has certified a given license as "open source," then that's a good benchmark; otherwise, you'll have to read the license yourself and decide whether you like it.

A License to Code

So what does all this mean for people who are only interested in using (and tuning and customizing) a Linux system? Well, the one thing that all open source and free software licenses have in common is that they are free for use for any purpose. Most of the snags that arise in open software licensing generally involve redistribution and modification. Parties that are simply using the software are safe.

But, with all this question and rhetoric over free software vs. proprietary, should we really be so careless about the licenses we use? The answer is that it's up to you. Some people object to animals being used to test the safety of cosmetics. Aside from suing these companies if they violate the law, the only recourse available to such activists is to boycott the offending companies' products. Similarly, if you don't care for a particular software license, you can simply

choose not to use that software. If you can't work without it, then you can write
(or commission) your own version under a license you prefer.

Users who are truly concerned (or perhaps just curious) about free software
licenses are encouraged to look at the web sites of the Free Software Foundation
and the Open Source Initiative, read their respective positions and definitions,
and perhaps make a donation. The best choice is always the one you make
yourself.

Part Two

Linux Distributions

Welcome to Part Two of *Tuning and Customizing a Linux System*! Part Two introduces the concept of a distribution of Linux software and then explains three such distributions in detail. After reading Part Two, you'll have a generalized understanding of what a Linux distribution actually is, which in turn will enable you to work with any distribution you encounter and figure it out. Additionally, you'll come away with a basic functional knowledge of the three distributions discussed.

The three distributions studied in detail are Red Hat Linux 7.3 (in Chapter 4), Slackware Linux 8.0 (in Chapter 5), and Debian GNU/Linux (in Chapter 6). The distributions are compared to one another, and both their similarities and their differences are highlighted. The ultimate goal is to provide you a basic mastery of three different Linux distributions and by extension *all* distributions. After reading Part Two, you'll be able to either use these distributions themselves or draw upon your knowledge to learn some other distribution not directly covered in this book.

Part Three builds on the material discussed in this part. That is, where Part Two teaches you everything you would want to know about the workings of a distribution, Part Three will show you how to customize a distribution by installing and configuring software on it. Finally, Part Four will put it all together and demonstrate some real-world case studies. For these reasons, Part Two is an absolutely crucial part of this book, since it's the foundation of so much else.

CHAPTER 3

The Nature of a Distribution

In Chapter 1 you learned what a Linux system is, what the various parts are, and how it all fits together. That should go a long way toward understanding Linux systems in general, right?

Well, it does, but there's more to it than that. For each of the components of a Linux system we've seen, there are several options. The kernel, system libraries, and other parts of the system usually have many different "live" versions; some are stable and well tested but no longer "current," while the cutting-edge versions may be buggy or unstable. Plus, sometimes there are competing options even for the same program, as in the case of desktop software where GNOME and KDE are both excellent choices.

The responsibility of a Linux vendor is to produce a system that works. This means selecting the best possible software products and versions for the task at hand. A particular configuration of such a collection of software is known as a *distribution*. This chapter will discuss the notion of a distribution and what makes up a distribution, and will describe how distributions are created.

Taking a Snapshot of the Linux Continuum

The phrase "Linux Continuum", is not from a science fiction book nor is it a bizarre cultist rite. Rather, it is really just a way of describing the overall state of the software that collectively becomes a Linux system. A lot of software packages from a lot of different sources go into a Linux system. All this software isn't just out there growing on a tree or falling like manna from heaven. It's actually out there growing on a million different trees, and the real manna is sometimes hidden under mud and grime. It can be hard work hunting down all this software and cobbling it together into a usable system. This is what Linux vendors do, and the end result is a distribution.

The vast majority of software packages aren't written explicitly to become part of a particular Linux distribution. Because of this, at any given time, each of these software packages has its own version, and even its own versioning scheme.

For example, at the time of this writing the current version of the emacs editor is 21.2, while the current stable version of XFree86 is 4.2.0.

Figure 3-1 depicts how a distribution is really just a sampling (or a "snapshot") of the larger overall continuum of Linux software. You can see from this figure how Red Hat Linux 7.3 is made up of a number of different packages, each with its own version. Obviously, Red Hat Linux consists of far more packages than just the few shown in Figure 3-1; however, it does show three important software packages:

- XFree86 implementation of the X Window System

- The Linux kernel

- KDE desktop

Each of these packages has its own version history, release cycle, etc. Red Hat Linux, meanwhile, constructs its distribution from particular versions of the software. The three packages represent an example continuum, while Red Hat Linux represents a snapshot. In this case, Red Hat Linux 7.3 shipped with XFree86 4.2.0, Linux 2.4.18, and KDE 3.0. Remember that this is a *snapshot* of the continuum and doesn't (usually) change over time; Red Hat may choose the latest version of a package available at the time it was released, but later versions may be released after Red Hat has released their own snapshot.

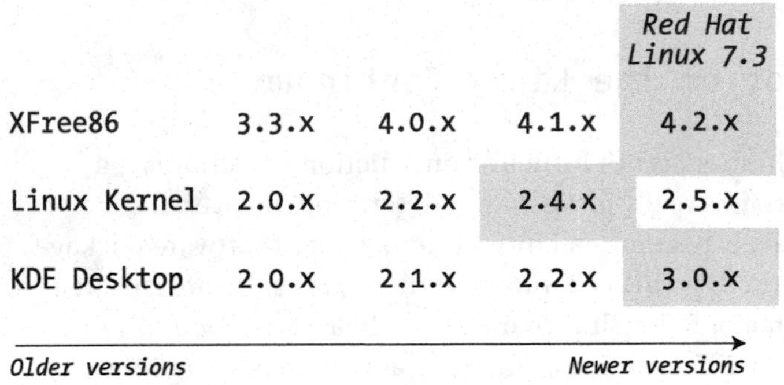

				Red Hat Linux 7.3
XFree86	3.3.x	4.0.x	4.1.x	4.2.x
Linux Kernel	2.0.x	2.2.x	2.4.x	2.5.x
KDE Desktop	2.0.x	2.1.x	2.2.x	3.0.x

Older versions ———————————————————→ *Newer versions*

Figure 3-1. Example software continuum

NOTE *A Linux distribution is a collection of software that makes up a Linux-based operating system. Because each of the software packages in a distribution has its own independent version, the version number that a vendor assigns to its distribution does not bear any relationship to the versions of the software packages which comprise it.*

If all these various software packages and versions are starting to get blurred together in your mind, that's great, because it's the perfect way to view things. You really can view the state of open source software as one great big "space" of software and version numbers: a continuum. This continuum is constantly evolving and changing, as individual software packages develop and change versions. What a vendor calls a production-quality release is really just a snapshot taken of this continuum at one particular instant.

The responsibility of a vendor is to craft the snapshot so that the overall system is as useful, flexible, and bug-free as possible. Vendors do this by first identifying which software packages are going to go into the distribution at all, and then selecting the most recent stable version of that software that meets their goals.

Understanding the Goals of a Distribution

Linux systems are extremely flexible. Linux (the kernel) can be scaled up to large multi-processor systems, or scaled down into tiny memory-constrained PDAs. Obviously, the software requirements for a distribution running on the multi-processor system are going to be rather different that the software requirements for a PDA—unless, of course, someone's lucky enough to have a 32-processor PDA with 8GB of memory (that won't spontaneously burst into flames!).

So, the first decision that a distribution vendor has to make is what, exactly, are the goals of the distribution. Is the distribution to be for servers, or workstations? Is the goal a highly user-friendly environment suitable for desktop office use, or is the goal a high-performance traditional Unix environment for engineers? Is the distribution supposed to run on Intel, Alpha, PowerPC, SPARC, MIPS, ARM, or IBM S/390 mainframe?

This is, of course, a marketing decision (whether for a commercial entity or for a volunteer free effort), and different vendors target different markets. Red Hat Software, for example, produces a well-rounded distribution suitable for use as either a server or a desktop system. The Debian project produces a distribution similar in scope to Red Hat, but consisting entirely of free software. Mandrake Software produces a desktop-focused distribution, and TurboLinux produces a high-end distribution for clustering and parallel computing. The Slackware distribution aims to create a traditional Unix-like system. In other words, the market each vendor targets defines the overall requirements of the distribution, and the particular selection of software that goes into the distribution.

Each user, meanwhile, also has specific needs. Some users need to set up a workstation for their own personal use, others need to set up a local file server, and still others need to set up extensive server farms to run a web site. Some Linux distributions, of course, are good at some tasks, and others are better at other tasks. Sometimes, the user has the luxury of picking the best distribution for the task. Frequently, however, the user prefers to use a specific distribution (perhaps by personal preference or corporate mandate) that might not have been optimized out of the box for the task. In these cases, it helps the user immensely to understand how the distribution was built and what its goals are, in order to customize the system for the desired task. This book will help the reader understand and customize the system, but it's up to the reader to know what her own goals and needs are.

This book covers three sample distributions:

- Red Hat Linux

- Slackware Linux

- Debian GNU/Linux

These distributions were chosen because of their huge influence on the evolution of Linux systems; almost every other distribution out there is derived from, inspired by, or related to one of these three. Despite their different focuses, however, each of these distributions consist of the same general set of software; they're snapshots of the same continuum, just from different angles. The rest of Part Two (in Chapters 4 through 6) is dedicated to discussing each of these distributions in detail, but first you need to understand exactly what a distribution is; that's the focus of the remainder of this chapter.

Dissecting a Linux Distribution

This section will describe the key components of a Linux distribution, which are:

- Linux kernel version

- Packaging format

- Filesystem layout

- System startup scripts

- System library versions

- X Window Desktop

- Userspace software

After reading this section, readers will understand the basics of what goes into a distribution; later chapters cover specific sample distributions in depth, but this section provides an introduction. Users who are already familiar with a Linux distribution or are experienced Unix users should be able to skim or skip this chapter, and proceed to the detailed discussions of the sample distributions, starting with Red Hat Linux in Chapter 4.

Linux Kernel

The Linux kernel is the core of the operating system (see Chapter 1). Generally, the Linux kernel has two "trees": the stable version and the development version. The *stable version* is a production-ready kernel, and is debugged and well tested by millions of users all over the world. The *development version*, in contrast, is where the key kernel developers do their tinkering and feature enhancements. The development tree is thus highly unstable, and is not for production systems, daily use, or people prone to apoplexy.

 CROSS-REFERENCE *See Chapter 1 for a discussion of the Linux operating system.*

The Linux kernel has a numbering scheme of X.Y.Z, described as follows:

- X is the major version, representing major architectural changes

- Y is the minor version, indicating functional enhancements but few architectural changes

- Z is the build version, representing bug-fix or development patch levels

If Y is an even number, the kernel is stable; if it is odd, the kernel is in development. The current stable kernel series at the time of this writing is 2.4.*x*, and the current development series is 2.5.*x*. (A "series" is simply a series of similar versions.)

Generally speaking, distribution vendors are interested in producing stable, bug-free systems. Thus, any formal releases should obviously make use of only stable Linux kernels; otherwise the vendors risk exposing their users to excessive bugs in the kernel—the most sensitive and critical part of the system.

On the other hand, the Linux kernel, like many open source projects, has a long release cycle, when compared to many commercial efforts. This means that many of the distribution vendors often find that they need features that are new or experimental, and exist only in the current development kernels. Distribution vendors often must decide whether they will opt for a stable, less fully featured kernel, or a more fully equipped but probably less stable version.

Many distribution vendors adopt a compromise, by *backporting* features from development kernels to the previous release kernels. (The process of adding such advanced features to an older kernel is known as *backporting*.) Since a development kernel that is to become the next stable kernel was originally derived from the current stable version, it still shares many similarities with the older kernel. Thus, many of the features and bug fixes that are added to a typical development kernel are not strictly incompatible with the previous stable kernel.

The core kernel developers (led by Linus Torvalds) do not have enough time to try and manage these backports to older kernels; they are already spending all their available time on improving the new kernel. Many distribution vendors therefore do this work, and release customized kernels with their products. For example, universal serial bus (USB) support was added to the Linux kernel in the 2.3 development series, but Red Hat wanted USB support for their 2.2-based Red Hat Linux 7.0 distribution. They chose to do the work to backport the 2.3-version USB functionality, and shipped Red Hat 7.0 with a custom kernel. Moreover, distribution vendors sometimes even add functionality that isn't in the kernel at all, in either the development or stable trees; for example, Mandrake software has kernel patches used to make removable media easier to manage. This really isn't isolated behavior, and many distributions ship with customized kernels.

Backporting development kernel features isn't always possible, of course; sometimes new features in a development kernel depend on architectural changes that were made to the kernel that don't exist in the previous stable version, and so can't be backported. Still, in a lot of cases development features are considered unstable only because they are new and not yet extensively tested. Some vendors may disagree and regard these features as suitable for production or may have features of their own that they wish to add. In such cases, vendors may choose to ship a custom kernel in their distribution.

Some people disapprove of this behavior, citing the danger of fragmenting the kernel into many custom derivatives, and compatibility issues that might arise when vendors customize a kernel so much that it differs from the "standard" kernels in subtle ways. However, you can view the "official" kernel as a sort of starting point for distribution vendors to begin with for developing their systems. After all, does it really matter whether the USB features you're using came from the 2.3 kernel or a 2.2 kernel, as long as your USB digital camera works?

Packaging Format

A distribution's *packaging format* is the mechanism used to install and manage the software that comes with a distribution. Since many of these software applications are placed side-by-side in the same directories, it is extremely useful to have a way to track which particular files were installed by which packages. Package managers also provide the ability to uninstall or upgrade software, and query the system for which software is installed.

Package management tools also generally provide versioning and dependency information. For example, a particular version of the KDE X Windows desktop requires a particular version of the Qt widget library. For KDE to run properly, the appropriate version of Qt must also be installed, but determining version information isn't always easy. Package managers can track this information, helping users and system administrators keep their software and versions in sync.

Every flavor of Unix—including the commercial ones—has its own packaging format or software maintenance mechanism. However, as with many other areas, the Linux package formats are far more functional and easier to use than most of the commercial Unix equivalents. Indeed, some commercial Unix vendors have even announced plans to include the RPM packaging format with their own systems.

Red Hat Package Manager

The first sophisticated packaging manager for Linux systems was the *Red Hat Package Manager* (RPM), developed by Red Hat Software for their distribution. RPM supports all of the standard packaging tasks, and has an extensive list of features. It installs, uninstalls, and upgrades packages, runs scripts during installations and upgrades that do extra work to configure the software, and supports package dependency tracking and version enforcement. RPM also supports extensive querying of package contents and documentation, has facilities for verifying the integrity of installed packages, and can even generate "source RPMs," for supporting users who wish or need to customize the RPMs. RPM's largest contribution to packaging software was probably its ability to reliably perform package upgrades and extensive dependency checks.

Deb Files

The Debian project has its own alternative packaging format. Since these files have the extension .deb, they are frequently known as "Deb files." The Debian packaging format is similar in functionality to RPM, but has some additional features, such as more extensive scripting capability and the ability to create "meta" packages for encapsulating other packages. Debian systems also have additional user-interface tools intended to make the packaging system easier to use.

RPM and the Debian format are the two most popular packaging formats around. Most other distributions use one of these two formats. A notable exception is Slackware, which uses its own format based on traditional tar files and searchable text databases. There are also supporting tools for these packaging systems that provide additional features; for example, both RPM and Debian's system have tools for searching servers for particular packages and automatically downloading and installing them.

Packaging Format vs. Distribution

It's important not to confuse the packaging format with the distribution itself. Two distributions can use the same packaging format, and yet have incompatible versions of the same software. For example, both Caldera and Red Hat use the RPM format for their distributions. However, an RPM created for a Red Hat system may not necessarily work on a Caldera OpenLinux system, which may have different versions of the libraries that the package requires. In other words, a packaging format only manages the installation and configuration of software, not the software itself. The packaging format doesn't change the fact that a piece of software requires another piece, it just lets you install it.

Functionally, there isn't that much difference between the various packaging formats. They all do the same things. Therefore, the choice of which format to use isn't made on technical or quality issues, but really on package availability issues. That is, whom do you want to be compatible with? Currently, the majority of software that is packaged for Linux is packaged in the RPM format. This doesn't mean that users of other formats (such as Debian) can't use the software; for a lot of software, .deb packages can be found in addition to RPM, and you always have the option of installing the software manually (or building it from source code) without using the packaging tool at all. However, if you're browsing the Web and find a random piece of software, you're more likely to find the Linux version packaged in RPM than in Debian's format.

Even this distinction is somewhat moot, since Debian's distribution also includes tools that can convert RPM files into Debian-compatible packages and vice versa. As a user, you're far more likely to run into compatibility problems with required libraries than you are with the format used to package the software. Once either of these formats is installed, the same files are extracted anyway, after all.

That said, it currently appears that RPM has the greater momentum. More distributions use it, and it appears to be the de facto standard software-packaging format for Linux systems. However, the open source community is nothing if not dynamic, and this situation could change the week after this book is published.

Filesystem Layout

Even the greatest Linux distribution is worthless if you can't find the file you're looking for. From the very earliest days of Unix, the conventions for which files and programs go where on the disk have been a major consideration. Your average Unix-like system is a lot more complex than many other operating systems, and so having standards for where to find things is a big deal. The particular filesystem convention chosen by a vendor has a big impact on the rest of the system.

There is any number of ways to lay out the contents of a distribution on the disk, so there isn't really a set number of options to choose from. The Unix legacy has left behind a basic set of conventions for what programs go in what directories, but traditionally those have been rough guidelines at best, and the various vendors of both commercial Unix flavors and free systems alike have followed these loose conventions with varying degrees of rigor.

Directories

The /etc directory on Unix systems generally contains configuration files, scripts, and similar contents. However, Solaris systems place some administrative programs in this directory as well, whereas Linux systems and BSD systems typically place such programs in /sbin. Additionally, sometimes it's the software itself that determines where to place its files: on BSD systems, some third-party software such as Apache puts its configuration files in /usr/local/etc, where on most Linux systems even third-party software puts its configuration files in /etc.

Filesystem Hierarchy Standard

There is an ostensible convention for directory layout on Linux systems. The Filesystem Hierarchy Standard (FHS) addresses the confusion surrounding directory layouts on Unix systems, and has a set of standard guidelines for which types of files should go in which directories. The FHS aims to be applicable to any Unix-like system, though it was originated and tailored for Linux systems. Most Linux distributions follow the FHS reasonably well, though there are a few exceptions. The open-source BSD systems also generally follow the FHS, but commercial vendors are proving to be somewhat slower to adopt the FHS, probably due to concerns for backward compatibility.

Table 3-1 summarizes the major aspects of the FHS, by showing the major directories identified by the FHS. This is a good place to start, but users who truly want to master the "Zen of Linux" should definitely read the entire document. The FHS can be found at www.pathname.com/fhs/. Once you've digested the FHS, you'll have made the first step to understanding a Linux system, which is simply knowing where to find things.

Table 3-1. Filesystem Hierarchy Standard Summary

DIRECTORY	NAME	TYPICAL CONTENTS	EXAMPLES
/etc	"etcetera"	Configuration files	/etc/passwd: user account information; /etc/resolv.conf: network lookup information
/boot	Boot files	Files required for the system to boot up	/boot/vmlinuz: the Linux kernel image
/dev	Device nodes	Files representing hardware devices on the system	/dev/sda: the first SCSI disk in the system; /dev/audio: the sound device
/lib	System libraries	Shared library files required by user programs	/lib/libc.so: the shared library (.so) for C programs; /lib/libpthread.so.0: the POSIX threads library
/bin	Program binaries	User application programs	/bin/ls: file listing utility; /bin/bash: the "Bourne Again SHell" command shell
/sbin	Administrative	Programs used primarily for administrative tasks programs	/sbin/ifconfig: network device configuration tool; /sbin/mkfs: filesystem formatting tool
/home	User home	Home directories for users	(Optional) /home/morrildl: the home directory for the user "morrildl"
/mnt	Mount points	Contains subdirectories where temporary filesystems can be mounted	/mnt/cdrom: mount point for the CD-ROM drive; /mnt/floppy: mount point for the floppy drive

Table 3-1. Filesystem Hierarchy Standard Summary (continued)

DIRECTORY	NAME	TYPICAL CONTENTS	EXAMPLES
/usr	User partition	Files useful to users once the system is running	/usr/X11R6: files related to the X Window system; /usr/bin: end-user program binaries
/var	Runtime programs	Files and directories for storing control information or data for programs and services	/var/spool/mail: email-related files; /var/log: system log files
/tmp	Temporary files	Files that are not persistent or important	

A bit of explanation of Table 3-1 is in order, especially with respect to the "/" directory and the "/usr" directory. Unix paths begin with a "/" character, and the top-level directory itself is "/". This is known as the *root directory* or *root partition*; if someone asks you to "cd into the root directory," they're actually asking you to type the command cd /. Similarly, the /usr directory is pronounced "slash user."

When you read the FHS, you'll probably notice that it defines two copies of most directories, for example, /bin and /usr/bin. The reason for this is related to the way the system boots up. During boot-up, Unix systems typically mount the root partition first, and only mount the user partitions later on in the process. Also, an administrator will occasionally boot the system into single-user or maintenance mode, to perform major upgrades, configuration maintenance, or security examinations. In this case, the system might stop at the root partition, and not mount any others at all. In both of these cases, a set of core programs (such as ls, mount, cd, vi, echo, etc.) is required for the system to function.

Since the system requires access to these core programs and files before mounting the rest of the volumes, they obviously have to be located on the root partition. Thus, the top-level directories such as /bin, /lib, and /sbin are there to contain a basic set of commands required for the system to complete the bootstrap process, while /usr/bin, /usr/lib, and /usr/sbin contain additional programs that are most commonly used by administrators on a running system.

For example, the ls command is required, so it is in /bin. However, the find command is not strictly required (though it is convenient), so it is located in /usr/bin. As a rule of thumb, if you're trying to find a program or are trying to decide where to place a new program, first decide whether it's critical for the system to function. If it is, use /bin, /lib, or /sbin; if it's not, use /usr/bin, /usr/lib, or /usr/sbin.

There is, in fact, even a third case here: the /usr/local directory. /usr/local is used for the same type of files as /usr (that is, files that aren't strictly required for the system to run or start up), but for files that are local to the particular system. For example, the X Windows software is fairly common and standard across all installations, so it should be placed in /usr. However, an installation of the Apache web server that has been customized for a specific system is not standard and should be placed in /usr/local, rather than /usr.

There are a several rules of thumb to apply when trying to decide where to place a particular file. One approach is that anything that was included with the distribution as it was shipped should be placed in /usr, and everything else should be placed in /usr/local. Alternatively, if it is managed by the system packaging tools, it belongs in /usr; otherwise, it belongs in /usr/local. The point is that the FHS is a somewhat flexible standard, and you can really place a file anywhere you want, as long as you're consistent.

The way that the FHS breaks the filesystem up into these parallel, almost mirror-image directories may seem excessively complicated. However, there is good reason for the added complexity: it makes life easier for system administrators, and more recoverable in the case of disk failures. By breaking up the filesystem into core (root), non-core (/usr), and local (/usr/local) directories, the FHS establishes an easy way for administrators to place different types of files on different disks.

Partitioning with Upgrades in Mind

Recall that the placement of core files on the root directory allows the system to boot up and be managed without having to bother during the boot process with the other partitions on the system. However, this separation of the root directory and /usr means that either the core system or the user-level files and programs could be upgraded independently of each other.

Perhaps more importantly, this separation also means that the core system (the root and /usr volumes) can be upgraded independently of /usr/local and /opt. This allows administrators to upgrade a system without disturbing custom software installed on the system, and also means that the custom software can be preserved if the main system disk containing the root and /usr volumes goes bad. (It's easy to reinstall an operating system, but hard to recover months of work on the Apache web site you had running. It's even worse if the site was intact but you have to overwrite it to reinstall the operating system because they shared the same partition or disk.)

System Startup Scripts

What good is a computer if it won't start up? Following that thought, what good is a startup script if you can't figure out how to use it to start your own software? Linux systems, like all Unix systems, configure their startup and shutdown activities via a set of scripts. The system itself would be perfectly happy to just start up or shut down without doing anything for you, but that would be pretty annoying (and dangerous, if it meant disk partitions don't get properly managed). The startup and shutdown scripts—known as *runlevel command* or *rc* scripts—do the grunt work of starting and stopping your Linux system.

When a Unix system starts up, the kernel is the first thing to get loaded. It then kicks off a program known as *init*, which is responsible for starting up the rest of the system. This init program essentially manages runlevels. A *runlevel* is simply a configuration of programs and services that are to be run; usually, these configurations are geared toward a specific goal, such as normal multiuser operation, shutting down the system, starting it up, entering into maintenance mode, etc. Each runlevel corresponds to a different state; for example, runlevel 0 might mean "system halt" while runlevel 4 might correspond to "normal server mode." The init program is responsible for starting up any services (such as web servers, DNS servers, databases, and so on) and setting up the user environment (such as mounting all the partitions, allowing the user to log in, and starting up X Windows if necessary).

The kernel doesn't actually care how init does this; init could do the work itself, of course, but that's not very customizable, so init instead delegates the majority of its startup tasks to an external program. All init usually does is look for a configuration file in the /etc directory (named /etc/inittab) that tells it which runlevel it should enter into by default, and then invokes a program (almost always a shell script) for that runlevel. In fact, the init program itself is simply a configuration parameter for the kernel. The kernel can just as easily kick off a different program instead of init that has different behavior for setting up the system. For example, if the system has been damaged and needs to be recovered or maintained, the kernel can simply start an interactive command shell instead of init.

Normally, though, the kernel starts init, which runs the scripts for the current runlevel. There are actually seven of these system runlevels, summarized in Table 3-2. Whenever init changes to a new runlevel, it invokes the scripts for that runlevel, and the scripts start and stop programs as required by the new runlevel. Actually, init doesn't even distinguish between which runlevel is which; it just has up to six "modes" it can be in. By Unix convention, the runlevels usually have the meanings expressed in Table 3-2. Sometimes the runlevels will vary by Unix flavor or distribution; to find out exactly what runlevels your system supports, look at the configuration file for init, which is usually /etc/inittab.

Table 3-2. System Runlevels

RUNLEVEL	MEANING	BEHAVIOR
0	Halt	Shuts down all programs and services, unmounts filesystems, and halts the CPU
1	Single-User Mode	Shuts down most programs and services, permitting only root logins; frequently used for system maintenance
2	Networkless Multiuser	Starts all programs and services except network-related ones; allows all local users to log in
3	Normal Multiuser	Starts all programs and services, except X
4	Normal Multiuser	Frequently unused; otherwise just like runlevel 3
5	Graphical Multiuser	Just like runlevel 3, but also starts the X Window system for user logins
6	Reboot	Shuts down all programs and services and reboots the system

Each runlevel has a different meaning, which reflects what programs and services are started in that runlevel. An important concept is that any runlevel can be entered from any other runlevel. For example, runlevel 1 (single-user mode) can be entered either on system startup, or from another runlevel on a running system, such as runlevel 3. From init's perspective (and the perspective of the shell scripts that get run by init), the two cases are identical, and runlevel 1 has the same meaning and runs the same scripts. In other words, the terms "shuts down" and "starts up" are relative; if the system just started up, there's nothing to shut down, and vice versa. The ways in which you instruct init to switch runlevels vary by system; the most "portable" method is to use the `telinit` command, but most systems provide alternative commands such as `shutdown`.

 NOTE *Remember, init doesn't do any work itself, but simply invokes the appropriate script for the current runlevel. What actually happens when that script is run is up to the script. This script is like any program, and can be as complex or as simple as the author chooses to make it.*

The format of the init scripts is one of the areas where you can trace the origins of a Unix flavor back to either the original AT&T SysV Unix or BSD operating systems. Each of these systems, though they share the same behavior and usage of init, has different architectures for the actual scripts that get run by init. Though they fulfill the same purposes, they are fairly different in the details.

Most Unix-like systems, including Linux systems, choose one or the other of the SysV or BSD init-scripts models, and emulate it with varying degrees of accuracy. Red Hat Linux, for example, uses the SysV initscript model, whereas Slackware uses the BSD model. Since we will be covering both of these distributions in depth in Chapters 4 and 5, we'll cover the details of the SysV and BSD mechanisms there, rather than duplicate it here.

Like many scripting activities, whether an individual prefers the SysV or BSD initscript model is really a matter of personal taste. The SysV model can be described as more "modular," which some people prefer, whereas the BSD model is simpler, which other people prefer. It's hard to make a case that either is fundamentally better than another, though, so the initscripts model used by a particular Linux distribution is really immaterial, though it probably reflects which Unix flavor the distribution is trying to emulate.

System Library Versions

As mentioned in Chapter 1, it's really the system libraries that define the character of an operating system. If you chose to spend the time and effort, for example, you could write a set of system libraries that provide a clone of Windows, running directly on a Unix kernel (such as Linux). This would provide a completely different user interface and programming API, but would still have a POSIX-compliant kernel running underneath it all. In other words, by changing the system libraries you can completely alter the nature of an operating system.

You may be wondering what these system libraries are. The system libraries make application development and use easier by encapsulating a body of functionality into, well, a library. This allows end-user programs to reuse functionality by using the library, instead of having to interact with the kernel directly. There are system libraries for most aspects of the operating system, including network access, multithreading and process management, program linking and loading, and so on.

Actually, the term "system libraries" is a bit fuzzy. Libraries like those just mentioned are pretty much required for the system to work. However, there are additional libraries that aren't strictly required, but can still be considered system libraries. The most obvious example is shown in the libraries required for the X Window system to work; these libraries aren't required for the system to run, but they *are* required for the system to run a GUI. Other examples include the ldbm database libraries used by many programs, or the tcp_wrappers library used for security for some network programs. These libraries aren't required, but are still system libraries.

For the vast majority of cases, the only real option for system libraries for a Linux system is the GNU C Library package, known as *glibc*. The glibc package provides most of the libraries that are absolutely critical for the system to run. glibc doesn't include some of the optional system libraries; these other libraries are usually installed individually, as separate packages.

> **NOTE** *Traditionally, Unix systems name their libraries libfoo.o, where "foo" is the name of the library. By this convention, libc refers to the C libraries. The glibc package provides many other libraries in addition to the basic libc.o, so it is somewhat poorly named.*

System libraries are probably one of the three most difficult pieces of software to write, along with a kernel and a compiler. So, once you have a functional set of system libraries (or kernel or compiler), think long and hard before going off and starting your own. For this reason, no one has written a serious competitor to the glibc for Linux systems, and every major distribution out there uses some version of the glibc for the core system libraries.

At least, no one has written a serious competitor for traditional desktop or server distributions. There are, in fact, several efforts to produce a set of system libraries for other hardware environments, such as PDAs, set-top "network appliances," and so forth. Many of these efforts are quite innovative. Transvirtual's PocketLinux, for example, consists of a Linux kernel that essentially uses a Java VM (name Kaffe) as the system libraries; the uCLinux project, meanwhile, has as a goal—a "Linux-on-chip" system—where a stripped-down but functional Linux kernel and rudimentary system library can be embedded into a piece of equipment.

Again, however, these are really still exceptions. As interesting as these efforts are, they only demonstrate the versatility of the Linux kernel, whereas we're interested in a more traditional Linux-based desktop, workstation, or server operating system. For such systems, the glibc is where it's at.

X Window Desktop

Ah, X. The X Window system may be one of the most beloved and reviled pieces of software in history. X has become the de facto (and some people would argue more than de facto) standard windowing system for Unix-like operating systems. X can seem bizarre to those new to it, can seem primitive to casual observers, and can seem incredibly powerful to experienced users.

The X Window system was first released in 1984 by the Massachusetts Institute of Technology's Laboratory for Computer Science, and is now governed by a consortium of industry and other public and private groups. Since 1984, it has become the GUI of choice for Unix systems. Commonly referred to simply as "X," it has legions of zealous supporters, as well as staunch opponents. Indeed, the fortune cookie amusement program that ships with Red Hat Linux has many anti-X quotes in it; "X Windows: You'll wish we were kidding." and "X Windows: More than enough rope." Love it or hate it, however, everyone admits that X introduced several important architectural features to the GUI scene, including network transparency and a layered design for user interfaces.

Network Transparency

Network transparency means that you can view the output of an X program running on a different machine across the network. That machine, in fact, doesn't need to have X running, or even have a monitor at all. This network transparency was standardized in the X protocol, which allows any GUI to support the viewing of X apps simply by implementing the protocol; for example, you can purchase X servers for Windows that will let you view X applications on your Windows box. This network transparency is one of the primary reasons why X has survived as long as it has; without it, X would have been left in the pixilated dust of its competitors.

Layered GUI Model

X's other major claim to fame is the layered GUI model. The X Window system itself is essentially just an event framework for managing windows and window events. Managing windows involves keeping track of where on the screen windows are located, window dimensions, and so on. Managing window events means sending notifications when buttons are pushed, when windows are resized, when repainting or redrawing windows, and so on. These window management events, together with the network transparency functionality, comprise the *X- Window protocol*. This protocol itself knows nothing about video cards, framebuffers, 3D acceleration, or any other aspect of actually rendering graphics to a display. These lower-level tasks are the responsibility of the X server, which is a program that interacts with the video card, implementing the X protocol.

Neither the X protocol nor the X server has knowledge of what actually goes on in a window, however. That is, X has no facilities for drawing buttons, check-boxes, or any of the other "widgets" that users are familiar with. The X protocol only manages events for these widgets, and the X server only handles drawing the widgets to the video card. X also doesn't provide any user interface components, such as icons, desktops, start menus, and so forth. X itself is very stripped-down (when compared to other GUIs such as the MacOS or Windows) and relies on two others layers to do the real work: the widget set and the window manager. In other words, the X Window system consists of three parts:

- An X server

- A widget set

- A window manager

These layers are discussed in more detail in the rest of this section.

Widget Set

The *widget set* is a library or a sort of palette of elements commonly used in GUIs. Examples of widgets include the buttons and checkboxes mentioned in the previous section, as well as selection lists, radio buttons, and so forth. Since X imposes no restrictions on what these widgets have to look like, developers and artists are free to make widget sets look however they choose to. There are a lot of widget sets out there, with a very wide variety of appearances. Motif (developed by the Open Software Foundation, with no relationship to the Free Software Foundation) was the first highly popular widget set, and became the *de facto* standard widget set for many years. There are many widget sets available to choose from today; so many, in fact, that it's hard to keep track of them all!

Recently, GNU's GTK+ and TrollTech's Qt toolkits are emerging as modern, full-featured, and open-source libraries. These toolkits are really more than simple widget sets, since they are also providing fairly extensive frameworks for actually building applications. GTK+ was popularized by the GNOME desktop, and Qt was popularized by the K Desktop Environment (KDE).

GNOME and KDE

GNOME and KDE, in turn, are examples of the last layer of an X GUI: the window manager. A *window manager* is responsible for drawing window decorations such as borders, title bars, and the ubiquitous minimize and maximize buttons, as well as the "softer" aspects of providing the icons, desktops, menus, etc. that really characterize a user interface. There are probably as many or more window managers out there as widget toolkits, and frequently there is a window manager for each widget set. For example, in addition to KDE/Qt and GNOME/GTK+, the mwm window manager is based on Motif, while the fvwm and twm window managers have their own internal widget sets.

Window Manager vs. Desktop Environment

While I described KDE and GNOME as window managers, it's actually a little white lie. In reality, they're both examples of software suites that make up a desktop environment. The suites include several different programs, of which a window manager is only one. Typically, KDE and GNOME include:

- Window manager

- Desktop program (for placing icons on the background)

- Button panel (for containing buttons to launch programs)

- Taskbar or window list (for switching between running applications)

- Desktop pager (for switching between virtual desktops)

- Utility programs (for controlling and configuring all the rest)

Different desktops and window managers (including not only KDE and GNOME but others as well) will have some subset or superset of this list. To really unlock your productivity when using your desktop, you should learn about what features are available to you with your environment. Throughout the rest of this book, these suites will be referred to as desktop environments.

In a nutshell, the window manager handles moving, resizing, and closing the windows, while the widget set manages the appearance and behavior of the windows. X, meanwhile, provides the framework to run all of this. This componentized model for the GUI gives developers and users a truly staggering, and even daunting, degree of choice in GUIs. Some of these GUIs are very simple and lightweight, such as twm, short for "Tom's window manager." Others, like KDE and GNOME, are more than window managers and are better described as desktop environments.

Choosing an X Server, Widget Set, and Window Manager

Since there are three "layers" to an X Window environment, there are essentially three choices you need to make regarding the following:

- Which X server to use

- Which widget set to use

- Which window manager to use

For Linux systems and most of the BSD systems, the XFree86 package is the de facto standard X server and library set, so that's an easy choice, leaving only the widget set and window manager to be determined. However, since the widget set and window manager are usually closely related, there's only one choice to make here. In other words, the only choice you really have to make is which window manager or desktop you want to use.

The choice of window manager depends largely on what you want to do with the system. (Now where have we heard that before?) If you're reading this book, you are probably most interested in using it as a desktop, server, or workstation. In these cases, your alternative is Windows or a Macintosh, so the competition is pretty stiff. If this is what you're after, your best choices are KDE or GNOME.

KDE and GNOME are both very complete environments. They provide not only a window manager, but also various applications such as icon panels (for launching applications), task bars, and various other features that will make most Windows users feel right at home. KDE and GNOME also have features that competitors can't touch—even Windows and the Macintosh—such as the ability to support custom "themes" or "skins" that let the user customize the desktop right down to the widget set level. Figures 3-2 and 3-3 show the same KDE desktop running two completely different themes. Figure 3-2 depicts Alessandro Rossini's "Acqua GRAPHITE" theme, while Figure 3-3 depicts Martin Doege's "LCARS ACCESS 411" theme. Both themes can be obtained from the site `kde.themes.org`.

KDE and GNOME generally lag Windows only in some of the infrastructure aspects. For example, Windows has a more extensive, pervasive, and robust component object model (COM) for embedding application functionality and communicating between applications, which KDE and GNOME are just now starting to address. This becomes especially evident in the realm of office productivity applications, where COM is used extensively. However, both KDE and GNOME have embeddable component framework efforts underway, and are gaining ground quickly. The 2.1 version of KDE, for example, offers some features that even Windows doesn't have. Additionally, industry consortiums have recently formed behind both KDE and GNOME, including support from all the major commercial Unix vendors; this support could accelerate the progress of these environments even further.

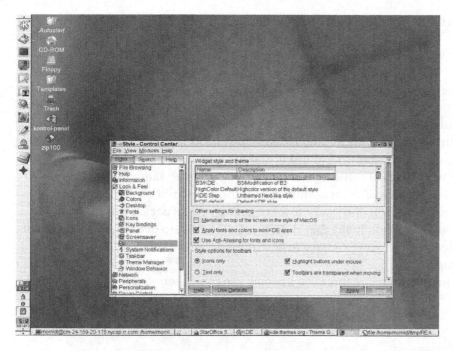

Figure 3-2. Example KDE theme: Acqua GRAPHITE

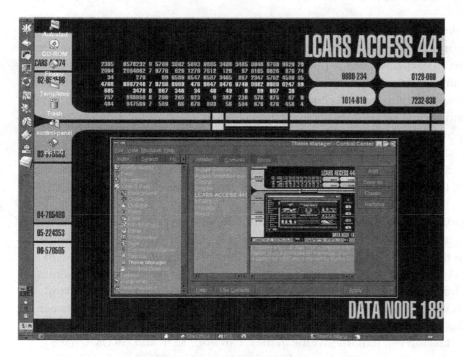

Figure 3-3. Example KDE theme: LCARS ACCESS

Application Software

So far, I've talked a lot about the system itself. That's fine if you're an enthusiast interested in technology for the sake of technology. However, the rest of us are interested in technology for our own sakes: what can it help us do? (Hopefully you've noticed this recurring theme by now.) On this note, a Linux system is only as useful as the productivity software installed on it. The real objective of a Linux distribution is to provide as much useful software as possible; everything up to this point is just enabling us to install and run what we really want to get at.

So, what kinds of software can you actually use with Linux? The answer is, all kinds. However, there's a lot of software out there, and not all of it is useful to everyone. Just as you don't want to leave out a software package users want, you don't want to add too many they don't need, either. So, to determine what kind of software to install, you first have to determine what kind of system you're installing.

Generally, there are three ways people use computers:

- Desktops (or personal computer)

- Servers

- Workstations

A *desktop* is generally used by very non-technical people who just want to get work done. *Servers* are run by individuals or organizations that need to provide services to each other or the public. A *workstation*, though, is a hybrid: it's part server and part desktop. A workstation is generally a desktop that frequently runs heftier applications (such as engineering design applications or scientific computing) and sometimes a few services (such as a low-volume web server). Microsoft Windows ME and the Macintosh OS are good desktop operating systems; Windows NT is a good workstation OS; Solaris and Linux are good workstation and server operating systems. (These examples are just generalities, of course; there's nothing that says the Mac OS can't be a workstation operating system.)

Why doesn't Linux make a good desktop operating system? Well, some people will argue that it does. However, there's a good deal more complexity to a Linux system than your average desktop OS, and users of desktop operating systems generally eschew complexity in all its myriad forms. The proof is in the pudding: Linux has exploded on the server and workstation, so if it's not on the desktop, there must be a reason. However, it's important to note the distinction between "has not" and "can not": Linux systems "have not" experienced vast penetration on the desktop yet; that doesn't mean they "can not." KDE and GNOME have extremely strong stories on the desktop, and only time will tell.

Why are KDE and GNOME so strong? Well, because contrary to popular belief, there is software for Linux systems. From office suites to digital camera software to image editors to web browsers and email clients, it's there on the desktop. From web servers to databases to LDAP directories to network file-sharing software, it's there on the server. From scientific computing and visualization to engineering applications to software development, it's there on the professional workstation. The main problem is that this software can be rather hard to locate and install; it sometimes takes a software developer just to get a program to run. Well, either a software developer or someone who's read this book, that is.

Enter the Linux Standards Base

It's probably becoming clear at this point that there are a lot of variables in creating a Linux distribution. Each distribution is independent, and the fact that two different distributions are based on the same Linux kernel does not by any means imply that they are compatible with one another. In fact, they frequently are not. Software compiled for one distribution may not run on another, and this increases the burden for software developers, who may end up having to support their software on multiple distributions.

To address this fact, the Linux Standards Base (LSB) project was created. This project is a collaboration between individuals and companies involved in Linux systems and other open-source or free software activities. The goal of the organization is to establish a basic set of core software that distribution vendors can include in their products—in essence, a sort of "mini-distribution" that vendors can use as the core of their own systems. By standardizing on the LSB, the various distributions can improve interoperability and compatibility between systems. At the time of this writing, the LSB had only recently released a formal 1.0.0 specification, and so no major distribution vendors support it yet. However, the LSB (and its sponsoring organization, the Free Standards Group) may become a major influence on Linux systems in the future. The LSB can be found at www.linuxbase.org.

Summary

In this chapter, you read about the basics of a distribution. You learned that as different as the various distributions are from each other, in the end they all must solve the same set of problems, such as which software to include and how to lay out the filesystem. Once you understand this, the task of mastering a new distribution is as simple (or as hard!) as figuring out how the distribution solves each of these problems.

In the next three chapters, you'll read about three actual distributions. These chapters discuss the distributions in detail and dissect them to illustrate how each solves these same basic problems. After reading these chapters, you'll have a broad set of real-world details to flesh out the general understanding you gained from this chapter.

#### CHAPTER 4

Red Hat Linux 7.3

One of the most successful commercial Linux vendors is Red Hat, Inc., makers of the eponymous Red Hat Linux distribution. In this chapter, you will read about Red Hat Linux version 7.3 and focus on the characteristics that make it unique and useful. Since Red Hat Linux is one of the more popular and most well-known distributions, it's a good place to start learning about Linux systems in general.

This chapter is the first of three distribution-focused chapters in Part Two of this book. The goal of these sample distribution chapters is to provide three perspectives on Linux systems, offer insight into their construction, and illustrate the general concepts of distribution design. Most important, examining these different sample distributions will provide you with a broader base of experience from which to draw when you work with any other distribution, current or future.

Red Hat's Background and Philosophy

Red Hat, Inc. was founded in 1994 by Bob Young and Marc Ewing, who were intrigued by open source software and thought it would make a great business model. Their primary activity at the beginning was the production and marketing of Red Hat Linux, their flagship product. Since Red Hat's inception, the company has branched out into a number of additional markets, including embedded systems and professional services. As a company, however, Red Hat remains aligned with and dedicated to the open source model. Almost all of their own software is released under an open source license, and they fund various open source development efforts that are not necessarily core to the Red Hat Linux distribution.

 CROSS-REFERENCE *See Chapter 2 for a discussion of the open source model.*

However, Red Hat Software is a business, so they have to make money. Because Red Hat Linux itself is free, Red Hat makes profit by adding value to the distribution through support contracts, subscriptions for priority access, and so forth. In fact, these other activities are Red Hat's primary source of funding, and their Linux distribution can be viewed simply as a platform that enables these other sources of revenue.

Regardless of whether it's their primary moneymaker or not, Red Hat's Linux distribution still has to be of quality, or else it won't succeed. To ensure the best overall quality, Red Hat views their distribution as a holistic system that must be as full-featured and bug-free as possible in the aggregate, rather than state-of-the-art in terms of each individual component (such as the kernel or the system C compiler). Consequently, Red Hat takes a more conservative approach to their software than do many other free software and open source organizations. Red Hat frequently incorporates software versions and patches that aren't technically "stable" but that Red Hat deems production-ready. Conversely, Red Hat just as frequently elects not to include software that others might claim is stable if it doesn't meet Red Hat's own quality standards. In other words, in order to enhance the quality and functionality of the Red Hat distribution, the company makes various tradeoffs with that goal in mind.

Linux Kernel

Red Hat Linux 7.3 shipped with a kernel based on Linux 2.4.18 and in general is intended for use with the 2.4 series of kernels. When the next series is released (which will probably be either 2.6 or 3.0), Red Hat's 7.*x* series might or might not work with the newer kernels; Red Hat generally engineers their distributions to function with a specific kernel series. Though they may strive for forward compatibility, Red Hat's ultimate goal is an overall robust, functional system, so they occasionally forgo forward compatibility when they think the required changes would reduce the quality of their distribution. (Red Hat takes this attitude toward all parts of their system, not just the kernel, as you will see as you read on.)

Because Red Hat is intent on producing a high-quality distribution, they rarely ship a "stock" Linux kernel with their operating system. Instead, Red Hat puts the kernel through extensive quality assurance tests, and they usually apply customizations and bug fixes intended to improve the quality of the distribution or to add some functionality that they deem useful. Red Hat is not alone in this practice; most of the commercial distribution vendors have similar practices, though some other distributions (such as Slackware, which is covered in Chapter 5) focus on stock kernels.

Red Hat does, of course, submit any changes they make to the Linux kernel back to the kernel development community. In fact, Red Hat employs developers who are regular and crucial contributors to the stock Linux kernel. Generally, any changes Red Hat makes are eventually included in the stock kernel sources, but occasionally they are not, which rouses fears of a "kernel fork" or incompatibilities.

To date, though, Red Hat has never shipped a kernel that was a truly significant departure from the stock kernel.

Packaging Format

Red Hat Linux uses the *Red Hat Package Manager* (RPM) format as its package manager. RPM was developed explicitly for Red Hat Linux. This section discusses the Red Hat Package Manager in detail, first describing some of the general properties of the format and then covering the important features in detail. Once you've read this section, you'll have a working understanding of how to manage software on an RPM-based system, and you'll know where to look to find out how to do the more esoteric tasks.

RPM was one of the first package management tools for Linux systems, but it is currently at version 4, meaning that it has been significantly overhauled three times since the original version. RPM is consequently a relatively mature package management tool and compares favorably to most commercial package management tools. In fact, it's such a solid product that even commercial Unix vendors are beginning to include tailored installations of it. RPM is really only rivaled or exceeded by the Debian packaging system.

RPM is a pretty typical example of a package management tool for Unix systems, though it far exceeds most in actual functionality. Such utilities typically allow you to install and uninstall software packages. RPM provides rich functionality for these basic tasks, but it also goes beyond them by providing upgrade- and dependency-validation semantics, as well as a way to list installed packages and even query packages (both installed and uninstalled) for documentation. In addition, RPM has functionality supporting *source RPMs,* which are packages containing the source code for a particular software package. Users can use source RPMs to build software with customizations different from the defaults for a given package or to build the software on an architecture or platform not supported by a given package.

You can think of RPM in a certain sense as a sort of database for software information. Relational databases (such as those used for web sites or other applications) store their data so that it can be queried or updated in a variety of ways. Similarly, the RPM format allows administrators and users to query installed packages for a variety of information and to "insert" or "remove" applications by installing or uninstalling them. Also, just as relational databases enforce transactions and atomic operations, RPM enforces software dependency requirements and tries to ensure atomic operations.

NOTE *An **atomic operation** is one that can't be interrupted and is guaranteed to either complete successfully or not at all—an atomic operation can't partially succeed and leave behind a mess.*

Technical Summary

This section covers some of the basic details of an RPM package. In particular, the conventions for naming RPM files and the properties of the file format itself are discussed.

File Naming Conventions

By convention, RPM file names have this format:

```
package-version-build.arch.rpm
```

where "package" is the name of the software, "version" is the release version of the software, "build" is the version of the particular RPM package, and "arch" is the architecture that the RPM was compiled for.

For example, an RPM file for glibc v2.2.5 as shipped with Red Hat Linux 7.3 and built for Intel-based systems might have the file name glibc-2.2.5-.i386.rpm. The version of this file that actually shipped with Red Hat 7.3 is glibc-2.2.5-34.i386.rpm; in this case, "-34" indicates that this was the thirty-fourth version of this RPM Red Hat created before releasing Red Hat 7.3. (Generally, these miniversions include minor tweaks to the package layout or configuration options, and occasionally minor bug fixes.)

Architectures

As mentioned in the previous section, RPMs are built for specific architectures. An *architecture* is usually simply a type of microprocessor. Most installations of Linux are on systems with Intel microprocessors in the i386 family, but Linux runs on many other processors, and you can find RPMs for these platforms as well. Table 4-1 lists some common architectures and the name of that representation in an RPM file name.

Table 4-1. RPM Architectures

ARCHITECTURE	VENDOR	NAME IN RPM	COMMENT
Intel 386 family	Intel	i386	Most common RPM format.
Intel Pentium	Intel	i586	Makes use of Pentium-specific performance optimizations.
Intel Pentium Pro	Intel	i686	Makes use of optimizations for Pentium Pro, Pentium III, or Pentium IV.
Alpha	Compaq	alpha	Compaq's high-performance RISC processor. This is an actual architecture and it does *not* indicate a test version of the software!
PowerPC	IBM, Motorola, Apple	ppc	IBM's PowerPC architecture used in Apple Macintoshes and certain IBM workstations.
SPARC	Sun Microsystems	sparc	Processor used in Sun workstations and servers.
Generic	N/A	noarch	The RPM does not contain any processor-specific binary files— for example, it might consist entirely of shell scripts.
Source code	N/A	src	Contains only source code. When compiled for a specific architecture, the output will be a binary RPM for that platform.

Package File Format

The RPM file format is based on cpio; that is, an rpm file is simply a cpio file with some extra header bytes prepended to it. The RPM package itself comes with a tool (rpm2cpio) that can actually convert an RPM file into the underlying cpio file. The cpio command on a Unix system is similar to tar, but it has a slightly different usage.

RPM is more than just a fancy file storage format, however. RPM archives (sometimes called *packages*) include additional information on dependencies that the software has. RPM also allows for scripts to be run when the package is installed or uninstalled, and these scripts can perform additional work that RPM itself doesn't do automatically. An RPM installation will enforce these dependencies and reject an administrator's attempt to install a file if the dependencies are not met (unless the user explicitly overrides this behavior).

The cpio and tar Commands

Two common formats for packaging and distributing files on Unix-like systems are cpio and tar. These formats are named after the programs used to create and manipulate them. The `tar` command is short for "tape archive" and was originally used to shuffle data to and from magnetic tapes, usually for backup purposes. However, the tool can also be used to create and manipulate archives of ordinary files. The `cpio` command is very similar to tar, and its name means "I/O (input/output) copy."

These two commands are used to create files that contain other files. They are very similar to the ZIP file format commonly used on other operating systems such as Windows and IBM's OS/2. Unlike ZIP, however, they do not themselves provide any compression of the data, but rather are simply "containers" of other files. Typically, one of these archives is compressed via a command such as the GNU Zip (gzip) program—for example, a gzip-compressed tar file becomes the ubiquitous .tar.gz file.

These file formats differ from a more sophisticated packaging format such as RPM. Whereas a tar or cpio archive simply contains other files for "transportation," an RPM archive augments the files themselves with additional information (such as dependencies on other files not included in the archive or installation scripts) that is required to correctly install or use the files.

Using RPM

This section covers the basics of using RPM to manage software installations. Red Hat's documentation on RPM is quite good, so rather than duplicate that information, this section and the following ones cover only the basics. Readers who need more detail should consult the RPM manual page (via the `man rpm` command) or the excellent documentation on Red Hat's web site (`www.redhat.com/docs/books/max-rpm/index.html`).

Program Modes

The command for managing RPM packages is simply `rpm`. This single program has the five following "modes" that it operates in to perform its various tasks:

- Query

- Install

- Upgrade

- Verify

- Erase

- Rebuild

Each of these modes has additional options that let users perform specific tasks. Again, for full documentation, consult the information available from Red Hat. The following sections present details on how to perform several common, useful tasks.

Access Permissions

The RPM database is a tool for managing the software installed on the system. Obviously, if a system is shared among many users, only an administrator should be able to install software. However, users may still wish to be able to check on installed packages; for this reason, the RPM database is usually installed with "world-readable" but only "root-writable" permissions. Thus, as a general rule of thumb, normal users may execute any query, but only the root user will be able to execute any command that would modify the contents of the disk, such as an installation or deletion.

Dependency Checks

Many of the commands described in this section rely on *dependency checks.* That is, RPM will determine whether it can perform an operation based on whether or not the operation would result in software with broken or unfulfilled dependencies. As a convenience, RPM will also include all package or file names given to it in this dependency checking. For example, the command

```
rpm -i foo.i386.rpm bar.i386.rpm
```

will install both RPMs at the same time. Aside from saving the user the effort of issuing two rpm commands, this allows users to install multiple RPMs at the same time that might be mutually dependent on each other. Most of the RPM operations have this behavior.

Understanding Dependencies

A package has a *dependency* on another package or file if it requires the presence of that package or file to properly function. These dependencies can take any form. A program might require a particular shared library in order to function, or it might require that another program first be installed. (This program might be used in configuring or operating the new program.) Alternatively, a package of documentation files might require the presence of a reader program for those files.

As a concrete example, the KDE window manager and desktop system requires that XFree86 be installed, as well as the Qt windowing toolkit library. Meanwhile, the Washington University FTP server (wuftpd) requires that an inetd program (such as xinetd) be present. Keeping track of all these dependencies can become burdensome, and so the RPM system (and other packaging formats) was created to automate these tasks.

Querying Uninstalled Packages

RPM is a distribution format as much as it is a package management format. That is, an important goal of RPM is to provide a canonical, standardized way for distributors of software to package their applications so that end users can easily install those applications. To this end, the RPM format and the rpm program provide the capability to query uninstalled RPM packages for information about the software. This allows users to find out what the RPM will do and what it will install before they actually install it.

This is the general form of an RPM query command:

```
rpm -q<options> <target>
```

<target> is either the name of an installed package or a path to an RPM file, and *<options>* are additional letters specifying the type of information to be retrieved and whether the desired package is already installed.

To query a package that has not been installed yet, the form is

```
rpm -qp<options> <filename>
```

<options> in this case must indicate what information is to be retrieved, and *<filename>* must be the path to the RPM file to be queried. There are many options for obtaining information, but these four are particularly useful:

- General information

- File listing

- Requirements

- Provided capabilities

Table 4-2 lists the RPM commands required to retrieve these query types and describes what details are provided by each.

Table 4-2. RPM Package Querying

QUERY TYPE	RPM COMMAND	INFORMATION PROVIDED
General information	rpm -qpi	General information about the package, such as size in bytes and a text description of the package
File listing	rpm -qpl	A list of all files the package will install
Requirements	rpm -qpR	A list of all capabilities (such as shared libraries) required by the software
Provided capabilities	rpm -qp --provides	A list of all capabilities the software provides

Note: Each of these RPM commands must be followed by the file name of the RPM package to be queried—for example, rpm -qpi glibc-2.2.5-34.i386.rpm.

Additional queries that you can perform on uninstalled packages include listing configuration and documentation files, listing the scripts used by the package, and so forth. Some of the more advanced RPM queries are actually quite powerful but can become a bit arcane. Interested readers should consult Red Hat's documentation on RPM.

Installing Packages

Installing packages with RPM is quite easy. The command used is simply

```
rpm -i <filename>
```

Two useful options are --force and --nodeps, which respectively force the package to be installed even if it conflicts with existing files and instruct RPM to ignore dependency checks when installing the package.

CAUTION *Use the* --force *and* --nodeps *options with great care, since they are overriding RPM's default behavior.*

Users may take advantage of additional options to instruct RPM to customize the installation of a package, but generally installations are as simple as executing the previous command.

RPM goes through the following routine when installing a package:

1. It extracts a file list from the package and checks it against its database of installed files, looking for conflicts.

2. It checks the dependencies listed by the package to make sure they are met. If all is well, RPM then executes any preinstallation scripts identified by the package.

3. The files are extracted from the archive and placed in the appropriate locations on the disk.

4. Finally, RPM executes any postinstallation scripts identified by the package.

After these steps are completed, the package is installed. However, sometimes a given package that has already been installed may need to be notified when a related package is installed. For example, the xinetd package may need to be notified whenever any applications that use xinetd are installed. In cases such as this, RPM allows a package to designate trigger scripts that get executed whenever certain conditions are met during a subsequent package installation. Executing any relevant triggers is the last step in installing an RPM package. In practice, comparatively few RPM packages actually use triggers, but the functionality is available.

Upgrading Packages

If one thing is true of software, it's that it's never finished. Whenever a new version of software is released, users will probably want to upgrade their copies. RPM allows users to upgrade the packages installed on their system to a later version.

The command for an RPM upgrade is

```
rpm -U <filename>
```

The process for upgrading an RPM is similar to installing one, except that RPM first checks to see if the software is already installed. (RPM will abort the process if the software is not already present.) Most of the same commands available for an RPM installation also work for an upgrade. Using an RPM upgrade essentially saves the user from having to manually erase the old RPM and install the new one.

....

Beware the Case!

The syntax for an RPM upgrade is `rpm -U <filename>`; however, older versions of RPM used a lowercase "u" to mean "uninstall"! Current versions of RPM use the `-e` option (for "erase") instead of `-u`, but you should take care nonetheless, especially when using older Red Hat Linux systems.

....

Querying Installed Packages

One of the most powerful features of RPM is its capability to query the system for installed packages. This allows users to easily check whether a given piece of software is installed (and if so, where it is located), rather than have to hunt around the system to find out the hard way. It also allows administrators to keep track of a system, since they can generate a list of all software installed. Because the RPM database also keeps track of the additional information described earlier in this chapter under the "Querying Uninstalled Packages" section, RPM also provides access to documentation and dependency information on installed packages.

Querying an installed package is almost identical to querying a package that hasn't been installed yet. The only difference is that instead of executing the command

```
rpm -qp<options> <filename>
```

users simply execute the command

```
rpm -q<options> <package>
```

and substitute the name of an installed package for the file name of an uninstalled package. Otherwise, all of the query options listed in Table 4-2 can be used.

One notable variant of the package query command is the option to query all packages. The command

```
rpm -qa
```

allows users to perform a query on all packages. Normally, this is used to obtain a list of all installed packages, but users can also add the query options listed in Table 4-2. Be forewarned, though: Commands such as `rpm -qai` will generate *a lot* of output!

Verifying Installed Packages

Over the course of a system's normal usage, files get changed. This could be as innocent as simply changing a configuration file in the /etc directory or as problematic as a file being corrupted by a power failure. To assist in the detection of these changes, RPM allows users and administrators to verify the integrity of an installed package.

The command

```
rpm -V <package>
```

or

```
rpm -Va
```

will verify all installed packages. RPM then computes the MD5 checksum of all files on the disk and compares them to the stored MD5 sums from the original RPMs. The output of the command is a line indicating any files that differ from the versions that were originally installed and a code indicating how the file has changed.

RPM verification is useful for detecting accidentally damaged files and for maintaining a list of files that have been manually changed. It is important to note that many files (such as the device node files in /dev) get changed almost immediately after installation, so there will almost always be changed files on any given system.

Also, while RPM verification can be a crude first line of defense in detecting an unauthorized intrusion (such as a cracker gaining root on the machine), there are better tools available, such as Tripwire, which comes with many distributions, including Red Hat 7.3. RPM's package verification functionality should be used strictly as a damage detector, and should not be relied on as a security tool. You can find the open source version of Tripwire at www.tripwire.org.

Rebuilding Packages

Sometimes a user will want to install a piece of software with different customizations than those contained in the default RPM as distributed or is using a Linux system on an architecture for which there is no binary RPM. Sometimes a software vendor simply can't keep track of all the possible target configurations of their software and wishes to provide a convenient package of source code for their product. To handle these cases, Red Hat's RPM format includes support for *source RPMs* that contain source code for software. These RPMs have the extension .src.rpm and they can be rebuilt into binary RPMs.

Recall that an RPM file is really a cpio file with some additional information. This additional information is contained in a file called a *spec file* (which is short for "specification file"). A spec file contains all the information needed to build an RPM, such as the list of dependencies, the list of required capabilities, and so forth. Spec files are written by the developers of the software or by the packager of the RPM file. All that is needed to build a binary RPM file is the spec file and the source code.

There are two ways to rebuild an RPM package. If a source RPM is available, the command

```
rpm --rebuild <filename>
```

will rebuild that file into a binary RPM (assuming no errors occur during the build). This is the simplest case, and it will work for almost all source RPMs. However, the RPM command supports additional options for conveniently building RPM files out of other formats.

Sometimes, the developers of a piece of software will release their application in some neutral format, such as a tarball, but include a spec file with it. In this case, the tarball can be placed in the special directory /usr/src/redhat/SOURCES, and the spec file can be placed in /usr/src/redhat/SPECS. Then, the command

```
rpm -ba /usr/src/redhat/SPECS/<filename>
```

will rebuild the tarball according to the directions in the spec file. The output will be an RPM file in /usr/src/redhat/RPMS/<arch> (where <arch> is the architecture of your system, such as i386, as listed in Table 4-1). This RPM file can then be installed normally, like any other RPM file. It can also be copied to another system and installed there (assuming any dependencies are met); in fact, this is generally how most RPMs are created for distribution.

Uninstalling Packages

Occasionally software must be uninstalled from a system. This is historically one of the most difficult tasks about managing a computer system. Windows users are familiar with *DLL hell,* which refers to the problem of "orphaned" shared libraries and multiple (incompatible) versions of libraries installed or left behind by several programs. On RPM-based systems, however, this problem is greatly reduced.

Because the RPM database keeps track of all the files installed by a given package and ensures that one package doesn't replace a file owned by another package, RPM always knows which files belong to a given package, making it easy to uninstall a package. RPM's capability to track the dependency information of packages also allows it to make sure that a user doesn't delete a package that provides a capability required by another package. These behaviors can be overridden or ignored, but generally RPM is very successful at uninstalling software.

The command to uninstall an RPM package is simply

```
rpm -e <package>
```

Most of the options for install and upgrade (for example, `--nodeps` and `--force`) are also supported by the erase operation. If RPM determines that it is safe to uninstall the software, then the command will simply return. If a dependency check fails or some other error occurs, however, RPM will indicate what the error is and will not remove the package. If the problem is that another package depends on the package being removed, the user must decide whether both programs can be removed.

Creating New Packages

Creating a new RPM package generally involves creating a spec file and using the RPM program to build an RPM file from a source code archive according to the directions in the spec file. Creating a spec file requires extensive knowledge of the software being distributed, and so it generally must be created by a developer or other individual familiar with the software. There are many sources of documentation on how to create a spec file and RPM, so interested readers and developers should consult these sources. One excellent source is Red Hat's book *Maximum RPM,* which you can find at www.rpm.org/max-rpm.

Additional Functionality

RPM has some extra features that make it easier to use. These features don't include any extra functionality beyond the basic operations discussed earlier in this chapter, but rather make it easier and safer to user RPM for those operations. Specifically, RPM supports cryptographically signed RPM files and operations on RPM files over a network.

Most users of Red Hat Linux either install the system off of some physical medium such as a CD or install it over the network from a public server. In either case, it is extremely common for users to download RPM files from the Internet and install them on their systems. After all, network connectivity is a large part of the success of Linux systems. As a convenience for these operations, RPM has built-in support for automatically downloading RPM files from FTP or HTTP servers. This allows users to install an RPM package in one command rather than having to manually download a file. For example, the rather ponderous command

```
rpm -i ftp://ftp.redhat.com/pub/redhat/redhat-7.3-en/os/i386/RedHat/RPMS/zsh-
4.0.4-5.i386.rpm
```

will install the zsh package for Red Hat Linux 7.3 from Red Hat's public FTP server.

However, downloading files over the network can be dangerous, as it's possible that hostile users could place "Trojan horse" packages that appear to be authentic but in fact contain hostile code that could damage a user's system or expose it to attack. To ameliorate this risk, RPM is able to use the GNU Privacy Guard (GPG) program to verify the authenticity of RPM files that have been cryptographically signed. You can access the GPG program via the gpg command. For more information, visit the GNU Privacy Guard web site at www.gnupg.org.

Mechanism vs. User Interface

So far, RPM has only been discussed as a tool for managing packages that the user already has in hand. RPM itself is also only a command line tool, and has no graphical user interface. The reason for these limitations is that RPM is focused strictly on package management. Red Hat's philosophy is to keep mechanism separate from user interface, and so RPM relies on additional tools to provide a pretty user interface.

Red Hat's up2date Program

Red Hat's preferred user interface tool is the up2date program. *up2date* is both a command-line program and a graphical program that communicates with a server to obtain software updates and install them. up2date keeps track of a system's *profile* (which is essentially a list of what RPMs the system has installed) and will update any packages for which there is a later version on the server. This allows users and administrators to closely track security and bug fixes released by the administrators of the server.

In a default Red Hat Linux installation, up2date is configured to use Red Hat's servers. Red Hat allows basic access to their servers for free but has a subscription fee plan based on up2date. Users who do not wish to pay for Red Hat's service (such as those managing a base of Red Hat Linux installations at a business) may either set up their own server or choose another provider if one is available.

Other GUI Programs

A myriad of other GUI programs act as a front end to RPM. For example, the GNOME and KDE projects each have their own such tools, named gnoRPM and kpackage, respectively. These programs are fairly similar in functionality and provide a point-and-click, drag-and-drop interface for managing RPM packages. Generally, these applications are also integrated into their desktops in various ways.

Fundamentally, RPM really is just a specification of a file format and a database of information on the RPMs installed in a system. Another packaging system can be compatible with the RPM format by simply supporting the file format. The Debian packaging format has some support for RPM files in their own tool, apt-get.

Examples of Using RPM

Like many tools on Unix systems, RPM is pretty sophisticated and even—dare I say it—arcane. Typically, much of the true power of RPM comes from using it with other commands. This section demonstrates some useful examples of RPM to perform common tasks. Table 4-3 lists some common commands and describes their output. Except where noted, these commands are generally safe—users should feel free to experiment with them.

Table 4-3. Useful RPM Commands

COMMAND	DESCRIPTION
rpm -qf `which <command>`	Shows the package that installed <command>.
rpm -ql <package> | grep /bin	Locates program binaries (e.g., files in /usr/bin) installed by <package>.
rpm -qfi `which <command>`	Shows the description of the package that installed <command>; may be useful for commands with no man page.
rpm -qfl `locate <file>`	Shows all files in the same package as <file>. (Watch out—locate may return more than one result!)
rpm -qa | grep <package>	Displays the exact package name for <package>; useful when you know a package is installed, but don't know its exact name.
rpm -qi `rpm -qa | grep <package>`	Shows the description of a package whose name isn't fully known.
rpm -e `rpm -qa | grep <package>`	Useful for erasing a package whose name isn't fully known. This command can be *very dangerous*—use it with caution.

If you have read this entire section, you should now have a working knowledge of Red Hat's packaging format, RPM. With this knowledge, you should be able to manage the software installed on your system, and with a little exploration of the detailed documentation available from Red Hat, you'll be using RPM like a pro. The rest of this chapter gives you a similar understanding of the other key aspects of Red Hat Linux.

Filesystem Layout

Perhaps the most immediately obvious idiosyncrasy of any Unix-like system (including Linux systems) is the layout of the filesystem. In Chapter 3, I discussed the Linux Filesystem Hierarchy Standard (FHS). In this section, you'll learn how closely Red Hat Linux follows the FHS. When you've finished this section, you'll be able to find anything on a Red Hat Linux system. If you haven't already done so, it would be useful to review the FHS and my discussion of it in Chapter 3 now. Generally, Red Hat closely follows the FHS. Table 4-4 summarizes the key points of Red Hat Linux's filesystem layout.

Table 4-4. Red Hat Linux and the Linux FHS

DIRECTORY	FHS CONTENTS	RED HAT COMMENTS
/etc	Configuration files	Follows FHS; general strategy is to have a separate subdirectory for each component
/boot	Files required for the system to boot up	Follows FHS
/dev	Files representing hardware devices on the system	Follows FHS
/lib	Shared library files required by user programs	Follows FHS
/bin	User application programs	Follows FHS
/sbin	Programs used primarily for administrative tasks	Follows FHS
/home	Home directories for users	Follows FHS
/mnt	Contains subdirectories where temporary filesystems can be mounted	Follows FHS
/usr	Files useful to users once the system is running	Generally follows FHS, but occasionally deviates for specific special cases
/var	Files and directories for storing control information or data for programs and services	Generally follows FHS, but occasionally deviates for specific special cases
/usr/local	Installation-specific files	Present per FHS, but no contents by default
/opt	Installation-specific "optional" software	Present per FHS, but no contents by default
/tmp	Files that are not persistent or important	Follows FHS

Having a filesystem standard for the base installation of an operating system is all fine and well, but it's pointless if it's ignored during subsequent software installations and system maintenance. That is, it's just as important to keep track of where RPMs place files as it is to keep track of where the base installation places files. Fortunately, the convention for RPMs is to follow the FHS; most RPMs downloadable from the Internet (and all of Red Hat's own RPMs) will place their files in /usr or /, as appropriate.

Another point it is worthwhile to cover is how Red Hat Linux treats the /usr partition. The FHS standard indicates that /usr should contain only "static" files that don't need to change frequently. Any "variable" files should go into another directory, such as /var. If this rule is closely followed, then the /usr directory should never be modified, because any nonstatic files belong in another directory. Thus, if the /usr directory was placed on its own partition, it should be possible to mount this partition as read-only; this helps prevent intrusions and accidental damage. This is a feature supported by many other Unix-like systems and even some other Linux distributions. Previous versions of Red Hat Linux were not quite able to support a read-only /usr out of the box, but Red Hat 7.3 does support this technique.

As you've seen, Red Hat Linux follows the FHS fairly closely, with a few exceptions. As a user of a Red Hat Linux system, you should be aware of the conventions established by the FHS. Whenever you need to find a particular file or figure out how a piece of software is installed, you can follow this rule of thumb: First check in the place where the FHS says it should go, and then check in the place where you would expect to find it on a different Unix system. If all else fails, you can try using the locate command if you know the file name you're looking for.

System Startup Scripts

Chapter 1 covered the origins and history of Linux, including a brief history of Unix systems. Chapter 3 discussed the basic components of a Linux distribution, including a brief mention of the startup scripts run by the init superprocess. In this section, you will learn about the startup script architecture used by Red Hat Linux, and you will also learn how to customize a system's startup behavior, both manually and by using the provided tools.

One of the two archetypical Unix systems was AT&T's System V (SysV) Unix. This system introduced a particular technique for laying out the scripts that get run by init on startup. The other major approach was introduced by Berkeley Software Distribution (BSD). These two models serve the same ultimate purpose but differ significantly in how they accomplish it. The SysV approach is a more complicated framework that is fairly easy to automate (but harder for humans to modify), whereas the BSD approach is comparatively simpler and easier for humans to manage (though harder to automate). Red Hat Linux uses the SysV approach, and the remainder of this section describes the details of this mechanism.

Red Hat Linux is not the only Unix-like system to use the SysV init scripts model; some commercial Unix flavors use it as well. Once you've read this section, you'll have a working knowledge of the SysV init model in general, so you should be able to apply your knowledge to any system that uses that model, not just Red Hat Linux. Conversely, if you've used one of these other systems previously, you may already be familiar with the SysV init model. In this case, you may wish to skim or skip this chapter; however, the "Using Red Hat's Tools" section is worth reading as it may offer you some additional information.

Understanding Init Runlevels

The init process is the parent of all other processes—it is the *superprocess*. Consequently, you can think of init as the master process governing the system. As this master process, init controls the lifecycle of all other processes and therefore of the system itself.

Generally, however, init is not directly involved in the activities of its child processes. Instead, after doing its work, init generally sits idle in the background, only waking up when the user requests certain actions or when a crucial process (such as a tty console used for logging in to the system) needs to be "respawned."

At any given time, init is one of seven general states; these states are the system runlevels. The runlevels are numbered 0 through 6, and each level typically corresponds to a certain mode of usage of the system (such as maintenance mode, single-user mode, or even system reboot mode). Init can be configured to perform different actions based on which runlevel it is entering, and the root user can instruct it to switch between runlevels.

The POSIX standard defines the general behavior of init, but it does not specify what states the seven runlevels represent. Traditionally, Unix systems use runlevel 0 for system halt, runlevel 1 for single user, and runlevel 6 for system reboot. The remaining runlevels (2 through 5) are generally multiuser runlevels, but what actually happens in these runlevels is up to the operating system vendor. Table 4-5 summarizes the meanings Red Hat Linux assigns to these runlevels; this information is from the file /etc/inittab.

Table 4-5. Red Hat Linux Runlevels

RUNLEVEL	MEANING	BEHAVIOR
0	System halt	Terminates all processes, flushes the filesystem caches, and shuts down the system.
1	Single-user mode	Opens only a root console; used for system maintenance.
2	Multiuser, no NFS	Normal multiuser mode, except that the Network Filesystem (NFS) is disabled. Typically used for servers or workstations that have only local users.

Table 4-5. Red Hat Linux Runlevels (continued)

RUNLEVEL	MEANING	BEHAVIOR
3	Normal multiuser	The typical mode for systems (such as servers) that do not normally need a graphical desktop.
4	Unused	
5	Multiuser with X11	Normal multiuser mode with an X11 graphical login screen. The only difference between this runlevel and runlevel 3 is that the X11 login manager is started automatically.
6	Reboot	Like runlevel 0, but reboots the system instead of shutting it down.

Init can be instructed to switch between runlevels on a running system via the `init` or `telinit` commands. For example, the canonical way to reboot a Unix system passed down from antiquity is via the command sequence

```
sync; sync; sync; init 6
```

which manually flushes the filesystem cache and then instructs init to reboot the system. Whenever init switches runlevels, it first terminates or kills all processes that do not belong in the new runlevel, and then it starts all processes that should be running. Through this behavior, shutting down and rebooting the system via runlevels 0 and 6 is actually accomplished by simply defining no processes that may run in those runlevels. Init then terminates everything and starts nothing, except a simple reboot or halt script.

Using init to switch system runlevels actually solves only half the problem of managing the system's running software. The actions that init actually takes (which mostly amount to which processes init runs) must also be established. This is where the shell scripts mentioned in Chapter 3 come in. For each runlevel, init can be configured to execute a corresponding program or take some other action. The next section covers the important files in Red Hat's init scripts package.

File and Directory Layout

Red Hat's installation of init and the scripts comes in two RPM packages: SysVinit and initscripts. In Red Hat 7.3, the actual RPMs (for i386 systems) are SysVinit-2.84-2.i386.rpm and initscripts-6.67-1.i386.rpm. SysVinit installs the init program itself and the related support programs; initscripts installs the actual shell scripts invoked by init.

The SysVinit Package

SysVinit is just an implementation of the init program and doesn't dictate anything about how the actual shell scripts must look—it's the initscripts package that establishes the actual framework used by Red Hat Linux. In fact, most Linux distributions use SysVinit for the init program, whether their actual shell scripts are SysV-like or BSD-like. Table 4-6 lists files installed by SysVinit. This list is not complete; you should use the `rpm -ql` command to obtain a complete list.

Table 4-6. Important Files from the SysVinit Package

FILE	PURPOSE
/sbin/init	The init program itself
/sbin/telinit	Used to instruct init to change runlevels
/usr/bin/wall	Used to send warning messages to all users on a system when init changes runlevels
/sbin/pidof	Useful tool used to retrieve the process ID (PID) of a program by name; try `pidof init`

Most of the files in the SysVinit package can be found on any Unix-like system that uses a SysV-compatible init program. The major exception is probably the pidof program, which is used to retrieve the process ID (PID) of a process by name. For example, the command

```
pidof init
```

will return 1 because init always has the PID of 1. This program is useful in any script that needs to retrieve the PID for a particular process, and it is a bit more convenient to use than a pipeline of commands. `pidof myprocess` is easier to type than `ps aux | grep myprocess | cut -f 1 -d ' '` and quite a bit less error-prone as well, since the latter command will return any process with "myprocess" in its name (such as "notmyprocess"). The pidof command is obviously not required for the system to operate correctly, but it is a typical example of the incremental improvements that open source software makes on the quality of an overall package—init in this case.

Generally, users will not interact directly with most of the files in SysVinit; if you need more information than is contained in Table 4-6, you should consult the man page for the command you need. However, the initscripts package contains the actual scripts that control the system and so bears some discussion.

The initscripts Package

Table 4-7 lists files installed by initscripts. This list is not complete; you should use the rpm -ql command to obtain a complete list.

Table 4-7. Important Files from the initscripts Package

FILE	PURPOSE
/etc/inittab	Configures init; specifies which shell scripts init invokes for each runlevel.
/etc/sysconfig	Contains files that specify values for configuration variables in the scripts. Each file sets values for a particular aspect of the system, such as the network.
/etc/rc.d/rc.sysinit	Invoked by init once when the system boots up.
/etc/rc.d/rc	Invoked by init when switching runlevels.
/etc/rc.d/rc.local	A script invoked last in the process; configures machine-specific details.
/etc/rc.d/rc{X}.d	Contains links to service control scripts used to start the services for a given runlevel X (e.g., /etc/rc.d/rc5.d).
/etc/rc.d/init.d	Contains the actual shell scripts referenced by the rc.{X} directories.
/sbin/service	A utility used for conveniently starting and stopping services manually while the system is running.
/etc/X11/prefdm	Used to indicate which X11 desktop manager to use; specific to runlevel 5 on Red Hat systems.

Note: With version 8, Red Hat will probably move the /etc/rc.d/rc{X}.d directories to simply /etc/rc{X}.d; in fact, the symbolic links to these directories are already present. You should be aware of this impending change for forward compatibility.

/etc/inittab

The file /etc/inittab contains the init table (inittab) for the system. This file specifies which scripts get invoked for which runlevels. It also specifies scripts that get invoked globally, such when the system boots up or when a user signals a reboot via the "three-fingered salute" Ctrl-Alt-Delete combination. The /etc/inittab file also sets the default runlevel that init enters on startup.

/etc/sysconfig

The /etc/sysconfig directory contains basic configuration data specific to a system. The scripts for a given runlevel are configuring the services and system itself for operation. These scripts must be generic since they are written to run on any system; however, many services require specific values to function correctly. For example, the script for configuring the network should be generic so that it can be reused on any system. However, the IP address of a system is obviously specific to that system. To keep the scripts reusable, data such as IP addresses are placed in the /etc/sysconfig directory and are read by the scripts. The file /etc/sysconfig/network contains data for the network script, for example.

/etc/rc.d

The /etc/rc.d directory contains all of the shell scripts and the directory tree used by init. There is a subdirectory for each runlevel under /etc/rc.d, named according to the level number. For example, the "rc directory" for runlevel 5 is /etc/rc.d/rc5.d. There is also an additional directory named /etc/rc.d/init.d that contains the physical shell script files; the contents of the individual rc directories are symbolic links to scripts in the init.d directory. Note that there are symbolic links to each of these directories from the base /etc directory; however, those links point to the corresponding directories in /etc/rc.d, and are present for convenience and forward compatibility. (A later version of Red Hat will probably move the rc directories to /etc permanently.)

rc.sysinit

The rc.sysinit file is a script that is run once when the system boots up, before any runlevel is entered. This script is specified in /etc/inittab and performs tasks such as checking the disks and filesystems for errors, loading any kernel modules or drivers that are required, restoring the system clock and random number seeds, and other work that is required by the system, regardless of which runlevel is going to be entered. If you watch a recent Red Hat Linux system as it boots, it has two "phases": one phase that always proceeds the same regardless of what the default runlevel is and a second phase where the actual services are started. The first phase (where you are prompted to "Press I to enter interactive mode") corresponds to when rc.sysinit is executing; the next phase begins when rc.sysinit completes, and init enters the default runlevel.

When init enters a particular runlevel, it executes the script matched to that runlevel in /etc/inittab. (In fact, init could be configured to execute more than one script in a particular sequence, but Red Hat has a different approach.) This script is then responsible for starting any services that are appropriate for that runlevel. The next section describes this process in more detail.

Tracing an Execution

Perhaps the best way to illustrate the Red Hat initscripts behavior is to examine the copy of /etc/inittab that comes with Red Hat Linux and track it through a sample boot-up sequence. The remainder of this section dissects the inittab file and maps its contents to the individual events that occur as a Red Hat Linux system starts up. For full documentation on the inittab file, you should consult the man page. All that you need to know for the purposes of this discussion is that the first column (before the first colon) in the lines that follow is simply an identifier and can be arbitrary.

The first noncommented line in inittab specifies the default runlevel. In the case of Red Hat Linux, this is normally 3 or 5. It is 5 if the user selected the Graphical Login option during installation and 3 otherwise. In Table 4-5 (and in the /etc/inittab file itself), runlevel 3 is indicated to be normal multiuser mode, while runlevel 5 is multiuser mode with graphical login. The difference is in the services that get started in each runlevel. The line setting the default runlevel is this one:

```
id:5:initdefault:
```

The next line specifies the rc.sysinit global script to be invoked by init before entering the default runlevel. This script, as described in the previous section, is responsible for checking the disks for errors, cleaning up the /tmp directory, loading any required kernel modules or drivers, and other similar administrivia. This file is also the one that generates the "Press I to enter interactive mode" prompt during startup. This file is not too complicated, so readers interested in the details should simply scan through this script. It is actually possible to define more than one of these global scripts to execute; however, Red Hat chose to use only one such script. The line specifying this global startup script is this:

```
si::sysinit:/etc/rc.d/rc.sysinit
```

The next group of lines maps runlevels (in the second column) to scripts (in the last column). As is immediately obvious, Red Hat Linux uses the same script for all runlevels and simply passes the script a different argument depending on which runlevel was entered. The behavior of this script is rather simple: It looks in the corresponding rc directory for the runlevel it was passed as its argument, and then it invokes any programs it finds in that directory. The /etc/rc.d/rc script is covered in a bit more detail in the "Runlevel Configuration Script" section, so for now here are the relevant lines:

```
l0:0:wait:/etc/rc.d/rc 0
l1:1:wait:/etc/rc.d/rc 1
...
l6:6:wait:/etc/rc.d/rc 6
```

The next few lines configure init's behavior when it changes runlevels or when it receives certain significant events. The first line starts the kernel's update daemon to periodically synchronize memory cache with the disk, the second line tells init to execute the shutdown command whenever the user presses Ctrl-Alt-Delete, and the last two lines specify commands to run if the system is notified of a power failure. (These last two events can only be triggered if the system is connected to a properly configured uninterruptible power supply [UPS].)

```
ud::once:/sbin/update
ca::ctrlaltdel:/sbin/shutdown -t3 -r now
pf::powerfail:/sbin/shutdown -f -h +2 'Power Failure; System Shutting Down'
pr:12345:powerokwait:/sbin/shutdown -c 'Power Restored; Shutdown Cancelled'
```

The next group of lines instructs init to create several virtual text consoles (known as *ttys*), but only for the four multiuser runlevels. These tty consoles are the six text-based consoles that users can use in lieu of an X Window graphical interface; users can switch between them via the Alt-F1 through Alt-F6 key sequences. The ttys are defined to respawn, meaning that init will restart them when they exit. Once the user logs out, the tty exits, and init will start another in its place, which will display the login prompt again. Here are the lines defining the ttys:

```
1:2345:respawn:/sbin/mingetty tty1
2:2345:respawn:/sbin/mingetty tty2
...
6:2345:respawn:/sbin/mingetty tty6
```

The last line in the file instructs init to start the prefdm graphical login program. The second column, however, restricts this behavior to runlevel 5, so it won't be invoked for any other runlevel. This is the line that causes the graphical KDE or GNOME login screen to appear after the system boots up. (Because this line occurs after the previous rc script line, it gets invoked after init has entered runlevel 5.)

```
x:5:respawn:/etc/X11/prefdm -nodaemon
```

TIP *If you told Red Hat Linux to start the graphical login on startup but have since decided you don't like this (or vice versa), you can fix it by editing /etc/inittab and changing the "initdefault" default runlevel to 3 (to disable the graphical login) or 5 (to enable the graphical login).*

All of this information can be brought together into a trace through a Red Hat system startup according to the following steps:

1. The kernel boots and starts init, which then reads /etc/inittab.

2. The /etc/inittab file instructs init to invoke /etc/rc.d/rc.sysinit; if that script completes successfully, init proceeds on to the next line. If that script returns an error (due to an error located on disk, for example), then init stops and enters single-user mode.

3. Once rc.sysinit completes successfully, init checks the default runlevel (which is 5 in this example) and then invokes the script defined for that runlevel.

4. The rc.sysinit script will start any services that are required by the runlevel. Once it completes, init registers the next few lines of the file, defining how it should react to various events, and then reaches the lines defining the ttys. If the runlevel is one of those defined by these lines (which it will be for any runlevel except single-user, halt, or reboot), init starts /sbin/mingetty on the ttys to let users log in, and then watches for them to exit.

5. Finally, init does the same check against the last line, which determines whether it should start the "preferred desktop manager" program /etc/X11/prefdm (which in turn invokes either the KDE or GNOME graphical login programs if they are present).

At this point, the system is fully booted up and ready for use. A very similar sequence of events occurs if the root user instructs init to switch to a different runlevel; the only difference is that the rc.sysinit script will not be invoked, since it was defined to be invoked only once, on system startup. The only part of this sequence not yet described in detail is the behavior of the /etc/rc.d/rc script invoked when init enters a runlevel—this script is covered in the next section.

The Runlevel Configuration Script

Everything described in the previous section is automatic on a Red Hat Linux system. End users (and in the majority of cases, system administrators) generally don't need to modify any of the scripts invoked by init when it starts up. In fact, it's one of Red Hat's general design goals for the system: Users should be able to configure the system without having to edit scripts. By far, the most common customization users make to a system is simply changing which services are started for a given runlevel. This section describes the mechanism used to automate this in Red Hat Linux.

Recall that the /etc/inittab configuration file for Red Hat Linux uses the same shell script—/etc/rc.d/rc—to configure all runlevels. This shell script takes the runlevel number as its input and configures the services as appropriate for that runlevel. It accomplishes this by looking for files in the rc directory corresponding to the runlevel—/etc/rc.d/rc5.d in our example. This directory should contain files whose names match a certain pattern; the rc script uses this pattern to start and stop services as appropriate. The files themselves should be, but need not be, symbolic links to physical shell scripts in the /etc/rc.d/init.d directory. Table 4-8 summarizes the naming pattern.

Table 4-8. SysV Init Scripts File Naming Pattern

FORMAT	MEANING	EXAMPLE
KXXfoo	Stop service named "foo," in order XX	etc/rc.d/rc3.d/K87portmap: stops the portmap /service for runlevel 3
SYYbar	Start service named "bar," in order YY	/etc/rc.d/rc5.d/S55sshd: starts the sshd service for runlevel 5

Essentially, if a file name starts with "K", the corresponding service is "killed" (actually, shut down, not really killed) when init enters that runlevel. If the file name starts with "S", it is "started" whenever init enters that runlevel. After the "S" or "K" comes a two-digit number that has no meaning except to order the files with respect to each other, so that the user can control which order services get invoked in. The remainder of the file name is the service name.

The rc script /etc/rc.d/rc simply scans the appropriate directory for the new runlevel, stops any services whose file names start with "K", and starts any services whose file names start with "S". The file names are invoked as shell scripts and are passed either "stop" or "start" as input, depending on whether they are being killed or started, respectively. Thus, to function correctly, any shell scripts in an rc directory must be capable of interpreting these inputs. Actually, there are two more inputs as well: "status," which indicates whether the service is running, and "restart," which is shorthand for a "stop" followed by a "start." If you wish to add a new service to the system, all you need to do is place a shell script honoring these four inputs into the /etc/rc.d/init.d directory and then create symbolic links as appropriate in the other rc directories.

"Dropping in" New Configurations

The notion of configuring the system by placing files in a certain directory is worth a second look. It's one of Red Hat's most common techniques because it makes it easy to install software and connect it into the system.

RPM is the package format for Red Hat Linux, and this format can generally only install files in preordained locations. It quite frequently happens that two programs need to hook themselves into the startup framework to function correctly. Thus, there are two programs that need to modify the system configuration, and meanwhile the system administrator may already have modified the same file while installing a package that doesn't use RPM. It is extremely inconvenient when two separate programs "clobber" each other's changes by modifying the same file. You might be able to solve this problem with extensive use of "intelligent" text processing, but that is a good deal of work to implement, and since Red Hat doesn't write most of the software they ship, they can't enforce a universal use of a single centralized approach anyway.

The SysV init scripts model solves this problem by allowing each program (in this case, system service) to have its own separate configuration file that no other program would need to modify—the shell scripts in /etc/rc.d/init.d. The core framework scripts are untouched and can be managed by the system, and configuration occurs by simply "dropping in" a new configuration file for a new program.

Red Hat engineers took inspiration from this solution and have started using the technique in many other places. This can be considered a pretty successful best practice used fairly rigorously by Red Hat.

The next section presents an example of how to manually configure the services for a Red Hat Linux system.

Manually Configuring the System

At this point, you know enough to customize the list of services started up by your Red Hat Linux system. However, just to drive home the point, this section presents an example of how to hook a new service into the system. The example is based on the following characteristics of the hypothetical software that is being added to the system:

- Represents a service (i.e., server or daemon) named "myservice" and installed in /usr/local/myservice

- Includes a script obeying the start/stop/restart/status semantics

- Runs only in the multiuser runlevels—2 through 5

- Depends on the portmap service, so it must be started after that service

The first step is to copy the shell script from the installation into the /etc/rc.d/init.d directory. This is actually not required; you could create a symbolic link directly from the various rc directories straight to the installation directory in /usr/local/myservice. However, it is a good practice to have all your shell scripts in a single, centralized location. This becomes especially important if you need the service to be running in single-user mode, since single-user mode may not mount your /usr/local partition at all, depending on how it was installed.

Once the shell script is located in /etc/rc.d/init.d, it must be activated by creating symbolic links to it in the desired multiuser rc directories. Because you are activating the service for these runlevels, the symbolic link name must begin with "S"; thus, "S00myservice" might be a good first try. However, because myservice depends on the portmap service, it must be started afterward. Since portmap is S13portmap on Red Hat Linux 7.3, the link for myservice needs to be something like S15myservice. (Any number will work, as long as it's greater than portmap's 13.) A link of this name must be created for each multiuser runlevel. Listing 4-1 contains a simple bash shell script that can be used.

Listing 4-1. Creating Symbolic Links to Configure a Service

```
#!/bin/sh
cd /etc/rc.d
for i in 2 3 4 5; do
    cd rc${i}.d/
    ln -s ../init.d/myservice ./S15myservice
    cd ..
done
```

Next, equivalent "kill" links must be created in the rc directories for runlevels 0, 1, and 6. Because portmap is run as K87portmap, the "K value" for myservice must be less than 87 (for example, 85). This can be accomplished by simply modifying the script in Listing 4-1 to use 0, 1, and 6 instead of 2–5 and changing

"S15myservice" to "K85myservice". Now the newly installed service will be properly started and stopped by runlevel. If you wish to manually start or stop the service once the system is running, you can do so as you would for any service—for instance, `/etc/rc.d/init.d/myservice restart`.

Sometimes you need to configure something that isn't a long-running server. In that case, it might be overkill or even inappropriate to treat it as a service and use the preceding approach. For example, you might need to simply run a program on startup that records the data and time, erases a file in /tmp, or so forth. There is a file where these changes can be placed: /etc/rc.d/rc.local. All runlevels invoke this script on startup, which by default sets up the /etc/issue file (whose content gets displayed as part of login prompts). You can add small "miniscripts" to this file if you like; however, be aware of the fact that this file is shared and suffers from the difficulties described in the previous section. Any changes you make to rc.local could potentially get clobbered by an upgrade or another program or user.

This whole "symbolic-link-to-shell-scripts" thing saves a lot of work, but it can still be a bit of a pain in practice. If you find yourself managing these services a lot, you will probably end up writing some shell scripts (similar to Listing 4-1) that automate much of the work. Red Hat engineers recognized this, as well, and included some small programs that make life quite a bit easier. The next section describes these utilities.

Using Red Hat's Tools

Red Hat ships the three following commands with its distribution:

- `/sbin/service`

- `/sbin/chkconfig`

- `/sbin/shutdown`

These commands are targeted toward managing the configuration and usage of init and its scripts. These commands are niceties—the system can be managed without them, and they don't let users do anything they couldn't do already. For this reason, some of the more hard-core Unix hackers scoff at them. However, the beauty of these commands (and Unix systems in general) is that if you don't like them, you don't have to use them; the old-fashioned way works just as well. This section describes what these commands are and what they do.

/sbin/service

The /sbin/service command is included in the initscripts RPM, so it is available on every recent Red Hat Linux installation. This program is essentially a short-hand for manually starting and stopping the services in /etc/rc.d/init.d. Instead of typing /etc/rc.d/init.d/myservice start, for example, you can simply type service myservice start. In other words, service saves you from having to type /etc/rc.d/init.d. The command lets you perform all the standard actions—start, stop, restart, and status.

/sbin/chkconfig

The chkconfig command is included in its own RPM (chkconfig-1.2.22-1) and is installed in /sbin/chkconfig. This program manages the symbolic links in the rc directories; that is, it can manage which services are configured to run in which runlevels. It is essentially a full-featured version of the shell script in Listing 4-1 (except with a lot more sophistication), in that it creates and removes the symbolic links according to user input.

The chkconfig program also provides a way to automate the process of adding in a new shell script by placing a properly formatted comment in your shell script. The format is

```
# chkconfig <runlevels> <S value> <K value>
```

When run, chkconfig will scan these values and use them when constructing the symbolic links. The line for portmap, for example, is # chkconfig 345 13 87, which shows where the "magical" values of 13 and 87 come from for runlevels 3 through 5. To add in a new service with chkconfig support, you would simply create one of these lines with appropriate values for where in the script sequence your service needs to be run.

/sbin/shutdown

The /sbin/shutdown command is included in the SysVinit package. This program is used to instruct init to go to either runlevel 0, 1, or 6 (i.e., shut down, reboot, or go into single-user mode). Again, this command is really just a shortcut for some-thing longer (such as wall "System is shutting down.";sync;sync;sync; init 0) but it is a convenience that is often overlooked by administrators who are used to dealing with other flavors of Unix.

If you've read this entire section on the init mechanism for Red Hat Linux, then you have taken a huge step toward bringing the system under your control.

After all, once you know how the system is configuring itself, you can use that as a starting point for finding out almost anything else. The rest of this chapter covers other aspects of Red Hat Linux in equivalent detail. Next up is the core system libraries.

Core System Libraries

As discussed in Chapter 1, Linux is merely the kernel of an operating system; the system libraries are what give an operating system the majority of its functionality. In this section, you will learn a bit about the core libraries used by Red Hat Linux 7.3.

Generally, users don't have to pay much attention to system libraries; they tend to be pretty static for the life of a release. That is, most bug fixes and similar upgrades occur in the userspace applications rather than in the system libraries. However, it is still important to know what system libraries are installed on your system, what they do, and any issues they might have.

Table 4-9 lists the most important RPM packages for Red Hat Linux 7.3 and some brief comments. This list includes not only the shared libraries that other programs link against, but also some of the key utility programs, such as the bash command shell and the fileutils package. Table 4-9 is actually organized by RPM package name—each entry in the table is packaged as its own RPM. Each RPM package, meanwhile, also contains many actual libraries (which are files with an extension of ".so") and related support files. This table should be viewed as a starting point rather than a comprehensive reference. The hardest part of learning about the core system libraries is just figuring out which libraries are the most important; that's what this table is providing. Readers should check the web sites, man pages, and other documentation to learn about the actual libraries.

Table 4-9. Red Hat Linux 7.3 Core Library Packages

PACKAGE	VERSION	COMMENT
XFree86	4.2.0	X Window System; v4 contains 3-D acceleration and new rendering extensions
glibc	2.2.5	Core runtime system libraries; contains linker/loader, math libraries, security libraries, network libraries, and multithreading libraries
bash	2.05a	Bourne Again SHell; primary system shell (used by root)
util-liunx	2.10s	Linux-specific disk, process management, and user tools

Table 4-9. Red Hat Linux 7.3 Core Library Packages (continued)

PACKAGE	VERSION	COMMENT
PAM	0.75	Pluggable Authentication Modules; used to log users in against various data stores (e.g., LDAP, RADIUS, and so forth)
gdbm, db2, db3	1.8.0, 2.4.14, 3.3.11	File database libraries; used by other programs to index and store data
fileutils	4.1	Binary utilities; contains basic programs such as `ls`, `cp`, `rm`, and so forth

It's worth noting the origins of some of these packages. As you know from reading Chapter 1, the Free Software Foundation's GNU project provided much of the software that made Linux usable. Linux, meanwhile, provided the kernel that GNU lacked. Libraries and programs such as these are concrete examples of the GNU contribution. The gdbm, fileutils, bash, and glibc packages are all GNU software. Notably, XFree86 is not; the GNU project still lacks its own X Window implementation. (XFree86 is discussed in more detail in the next section.)

The X Window System and the Desktop

One of the hotspots in the technical media these days is the so-called battle for the desktop, in which "David" (the Linux community) faces off against "Goliath" (desktop software companies such as Apple and Microsoft). Melodrama aside, providing a solid user interface is crucial to any operating system, and Linux systems are no exception. This section describes the desktop solutions provided by Red Hat Linux 7.3.

The GUI of choice for a Unix-like system is almost always based on the X Window system. Most commercial systems, however, typically "support" only one desktop environment that runs under X. In the past, the Common Desktop Environment (CDE) was put forward as the standard desktop for Unix-like systems, and many vendors adopted it. However, CDE was eventually supplanted by products, such as Microsoft Windows, in terms of user interface and component architecture. This, combined with the typically higher costs of Unix systems, caused Unix to lose market share to Windows in the desktop workstation market. Today, however, there are several desktop environments that far surpass CDE and rival any commercial desktop. Red Hat Linux 7.3 supports two of these environments: the K Desktop Environment (KDE) and the GNU project's GNOME. (Both of these desktops are discussed later in this section.)

XFree86

Like most of the free Unix-like systems, Red Hat Linux uses XFree86 as its
X Window implementation. The version shipped with version 7.3, 4.0.*x*, introduced
several important enhancements. XFree86 4.0 introduced support for 3-D hardware accelerator cards and an API for various enhanced graphical effects, such as
transparency and antialiased text. The 3-D hardware support makes XFree86
much more viable for 3-D visualization applications and games, making it more
competitive against both commercial Unix vendors' offerings and other desktop
environments. However, the number of graphics cards actually supported by the
3-D acceleration functionality is small at the time of this writing. The number of
supported cards will undoubtedly grow over time.

In addition to the hardware support, the enhanced rendering capabilities of
XFree86 4.0 (known as the *render extensions*) support advanced visual eye-candy
effects, such as transparent and translucent windows, as well as support for
antialiased fonts. This support addressed one of the most frequently cited and
conspicuous shortfalls of XFree86.

Red Hat Linux ships with some useful tools for configuring XFree86 and all
the included desktops (such as GNOME, KDE, fvwm, and others). Table 4-10
summarizes these tools.

Table 4-10. XFree86 Related Tools

PROGRAM	PURPOSE
Xconfigurator	Configures XFree86 for a particular system
switchdesk	Automates the process of switching between desktops
xev	Used to track and display mouse and keyboard events; useful for debugging and testing
xdpyinfo	Shows information about the current X display
xvidtune	Used to tweak the X configuration for a monitor

Xconfigurator is a tool written by Red Hat to manage the XFree86 configuration. XFree86 is typically installed and configured to run the program /etc/X11/X
as the correct X server for the video card. This file is actually a symbolic link to the
correct X server, which is usually installed in /usr/X11R6/bin. If you upgrade the
video card or simply need to alter your configuration, you first need to update this
symbolic link to the new X server binary and then alter the XF86Config-4 file with
the new settings. Xconfigurator automates these tasks. Xconfigurator supports
both XFree86 4.0 and earlier 3.*x* versions, but it defaults to 3.*x*, so in order to use it
to configure XFree86 4.0 you must use the `-preferxf4` argument.

The other programs in Table 4-10 are intended to be used for less extensive configuration tasks. The switchdesk package is used by users to change their default desktop (for example, from GNOME to KDE). The other programs are actually included with XFree86: xev is used to monitor keyboard and mouse events and is useful for debugging keyboard mappings or mouse configurations; xdpyinfo displays information (such as resolution and color depth) about the current display; and xvidtune is used to tweak the height, width, centering, and other aspects of the current display, and it can print out a line to be added to the XF86Config file to make the change permanent.

GNOME and KDE

XFree86 is just an implementation of the X Window system, however, and so requires a window manager and widget set to actually provide the desktop environment. Red Hat Linux 7.3 ships with KDE 3.0 and GNOME 1.4 as alternative desktop environments. Red Hat Software provides some financial support of the development work on the GNOME project, and so GNOME is the default Red Hat Linux desktop. However, Red Hat is actually "desktop agnostic," and so it provides various tools that allow users to easily switch between GNOME and KDE as their desktop. Red Hat believes in shipping "best of breed" software, irrespective of its origins, and so includes both KDE and GNOME.

Information about these environments could easily fill an entire book, but a few points are worth making. The latest versions of KDE and GNOME both support (or will soon support) antialiased fonts, giving them a smoother look than earlier versions. Both desktops also have evolving component-embedding models, allowing application developers to start using some of the enhanced techniques of component architectures seen on Windows. Additionally, both environments have very extensive support for "themes" or "skins" that allows users to customize the look and feel of their desktops. In this way and several others, both KDE and GNOME are actually ahead of their commercial competition. The argument that Linux systems are not viable as desktop systems is becoming increasingly unfounded.

The user desktop is an important part of the system, but in the end it is really just an interface. The true value of the system comes from the actual applications that are installed on it for the users to work with. The next section discusses some of the applications that come with Red Hat Linux, as well as a bit of Red Hat's approach to distributing these programs.

Userspace Applications

Red Hat ships a lot of software with their system. Generally, this is true of most Linux distributions; they tend to be very complete software packages. On a commercial system such as Microsoft Windows or a commercial Unix, you typically must pay for things such as compilers, office productivity software, and web servers in addition to the base operating system; but this type of software for Linux systems is usually just as free as the operating system itself. This section describes the software that ships with a Red Hat Linux system.

Generally, Red Hat Linux contains the usual fare common to Linux systems:

- emacs text editor (as well as its cousin, xemacs)

- gcc compiler suite

- Apache web server

- Samba software for Windows-compatible SMB file sharing

Red Hat follows the "leading edge" without being "bleeding edge" (most of the time, anyway). For example, back in the early days, theirs was one of the first distributions to switch to the GNU libc package from the original libc5 package typically used with Linux. Red Hat also follows the latest kernel; for example, Red Hat Linux 7.1 shipped with the 2.4.*x* series of kernels shortly after they were released. Version 7.3 also included the latest XFree86 and KDE desktop, even making use of their support for antialiased fonts, even though that feature was still technically beta. On the other hand, Red Hat's quality assurance process does sometimes prevent them from releasing "undercooked" software. Testing on the 2.4 series of kernels, for example, exposed a few problems with the ReiserFS journaling filesystem, preventing its default inclusion in Red Hat Linux 7.1.

Red Hat Linux, like most distributions, contains a large amount of software. Some of it is considered core to the distribution, while some of it is considered mainly of interest to so-called power users. There is so much software, in fact, that the whole distribution (including optional packages) now consists of three compact discs, with even more for source code and documentation! To get a feel for what you actually get with Red Hat Linux, simply look at the lists of RPM files on the installation CDs. The remainder of this section discusses how Red Hat organizes their distribution as follows:

- Core distribution

- Source code and documentation CDs

- Red Hat Linux editions

Understanding the Core Distribution

The core Red Hat Linux distribution contains software that is frequently used by many or most users. As recently as version 6.2, Red Hat Linux could fit on a single CD. However, due to the inexorable increase in size of existing packages and the introduction of new packages, the core distribution now consists of three CDs, not including the source code.

Of course, the more discs a user has to deal with, the more confusing installation and maintenance become. For example, there are so many packages now that performing a custom installation and selecting individual packages can take quite a while, even for expert users, simply due to the sheer number of packages available. To ameliorate these difficulties, Red Hat identified some common profiles of system usage, such as Workstation, Web Server, File Server, and so on. Each profile is oriented toward a different usage pattern and is associated with a list of packages for that profile. Red Hat's installation program, anaconda, allows users to select one or more of these predefined profiles to produce a configuration that meets most of their needs. The issue, of course, is that these configurations are inevitably someone else's idea of what a system of that type should contain. However, even if most users end up customizing a default configuration, at least they are starting points.

For users (generally network and system administrators) who need to install many instances of the same configuration, Red Hat provides a package known as kickstart that allows these administrators to essentially create their own "canned" configurations. Administrators can then set up a server machine containing the software packages and use a floppy disk to boot each target machine. The target machines then fetch their packages from the server for the installation. Additionally, the up2date software can be customized to work with a server local to a network, so that administrators can easily upgrade their installations according to their own needs. (Of course, Red Hat does not provide a customizable version of the up2date server, so work would have to be done to obtain or create one.)

Source Code and Documentation CDs

The core distribution Red Hat Linux CDs contain typical software, for both desktop and server applications. However, some users need additional information on the distribution and the software included with it, while other users may need access to the original source code for the system (which is almost always available, since this is open source software). To accommodate these needs, Red Hat Linux 7.3 includes not only the three installation CDs, but also two source code CDs and a documentation CD. That's a total of six CDs, for those keeping track.

Red Hat Linux Editions

Red Hat actually produces several different editions of their distribution. Each edition has a different focus, and some editions contain some non–open source commercial software add-ons. The editions tend to change a bit from release to release, but as of version 7.3, they are as follows:

- Red Hat Linux Personal

- Red Hat Linux Professional

- Red Hat Linux Advanced Server

The Personal edition is suitable for home users and individuals. The Professional edition is for more corporate-oriented and other larger-scale users, and it contains some tools and software that are useful in those contexts. The Advanced Server edition, meanwhile, contains various high-end features and software, such as the ability to cluster servers for web sites, databases, and other server tasks. In addition, the Advanced Server edition includes premium support options. Red Hat also publishes distributions for several non-i386 architectures, such as IBM S/390 mainframes and Intel's Itanium processor.

Finding Additional Software

Eventually, almost every user will find that he or she needs software not included with Red Hat's distribution. In these cases, users usually end up going to the Web to search for software. There are, however, several software applications that make this process easier. The Debian package management tools actually integrate searching for packages over the network and automatically downloading and installing them; RPM doesn't support this inherently, but there are several tools available that add this behavior.

One such tool is rpmfind. This tool is both a program used to search for, download, and install RPM packages and a web site that can be used for convenient searches for RPMs. Both the tool and the web site are maintained by Daniel Veillard of the World Wide Web Consortium (W3C). The web site is located at www.rpmfind.net. The rpmfind tool on Red Hat Linux systems can be viewed as a sort of last resort; most users will (but need not, of course) treat Red Hat itself as the primary source of RPMs via up2date, simply as a matter of convenience. However, for those cases where Red Hat doesn't maintain official RPMs for a given piece of software, rpmfind can be very useful indeed.

Red Hat Linux Idiosyncrasies

So far, everything that's been discussed in this chapter is more or less applicable to other Linux systems and even some other Unix-like systems. That is, so far I've only covered the ins and outs of particular software packages and tools that Red Hat Linux uses. In this section, I cover some idiosyncrasies specific to Red Hat Linux.

Using the GRUB Boot Loader

All operating systems require a boot loader to start up. A *boot loader* is a very small program that is executed automatically by the system hardware and is responsible for locating, setting up, and executing the primary operating system—in this case, the Linux kernel. Most distributions use the Linux Loader (LILO) as their boot loader, but as of version 7.2 Red Hat Linux uses GRUB.

GRUB, the "GRand Unified Bootloader," was developed by the GNU project. It is a very full-featured boot loader that contains features frequently only found in higher-end commercial systems and hardware. For example, GRUB allows users to edit the boot configuration manually when the system starts up, while LILO can only set up boot configurations from within an already-running system. GRUB's feature is extremely useful in cases where you accidentally misconfigure your boot configuration. Installing GRUB is as easy as installing the appropriate RPM. (Of course, you should probably uninstall LILO just in case.) GRUB is also the default boot loader, so unless you manually change it during installation, you'll have it already.

GRUB is configured via a text file. Because this file has to be accessible to GRUB during system bootup, it has to be located on the /boot partition. (The RPM for GRUB also creates a symbolic link in /etc/grub.conf that points to the real file in /boot/grub/grub.conf.) Managing the operating systems installed on your computer is then as easy as editing the contents of this file. However, GRUB is very adequately documented in its manual page and via its home page at www.gnu.org/software/grub/, so I don't cover the details of configuring GRUB here.

Managing Similar Software

Sometimes you might find yourself needing or wanting to install two independent but similar programs. For example, both KDE and GNOME include "desktop managers" that allow users to log into the X Window system. However, only one of these programs can be used at a time, so one of them has to be designated as the default.

Red Hat Linux addresses this situation through the use of the *alternatives mechanism.* This is simply a directory (specifically, /etc/alternatives) that contains symbolic links to the default version of a particular program in cases where more than one program fulfills a given need. (For instance, the /etc/alternatives/mta link points to the system's default mail transfer agent.)

The alternatives system was actually borrowed from the Debian GNU/Linux distribution. Because Debian is discussed in Chapter 6 (along with the alternatives system), you should consult that chapter for more information.

Upgrading to a Stock Kernel

Red Hat does extensive quality assurance tests on any kernel they officially ship. However, since Red Hat's focus is on the operating system as a whole, they generally don't release updated kernels unless they must in order to address some important bug or functionality. So, it is not uncommon to need to install a stock kernel on a Red Hat Linux system if the need for a new feature or bug fix in the kernel is too urgent to wait for Red Hat's next release. This section describes how to install a stock kernel on a Red Hat Linux 7.3 system without breaking any other software that might be installed.

 CAUTION *Before performing any of these steps, it is important to understand the dangers involved. The kernel is the most crucial part of the operating system, and if it is misconfigured or damaged, the system will not boot up correctly, or at all. These days, Linux systems are becoming more and more stable, so users shouldn't upgrade the kernel just for the sake of doing so. However, if the kernel must be upgraded to a stock kernel, these instructions can be used. Be extremely careful in using these instructions, read all the documentation (both here and elsewhere), and make certain that you have a working rescue boot disk before beginning.*

To install a stock kernel on Red Hat Linux 7.3, follow these steps:

1. Install the required libraries, if needed (such as the dev86 package on Intel).

2. Remove the /usr/src/linux-2.4 symbolic link.

3. Extract the stock kernel into /usr/src.

4.   Create a symbolic link to the new kernel as /usr/src/linux-2.4.

5.   Copy the Red Hat kernel configuration into the new source tree (customize if necessary).

6.   Build the new kernel.

7.   Copy the bzImage and System.map files into /boot, named appropriately.

8.   Update //etc/grub.conf to use the new kernel.

9.   Rebuild the system initrd via the `mkinitrd` command, if the system uses one.

10. Install the new kernel for bootup by running lilo.

Note that this list is probably not detailed enough to follow verbatim; however, Red Hat and other sources provide documentation on upgrading the kernel. You can use the steps here as a checklist when performing one of these installations. Note that if you wish to switch back to a stock Red Hat kernel later, you will have to undo some of these changes (notably step 7, since that symbolic link will conflict with a kernel-source package of a Red Hat kernel).

The first step is to make sure the required software is installed. Intel systems need the dev86 package installed. If the kernel source code is already installed, this package will also be installed. If you do have the kernel source code installed, you should leave it installed until after you've completed the upgrade. Once you've verified that your new kernel is working properly, you can reclaim the disk space if you really need to by erasing the kernel-source RPM.

The kernel-headers RPM

You may notice a second RPM installed on your system called kernel-headers. This package, even though it appears to be related to the kernel, does not actually need to be upgraded or uninstalled. This package contains the kernel include files used by certain userspace software, such as the system C libraries (glibc). The version of glibc installed on the system is dependent on a particular version of these kernel header files, and there is generally no reason to upgrade them in normal use, even if the kernel itself is upgraded. In fact, doing so might cause problems. Since these files are unrelated to the process of building or running a new kernel, there is no need to update them, unless there is a strong legitimate need. In order to build a new kernel, only the kernel-source package needs to be upgraded.

The /usr/src/linux-2.4 Symbolic Link

Various software and other parts of the system expect to find kernel source for a 2.4-series kernel in the directory /usr/src/linux-2.4. This directory should be a symbolic link to the actual directory where the source code is installed. So, after removing the source code RPMs, the next step is to extract the stock kernel source code into a directory in /usr/src, and then update the /usr/src/linux-2.4 symbolic link to point at the new stock kernel directory.

A related issue worth mentioning is that Red Hat's approach is to install the kernel source code in the /usr directory. However, it doesn't strictly need to be there; a normal user can (and perhaps should) build a kernel in her own home directory and then become root to actually install the kernel. On the other hand, the whole process of upgrading a kernel *is* a system administration task, so an argument can be made for placing the source code in /usr/src. For the purposes of this chapter, let's try and stay within Red Hat's own conventions.

Building the Kernel from Source Code

At this point, the kernel source code will properly installed. The next step is to actually build the kernel from the source code. In order to do this, the kernel must be configured. You can use the standard make menuconfig or other methods to configure the source code, but Red Hat also provides their standard kernel configuration files with the system. By reusing these files, you can make sure that your new stock kernel configuration will match Red Hat's, reducing the chance that you will accidentally omit a kernel option required by the system. (However, the Red Hat configuration may require minor customizations because Red Hat kernels sometimes include options that stock kernels do not have. This will vary on a case-by-case basis.)

Red Hat's configuration files is located in /lib/modules/<version>/build/configs; copy the file appropriate to your system to /usr/src/linux-2.4/.config and it will be located by the build process. (The <version> in the path refers to the version of the old kernel being upgraded: 2.4.2-2 on a stock 7.3 system. These files will not be present if the kernel source RPM has already been uninstalled, which is why that should be done last.)

Once the Red Hat configuration file has been copied (or the kernel source otherwise configured), the actual kernel can be built. At this point, the instructions for building a standard kernel apply; users should consult that documentation for more detail. Essentially, this involves running the build, which creates a new kernel in arch/i386/bzImage (on Intel systems, or something else on other architectures) as well as a System.map file. These files must be placed in the /boot directory, the boot loader configuration file (/etc/grub.conf or

/etc/lilo.conf on Intel systems) must be updated, and on systems that require it, a new /boot/initrd file must be built via the mkinitrd command. When configuring the boot loader, make certain to *add* the new kernel, rather than *replace* the old; if the new kernel is bad for any reason, you can recover by booting the old configuration.

> **TIP** *These instructions are somewhat skeletal. However, you can find extensive documentation at the Linux Documentation Project (LDP) at* www.linuxdoc.org/HOWTO/Kernel-HOWTO.html *and at Red Hat's web site. The LDP actually has documentation on many aspects of Linux systems and is a great resource to bookmark.*

Once you've completed the preceding steps, you can reboot the system (via the shutdown command, running telinit 6, or simply using the Ctrl-Alt-Delete sequence), and the new kernel should be running. After the system is rebooted, you can log in and use the command uname -a to verify the upgrade.

User Environment

Users of Unix-like systems get especially ornery about their command shells; perhaps the only issue touchier than this is the stalwart emacs vs. vi text editor debate that has plagued Unix users since the very earliest days. Almost invariably, the first thing a Unix hacker does when given an account on a new system is customize his shell environment. This section is dedicated to these hackers and describes how the Red Hat Linux user environment configuration—you can't customize what you don't know.

Every command shell reads its configuration from specially named files. Generally, they start with a file in the /etc directory containing global and system-specific configuration information and then move on to a given user's personal files. What actually goes on in these files is totally up to the user (and the system administrator). One of the hardest things to handle, though, is the case where new software is installed that requires users to set some environment variables. In this case, the global configuration files must be modified, for the changes to take effect for all users. However, the administrator may have customized these files, and so automatically installing new files may clobber those customizations.

This should be starting to sound familiar; it's the same problem that motivated the "drop-in files" approach to the SysV init script configuration. (I first mentioned this technique in the section "The Runlevel Configuration Script.") It isn't surprising, then, that Red Hat approached this similar problem in a similar way: with the /etc/profile.d directory. The global shell configurations on Red Hat Linux systems are constructed to read any files placed in /etc/profile.d as part of their execution.

The global configuration files /etc/profile and /etc/bashrc (for bash), and /etc/cshrc and /etc/csh.login (for tcsh) are fairly simple files. (Actually, these files are for sh and csh rather than bash and tcsh, but most Linux distributions use bash and tcsh as their sh and csh implementations.) They set some basic parameters such as a prompt and some system defaults and then simply source any files present in /etc/profile.d with a certain extension. (The bash configuration reads any files ending in ".sh", while the tcsh configuration reads any files ending in ".csh".) Each such file serves a specific purpose. For example, kde.sh configures KDE for bash users, while colorls.csh configures the color-ls program for tcsh users.

Whenever new software is installed on the system that requires configuration in users' shells, the administrator can simply write two shell scripts (one in sh syntax and another in csh syntax, but otherwise functionally identical) containing the required configuration, and place them in the /etc/profile.d directory as executable files. They will be picked up automatically by the users' shells on their next login. This work can obviously be automated within RPM packages, making it very easy to hook new software installations into a user's shell environment.

Red Hat Linux and Inetd

There are a lot of venerable programs in the Unix world, hailing from the very earliest days of the first systems. Except for init and sh (the first command shell) perhaps the most venerable program on Unix systems is inetd, the Internet super-server. This section describes xinetd, the implementation of inetd used on Red Hat Linux 7.3.

Readers who are already familiar with Unix-like systems will most likely be intimately acquainted with inetd. This program is responsible for listening on various TCP/IP ports and kicking off server processes when client connections are received. Client programs using inetd can be a bit simpler to write than those that handle their own TCP/IP connections. The configuration file for inetd is traditionally /etc/inetd.conf, and is essentially a large list of ports and commands; inetd binds to each port, and executes the indicated program whenever a connection is received.

Versions of Red Hat Linux earlier than 7.3 used the traditional inetd program, with a traditional inetd.conf file. As of version 7.3, however, Red Hat Linux switched to a program known as xinetd, which, though it serves the same function, is quite a bit different than the traditional inetd.

CROSS-REFERENCE *Other Linux distributions, including Debian and Slackware, still use the traditional inetd. If you are interested in the older inetd, see Chapter 5.*

Why did Red Hat switch to xinetd? The long and the short of it is that xinetd is easier to work with. Traditional inetd implementations (including the one commonly used on Linux) have various restrictions (such as a limit on the number of arguments you can pass to a program) that make them inconvenient to use. Also, the /etc/inetd.conf file has to be modified for each program that wishes to make use of inetd; this leads to the same problems already described for the SysV init scripts and user shell environment.

The version of inetd that Red Hat switched to (xinetd) nicely solves all these problems. The directory /etc/xinetd.d contains configuration files for inetd services; this is another example of Red Hat's "drop-in configuration file" approach, which I first mentioned earlier in this chapter in the context of the runlevel configuration script. Additionally, the syntax of these configuration files is much richer than that supported by the older inetd.conf format, allowing for more flexibility in configuring the services.

xinetd is also supported by the chkconfig program mentioned earlier in this chapter. The chkconfig program is used to configure which services are enabled for a given runlevel. Normally, chkconfig works on the SysV init scripts to enable or disable services for specific runlevels. However, chkconfig also supports similar functionality for xinetd services, with the same syntax for enabling and disabling services. This integration makes chkconfig a truly one-stop shop for service configuration and was made much easier to implement with the switch to xinetd.

Mastering Red Hat's Configuration Directories

So far you've seen the "drop-in configuration file" mechanism used on Red Hat Linux in the SysV init scripts, the user environment, and the xinetd Internet superserver. There are, in fact, other examples of this technique. Simply looking in the /etc directory reveals several of them. Table 4-11 summarizes the most important examples. Understanding Red Hat's use of this technique will lead to a much better understanding of Red Hat Linux systems.

Table 4-11. Red Hat Linux Configuration Directories

DIRECTORY	PACKAGE	BEHAVIOR
/etc/rc.d	initscripts	All scripts in the directory corresponding to a runlevel are executed when that runlevel is entered.
/etc/profile.d	Red Hat Setup	All scripts are sourced when a user opens a shell.
/etc/xinetd.d	xinetd	Each file contains configuration information for a particular service.
/etc/cron*	crontabs	Each directory contains cron scripts that get run at that periodicity (e.g., /etc/cron.weekly contains scripts that get run on a weekly basis).
/etc/pam.d	pam	PAM is the Pluggable Authentication Modules. Each file configures the PAM permissions for a particular program or service.
/etc/logrotate.d	logrotate	Each file contains log rotation parameters for a given log file or service.
/etc/makedev.d	Core Red Hat	Each file contains information on generating a particular class of device files in /dev.
/etc/sysconfig	Core Red Hat	Each file contains system-specific configuration data for a particular aspect of the system.

Each of the directories in Table 4-11 has the same basic contents: Each contains a set of files that individually configure some small part or subset of the package. For example, the individual files in /etc/pam.d each configure some service to work with the Pluggable Authenticating Module (PAM) system, while the contents of /etc/logrotate.d configure the policies on rotating and cleaning the log files for a particular service. Even though each directory configures a different high-level service, they all use the same "drop-in individual configuration file" technique.

Working with Kudzu

Kudzu is a vine that was imported to the United States from overseas that has rapidly become ubiquitous in the southeastern part of the country. In a quest for similar "rapid ubiquity," Red Hat chose "kudzu" as the name for their program that scans the computer for new hardware and configures the system if any is detected. Of course, kudzu the vine also attacks trees, blocking their sunlight and causing them to slowly die. This section will help you avoid letting the same thing happen to your Red Hat Linux system.

Generally, kudzu does a fairly good job of checking for new hardware. Almost by definition, no hardware scanner can be perfect, but kudzu has been becoming steadily more reliable over the past few versions of Red Hat Linux. However, every now and then, users run into a particular hardware configuration that causes kudzu to behave incorrectly. Fortunately, kudzu is configured to run as a service via the SysV init scripts. If you find yourself in a situation where kudzu is doing more harm than good, you can disable it by using chkconfig: A quick `chkconfig kudzu off` and it will no longer be invoked for your current runlevel. (Of course, if you add new hardware, you will have to configure it manually.)

If you want to look at the files kudzu uses to do its work, they are installed in /usr/share/kudzu. Generally they map hardware device ID strings to kernel device driver modules. When it's run, kudzu scans for new hardware and configures the system to use any kernel modules mapped to the device. In theory, you could hook in support for new hardware by modifying these files, but that is definitely something that should only be attempted by developers. During system startup, the filesystem-management portion of kudzu is kicked off from /etc/rc.d/rc.sysinit, so if that is causing problems, you can disable it by commenting out the call to /usr/sbin/updfstab in that file.

Installing TrueType Fonts

One of the most highly anticipated features of recent Red Hat Linux versions has been the inclusion of support in XFree86 for the TrueType fonts that are ubiquitous on Windows systems. However, it isn't necessarily obvious how one goes about installing these fonts on a Red Hat Linux system. This section explains how this is done.

To install TrueType fonts on Red Hat Linux 7.3, follow these steps:

1. Create /usr/share/fonts/default/TrueType if it does not already exist.

2. Place the font (.ttf) files in /usr/share/fonts/default/TrueType.

3. Run `ttmkfdir > fonts.scale` in /usr/share/fonts/default/TrueType.

4. Run `mkfontdir` in /usr/share/fonts/default/TrueType.

5. (Optional) Modify the font directory order in /etc/X11/fs/config to list the TrueType fonts first.

6. Restart the X Font Server (xfs) service (`service xfs restart`).

The preceding instructions describe how to install the TrueType fonts in the standard location. You can actually place these files in any convenient directory; however, if you place them anywhere other than /usr/share/fonts/default/True-Type, you must modify the configuration file for the X Font Server (xfs) to include the new directory. (The xfs configuration file is /etc/X11/fs/config.) You can also use this file to change the order in which font directories are searched when a font name is being located. This allows users to give priority to TrueType fonts over other types if they happen to have the same name. It should be noted, however, that not all programs use the X Window font services; some (such as TeX, ghost-script, and the OpenOffice application) use their own mechanism. Such programs will still not be able to use the TrueType fonts, even after they have been installed.

Ensuring System Security

One of the major concerns about older versions of Red Hat Linux was the company's comparatively weak emphasis on security. In the past, Linux systems have traditionally been the playgrounds of technical experts. The various distributions generally took the stance of providing maximum functionality and let the users customize and secure the systems. However, as the market penetration of Linux systems increases, so does the number of less experienced users, who may not be able to secure their systems, or worse, might not even know their systems need to be secured! So, along with most vendors, Red Hat is gradually becoming more security conscious in their distributions.

Using a Firewall

Recent versions of Red Hat Linux no longer leave all the standard inetd services enabled, and version 7.3 actually includes a firewall by default. A *firewall* increases security by preventing attackers from accessing any potentially insecure servers that may be running, either intentionally or inadvertently. The installation process prompts the user to select a firewall security level and allows him or her to exclude specific ports from protection for specific applications (such as for the SSH protocol for remote access). This firewall can be configured after the system is up and running via the `lokkit` command. (Red Hat Linux firewalls are currently based on the ipchains system developed in the older 2.2 kernel series; Red Hat has not yet ported the configuration to the newer iptables system created for the 2.4 series, though there is no loss in functionality.)

CROSS-REFERENCE *An actual network firewall server configuration is one of this book's case studies. See Chapter 16 for much more detailed information.*

Managing Security Settings with PAM

While firewalls help protect the system from external attackers, they don't do much for keeping users who already have accounts on the system from attacking other users or the root account. This type of security is handled on Red Hat Linux systems (like most other distributions) via the *Pluggable Authentication Modules* (PAM) package.

PAM provides an extensible, pluggable, and transparent mechanism for adding authentication methods against various sources. For example, PAM modules exist for authenticating against LDAP and RADIUS servers as easily as against the traditional Unix /etc/passwd mechanism. PAM also allows for specific services and programs to have specific requirements for authentication. Finally, PAM also allows administrators to configure things such as the times of day when users may access a system.

PAM is configured via the /etc/pam.d and /etc/security directories. The first directory contains application-specific security parameters. As listed in Table 4-11, this directory uses Red Hat's typical drop-in-files scheme: Each file in /etc/pam.d contains security configuration information for a particular program. The second directory contains more global configuration options, governing how users are granted permissions to various resources and when they may log in.

The files end users are probably most likely to interact with are /etc/security/console.perms and /etc/pam.d files. The console.perms file specifies which devices users gain access to when they log in on particular consoles. For example, users are granted read and write access to the /dev/floppy device (which represents the floppy disk drive) when they log in either on the console or via X, but not when they log in remotely (since they would not be sitting at the machine in that case and would not need the floppy drive). The files in /etc/pam.d, meanwhile, control access for specific programs, such as the Apache HTTP server: Users who install software that has specific or nonstandard security requirements may need to create or modify files in this directory. Most of the time users will not need to modify these files. However, it is important to know that they exist for future use. When the time comes, users can consult the documentation for more detailed information.

Derivatives of Red Hat Linux

Red Hat is not the only game in Linux town. Red Hat Linux is one of the most popular distributions, however, and the company has had a tremendous impact on the open source community in general and on Linux distributions in particular. Many distributions are derived from Red Hat Linux; some are direct "knock-offs," and some merely use the same packaging format. This section lists a few popular derivatives or cousins of Red Hat Linux.

Mandrake

Mandrake is a Linux distribution produced by MandrakeSoft. Mandrake is focused on the desktop market and provides some financial support to the KDE project in the same way that Red Hat supports the GNOME project. Mandrake was originally based on a version of Red Hat Linux but has since diverged. Mandrake still tracks Red Hat Linux, but only loosely, to maintain feature-by-feature parity. Mandrake generally eschews most of Red Hat's custom software (such as kudzu and anaconda, the installer) in favor of its own versions. Mandrake also includes additional tools addressing how the user interacts with the system; for example, Mandrake includes a "supermount" program that aims to make it transparent for users to mount various devices. Finally, Mandrake also includes a wide variety of software, including a great deal of beta or alpha quality software.

Caldera

Caldera's OpenLinux distribution is aimed squarely at the corporate market. Caldera is not as rigorous about remaining strictly open source as is Red Hat, and so Caldera ships a number of proprietary (non–open source) software packages with their distribution. Caldera also provides support and professional services for their distribution. Caldera has other Unix-like offerings in addition to their Linux distribution; notably, Caldera now owns UnixWare, which is the only true direct descendant from the original AT&T SysV Unix. Caldera's OpenLinux was originally based on an older version of Red Hat Linux, but diverged fairly early on.

TurboLinux

TurboLinux produces a distribution focused on clustering and high-availability servers. Their distribution is typically used in either large, Beowulf parallel "number crunchers" or in server clusters for web sites or application servers. TurboLinux does not track the latest and greatest software as aggressively other distributions, but instead focuses on its own clustering solutions.

Summary

This chapter covered the details of Red Hat Linux, focusing on version 7.3. Red Hat is one of the big three Linux distributions that users will encounter. There are other distributions derived from Red Hat Linux, but in these cases a knowledge of Red Hat Linux itself is useful in working with the derivatives.

Having read this chapter, you are now well prepared for tackling any Red Hat Linux system. You're now able to find the files and programs you need to use, install and manage software packages, and customize the system for your own needs. You can install a stock kernel, customize how the system boots up, tweak the user environment, and customize various other aspects such as the firewall configuration. You also now have a familiarity with the Red Hat Package Manager (RPM) and the set of software shipped with the distribution. Probably the most immediately useful thing you've learned is the canonical Red Hat config.d drop-in configuration file technique.

Since no single book can include every single detail about a system as sophisticated as Red Hat Linux, perhaps the most important thing you've learned is the ability to navigate a Red Hat Linux system. Someday, you'll undoubtedly want to do something with your system not covered by this book; fortunately, you now know how to start and where to look. The next two chapters will provide you with a similar level of mastery over Debian and Slackware systems.

CHAPTER 5
Slackware Linux 8.0

Slackware Linux is one of the older distributions that is still actively developed. It was created in 1993 by Patrick Volkerding, making it a predecessor to both of this book's other sample distributions, Red Hat Linux and Debian. Due to this longevity (as well as the reliable quality of the distribution), Slackware is generally considered one of the most stalwart Linux distributions.

After reading this chapter, you will have a working understanding of a Slackware system. After reading Chapters 4 and 6 as well, you will have seen three different Linux distributions, and should gain some significant insight into the functioning of any Linux system, as well as their power and flexibility.

This chapter will discuss Slackware Linux 8.0 (sometimes referred to simply as Slackware) in detail. To get a basic understanding of what goes into a distribution, readers should review Chapter 3. Additionally, much of this chapter is based on illustrating features of Slackware by comparing them to the equivalent features in Red Hat Linux; that is, this chapter builds on Chapter 4 in part by contrasting the two distributions, so it may be useful for you to also review Chapter 4. It's important to remember throughout your reading that these comparisons are not intended to argue that either distribution is superior, but only to illustrate different techniques.

Slackware's Background and Philosophy

The web site for Slackware Linux (www.slackware.com) has a section on "Slackware Philosophy." There can be no better summary of a project's philosophy than the one they explicitly espouse, and so their own words from their site are reproduced here:

> Since its first release in April of 1993, the Slackware Linux Project has aimed at producing the most "UNIX-like" Linux distribution out there. Slackware complies with the published Linux standards, such as the Linux File System Standard. We have always considered simplicity and stability paramount, and as a result Slackware has become one of the most popular, stable, and friendly distributions available.

A notable phrase is the term "Unix-like." Many (if not most) Linux distributions today are aggressively focused on adding functionality and features—essentially modernizing Unix, as embodied in a Linux system. However, there has traditionally been a sort of "hacker mystique" around Unix, reflected in a rigorous philosophy of simplicity and self-sufficiency. (Believe it or not, it is easy to use the advanced features of Unix, once you understand the basics.) In the mad rush toward modernization, it can be argued that much of this traditional Unix philosophy is being lost.

Because of this, Slackware's goal to be Unix-like speaks volumes about its philosophy. Users of other Unix systems (commercial or otherwise) may find Slackware the easiest Linux distribution to migrate to, because it is Unix-like. This philosophy is typically manifested in practice by choosing simple, standard ways to accomplish tasks, rather than reinventing the wheel. For example, Slackware uses the traditional compressed *tarball* (Tape ARchive) format (which is simply a .tar.gz file) as its packaging mechanism, rather than make use of an enhanced package management system such as RPM or Debian's system. Slackware's use of standard tarballs make it possible to manage all the software by hand, but sacrifices some more sophisticated features such as enforcing dependencies and file conflict resolutions.

On the one hand, Slackware lacks many of the newer features that many other distributions have introduced. On the other hand, it's possible to manage an entire Slackware system with nothing more than a text editor and a little know-how. This sort of self-sufficiency appeals to many experienced Unix and Linux users. It also makes Slackware a good "training crucible" for new users—if you can make it on Slackware, you can make it anywhere, so to speak. Many experienced Unix and Linux users (including myself) learned most of the basics on a Slackware system. For these reasons, Slackware maintains a sizable and occasionally ornery following of users who look affectionately on the distribution.

Linux Kernel

One of Slackware's stated goals is simplicity and stability. Distributing a customized kernel actually introduces an additional idiosyncrasy to the system that administrators (and occasionally users) have to be aware of and manage. Slackware, therefore, does not use or distribute customized kernels, as some other distributions do. Occasionally, however, Slackware will ship a kernel with a patch fixing a crucial bug that hasn't yet made it into the official stable kernel.

Since Slackware relies solely on standard kernels, it's actually very easy to upgrade the kernel on a Slackware system. The source code for the kernel is placed in /usr/src; this is the same location as on Red Hat Linux. Unlike Red Hat's kernels, however, there are really no hoops to jump through when you want to upgrade your kernel; you simply remove the Linux symbolic link, extract the new kernel, and recreate the symbolic link so that it points to the new kernel directory. After that, you simply build the kernel normally.

There is a significant way in which Slackware differs from Red Hat in kernel management, however. As was mentioned briefly in Chapter 4, the GNU glibc system library relies on certain Linux kernel headers. These headers should match the version of the kernel that glibc was compiled against, rather than reflect the currently running kernel. (In fact, Linus Torvalds and other kernel developers would much prefer that glibc remove this dependence on Linux kernel headers.) Red Hat works around this problem by providing a special *kernel-headers* RPM package; Slackware, however, handles this by creating a symbolic link in /usr/include/linux that points into the kernel source code installation. This means that Slackware essentially requires that kernel source code is installed on the system in order to use the compilers, and also means that the kernel headers will change with the current kernel version. Red Hat's solution is probably more "correct," but Slackware's is certainly simpler, illustrating again the differences in philosophy between the two distributions.

At any rate, Slackware is focused on stability and simplicity. Thus, Slackware occasionally lags behind other distributions in adopting major new releases of key components such as the kernel and system libraries. Slackware 8.0, for example, ships with two kernels: the current 2.4.5 kernel and the older—but tried and true—2.2.19 kernel. Even though both kernels are considered stable, Slackware 8.0 defaults to the 2.2 kernel, because it is a more extensively tested and debugged—and therefore reliable—kernel.

Packaging Format

Slackware uses standard tarballs (.tar.gz files) for its packaging format. Since tarballs can be read by any Unix system (and any Linux distribution), they are platform-independent (though, of course, their contents typically are not). This section will discuss how Slackware Linux 8.0 handles package management with tarballs.

Technical Summary

TAR files are not compressed, so they are frequently compressed before being distributed. In the early days of Unix, the most common compression format was the common Unix *compress* program, which gives files a .Z extension. The GNU project introduced the GNU Zip (gzip) compression format, with the .gz extension. Later, the bzip compression program introduced the .bz2 extension. A tarball is simply a TAR file compressed with one of these schemes; the extensions end up being .tar.Z, .tar.gz, or .tar.bz2. The most common format for Linux and other open source software is a gzipped TAR archive; sometimes the extension is shortened to .tgz. All of these file types (that is, simple .tar files as well as .tar.gz files, etc.) are sometimes referred to as tarballs; a tarball can be compressed or uncompressed.

Managing Installed Packages

Just as Slackware aims at simplicity in its use of tarballs as the native format for its package manager, it aims for similar simplicity in the tools for managing packages. This is most obviously evident in the package management tool, known simply as pkgtool, which is a console (text-based) menu program. It's really not much more than a user-friendly front-end for invoking the other tools described below. The pkgtool menu provides several installation options, an option to remove an installed package, and an option to view the contents of packages that are currently installed.

You can install packages from the following three sources:

- The current directory

- Another (arbitrary) directory

- A floppy disk

Each of the above options allows administrators to install multiple packages at once. This is actually the way packages are installed when the system itself is first installed. These are the actual activities that pkgtool performs when it installs multiple packages:

1. The Slackware installation program invokes pkgtool to install the packages selected by the user. (This step is only invoked during installation of the system—it's skipped if you just run pkgtool by hand.) This step sets the directory that pkgtool is to use in step 2.

2. pkgtool scans its input directory for all files it can find that end in either .tgz or .tar.gz, that is, it searches for any standard tarballs.

3. pkgtool then asks the user whether each tarball should be installed, and acts accordingly.

The other options supported by pkgtool allow the user to remove a package after selecting it from a list, and also allow the user to view a list of all installed packages, as well as their contents. This functionality is just a front-end for the other tools listed in the following sections. The tools can always be invoked from the command line, but the pkgtool command provides a consolidated user interface.

Installing Packages

Slackware packages can be installed via a command line with the installpkg program. This program takes a single parameter—the name of a tarball—to install and has several options that tweak where and how the package is installed. The command is very simple so we won't replicate all the options. The most useful option, however, is the -root <path> option. This parameter changes the root of the installation to <path>; for example, a package that would normally be installed in the root directory can be placed somewhere else, such as /opt via the command installpkg -root /opt packagename.tgz.

The installpkg command has additional options you can use that provide various interactive menu capabilities; these features are typically used when installpkg is called from another program or script, such as the pkgtool front-end command.

Upgrading Packages

Slackware packages can be upgraded via the upgradepkg command. This command is even simpler than the installpkg command. If the new package has the same name as the package already installed, then the command upgradepkg <file name> will upgrade the package. If the file names are different, then the command upgradepkg <old package name>%<new package filename> will upgrade the package. For example, if foo-2.0.tgz is an upgrade of foo-1.0.tgz, then the command upgradepkg foo-1.0%foo-2.0.tgz will accomplish the upgrade. In either case, the effect is the same: the tool consults the list of files that the old package had installed, and then installs the new (upgraded) package.

If there are any files contained in the original package that were not replaced by the upgrade package, then the old stale files are removed. If a package needs to be upgraded into to a different root directory, then the ROOT environment variable must be set to that effect (in contrast to the installpkg command, which accepts this setting as a command line option). Note that the package will have to be upgraded into the same root as it is installed, or else it's not really an upgrade.

Uninstalling Packages

The command to uninstall a package is removepkg. This command takes a single argument, which is the name of the package to be removed. As with upgradepkg, the root of the package can be altered by setting the ROOT environment variable. Of course, the root directory has to match the directory where the package is actually installed. To remove the package, the tool retrieves the list of files installed by the package and then simply removes them.

Creating New Packages

Slackware's package management system also provides a very easy way to create Slackware-compatible packages. A developer administrator, or other packager, simply creates the directory layout of the software to be packaged in a temporary scratch directory. For example, an administrator might compile a software package and place it in /tmp. Then, the makepkg command is run, which creates a tarball with the necessary structure, and even creates a basic installation script if one is required. This package can then be installed (or upgraded) by one of the other tools.

There are additional advanced features that can be exploited when creating Slackware packages. The makepkg command is useful for many or most situations, but if more extensive functionality is required (such as a custom installation script,) it can be taken advantage of. Interested users can consult the Slackware documentation at www.slackware.com.

Mechanism and User Interface

Slackware's package management tools are fairly basic when compared to Red Hat's RPM (discussed in Chapter 4) or Debian's *apt* tools (discussed in Chapter 6). However, even though Slackware's tools might not be quite state of the art among Linux distributions, they are still at least as sophisticated as most other Unix systems' tools.

It's important to remember the Slackware philosophy of simplicity and ease of maintenance throughout. There is literally nothing that these tools do that cannot be done manually with a text editor. When a package is installed, a file containing the description of the package and a list of all its files is placed in the directory */var/log/packages*. These files are human-readable, meaning that they can be viewed, or even accessed via various scripts if an administrator is feeling particularly clever. For example, you can grep for the string "etc" in

/var/log/packages to find a list of all files in the /etc/ directory that are owned by packages; Red Hat doesn't make this quite so easy.

The tools discussed in this section use these same files to do their work. In fact, the tools themselves are simply shell scripts! Slackware's package management mechanism is really shorthand for things that an administrator can accomplish by hand. That this fact is not immediately obvious to users of the tools is a tribute to the success of Slackware's elegant simplicity, and a great demonstration of that traditional Unix "hacker mystique" of self-sufficiency and simplicity.

Filesystem Layout

At this point, the importance of understanding how to navigate an operating system's file layout should be clear—if you can't find something, you can't use it. In Chapter 3, the Linux Filesystem Hierarchy Standard (FHS) was discussed; in Chapter 4, Red Hat's adherence to the FHS was also discussed. In general, there's not much to say about Slackware except that if anything, it obeys the FHS even more strictly than Red Hat. That is, you can expect no surprises when looking for a file on a Slackware system.

 CAUTION *Since Slackware's packaging tools support the installation of simple tarballs, administrators should be careful to make sure they know where in the filesystem non-Slackware packages are installed. Not everyone follows the FHS.*

The only other remarkable thing about Slackware's use of the filesystem is how it treats the /opt directory. Recall from Chapter 3 that /opt is to be used for "optional" system components. Red Hat treats this directory more or less like /usr/local, in that normally, Red Hat's RPM packages don't place anything in /usr/local or /opt (and this convention is obeyed fairly consistently in general). Those two directories are reserved for use by a system administrator to place local files.

Slackware also treats /usr/local as strictly for administrators; however, Slackware actually does place some software in /opt. Specifically, Slackware places optional packages in /opt (for which it's hard to fault them, obviously). For example, neither KDE nor GNOME is required for the normal operation of the system or for XFree86 to function; Slackware therefore installs these packages in /opt. In a way, you can actually claim that by placing optional packages in /opt, Slackware is doing a better job of logically partitioning its software installation than Red Hat. In the end, it's six of one and half a dozen of the other, so really what users should take away from this discussion is that if a particular package isn't located under /usr, it's probably under /opt.

System Startup Scripts

In Chapter 3, the two common models for system startup scripts—the BSD model and the SysV model—were briefly mentioned. In Chapter 4, Red Hat Linux's model, which is based on the SysV approach, was discussed in detail. That chapter contains enough information to reach proficiency with the startup mechanism of any SysV-based system. This chapter, meanwhile, will discuss Slackware's startup script model. Since Slackware is very BSD-like, this chapter will provide detailed information on the BSD model of initialization scripts. Finally, this chapter assumes that you've already read the "System Startup Scripts" section in Chapter 4, and relies on comparisons to that material.

File and Directory Layout

The first step toward understanding the BSD init scripts model used by Slackware is to list the relevant files. It's important to remember that fundamentally, both the SysV model used by Red Hat and the BSD model used by Slackware do the same things. Only the structure of the scripts varies between the two. This section will outline the following files used by the BSD model, and discuss how they compare to their SysV counterparts:

- /etc/inittab

- /etc/rc.d/rc.S

- /etc/rc.d/rc.K

- /etc/rc.d/rc.M

- /etc/rc.d/rc.0 and /etc/rc.d/rc.6

- /etc/rc.d/rc.modules

- /etc/rc.d/rc.inet1 and /etc/rc.d/rc.inet2

- /etc/rc.d/rc.sysvinit

The primary directory containing all of these files is /etc/rc.d—just as with the SysV model.

/etc/inittab

Remember that the ultimate purpose of the init scripts is to configure the various services that are to be kicked off by the init global parent process. Since both Slackware and Red Hat use the same implementation of the base init program, they share the same starting point, which is the */etc/inittab* file—the "init table."

As was discussed in Chapter 4, /etc/inittab contains lines that specify programs (usually shell scripts) that should be run when init enters a certain runlevel, or when various other events (such as a power failure) occur. The init program itself allows for there to be up to seven runlevels, numbered 0 through 6. A given Unix system can assign whatever meanings to these runlevels it desires, but traditionally runlevel 0 corresponds to system halt, and runlevel 6 corresponds to system reboot. The other runlevels are up to the system. Table 5-1 summarizes the meanings Slackware assigns to the runlevels.

Table 5-1. Slackware Linux Runlevels

RUNLEVEL	MEANING
0	System halt
1	Single-user (root-user only; typically used for system maintenance)
2	Unused, equivalent to runlevel 3
3	Standard multiuser mode (no X Window)
4	Multiuser mode with X desktop (via a graphical login)
5	Unused, equivalent to runlevel 3
6	System reboot

Many of the lines in the standard Slackware /etc/inittab file are the same as or similar to the equivalent lines in the Red Hat version. Since those lines were discussed in Chapter 4, they won't be rehashed here. However, there are some lines that are different, and these lines will be dissected in detail. First, though, it's useful to make a few generalities.

One way to characterize the SysV model of init scripts is as a framework of scripts you can plug services into. In essence, each runlevel in /etc/inittab is configured to invoke the same script, and the script itself does the work of starting and stopping services appropriate to the new runlevel. The BSD model, however, doesn't have the same kind of extensive script framework. Instead, the BSD model defines a separate script for each runlevel, and /etc/inittab binds each script to the corresponding runlevel. This is really what goes in most of the lines in Slackware's /etc/inittab file that differ from the Red Hat version. Here are the relevant lines:

```
si:S:sysinit:/etc/rc.d/rc.S
su:1S:wait:/etc/rc.d/rc.K
rc:2345:wait:/etc/rc.d/rc.M
```

The first line defines the file /etc/rc.d/rc.S as a script to run when the system starts up, regardless of runlevel; the second line defines /etc/rc.d/rc.K as the script to run when entering runlevel 1 (which is single-user mode); the third line defines /etc/rc.d/rc.M as the script to execute for all the multiuser modes. These are the three key scripts used by Slackware to configure the system.

Later in the file, this series of lines appears:

```
c1:1235:respawn:/sbin/agetty 38400 tty1 linux
c2:1235:respawn:/sbin/agetty 38400 tty2 linux
c3:1235:respawn:/sbin/agetty 38400 tty3 linux
c4:1235:respawn:/sbin/agetty 38400 tty4 linux
c5:1235:respawn:/sbin/agetty 38400 tty5 linux
c6:12345:respawn:/sbin/agetty 38400 tty6 linux
x1:4:wait:/etc/rc.d/rc.4
```

These lines define six text "virtual consoles" that run on all of the multiuser runlevels, except runlevel 4 (that is, runlevels 2, 3, and 5). Runlevel 4 is the one that includes X; the last line of code starts X via the /etc/rc.d/rc.4 script. Recall that Red Hat's "multiuser with X" is runlevel 5. Thus, runlevel 5 on Red Hat Linux is more or less equivalent to runlevel 4 on Slackware Linux.

There is one small difference: under Slackware, only one of the consoles (tty6) is configured for runlevel 4, while under Red Hat Linux all six consoles are present and X is simply added on the seventh console. The reason is that Slackware treats runlevel 4 slightly differently than the way Red Hat treats its runlevel 5. Whereas Red Hat leaves all six virtual consoles running and simply adds X to the seventh console, Slackware disables all but one of the text consoles. This is, of course, really just "administrivia," but it's a subtle difference: Slackware is viewing runlevel 4 as a different "mode of usage," where Red Hat views runlevel 5 as simply starting X for convenience.

> **NOTE** *On any distribution, you can always start X by first logging in to one of the virtual text consoles and using the xinit command, so in the end starting X automatically is really just a convenience.*

/etc/rc.d/rc.S

The */etc/rc.d/rc.S* file is the sysinit script that does very basic work such as activating memory swap space, checking local disk partitions for errors, and mounting non-networked filesystems. It also configures hardware such as the system clock and random number seed, and configures kernel modules for device drivers (by invoking the *rc.modules* file, which is described later) and PCMCIA devices.

It also configures the serial port hardware via the *rc.serial* script. This file is pretty low-level and generally straightforward, and chances are you won't have to modify it very much. The important thing to understand is that since it handles very basic tasks, this file is configured to be invoked no matter what runlevel is being used. It may be worthwhile to scan through the file just to get a sense of the kinds of tasks it performs.

/etc/rc.d/rc.K

The */etc/rc.d/rc.K* file is the script that is run when the system enters single-user mode (which is runlevel 1). The ".K" is short for "kill," because this script kills processes. It first terminates all currently running processes, and then simply switches to runlevel 1. The only processes that will be started in runlevel 1, therefore, are the tty consoles defined in /etc/inittab. This state obviously won't be all that useful (since it's not running any daemons or other processes) so it is primarily used for administrative mode.

/etc/rc.d/rc.M

The */etc/rc.d/rc.M* file is the script responsible for configuring the system for all the multiuser modes. It picks up where the rc.S sysinit script leaves off; once rc.S has finished configuring the hardware and preparing the system basics like mounting filesystems, the rc.M script begins starting server processes.

The /etc/rc.d/rc.M script begins by starting the basic processes, such as the syslog (system logging) facility, the crond and atd daemons for scheduling tasks, and also sets a few parameters for the login consoles and CD-ROM drive. It also starts various daemons, such as the printer daemon (lpd), mail server (Sendmail), and web server. One of the most important tasks that rc.M performs is activating the network. It accomplishes this by calling two other scripts: rc.inet1 and rc.inet2. (These scripts are described separately, later in this section.)

 NOTE *Many daemons (such as lpd and sendmail) can sometimes be security risks; for more information, see the section on "Ensuring System Security" later in this chapter.*

Finally, rc.M invokes other system scripts. Slackware, even though it primarily uses the BSD init scripts model, also supports scripts written for the SysV model. It supports these files through the script *rc.sysvinit*, which is described later in this section, in the "/etc/rc.d/rc.sysvinit" sub-section. The last step in the BSD model, meanwhile, is to invoke a script called rc.local, which is the same as the rc.local script discussed in Chapter 4 as part of the SysV model Red Hat Linux uses. This script simply contains whatever additional code the administrator requires for a particular system. It's intended to allow administrators to customize a system's configuration without having to make extensive modifications to the other init scripts. By default, this file is empty on Slackware (unlike under Red Hat Linux).

/etc/rc.d/rc.0 and /etc/rc.d/rc.6

These are actually the same file: *rc.0* is a symbolic link to *rc.6*. The script has a block in which it detects whether it was called for runlevel 0 (system halt) or runlevel 6 (system reboot). These runlevels are almost identical; they differ only in whether the system is automatically rebooted at the end. So, the two scripts are really a single file, to avoid duplicating code across two files.

In a certain sense, this file is just the "inverse" of /etc/rc.d/rc.M and /etc/rc.d/rc.S. That is, where rc.M has code that starts a variety of services, rc.6 stops them all. It also does a bit of work related to things that were initialized in the rc.S "sysinit" script, such as synchronizing the current time to the hardware clock, saving the random number seed, and deactivating the swap space. The rc.6 script also shuts down NFS (if it's running), turns off disk quotas and process accounting, and deactivates any RAID arrays that might be running. It unmounts local disks, and then reboots the system (if it was called as rc.6; if it was called as rc.0, it simply halts).

/etc/rc.d/rc.modules

The */etc/rc.d/rc.modulesis* file is responsible for configuring whatever kernel modules are required to support the system's hardware. The file actually contains lines for essentially every kernel module that is available with the Linux kernel. It has code to check for the presence of various kernel modules, and if they are found, it attempts to load them. It also has many lines for other kernel modules, which are commented out. Generally, an administrator would modify this file to activate support for the hardware for a given system. Most of the time, the appropriate lines simply need to be uncommented, but occasionally a line may need to be added. Red Hat Linux handles this functionality more or less automatically via the *kudzu* hardware detection utility, and so there is really no analog to this file.

The only other notable thing that rc.modules does is to call out to the *rc.netdevice* script. This script is responsible for configuring the device driver for the network card; usually it consists of a single line, which loads the kernel module for the network card (if one is present). This script is invoked from rc.modules, which is invoked from rc.S, and so the network device is guaranteed to be up before the network scripts (rc.inet1 and rc.inet2) are invoked.

/etc/rc.d/rc.inet1 and /etc/rc.d/rc.inet2

These scripts are responsible for configuring the network for the host. They are invoked in order: *rc.inet1* first, and *rc.inet2* next. The rc.inet1 script brings up the various network interfaces, and either configures the IP addresses and routing tables, or requests the settings from a DHCP (Dynamic Host Configuration Protocol) server. (These settings are set by the administrator during installation.) The *rc.inet1* script is roughly analogous to the /etc/rc.d/init.d/network file used by Red Hat Linux (discussed in Chapter 4).

The rc.inet2 script starts network-related processes and performs other network-related work, once the network is up and running. This script, for example, starts the *inetd* "superserver," the *portmap* daemon, and the Secure Shell (SSH) daemon for remote login, among other processes. This file also performs other tasks, such as mounting network filesystems. Some of the less common functions of rc.inet2 are commented out by default; for example, most systems don't need to run a Domain Nameserver (DNS) or router software, and so the corresponding lines, while present in the file as samples, are disabled by default.

The rc.inet2 file starts up most network-related servers. However, it doesn't handle quite everything that has to do with the network; it really only handles the basics. Some servers, such as the Sendmail server for SMTP and the Apache web server, are actually started directly from the rc.M file that calls rc.inet2.

/etc/rc.d/rc.sysvinit

Slackware Linux is based on the BSD init scripts model. However, some software packages come with pre-written scripts for starting and stopping (or otherwise managing) the software. If these scripts are written to use the SysV init framework, they might be a bit cumbersome to integrate into the BSD framework. As a convenience to administrators, Slackware Linux actually includes support for the SysV init scripts model. This support is kicked off by the *etc/rc.d/rc.sysvinit* file, which itself is invoked by the other scripts. (The rc.M script invokes rc.sysvinit to start the SysV processes, and the rc.6 script invokes it to shut them down.)

Any SysV init scripts that are started via this file must be placed in the directory corresponding to the runlevel—the same naming convention used in standard SysV init systems (such as Red Hat Linux). For example, the directory for runlevel 3 would be /etc/rc.d/rc3.d. In general, most of the functionality discussed in Chapter 4 is supported by Slackware's SysV init scripts support. When entering a new runlevel, the kill scripts (scripts starting with the letter "K") are executed, and then all start scripts (which start with an S) are executed for the new runlevel.

Slackware's support for SysV init scripts is pretty complete, but not sophisticated; it's an afterthought or a convenience, and so it's really only useful for easily hooking in scripts that you may already have written, rather than for managing the system itself. To complete most low-level tasks, you'll have to edit the BSD init scripts directly, as discussed in the rest of this section.

Other Files

There is a smattering of other files, mostly responsible for specific activities. For example, the *rc.httpd* file is responsible for starting up the Apache HTTP server. The *rc.sshd* script is responsible for starting the SSH server (which is OpenSSH on Slackware 8.0). These files are typically self-explanatory; a simple reading of them will reveal what they do, since they're not very complicated.

Modifying the Startup Scripts

The reason that Red Hat chose to use the SysV model was to allow administrators to add software into the startup process without having to modify shell scripts. The SysV model will automatically pick up any scripts placed in it. The advantage of this approach is that it's easier to automate system administration; the downside is that there's more structure to the files, and that can make the learning curve more difficult. The BSD model, in contrast, is very straightforward: there's one script for one task, and it's a very "shallow" structure—you don't have to dig very deep to find the script you're looking for.

Modifying Slackware's startup process means understanding which scripts are responsible for what tasks. If you want to change the network settings, you have to edit rc.inet1. If you want to start a new server process or disable one of the defaults you would edit either rc.M or rc.inet2. If you just want to add a small script snippet to clear stale files on each reboot, you might put the code in rc.local. The simplicity of the BSD approach makes it easy to tell where and what to modify. Once you've read this section and taken a look through the scripts themselves, you'll be managing Slackware's startup process with the best of them.

Tracing an Execution

The best way to understand how the BSD init scripts work together is to take a quick look at a typical boot process. We've already covered most of the actual contents of the script in the sections above, so we'll keep this section brief. In this example, we'll assume that the system is entering runlevel 4—normal multiuser mode with X.

/etc/rc.d/rc.S

When init starts, it processes /etc/inittab. It first encounters this line:

```
si:S:sysinit:/etc/rc.d/rc.S
```

This line instructs init to execute the /etc/rc.d/rc.S script, no matter what runlevel is being entered. This script, in turn, does basic system configuration, and invokes the /etc/rc.d/rc.modules script to load appropriate device drivers. The rc.modules script, in turn, invokes /etc/rc.d/rc.netdevice to configure the ethernet (or other network) hardware separately.

/etc/rc.d/rc.M

The next line in the file configures a script to be executed for runlevel 1; since that's not the current runlevel, it is skipped. Next up is the /etc/rc.d/rc.M script, which is configured to execute for runlevels 2 through 5:

```
rc:2345:wait:/etc/rc.d/rc.M
```

This script does the lion's share of the work in configuring the system. It activates the network (by invoking rc.inet1 and rc.inet2), configures things such as the system font and mouse (via rc.font and rc.gpm), and starts additional higher-level network servers. Finally, it activates any SysV scripts that may have been configured, by executing the rc.sysvinit script.

Other Actions

After executing the /etc/rc.d/rc.M script, init continues reading /etc/inittab. The next few lines define scripts to be run in response to various events, such as power failures or the "three finger salute" sequence (control-alt-delete) for rebooting the system. It also defines the scripts to be run on system halt and reboot (/etc/rc.d/rc.0 and /etc/rc.d/rc.6).

The last block of lines sets up the text consoles, as described in the section above on "/etc/inittab." However, since we're entering runlevel 4, the first five consoles are skipped. (Only tty6 is defined for runlevel 4.) The final line starts up X via the /etc/rc.d/rc.4 script, and is executed in this case since we're in runlevel 4.

That's pretty much all there is to the BSD init script model used by Slackware Linux. If you've read this whole section, you'll be able to bend Slackware to your will—or at least, bend its startup scripts. More importantly, if you've also read the equivalent section in Chapter 4, you'll now have exposure to both of the prominent models for init scripts on Unix-like systems in general. You might find some minor variants from system to system, but generally what you've learned will be applicable. This knowledge alone will probably prove useful on any number of occasions as you work with Unix systems. It might even be worth the price of this book by itself!

Core System Libraries

This section will discuss the core software that ships with Slackware Linux. Because Slackware's goal is simplicity and stability, Slackware Linux is a bit conservative in tracking the latest and greatest software. However, this is certainly not to say that Slackware doesn't keep up to date. In fact, Slackware follows the latest releases of software regularly—just not aggressively.

Slackware Linux ships with a selection of software similar to Red Hat's—in fact, similar to most modern distributions. Table 5-2 lists the major packages that come with Slackware Linux 8.0. For comparison, see also Table 4-9 in Chapter 4.

Table 5-2. Slackware Linux 8.0 Core Libraries

PACKAGE	VERSION	COMMENT
XFree86	4.1.0	X Window System. v4 contains 3D acceleration and new rendering extensions.
glibc	2.2.3	Core runtime system libraries. Contains linker/loader, math libraries, security libraries, network libraries, and multithreading libraries.
bash	2.05	Bourne Again Shell. Primary system shell (used by root).
gdbm	1.8.0	File database libraries. Used by other programs to index and store data.
fileutils	4.1	File manipulation utilities. Contains basic programs like `ls`, `cp`, `rm`, etc.

There are a few points worth making about Table 5-2. First, Slackware 8.0 does not include the Pluggable Authenticating Modules (PAM) libraries that Red Hat and others include. (This software is only an alternate way to handle system authentication, which is in a certain sense "reinventing the wheel.") Also, Slackware has different names and contents for other packages. For example, the user management tools are found in the "shadow" package on Slackware. For a full list of packages that are installed and their contents, simply look in the /var/log/packages directory on a running Slackware Linux installation.

X Window System and Desktop

Slackware Linux, like almost every usable Unix-like system, includes a version of the X Window System. This section will describe the implementation Slackware uses, and also cover additional related aspects, such as installed desktop environments.

XFree86

Slackware Linux 8.0 includes XFree86 4.1.0. This was the latest XFree86 version available at the time. Red Hat Linux 7.3, meanwhile, includes XFree86 4.2.0 (which was in turn the most recent XFree86 version available at *that* time). XFree86 4.0 introduced some enhancements (in the form of additional hardware drivers and some additional support software) and bug fixes, and it is the foundation for both versions 4.1.0 and 4.2.0.

CROSS-REFERENCE   *See Chapter 4 for information on XFree86 4.2.0; most of that material applies to XFree86 4.1.0, as well.*

Table 4-10 (in Chapter 4) lists several tools present on Red Hat Linux that are useful with XFree86. Most of these tools are also present with Slackware, but two are not and are worth mentioning.

First is the *Xconfigurator* program written by Red Hat. This program is a text-based application that guides the user through the process of configuring XFree86. However, Slackware does not include this program, relying instead on the *xf86config program* that is included with XFree86 itself. The xf86config program does essentially everything that Red Hat's Xconfigurator program can, but Red Hat's version is a bit more user-friendly.

Slackware also lacks the switchdesk applications present on Red Hat. These programs allow the user to change her preferred desktop environment. Slackware, however, relies on the traditional method for accomplishing this—the *xinit* mechanism. For more information on this, see "Slackware Linux Idiosyncrasies," later in this chapter.

GNOME and KDE

Slackware Linux, again like most modern distributions, includes both the GNOME and KDE desktop environments, and allows the user to select between the two. (The procedure for doing this is described in the "Slackware Linux Idiosyncrasies" section later in this chapter.) As with the version of XFree86, Slackware Linux 8.0 shipped the most recent versions of KDE and GNOME available at the time; in fact, Slackware was one of the first distributions to ship with GNOME 1.4! Slackware Linux 8.0 also shipped with KDE 2.1.2.

Userspace Applications

This section will discuss the actual user applications that are included with Slackware Linux. (Recall that a "userspace" application is a "normal" program, rather than one that runs in kernel space.)

Included Applications

Slackware Linux comes with a fairly modest selection of software, when compared to other distributions. That is, where Red Hat Linux comes on two full CDs with a third PowerTools CD, Slackware Linux ships on a single CD, with a CD of extras. Debian, like Red Hat Linux, ships on three CDs. At first, this might seem to imply that Slackware does not have as broad a palette of software as do Red Hat and Debian. However, it's important to remember that Slackware is about simplicity, and so including tons of software that the vast majority of users won't need is redundant. Slackware's packaging tools operate on simple tarballs; this makes it very easy to install software, no matter what its source is, and so Slackware avoids the need to include "the kitchen sink" by making it easy for users to install their own software.

That said, Slackware still ships with a large amount of software. (Remember, after all, that even the smallest Linux distribution comes with far more software than almost any commercial operating system.) The following list of packages that Slackware Linux includes is pretty typical of Linux systems:

- GNU Compiler Collection (gcc)

- Mozilla web browser

- emacs text editor

Any experienced user of a Linux system will feel right at home with Slackware Linux. Generally, Slackware simply lacks some of the more obscure programs included with other distributions.

ZipSlack

There is a variant of Slackware Linux known as ZipSlack. In Chapter 4, the various editions of Red Hat Linux were discussed. Slackware really has no equivalent to these editions; Red Hat uses them to delineate their product line, to support their commercial initiatives. Since Slackware isn't a commercial entity, there is no motivation to produce multiple editions. ZipSlack, then, is not so much an edition or variant of Slackware as it is a mini-distribution.

ZipSlack is intended to be small enough to reside completely on a small medium, such as an Iomega ZIP disk. By placing an entire Linux distribution on a portable disk, a user can carry a Linux installation in his pocket. ZipSlack also includes tools to boot directly into the Linux system from a Windows or MS-DOS machine. To accomplish this small footprint, ZipSlack simply restricts itself to only the absolutely critical components of the core system, and a minimal set of user tools. Due to its small size, ZipSlack is also useful in storage-constrained devices, such as personal digital assistants (PDAs) and network appliances.

Slackware Linux Idiosyncrasies

Like any distribution, Slackware Linux has its own peculiar quirks and ways of doing things. In Chapter 4, you learned some of the equivalent idiosyncrasies of Red Hat Linux; after you've read this section, you'll have seen some of the differences between two distributions, and will be another step closer to mastery of the concepts, and not just the techniques of using and managing a Linux system.

Configuring Inetd

The *inetd superserver* (sometimes called metaserver) was discussed in Chapter 4 in the context of Red Hat Linux. Red Hat uses the xinetd package as the inetd implementation for their distribution. Slackware, however, uses an older, traditional inetd implementation. This implementation will be very familiar to anyone who's ever worked with inetd on another traditional Unix-like system. In fact, users who have may wish to skip this section, since there will be no new material; less experienced users, however, will be able to apply the content in this section to other systems.

Recall that the purpose of inetd is to make it easy to write basic server applications. It's a sort of "cookie cutter" that can be used to stamp out similar servers. Software authors write small programs that handle operations, and then map their application to a port in the configuration for inetd. The inetd server, in turn, binds to all the ports indicated in its file and routes incoming requests to the appropriate service program depending on what port the request arrived on.

Generally, traditional inetd is pretty simple to configure. Slackware's implementation is in the tcpip1 package (along with a number of other things) and essentially consists of three files: the inetd program executable, the /etc/inetd.conf file which configures the server, and the /etc/services file that establishes meaningful names for port numbers.

The /etc/services File

The */etc/services* file is used to map names to port numbers. This is purely a cosmetic issue; it simply lets humans refer to port numbers by names, since keeping track of all the ports numerically can be confusing. (This is similar to how

Internet IP addresses are mapped to server names by the DNS system; the names are purely for human consumption.) Actually, the /etc/services file is used by more programs that just inetd; it can be used by any application that needs or wants to find a human-meaningful name for a port number. (An API is provided to applications to allow them to look up the name of a port number, or to locate a service by its human-readable name.)

Each line in the /etc/services file has this syntax:

```
<symbolic name>        <port>/<protocol>        <aliases>
```

The <symbolic name> is the human-meaningful term, such as "http" or "telnet." The port is the TCP/IP port number of the service, and the protocol must be either of the literal strings, "tcp" or "udp," depending on whether the service uses a TCP (i.e., stream-oriented) or a UDP (i.e., datagram-oriented) protocol. The aliases are optional, and simply indicate alternate names for the same port number.

TCP vs. UDP

Don't worry too much about the difference between TCP and UDP; generally, these are used only by server and client applications to establish connections of the appropriate type. A given protocol will be based on TCP or UDP depending on its needs. If you've written a server yourself and are adding it to inetd, you'll know whether it is TCP or UDP; if you're just installing one, the documentation for the software will state which it uses. In fact, many protocols listed in /etc/services have entries for *both* TCP and UDP, even though most only use one or the other. This mapping is mostly for human reference, and has no impact on the functioning of the software, anyway.

Here are some examples from the /etc/services file that is included with Slackware 8. This is the line for WWW servers:

```
www          80/tcp        http    # WorldWideWeb HTTP
```

This line indicates that the "www" protocol has port number 80, is a stream-based (TCP) protocol, and is also known as "http." Contrast this with the Trivial File Transfer Protocol (TFTP) line, which is a UDP-based protocol that runs on port 69 and has no aliases:

```
tftp         69/udp
```

A few moments' search through this file will turn up lots of familiar port numbers and protocols, such as telnet (for remote access) on port 23, HTTP (for web servers) on port 80, POP3 (for accessing email) on port 110, and SMTP (for transferring email) on port 25.

The /etc/inetd.conf File

The actual configuration file for the inetd server is */etc/inetd.conf*. The contents of the file are also straightforward. Each line in the file configures a separate service program and binds it to a port number. The lines have this syntax (which is also documented in the file itself):

```
<service_name> <sock_type> <proto> <flags> <user> <server_path> <args>
```

The `<service_name>` parameter is either a numeric port number, or the symbolic name of a port as specified in /etc/services. (If a non-numeric port is specified here, the /etc/services file will be searched to find a port number.). The `<sock_type>` must be either "stream" or "dgram" (which is short for datagram). The next field, `<proto>`, must be either "tcp" or "udp," and must match the `<sock_type>`field. That is, if `<sock_type>` is "stream," then `<proto>` must be "tcp" and *vice versa*; The "udp" and "dgram" fields are similarly linked.

NOTE *If a system used an underlying network protocol other than TCP/IP, it could use something other than "udp" and "tcp" for the datagram and stream protocols. However, the **vast** majority of computers today use TCP/IP, so it's really just a theoretical issue.*

The `<flags>` field must be either "wait" or "nowait" to indicate whether the inetd server should wait for the secondary program to finish before processing more connections. The "wait" flag means that inetd will essentially hand off ownership of that port to the designated program when a connection is received; the program will then manage (or not manage) additional connections on that port itself. This allows performance-critical applications (such as web servers) to manage connections themselves during times of peak usage. Doing so is more efficient and memory-friendly than having inetd spawn off a new process for each incoming request, since the service can essentially shut itself down when it's not needed, and be woken up by inetd again when additional connections arrive.

The <user> field is the username of the account that should own the secondary program; usually, this is the root user, but can be any user account with appropriate permissions. The <server_path> is the path to the secondary program that inetd is to kick off. Everything after the program name is considered to be arguments that get passed to the program when inetd invokes it.

Examples, as usual, are the best way to demonstrate this. The following line defines the entry for the telnet remote-login service, and creates it as a stream-oriented TCP server bound to the telnet port.

```
telnet  stream  tcp    nowait  root    /usr/sbin/tcpd  in.telnetd
```

This line also indicates that inetd should not wait for telnet to return before accepting another telnet connection. (If this were set to "wait," then inetd would wait for the telnet program to return before accepting another connection; in that case, the *in.telnetd* program would have to manage additional incoming requests itself.) The process runs as the root user (but the telnet program itself will switch to the appropriate user once she logs in), and the program to be run is */usr/bin/tcpd* with an argument of in.telnetd.

Installing a New inetd-Based Service

Installing a new service to be managed by the inetd superserver is done in just two steps:

1. Add an entry to the /etc/services file defining a name for the new service.

2. Edit the /etc/inetd.conf file to refer to the new service and assign a program to be run when a connection is received on the desired port.

CROSS-REFERENCE   *Chapter 12 will demonstrate a sample installation of the Concurrent Version System (CVS) as an inetd server.*

Passing Arguments

One important "gotcha" about inetd services is how arguments are passed from inetd to the secondary programs. Some implementations of the inetd program only allow a fixed number (typically five) of arguments to be passed to the secondary program—and the first argument is the name of the program to be run! If you're using an inetd implementation with that limitation (whether on a Linux system or another Unix system), you can usually work around it by writing a shell script that launches your *real* program with all the parameters it needs, and creating the entry in /etc/inetd.conf to invoke the shell script.

Ensuring System Security

This section will describe how to improve the security of a Slackware installation. Slackware's focus is on simplicity and stability. To a certain degree, moreover, the Slackware developers expect administrators to assume a responsibility for the system. This means that administrators are expected to understand and stay on top of all aspects of their system, including security. So, Slackware places the burden of securing a system in the hands of its administrator. In practice, this means that default installations of Slackware are optimized for maximum functionality, rather than security. They're a "vanilla" installation intended as a starting point for setting up the required functionality, rather than a "fire-and-forget" server.

A default Slackware installation is running many services; in fact, it runs essentially every service it *can* run! Many new users' first reaction to this is to ask, "So what? If I don't need it, I just won't use it. It's not hurting anything by running, right?" Well, no, the services aren't hurting anything. However, no software program is 100% bug-free, and the vast majority of security breaches occur when malicious attackers exploit these bugs to gain access to the system. The services themselves don't harm anything, but their bugs can be exploited. So, any server program that's running is a potential security hole. If they're left running, they are a security risk; if they're shut off, no functionality is lost because they're not being used, but the potential security holes are eliminated. In a nutshell, good security policy is to disable any services and processes that aren't absolutely necessary.

So, how does an administrator disable these processes on a Slackware system? In Chapter 4, the mechanisms used by Red Hat Linux were discussed—the *chkconfig* and *service* tools. These tools manipulate the shell script framework that Red Hat's system uses to manage the system and services. Slackware Linux, however, has no such tools. The absence of these tools means that the shell scripts have to be modified by hand. Earlier in this chapter, the Slackware system startup scripts were described. This section will draw on that material to describe how to disable unnecessary services.

Generally, a new Slackware installation will typically have these servers running:

- inetd services

- portmap daemon

- lpd printer daemon

- Sendmail SMTP server

- Apache HTTP server

This list may vary, depending on what software was selected during the installation; if you have a Slackware installation, your list may be different. Many of the services discussed in this section can be reconfigured to be more secure; for example, some can be configured to answer only to requests that originate from the local system (and not over the network). Administrators and users who need these services should read the documentation to learn what options are available to secure the software. In general, though, if you don't need a service running, it's a good idea to disable it, and so the remainder of this section will discuss how to disable each of these services.

Disabling the inetd Services

There are two ways to disable inetd services: either disabling them one by one in the configuration file for inetd itself, or simply disabling the entire inetd process outright, so that it never gets started. (If inetd isn't running, obviously neither are any of its services.) Disabling individual inetd services, as discussed earlier in this chapter, can be accomplished by simply placing a "#" character at the beginning of the line to be commented. If you find that you don't need any of the inetd services at all, however, you can disable the entire server outright.

Recall that Slackware has two files that govern most network configurations: rc.inet1, and rc.inet2. Both scripts are located in the /etc/rc.d directory. The rc.inet1 script configures the network itself, while rc.inet2 starts most of the network servers, including inetd. To disable inetd, then, you simply comment out the lines in the script that start the program. These are the lines you should look for:

```
# Start the inetd server:
if [ -x /usr/sbin/inetd ]; then
    echo "Starting Internet super-server daemon:  /usr/sbin/inetd"
    /usr/sbin/inetd
```

```
else
    echo "WARNING:  /usr/sbin/inetd not found."
fi
# Done starting the inetd meta-server.
```

Simply comment out the lines between (and including) the `if` and the `fi` statements by placing a "#" character at the beginning of each line, and inetd will not be started during the boot-up process.

Disabling the Portmap Daemon

The *portmap* daemon is the "portmapper" server originally developed by Sun Microsystems that is used by a number of programs, including NFS (Network File System) servers and clients. If a system is using NFS (either as a server or a client) to share disks across the network, then it will need the portmap daemon running. However, if NFS is not being used, then portmap can be disabled.

The actual program name is *rpc.portmap*, and like inetd, it is started from the rc.inet2 file during system boot. To disable portmap, simply locate and comment out these lines:

```
# This must be running in order to mount NFS volumes.
# Start the RPC portmapper:
if [ -x /sbin/rpc.portmap ]; then
  echo "Starting RPC portmapper:  /sbin/rpc.portmap"
  /sbin/rpc.portmap
fi
# Done starting the RPC portmapper.
```

Again, the lines can be commented by simply adding a "#" character to the beginning of the line.

The portmap daemon is actually notorious as a security risk. It's such a large risk, in fact, that it should never be run on a system exposed to the Internet at large (such as a home computer or a public server). If it's absolutely necessary to run portmap, then the system should be placed behind a firewall so that only local computers can access the daemon.

 CROSS-REFERENCE   *A firewall case study is discussed in Chapter 16.*

To Portmap or Not to Portmap

The portmapper is a standard for RPC (Remote Procedure Calls). The portmap service is a way to access a program running on a server across a network. It's used for many applications, but the most important one is the Network File System (NFS) protocol used on many networks. NFS is used to provide access to a single filesystem (such as a user's home directory) on many different machines, and NFS usually relies on portmap. If you're using an application such as NFS, then you will probably need to leave portmap running. If you're not, though, you should seriously consider disabling portmap, since it can be quite a security risk.

Disabling the lpd Printer Daemon

The *lpd* daemon is used to provide access to printers. It can either manage a local printer connected to the PC, or can provide access to a remote printer across the network, or can also act as a server, receiving print jobs from across the network that are to be printed on a local printer. Unless these printing services are required, the lpd daemon should be disabled. As with inetd and portmap, lpd can be disabled by commenting these appropriate lines in rc.inet2:

```
# Start the BSD line printer spooler daemon:
if [ -x /usr/sbin/lpd ]; then
  echo "Starting BSD line printer spooler daemon:  /usr/sbin/lpd"
  /usr/sbin/lpd
fi
# Done starting the BSD line printer spooler daemon.
```

Disabling the Sendmail SMTP Server

Sendmail is a popular SMTP server. SMTP servers are vulnerable to two types of security problems: In addition to the "remote exploit" vulnerabilities that other processes have, it's also possible to have Sendmail misconfigured to allow it to be abused by attackers as a way to send unsolicited email (that is, spam) to unsuspecting users. This typically causes the spam email to appear (at least upon casual inspection) as though it originated from the server used as the "relay." For these reasons, it's doubly important to make sure that the Sendmail installation is either current and properly configured, or disabled.

Sendmail is notoriously difficult to administrate, so unless it's actually required, it's generally a good idea to disable it. Generally, the only reason to leave Sendmail running on any system that is not a mail server is for the benefit of some email clients that can't make use of an SMTP server running on a host across the network. However, almost every graphical email client has this capability, so Sendmail can usually be disabled.

Unlike the other services, however, disabling Sendmail is not done in the rc.inet2 file. The rc.inet2 file is for core network services that absolutely must be running for the system to function normally. Other, less crucial servers (like SMTP and HTTP servers) are started from the file *rc.M*.

The rc.M file works by first checking to see if a given server program is installed. If it is present, it is executed; if it's not, it is skipped. There are, therefore, two ways to disable a server started from rc.M. You can either rename the program so that rc.M no longer "sees" it and therefore skips it, or you can simply comment out the lines in rc.M that look for the script in the first place. It's probably better to comment out the lines in rc.M than to rename a program executable, however, since renaming (or deleting) a program might cause issues later on down the road. For example, another administrator or user may wish to reenable the server, but may not if it was renamed something excessively cryptic. If the program was deleted, it can't be recovered at all, without reinstalling it!

To disable Sendmail, comment out these lines in rc.M:

```
# Start the sendmail daemon:
if [ -x /usr/sbin/sendmail ]; then
  echo "Starting sendmail daemon:  /usr/sbin/sendmail -bd -q15m"
  /usr/sbin/sendmail -bd -q15m
#fi
```

Disabling the Apache HTTP Server

The Apache HTTP server is a web server, and so is capable of serving up various types of static and dynamic content to web browsers and other clients. Like Sendmail, the Slackware startup scripts launch Apache from the /etc/rc.d/rc.M file. These lines need to be commented out to disable Apache:

```
# Start Web server:
if [ -x /etc/rc.d/rc.httpd ]; then
  . /etc/rc.d/rc.httpd start
fi
```

Astute readers will notice that in this case, Apache is not being started directly. Rather, a shell script (*/etc/rc.d/rc.httpd*) is being invoked, which in turn starts

Apache. That shell script is very simple, however, and itself simply invokes Apache's own "control" script, called *apachectl*.

Other Servers

Recall that depending on what software was chosen, a given Slackware installation may have a set of servers different than the ones discussed in this section. However, no matter what the server is, it will be started either from /etc/rc.d/rc.inet2 or from /etc/rc.d/rc.M directly. Since Slackware expects users to be on top of the administration of their own systems, it's vitally important to review these files for every new Slackware installation, to make sure unnecessary services aren't running.

Customizing the User Environment

This section will discuss how to tailor the login shell configuration scripts on a Slackware Linux system. In Chapter 4, Red Hat's login script framework was discussed. Readers should consult that chapter for comparison, but to put it briefly, Red Hat Linux makes use of the config.d drop-in configuration file model. Actually, this section is going to be very simple, since Slackware's user shell scripts are substantially similar to Red Hat's.

The basic model is the same as that used by Red Hat Linux. The main scripts (for both *csh* and *sh* shells) set some basic parameters, and then look in the directory /etc/profile.d for additional "drop-in" files for the shell. The sh-based shells (usually *bash*, *ash*, *ksh*, and *zsh* on Slackware) read files whose names end with .sh; the csh shell (which is almost always *tcsh* on Linux systems) look for files whose names end with .csh. This is the same mechanism used by Red Hat Linux, so readers should definitely consult Chapter 4.

However, there are some differences. First and probably most noticeably, Slackware's scripts are quite a bit simpler than Red Hat's, in keeping with the Slackware philosophy. Red Hat's, on the other hand, are arguably more sophisticated and do a bit more. It's the classic tradeoff of simplicity *versus* functionality, and we see yet again that Slackware leans toward simplicity.

The other major shell configuration difference between Slackware Linux and Red Hat Linux is in the use of the files. Red Hat uses the files /etc/bashrc and /etc/profile to manage bash and other sh-based shells, respectively. By using a separate /etc/bashrc file, Red Hat is able to configure the environments of bash users to take advantage of extended bash features. Slackware, in contrast, has no /etc/bashrc and simply "reuses" /etc/profile for all sh-derived shells. Also, Slackware curiously places all csh configuration in /etc/login—/etc/cshrc is empty.

Red Hat uses /etc/csh.cshrc for basic configuration and /etc/lcsh.login for configuration that's only appropriate for login shells (as opposed to shells that are started to run scripts).

Changing a User's X Window Desktop Environment

Chapter 4 mentioned the switchdesk program on Red Hat Linux that is used to change a user's preferred X Window desktop environment; this section will discuss how to accomplish the same task on Slackware Linux. Slackware doesn't have the switchdesk program (or any equivalent) and relies on a more traditional way of accomplishing the task.

By default, Slackware Linux uses the *desktop manager* from the KDE project, called KDM. KDM allows the user to select one of the installed desktop environments, and will use that environment for the duration of the user's session.

 NOTE *A desktop manager is the graphical program into which you enter your username and password to log into X. The other alternative is to start X from the command line via the xinit command.*

When the user logs in, KDM executes the script */etc/X11/xdm/Xsession* and gives it the name of the desktop the user selected as its first argument. The Xsession script then starts up the desktop environment corresponding to the user's choice. However, if the user has an executable program in her home directory called xsession, that program (which can be a script) will be executed instead, bypassing any selection the user made in KDM.

When the user selects a desktop from KDM, the selection is recorded in a file in the user's home directory called .wmrc. This file contains a single word indicating the user's most recently selected desktop. This file is used by KDM to "remember" the user's choice the next time he accesses KDM.

All that's fine and well, but it doesn't really answer the question of how a user changes her desktop environment. Well, given the mechanism just described, there are two ways. First, the user can simply edit the file *~/.wmrc* and change the word in that file to another environment. However, this is rather pointless since it's probably easier to simply select a new desktop from the pull-down menu in the desktop manager. The second way is to create a *~/.xsession* file that contains (or more frequently points to, via a symbolic link) a program to start the user's environment. This setting will always take priority over anything the user might select in the desktop manager. For example, the following link command will designate GNOME as the user's desktop environment.

```
ln -s /opt/gnome/bin/gnome-session ~/.xsession
```

If the user selected default and has no ~/.xsession file, the Xsession script simply executes the default environment by invoking */etc/X11/xinit/xinitrc* (which itself is a symbolic link to one of the other files in */etc/X11/xini/xinitrc*, each of which handles a different environment). It's probably becoming clear that the scripts that handle all this are fairly complicated. Other distributions, such as Red Hat Linux, are arguably even more complicated and elaborate. This complexity is why programs like Red Hat's switchdesk are written. Slackware keeps things comparatively simple, and users can change desktops manually by either creating a ~/.xsession file or selecting the desired environment from the desktop manager during the login process.

Adding New Hardware

One of the common complaints about Linux systems is that hardware support is occasionally spotty and sometimes difficult to configure. This section will discuss how to install and configure new hardware in Slackware Linux. In Chapter 4, Red Hat Linux's kudzu tool for automatically detecting and configuring new hardware was discussed; unfortunately, Slackware Linux has no equivalent tool, and the procedure is more manually intensive.

By now, we've seen several examples of the Slackware philosophy of simplicity and self-sufficiency. Perhaps the most explicit example of this is in its support for hardware. Recall that Slackware ships with stock Linux kernels. There's no easy way around it: the process for adding support for new hardware to a Slackware system is simply to configure the Linux kernel itself to support the new hardware (typically by configuring support for the device driver in kernel module form) and then load the module into Slackware.

In most cases, once you have the Linux kernel either compiled with the device driver built-in or compiled as a module, the kernel will either detect the device on startup or else automatically load it on demand. Slackware relies on this behavior for setting up hardware, and generally it's pretty straightforward to get the driver loaded. The main difficulty lies in configuring the rest of the system to make use of the rest of the new device; for example, adding a USB compact-flash card reader involves not only compiling and loading the kernel modules, but also creating a mount point and modifying the */etc/fstab* file appropriately.

Red Hat's kudzu tool automates most of these tasks. Unfortunately, there's no easy way to do this on Slackware, and so administrators have to roll up their sleeves and dig into the system configuration. If a mount point needs to be created, it'll have to be done manually; if a module needs to be loaded in a certain order, it'll have to be done from /etc/rc.d/rc.local or rc.M; if a new block device (i.e. a disk) is installed, it will need to be configured in the /etc/fstab file.

This is all fine and well, of course, but it doesn't help the administrator much. There's no checklist that an administrator can go through to install new hardware; when it comes right down to it, there are just too many cases to consider to make a truly comprehensive checklist. What's an administrator to do, then? Hopefully this book will provide the tools and knowledge that are required to do this.

Derivatives of Slackware Linux

This section will discuss some of the derivatives of Slackware Linux. A derivative of Slackware Linux is an alternative Linux distribution that is based on but not identical to Slackware. Some of these derivatives are more closely related to Slackware than others.

SuSE Linux

SuSE Linux is distribution that is especially popular in Europe, though it also has as strong following in the U.S. SuSE is actually a commercial organization, like Red Hat or Caldera. SuSE Linux was originally derived from Slackware (and in fact, started out simply as a translation of Slackware in German), but as the company grew, they eventually created their own distribution from scratch, based on Red Hat's RPM package management tool. Today, SuSE Linux bears little resemblance to Slackware Linux.

Peanut Linux

Peanut Linux is a derivative of Slackware Linux that is similar in scope to ZipSlack, which was mentioned earlier in this chapter. That is, Peanut Linux is a small-footprint distribution that installs to only a few hundred megabytes, and so is useful in space-constrained environments. Peanut Linux is a good example of how Slackware's simplicity lets it be scaled up or down to the needs of a particular niche.

Summary

Slackware Linux is a fully modern Linux distribution that is focused on simplicity and stability. Slackware is the most Unix-like of Linux distributions, meaning that it remains truer to the traditional techniques of Unix systems than most other distributions. For this reason, Slackware is probably the easiest way for a traditional Unix user to get into the Linux world. Slackware's simplicity makes it easily customizable, and also makes it a great way for new users to learn Unix and Linux systems.

If you've read Chapter 4 and this one, you've now seen two distributions in depth: Red Hat Linux and Slackware Linux. It's important to remember what was mentioned at the beginning of this chapter: by comparing the two distributions, the intent is not to argue that one is better than the other, but rather to illustrate differences. Once you understand the differences between the way these two systems work, you'll have two perspectives on the Unix world, and will be a very big step closer to achieving that remarkable state of Zen of being able to accomplish whatever you want with your system, regardless of how it's set up. You'll either already know how to do it, or be able to learn. Once you've read Chapter 6 as well, you'll have a working knowledge of several major Linux distributions, which will translate into a working knowledge of *any* Linux (or even Unix-like) system.

CHAPTER 6
Debian GNU/Linux 3.0

The Debian Project was founded in 1993 to create the Debian GNU/Linux distribution. Since then, the distribution has become quite prevalent, and in many polls rivals or exceeds Red Hat Linux in popularity. This chapter will discuss the Debian GNU/Linux distribution. However, there's an important caveat: This chapter only discusses a *beta* version of Debian 3.0. The final version was not released at the time this book was published. Even so, you will probably find the differences between the material in this chapter and the reality of the final Debian GNU/Linux 3.0 to be minor.

As was mentioned in Chapters 4 and 5, the goal of Part Two is to provide you with different perspectives and solutions to the problem of developing and using a distribution. This basic education and exposure to three example distributions will give you a base from which to draw when working with *any* distribution. At this point, you've read about two distributions: Red Hat Linux and Slackware Linux; after reading this chapter, you'll be familiar with Debian GNU/Linux as well, and one step closer to mastery. After this chapter, Part Three will discuss how to customize your system and install software on it.

Now, the idea here is that the more distributions you see, the better able you'll be to deal with *any* distribution. However, after a point enough is enough. Eventually you start seeing the same things over and over again, which really doesn't help that much. Between Slackware Linux and Red Hat Linux, you've almost reached that point. For example, Slackware uses the BSD model of init scripts, whereas Red Hat uses the SysV approach. Detailing yet another distribution's approach doesn't really pay off.

As a result, you'll find that this chapter is quite a bit shorter than Chapters 4 and 5. The reason is that in cases where Debian GNU/Linux is similar to Red Hat or Slackware Linux (or both), I simply cite any remaining differences and move on. However, I do go into full detail in cases where Debian does things differently.

The fact that this chapter is shorter than the others is evidence that my strategy is paying off. That is, now that you've seen two distributions, I can take a third and start pointing out places where your knowledge of the other distributions applies to this new distribution. This will allow you to focus on the areas where Debian is unique. Think of this chapter as a dry run for learning a new distribution.

Debian's Background and Philosophy

This section will describe the overall Debian Project and discuss the motivations and philosophies behind it; later sections discuss the distribution itself. Perhaps the best way to get started with Debian is to review two interesting documents: the Debian Social Contract (which outlines the philosophy of the project as a whole), and the Debian Policies (which specify in full the details of how the distribution is implemented).

The Debian Social Contract

The Debian Project is very closely related to the GNU Project, at least spiritually. The name of the distribution makes this explicit: "Debian GNU/Linux." As you read in Chapter 1, it can be argued that "GNU/Linux" is a more precise term than "Linux," because it more accurately reflects the GNU project's contribution to the system. Since Debian is closely related to GNU, you might (correctly) expect that to understand the goals and philosophy of the Debian Project, you need to understand free software, open source software, and how these concepts are alike and different. In other words, to understand Debian, first read Chapter 1 to grasp the context. (However, don't take this book as gospel; also view the relevant web sites and form your own opinion.)

From the start, it's clear that Debian is a socially conscious organization. If you think of Red Hat Software as a canonical "open source software" organization, then you might think of the Debian Project as a canonical "free software" organization. Let me be quick to point out, however, that that's just an analogy, and the differences are not really that black and white: the two organizations share many of the same ideals.

To illustrate its position, the Debian Project has published a "Debian Social Contract." This document states the Project's position on open source and free software, and establishes policies and commitments on the type of software that will be included in the distribution. This document is a commitment to a certain social ideal and standard of integrity in the contents of the Debian GNU/Linux distribution. You can find the Social Contract online at debian.org/social_contract.

The Debian Social Contract is also noteworthy in that part of it became the basis for the definition of open source software used by many organizations. This illustrates the close tie between the free and open-source software camps, and perhaps puts the whole issue in perspective. After all, most of the goals are the same; just a few differences exist in the details.

The Debian Policies

The Debian Social Contract outlines the basic philosophy of the distribution; the Policies define the details. The Debian Project has a comprehensive set of policies governing almost every aspect of the system. There are policies as general as defining the filesystem layout—which is dictated by the Linux Filesystem Hierarchy Standard (FHS)—and as specific as governing the preferred behavior of scripts in a Debian package archive (.deb) file.

All contributors to Debian GNU/Linux follow the Debian Policies, which makes most aspects of the system pretty consistent and reliable in behavior. (For example, it's rare to find a .deb package that installs files in an unusual location.) If you're not a contributor, then you'll probably be less interested in these policies. However, they *are* still useful to anyone trying to master Debian GNU/Linux; after all, they spell out the entire system in detail.

If you've read Chapters 3 through 5, then the actual contents of the Debian Policies (especially Section 10, "The Operating System") probably won't surprise you; they cover the packaging format, the installation of files, the init scripts model used, and so on. If you're using a Debian system (and even if you're not), then it's a good idea to at least skim over the Debian Policies. You can find them at www.debian.org/doc/debian-policy/.

The Debian Social Contract makes a commitment to a certain philosophy, and the Debian Policies define how these philosophies are implemented in the Debian GNU/Linux distribution. These documents are obviously the first and last words on the subjects. Consequently, rather than rehash these documents in detail, the remainder of this chapter focuses on illustrating how Debian GNU/Linux compares to Red Hat and Slackware Linux. For the rest of this chapter, any references to Red Hat Linux refer to discussions in Chapter 4, and references to Slackware Linux pertain to material in Chapter 5.

One of Debian's policies is that the distribution will follow the Filesystem Hierarchy Standard except where it conflicts with another Debian policy. The FHS is discussed in Chapter 3, and as mentioned in Chapters 4 and 5, Red Hat and Slackware also follow the FHS fairly closely. As a result, you'll find few surprises in Debian's filesystem layout. You may encounter the occasional quirk, but you shouldn't have any problems with it.

Linux Kernel

Since the kernel is the heart of the system, an unstable kernel makes for an unstable distribution. Selecting a kernel version to install with a distribution is always a balancing act between stability and feature completeness; if you want the latest features, you may have to tolerate somewhat less stability.

For the 3.0 release, Debian GNU/Linux opted for the 2.2.*x* series of kernels. Slackware Linux 8.0 also shipped with a 2.2.*x* kernel, but supports 2.4.*x* kernels for those users who require them. Likewise, Debian 3.0 also installs a 2.2.*x* kernel by default, but includes a 2.4.*x* kernel package for users who want it. Contrast this with Red Hat Linux 7.2, which includes a 2.4.*x* kernel by default. Debian's focus in this case is to provide maximum stability in the default installation, while providing adequate flexibility for those users who need it.

Debian Packaging

The Debian package management system may very well be the most sophisticated available for any Unix-like system. Debian's mechanism is even *network-transparent* (meaning that it can transparently install packages remotely across a network) and was among the first packaging systems to be so. Red Hat's up2date functionality is more recent than Debian's equivalent, and Slackware Linux doesn't reach the level of true network transparency. Users familiar with other operating systems such as Microsoft Windows may recognize similarities to Windows Update, although Debian's mechanism is arguably even more powerful. This section discusses Debian's package management system in detail.

Technical Summary

The Debian packaging system is built in several layers. At the lowest level is the actual physical package management, and at the highest level are user-friendly programs with various interfaces intended to automate the process of locating, obtaining, and installing software packages. Table 6-1 summarizes the major programs involved.

Table 6-1. Debian Packaging System Summary

PROGRAM	BASED ON	PURPOSE
dpkg	N/A	Physically installs and manages packages
apt-get	dpkg	Manages package source list and fetches packages for installation
dselect	apt-get, dpkg	Allows the user to select packages from the source list for installation
tasksel	apt-get, dpkg	Allows the user to select tasks (logical groups of packages) to install

The following sections discuss the Debian packaging programs in detail. For illustrative purposes, the Debian programs are compared with their equivalents from Red Hat Linux and Slackware Linux. This is purely for comparison, and is not intended to be a judgment as to which system is best. Debian's system is quite sophisticated, feature-rich, and correspondingly complex, so it helps to have a common terminology for the discussion.

Using the dpkg Program

The dpkg program is the where the rubber meets the road for Debian's packaging system. This program is responsible for physically unpacking and installing Debian package archive (.deb extension) files, and for managing the various databases related to package management.

You can use dpkg to install individual packages manually. For example, you may download a .deb file from a web site and install it with dpkg, or you may install a package off of a CD. Similarly, you can use dpkg to remove specific individual packages. You can also perform common query commands with dpkg, such as listing the files installed by a particular package or locating the package that owns a particular file.

You may have realized at this point that the dpkg program is essentially equivalent to the rpm program, in that you can install and remove packages and perform various queries on packages (both installed and uninstalled). Slackware Linux spreads the same functionality across multiple programs (namely installpkg, upgradepkg, and removepkg).

In Chapter 5, you read that Slackware Linux uses simple text files in the /var/log/packages directory to store information about which packages own which files. In Chapter 4, on the other hand, you learned that Red Hat Linux goes to the other extreme and stores all this information in a binary database that you can't really get access to except through the rpm command. Debian's dpkg falls somewhere in between: The actual lists of files installed by packages are stored in a database, but information on the packages is stored in the file /var/lib/dpkg/available, and information on installed packages is located in the directory /var/lib/dpkg/info. To some extent, you can consult these files for information without having to go through the dpkg tool (though you may find the dpkg tool to be more convenient).

One major difference between dpkg and rpm is that dpkg maintains an actual list of *available* packages that aren't yet installed—that is, the /var/lib/dpkg/available file. (Actually, Red Hat does provide a package known as rpmdb that includes some of these capabilities, but it is rather arcane to use, and isn't nearly as accessible.) This list is typically constructed from the contents of a CD or other media, and is consulted for various queries requested by the user.

(For example, the user might ask for documentary information on a package that hasn't been installed yet.) This is convenient because it means that you don't necessarily have to have the .deb package itself lying around in order to fetch information about it; with rpm you have to have the actual package present in order to query it with the rpm -qp commands. You'll be hearing much more about this list of available packages as you read further, so keep it in mind.

Another difference between Debian's system and Red Hat's RPM is in their handling of dependencies. You read in Chapter 4 that RPM can track dependency information—that is, which other packages a particular package depends on. For example, the OpenSSH package depends on the OpenSSL package. With RPM, a dependency is a "yes or no" proposition. The dpkg tool, however, supports several types of dependencies, such as "required", "recommend", and "suggested". This added flexibility can make it easier to communicate dependency information to end users. When you install a Debian package, be sure to check its dependencies carefully, since there may be recommended or suggested features you might otherwise miss.

Using the apt-get Program

The apt-get program builds on dpkg and manages package sources, providing most of the network transparency mentioned earlier. You can think of this program as keeping dpkg well fed. All those packages that dpkg installs have to come from somewhere, after all, and apt-get is that place. The other major responsibility of apt-get is to keep track of dependencies between packages (such as which packages are required by another).

Managing the Source Media

Typically, users install Debian from installation CDs or from an installation repository (such as an FTP site) on a network. These installation media really just consist of a collection of Debian packages; apt-get monitors these media and keeps track of the list of packages that is available from each source. When the user wishes to install a new package, she simply instructs apt-get to locate the package and hand it off to dpkg for installation. Locating the package might mean going back to that FTP site, or prompting the user to insert one of the installation CDs, or even something else.

This ability to keep track of available packages is a major convenience. Systems like RPM are really fairly myopic: rpm can't see any files that aren't sitting directly in front of it. Debian's apt-get, in contrast, has a much better view of the "terrain" of available packages, and can go fetch packages without the user having to bother with hunting it down. Red Hat does have a similar system known as up2date, but up2date typically only has knowledge of the package repository maintained by Red Hat, Inc., which it sells access to as a profit-making service. Debian's apt-get has a much more flexible package source list. You might think of up2date as a cousin of apt-get that can only handle one package source.

The list of source media that apt-get uses is itself maintained by several helper programs. The file that stores the source list is /etc/apt/sources.list; this file can contain a variety of sources, such as CDs, FTP or HTTP (web) sites, and so on. The contents of this file can be conveniently managed by the helper programs, such as apt-cdrom, which scans Debian package CDs and creates appropriate entries in /etc/apt/sources.list.

Network Transparency Revisited

Debian GNU/Linux contains the apt-get tool that, among other things, provides network-transparent access to software packages. Various other packaging systems include similar functionality, and there's a lot of work ongoing to "cross-pollinate" such tools. For example, there's at least one open-source implementation of Red Hat's server for its up2date program that would allow the use of up2date with providers other than Red Hat. Meanwhile, efforts are under way to configure apt-get for use with the RPM system so that users of Red Hat Linux systems can use apt-get to fetch and manage RPM packages the same way Debian users manage .deb packages. A number of other interesting efforts are also in the works, so the book is by no means closed on the future of package management.

Working with apt-get

When managing packages on a Debian system, many users work with apt-get most of the time. It's best suited for quickly and easily adding those packages that you forgot to include when you installed the system, or for upgrading current packages to a newer version when fixes or enhancements are released. However, apt-get is actually sophisticated enough that it can handle upgrading the entire distribution to a new version. These features of apt-get are discussed in more detail later.

Using the dselect Program

The dselect program is a menu-based interface for selecting packages to install. This is actually the same program that is invoked during the Debian installation process that allows users to tweak the list of packages to suit their needs. The program is also available to be run at any time after the installation to adjust the selected list.

This program is really just a view into the list of available packages maintained by apt-get and dpkg. That is, apt-get maintains a list of package sources, and dpkg maintains a list of available packages (which is compiled from the contents of the sources). The dselect program simply displays a list of all available packages, indicating which ones are already installed and allowing the user to flag available packages to be installed, or flag installed packages to be deleted. The menu of available packages also includes information on dependencies that each package has, and helps the user select packages to resolve any dependencies.

When the user makes his selections and exits dselect, apt-get (and in turn, dpkg) is then run to physically install and remove packages according to the user's selections. Red Hat Linux and Slackware Linux really have no tools equivalent to dselect.

Using the tasksel Program

The tasksel program is similar to dselect, but rather than allowing the user to select packages to install, it lets her select tasks. A task, in Debian's nomenclature, is essentially a collection of packages. For example, the XFree86 implementation of the X Window System actually consists of a number of different packages, including the core software, drivers for various video card models, and fonts (among other things). Debian has a notion of a task to permit the distribution designers to group collections of packages such as XFree86 into a single "virtual" package. When a user selects a task, he is actually selecting a set of multiple Debian .deb packages.

The tasksel program is pretty straightforward, and itself uses apt-get and in turn dpkg to handle the installation of the packages that make up tasks. As with dselect, Red Hat Linux and Slackware Linux don't really provide any similar functionality. (Red Hat Linux does allow users to select groups of software packages similar to Debian tasks during the installation process, but these collections are not accessible once installation has been completed.)

Getting Into the Details

The past few sections gave an overview of the capabilities provided by the various programs that make up the Debian package system. The next few sections go into a bit more detail and demonstrate some of the more common uses of the Debian packaging system. Each program, though, is pretty complicated, so for full details you should definitely check out the manual pages and other documentation on these tools provided with Debian GNU/Linux.

The following sections focus on illustrating the most common ways in which you'll use Debian's packaging system as a whole, rather than on the mechanics of the individual programs. By now, you probably have a pretty good grasp of exactly what tools like dpkg and rpm are doing (unpacking a bunch of files, recording where they went into a database so they can be removed later, and perhaps running a script). Rather than rehashing the same material you could get from reading a manual page, I'll focus on the distribution, not just the tools.

Managing Packages with Debian's System

Even though you can read the manual pages to figure out how to *use* them, the Debian packaging tools provide more power and flexibility than may be immediately obvious from the manual pages. Each of the next few sections focuses on a specific common task and outlines the general procedure for that task, in order to help you make the jump from knowing *how* to run the programs to knowing *when* to run them. It's important to bear in mind that with Debian's packaging system, there's more than one way to do almost anything, so much of this material boils down to a matter of preference.

It's generally possible to manage Debian packages on two levels: at the dpkg level, and at the apt-get and dselect level. This section will discuss each case, briefly demonstrating the mechanics of package management, and indicating when and why you'd want to use each level.

Working with dpkg

Debian's dpkg tool is the lowest-level tool in the packaging system. It operates at the individual package level, and can perform the typical packaging commands such as install, remove, and various queries. Table 6-2 summarizes some of the most common operations provided by dpkg; for full details, you should consult the manual page for dpkg, or other documentation.

Table 6-2. Common dpkg Operations

COMMAND	EQUIVALENT RPM COMMAND	FUNCTION
dpkg -i <filename>	rpm -i <filename>	Installs a Debian package file
dpkg -r <package>	rpm -e <package>	Removes an installed package
dpkg -l	rpm -qa	Lists all packages installed
dpkg -l <package>	rpm -q <package>	Checks whether a package is installed and provides its full name
dpkg -L <package>	rpm -ql <package>	Lists the files installed by a particular package
dpkg -S <file>	rpm -qf <file>	Identifies the package that owns a file that has been installed
dpkg -p <package>	None	Determines whether the indicated package is available to be installed

As you can see, using dpkg to manage individual packages is quite straightforward. If you've read Chapters 4 and 5, it's probably even familiar by now, since it's so similar to the equivalent mechanisms on Red Hat Linux and Slackware Linux. On Debian systems, you'll probably only use dpkg directly to install single packages that you obtain from somewhere other than the original installation or upgrade media, such as a specific piece of software you download from a web site. Most of the time, you'll probably use dselect or apt-get, which are discussed later in this section.

Globbing for Fun and Productivity

The term "globbing" refers to the expansion of wildcards like the "star" (*) character (or asterisk) to match specific patterns. Debian's dpkg program, like most of the packaging tools, supports globbing in the arguments you pass to it. For example, to list all installed packages with "libc" in the name, you can use this command:

```
$ dpkg -l "*libc*"
```

The asterisks will be "globbed" similar to the way filenames would be in a shell, and you'll get quite a list of packages with "libc" in their names. This is quite a convenient trick, so be sure to use it!

Managing Package Sources with apt-get

The only problem with using dpkg (or rpm for that matter) to manage the packages on your Debian system is that it's very laborious. After all, if you want to install a particular package, you first must *find* the package! This may involve inserting and mounting a CD—perhaps several times, if the package is not on the first disk you check—or downloading a file from a web or FTP site. Even if all you're doing is installing a package that you forgot to select during installation, you still have to shuffle CDs or URLs to locate it. Additionally, you also have to contend with any dependencies that the desired package might have.

For these cases, Debian GNU/Linux includes apt-get, which manages installation media for you. Since apt-get maintains a list of source media containing packages, and a list of the actual packages that are available, all you need to do is request that apt-get locate and install the desired package for you. Table 6-3 summarizes the common uses of apt-get. Again, you should consult the manual page for specific information.

Table 6-3. Common apt-get Operations

COMMAND	FUNCTION
apt-get install <package>	Locates and installs the indicated package from the list of available packages
apt-get remove <package>	Uninstalls the indicated package and any packages that depend on it
apt-get update	Refreshes the list of available packages (after the source list has been updated)
apt-get upgrade	Upgrades all packages on the system for which newer versions are available

The first two capabilities of apt-get—installing and removing packages—is pretty straightforward. Just type `apt-get install foo` and apt-get will check its list of sources and available packages in quest of a Debian archive named "foo". If it finds one, it will install the archive, resolving any dependencies along the way. Conversely, `apt-get remove foo` will uninstall the package. The remaining capabilities aren't quite so clear-cut, however.

Upgrading Installed Packages

One notable property of apt-get shown in Table 6-3 is that the `upgrade` function is not used on specific packages. Instead, it's a global command that upgrades all packages for which upgrades are available. This might seem like an odd restriction at first, since it makes upgrading to individual packages difficult. However, if you think about it, once you have a system that automatically updates itself you seldom need to worry about individual packages, so this turns out to be a nonissue in practice.

Refreshing the List of Available Packages

Another entry in Table 6-3 that may not be immediately obvious is the update command. This command differs from the upgrade command just described. The update command refreshes the list of *available packages*, but doesn't actually upgrade any packages. Typically, you'll run apt-get update after updating the /etc/apt/sources.list file, or when an FTP or web site updates its list of available packages. Once apt-get is aware that upgrades to installed packages actually exist, the upgrade command can be used to do the work.

Comparing apt-get to up2date

If you've read Chapter 4, you'll probably notice similarities between apt-get and Red Hat's up2date system. In fact, they are quite similar, but apt-get is rather more flexible, simply because up2date is currently only practical to use with Red Hat's own site, whereas apt-get lets you use any number of sources. (Ongoing work may always change this in the future, of course.)

In the end, apt-get is really just a convenience. However, it's a *big* convenience; after you spend a while maintaining the packages on a few Linux systems by hand, you'll be quite grateful for any conveniences you can get. Once you get used to apt-get, you probably won't care to use dpkg directly anymore. You'll quickly grow accustomed to running commands like apt-get install package and letting the system locate the package, download it or prompt you to insert the appropriate CD, and manage any dependencies for you.

Managing Packages with dselect and tasksel

Occasionally, you might need to install a number of packages at once, or you aren't quite sure of what the specific name of a package is. Sometimes you don't even know whether software even exists to fill a particular need, let alone what its name is. The dselect and tasksel tools address this issue.

Using dselect

The dselect program is first encountered early on in the life of a Debian GNU/Linux system, since it's the tool used to select individual packages during the installation. The dselect program is really just a menu-based front end that pulls together all the functionality discussed so far in this chapter.

Administrators can use dselect to browse the list of all available packages, and see instantly which are installed and which are not. By changing the list of selections, many packages can be installed or removed in one fell swoop. For such cases, working with dselect may be more convenient than using apt-get to manage each package individually.

Using tasksel

The tasksel program provides the coarsest level of granularity. A task is just a list of packages (or other tasks). For example, the XFree86 task includes a number of individual packages, such as the libraries, video card drivers, and fonts. The tasksel program can be used to install additional tasks after the installation is completed.

For example, a system may have originally been configured as some sort of server, and so XFree86 was not installed at all. If that system is then repurposed to be a desktop system, the XFree86 packages will have to be installed. This can, of course, be done manually with apt-get, but a lot of packages are involved. It might therefore be easier to use dselect to select all the XFree86 packages for installation, but even then you have to hunt them all down in the list. With tasksel, however, the entire suite of XFree86 packages—that is, the XFree86 task—can be installed quickly and easily.

Configuring Debian Packages

Packaging systems are very good at installing files, and upgrading and uninstalling them as necessary. Most are also capable of managing configuration files, though the degree of support varies. Red Hat's RPM system, for example, allows package creators to designate some files as configuration files. When later managing these files, RPM is careful to preserve them and never overwrite an administrator's custom files. Debian's system, however, includes more extensive configuration support.

Debian comes with the debconf package. This package is a set of libraries and utilities that implements a *protocol* that package designers can use to handle configuration of their packages. A protocol is a standardized contract controlling communication between programs; the debconf protocol essentially allows package creators to ask questions from the users in a standardized way. The debconf utilities and user interface front ends then gather the required information on behalf of the package, and pass the information to the installation scripts included with the package. The scripts can then do whatever is necessary, such as generating configuration files.

An example of a package that uses debconf is the x window-system package (which installs XFree86.) XFree86 requires a fairly large amount of information to configure the X server to work with the user's hardware. Red Hat wrote a program called Xconfigurator for its distribution, but Debian uses the debconf tools. The similarities between the two are fairly significant, at least inasmuch as both use a text menu–based user interface; they also ask similar questions and generate similar files (which makes sense, since they're different tools for configuring the same package).

Using debconf to Reconfigure Packages

Users and administrators frequently need to reconfigure packages after installation has finished. For example, a workstation may be upgraded with a new video card, requiring a reconfiguration of XFree86. To support this, debconf provides two tools: dpkg-preconfigure and dpkg-reconfigure. There is also a third tool, debconf-show, that displays the current configuration information for a package.

The two configuration commands—dpkg-preconfigure and dpkg-reconfigure—are fairly similar. Essentially, dpkg-preconfigure is used to gather information on a package before it is installed, and is most useful during the installation process; in fact, most users will seldom invoke it directly. The dpkg-reconfigure program, however, does basically the same tasks but can reconfigure already installed programs. For example, the command `dpkg-reconfigure xserver-common` can be used to reconfigure that workstation after the video card upgrade. Similarly, `debconf-show xserver-common` will display the configuration variables used by XFree86 and their current values.

Configuring debconf

The debconf program itself has a few configuration items. The primary components are the /etc/apt/apt.conf.d directory and the /etc/debconf.conf file. Each is described in the text that follows; however, most users will not have to deal with these very often, if at all. You should simply be aware of their existence, should you someday need them.

The /etc/apt/apt.conf.d directory is used by the apt packaging system (which includes apt-get, dpkg, and so on) as a hook for running programs when the apt tools are invoked. This directory contains files whose contents are used by the packaging tools during their operation.

The /etc/debconf.conf file configures the debconf system itself. This file really just specifies paths to database files that are used to store configuration information. The debconf system "remembers" previously entered answers to questions asked by packages via debconf by storing them in a database independent of the packages' contents. If a package is removed and then reinstalled (or simply upgraded), debconf fetches the configuration data from its database and uses those values to rerun the configuration scripts. To override this behavior, use the dpkg-reconfigure program.

Upgrading the System

So far I've covered a number of tools that provide a variety of ways to work with the Debian package management system. As you've probably noticed, generally this is similar to other systems, though Debian's may be a richer, more sophisticated system. However, there's one aspect I haven't touched on yet, and that is Debian's ability to be upgraded easily via the package management system.

For most distributions, an upgrade is a pretty intensive process. You typically have to boot from a floppy disk or CD that runs a special-purpose program that upgrades your system from the installation media. Debian systems, however, handle this rather differently.

The key is the list of available packages. Most of the time, you'll configure your system to use a set of sources that is largely static, but occasionally contains bug fixes, security fixes, and so on. On these occasions, you'll typically upgrade your installation with the new packages by a process similar to this:

1. If necessary, update the /etc/apt/sources.list file to reflect any new media. For example, you might have obtained a CD that contains updated packages and need to add the new CD through the `apt-cdrom` command.

2. Run `apt-get update` to cause apt-get to become aware of any updated packages.

3. Run `apt-get upgrade` to cause apt-get to fetch and install any updated packages that have been made available.

This procedure works well when all you need to do is upgrade a few packages. However, eventually you'll probably want to upgrade a Debian system to a new major release. This case, when you think about it, really isn't that different from the previous case; you just need to replace the currently installed packages with newer versions. The difference is just the scope of the upgrade: In a major version upgrade, a lot (perhaps all!) of the packages change simultaneously, most likely with significant changes made to the contents of each package.

Managing a full-blown upgrade like that isn't easy, so most distributions just produce new CDs, and you reboot the system to perform the upgrade. With Debian, however, you can use a procedure like this one:

1. Update /etc/apt/sources.list, removing all references to the current distribution's media, and adding the appropriate entries for the new major version. (For example, update the URLs for a web installation or add the new CDs for a local installation.)

2. Run `apt-get update` to refresh the list of available packages and versions.

3. Run `apt-get dist-upgrade` to actually upgrade the distribution. This command causes apt-get to enter an alternate upgrade mode suitable for handling the potentially complicated dependency issues that arise during a full system upgrade.

4. When the upgrade completes, reboot the system to complete the installation if necessary.

It's immediately obvious that this procedure for a full distribution upgrade is very similar to the procedure for handling minor updates to a particular distribution version. The system still has to be rebooted (if the kernel was upgraded, for example) of course, but it's a pretty elegant process nonetheless.

Manipulating Debian Package Archives

All these packages that you've been reading about have to come from *somewhere*, so it's logical to ask how they are created. Also, someday you may want or need to view the contents of a Debian package, or extract a specific file from it, or otherwise deal with it at a very basic level. To support all of these tasks, Debian includes a program known as dpkg-deb that manages individual Debian packages. Table 6-4 summarizes the usage of dpkg-deb. As always, consult the manual page for full details.

Table 6-4. Common dpkg-deb Operations

COMMAND	SIMILAR RPM COMMAND	FUNCTION
dpkg-deb --build	rpm -ba	Creates a new package
dpkg-deb --info <filename>	rpm -qpi	Extracts general information from a package
dpkg-deb --contents <filename>	rpm -qpl	Displays the contents of a package

As Table 6-4 shows, dpkg-deb is more or less functionally equivalent to RPM. However, it differs rather substantially in what happens when an archive is actually created. Recall from Chapter 4 that RPM packages are essentially built from special scripts contained in .spec (specification) files; these files contain all the information needed to re-create a binary RPM from pristine source code.

Debian packages, in contrast, are constructed with the `dpkg-deb --build` command, which creates the package by gathering the contents of the current directory and processing some specially named control files in the DEBIAN subdirectory. In fact, Debian's approach to creating packages is more like Slackware's than Red Hat's.

Managing Source Code

Some readers may be wondering whether Debian supports source packages, similar to the way that Red Hat's RPM supports .src.rpm files. The answer is "sort of." Since Debian packages are created to simply archive the contents of a particular directory, it's trivial to build a Debian .deb file that contains source code. However, there is no formal concept of a Debian source package; source code of Debian packages is distributed as standard "tarballs" (that is, gzipped tar archive files) containing the source along with files containing any patches that were necessary to build the software for Debian GNU/Linux.

 CROSS-REFERENCE *See Chapters 4 and 7 for information on Source RPMs.*

Installing Non-Debian Packages

As was mentioned in Chapter 4, you're probably more likely to find an RPM packaging of a particular application than you are a Debian package. Thus, Debian users frequently find themselves in the annoying situation of wanting to install a binary software package that's distributed in a different (non-Debian) format.

To address this issue, Debian GNU/Linux includes the alien program. This is a tool that converts between packaging formats. For example, it allows Debian users to convert an RPM file into a Debian .deb package. The user can then install the package on her Debian system (provided that it meets the software dependencies, of course). However, since each package format has its own peculiarities, there are bound to be some packages that alien doesn't quite handle correctly. It's not a perfect solution, but it definitely can help. Users who find themselves in this predicament may wish to check out alien.

Mechanism and User Interface

As you've probably noticed by now, Debian's package management system is rather substantially different from those of Red Hat Linux and Slackware Linux. Whereas Red Hat's and Slackware's systems more or less automate the process of *physically* installing (and otherwise managing) packages, Debian's system takes package management to another level.

The best way to illustrate this is to compare the installation processes of Debian GNU/Linux and Red Hat Linux. During the installation of Red Hat Linux, the user selects from one of a set of installation classes—for example, Server, Workstation, or Laptop. These options are templates that install a list of packages customized for the selected class. Users can tweak this list after the installation, but at that point it comes down to locating a required package on a CD or the Internet, and then installing it manually.

Debian GNU/Linux takes a similar approach, but with a twist. The Debian installer really only installs a very minimal set of packages—just enough to boot the system. The user is then prompted to use the dselect program to build a list of packages to be installed, selecting from a separate list of available packages. At any given time, only a subset of the available packages will be installed on the system. This approach also makes it easy to update the system with bug fixes, and even upgrade to a new major release; the process is almost fluid in nature.

Of course, all this flexibility comes at a price—namely, complexity. Some people swear by apt-get and the convenience it provides, and others swear just as loudly that RPM is a superior packaging format. Still others, of course, follow the KISS ("Keep It Simple, Stupid") philosophy and prefer Slackware's much more streamlined mechanism. There are vociferous advocates for each of these packaging systems, even though they have a great deal of overlapping functionality. In the end, users should use whatever they like best.

....

Which Tool Is Best?

So far, you've read about three different package management tools: Red Hat's RPM, Debian's .deb system, and Slackware's basic .tar.gz system. You've also read about a variety of tools that add a layer of functionality to these systems, providing features such as network transparency and various user interfaces.

If there's one thing you should remember, though, it's that there's more than one way to do something. Much of the "culture" of a given operating system is tied up in the way it handles updates; for example, Microsoft Corp.'s introduction of its Windows Update system was a major event for that community, despite the fact that Linux distributions had been providing such a mechanism for years. As another example, the FreeBSD Unix-like operating system has its own very powerful method that involves updating the source code for the entire operating system (and all applications!) via CVS, and then recompiling the whole thing. (This can take days for a full update!)

Working with a Linux distribution (or any other operating system) means that you're going to have to learn the way things are done on that system. So, try and avoid getting too attached to a particular distribution, because it's likely to be completely different on the system you use tomorrow.

System Startup Scripts

Debian GNU/Linux uses the SysV model for the system init scripts. Chapter 3 first discussed the SysV and BSD init scripts models, and Chapters 4 and 5 described SysV and BSD in detail. Like Red Hat, Debian uses an extensive SysV model, whereas Slackware is primarily BSD based with a few convenience hooks for scripts written to use the SysV model. Essentially, everything mentioned in Chapter 4 in the section "System Startup Scripts" about the init scripts is also true of Debian, with the few exceptions mentioned here.

Locating the SysV Directories

Debian GNU/Linux, like most systems that use the SysV model, has the relevant directories located immediately under the /etc directory. That is, the SysV directories are /etc/init.d for the scripts themselves, and /etc/rc1.d, /etc/rc2.d through /etc/rc6.d for the runlevel-specific directories. The script that manages all these is /etc/rc.d/rc.

Red Hat Linux 7.2, however, places the SysV directories all under the /etc/rc.d directory. That is, rather than /etc/init.d, Red Hat uses /etc/rc.d/init.d. For compatibility, Red Hat Linux has symbolic links from /etc to the corresponding directories in /etc/rc.d. (In a future version, Red Hat Linux will likely switch to the more common practice of putting the directories immediately underneath /etc.) Therefore, all the information in Chapter 4 in the SysV init scripts model also applies to Debian GNU/Linux, except for the change in directory location.

Working with Debian's Tools

Red Hat Linux includes several tools that automate the process of managing SysV init scripts—namely, chkconfig and service. Debian GNU/Linux does not include these tools, but provides similar alternatives: update-rc.d and invoke-rc.d.

Using update-rc.d

Debian's update-rc.d tool is similar to Red Hat's chkconfig. Whereas chkconfig is a binary program, update-rc.d is a Perl script. These tools have very different command-line options, but otherwise they perform very similar functions. Table 6-5 summarizes the usage of update-rc.d, though for complete information you should consult the manual page as always. (Note: To follow this section, it's imperative that you've read Chapter 4's content on the SysV init scripts model.)

Table 6-5. Using updated-rc.d

COMMAND	FUNCTION
update-rc.d -f <service> remove	Removes the service from all runlevels' configuration directories
update-rc.d <service> start <order> <runlevels>	Configures the service to be started with the specified ordering in a list of runlevels
update-rc.d <service> stop <order> <runlevels>	Configures the service to be killed (stopped) with the specified ordering in a list of runlevels

The biggest difference between update-rc.d and Red Hat's chkconfig is that update-rc.d is intended to set up all the runlevels' links to the service scripts in the /etc/init.d directory *en masse*, whereas chkconfig is capable of configuring services for each runlevel individually. Essentially, this just means that each time you change one runlevel with update-rc.d, you have to change them all. For example, the following sequence of commands is equivalent to the command chkconfig --level 2345 inetd off:

```
$ update-rc.d -f inetd remove
$ update-rc.d inetd stop 20 0 1 2 3 4 5 6 .
```

The first command removes all the runlevels' links to the service script /etc/init.d/inetd; the -f flag causes update-rc.d to proceed even though the ientd script itself is present. The second command then creates stop scripts in each runlevel with a service priority of 20; for example, this will create the symbolic link /etc/rc3.d/K20inetd to disable inetd for runlevel 3. (Note that you have to add the reboot and shutdown runlevels, 0 and 6, explicitly, even though almost all services should *always* be set to "stop".) As another example, the commands shown next will enable inetd for runlevels 3 through 5, and disable it for all others:

```
$ update-rc.d -f inetd remove
$ update-rc.d inetd start 20 3 4 5 . stop 20 0 1 2 6 .
```

Debian's update-rc.d can be a bit confusing at first, but once you figure it out, you'll see how well it works.

Using *invoke-rc.d*

Debian's equivalent of Red Hat's service command is invoke-rc.d. As it happens, the two commands are identical for most cases; for example, the commands service inetd start and invoke-rc.d inetd start have the same effect (which is to start the inetd service; the equivalent command to stop it would be invoke-rc.d inetd stop). The invoke-rc.d command does have a few extra command-line parameters that you can look into, but generally the two commands are equivalent.

Differences in /etc/inittab

As discussed in Chapter 3, the file that primarily configures the init system process is /etc/inittab. This file governs the scripts that get executed during system bootup. The /etc/inittab that is installed on Debian GNU/Linux systems should look pretty familiar, since it's somewhat similar to Red Hat's, as discussed in Chapter 4.

There are a few important ways in which Debian's /etc/inittab differs from Red Hat's and Slackware's:

- Debian's default runlevel is 2.

- Debian does not configure the X Window System display manager (that is, login widget) from /etc/inittab. (Read the section "Debian GNU/Linux Idiosyncracies" later in this chapter for more information.)

- Runlevels 2 and 3 are identical; runlevels 4 and 5 are identical.

- Runlevels 4 and 5 only launch one virtual console; runlevels 2 and 3 launch six.

By now, you should be able to verify the preceding points by looking at /etc/inittab; for details on how to do that, see Chapters 4 and 5, in which Red Hat's and Slackware's /etc/inittab files are dissected in detail.

Other than those points, Debian is a pretty typical SysV init system. For the nitty-gritty details, see the discussion of Red Hat Linux's SysV init implementation in Chapter 4; most of the details will apply to Debian GNU/Linux, though the contents of the scripts themselves may be different.

Core System Libraries

Debian GNU/Linux is a modern Linux distribution, so you won't find any big surprises here. The core libraries included with version 3.0 are listed in Table 6-6. If you compare this list with Tables 4-9 and 5-2, which list the core libraries for Red Hat Linux 7.2 and Slackware Linux 8.0, you'll see that they're pretty similar.

Table 6-6. Debian GNU/Linux 3.0 Core Libraries

PACKAGE	VERSION	COMMENT
XFree86	4.1.0	X Window System
glibc	2.2.5	Core run-time system libraries
bash	2.05a	Bourne Again SHell; primary system shell (used by root)
gdbm	1.7.3	File database libraries
fileutils	4.1	File manipulation utilities

The only thing that might give you a moment's pause is that Debian has alternate names for some of these packages. For example, the name of Red Hat's glibc RPM package is simply "glibc", whereas the name of Debian's equivalent package is "libc6". This is, of course, simply a matter of naming and has no bearing whatsoever on the contents of the packages.

You just need to be aware of this when you're using Debian's tools (or any distribution's tools, for that matter): if you can't find a package by name, don't assume it's not there. If you can't find the name of the package, then it's handy to use dpkg -S to locate the package from a file you know belongs to it. For example, dpkg -S /lib/libc.so.6 will reveal that Debian's package name is "libc6". In other words, there's a reason programs like dpkg support such query modes; learn to make good use of them.

The X Window System and the Desktop

Debian GNU/Linux 3.0 includes XFree86 4.1.0. Here again, there are no surprises. Slackware Linux 8.0 also supports XFree86 4.1.0; Red Hat Linux 7.3, meanwhile, supports a slightly later version of XFree86, namely 4.2.0.

Debian GNU/Linux 3.0 also includes the GNOME and KDE desktop environment, as do Red Hat Linux and Slackware Linux. Debian ships version 1.4.0 of GNOME, and version 2.2 of KDE. These are slightly older than the versions that ship with Red Hat Linux 7.3, but are concurrent with Slackware Linux 8.0.

Probably the only significant way in which Debian's X installation differs from Red Hat's and Slackware's is how the desktop manager is started. (Recall from Chapters 3 through 5 that the X desktop manager is the graphical login prompt that lets users log into X instead of the console.) There's more on this later in the section "Debian GNU/Linux Idiosyncrasies."

Userspace Applications

An extremely wide variety of applications is available for Debian systems. The Debian Project historically has strived to create Debian packages of as many software applications as possible. Whenever possible, these packages are included in the distribution, either on CDs, or over the network. (That is, they are provided in the list of available packages, as described earlier in this chapter, in the section "Managing Packages with Debian's System.") In fact, so many Debian packages are available, that you can even get an installation of Debian on a DVD! Clearly, Debian GNU/Linux does not lack for installation packages.

However, due to the way Debian's packaging system manages installation sources, there isn't really a way to distinguish between CDs. That is, whereas Red Hat provides clearly delineated core CDs and various ancillary CDs (such as PowerTools and so on), Debian GNU/Linux consists of a mad jumble of files spread out across multiple CDs. (It's not really that chaotic, but sometimes it can seem that way to new users!)

In other words, Debian doesn't have any additional CDs the way many other distributions do. So, there aren't any Debian editions or bonus discs or anything like that. However, this doesn't really matter; after all, the only point of labeling CDs like that is to make it easy for the user to figure out which CD contains a desired package. Since Debian removes from the user the burden of locating packages on CDs, there's little reason not to just drop all the files onto one big set of CDs. (Again, though, the organization is not that random; the most crucial packages are located on the first couple CDs, so that users who download the CD images and make their own CD copies don't have to download them all if they don't need them.)

Debian GNU/Linux Idiosyncrasies

This section will describe some aspects or features that are unique to Debian GNU/Linux. So far, you've seen that Debian GNU/Linux is quite similar to Red Hat Linux and Slackware Linux, but that a few minor differences exist in some areas. This section outlines a few more significant differences that you need to be aware of when using a Debian GNU/Linux system.

Touring the /etc Directory

Generally, you'll find everything in /etc that you would expect to find. There are a few things worth paying special attention to, though. Table 6-7 lists some note-worthy subdirectories of /etc that you should know about. The list does not include the common subdirectories defined by the Filesystem Hierarchy Standard (such as /etc/X11 and /etc/init.d), only Debian-specific directories. Each entry in Table 6-7 is discussed in the text that follows, except for /etc/alternatives, which has a whole section devoted to it later.

Table 6-7. Significant Subdirectories of /etc on Debian GNU/Linux

DIRECTORY	CONTENTS
/etc/default	Files containing configuration information for various programs
/etc/network	Files related to configuring the network interfaces
/etc/dpkg	Configuration information for the dpkg tool
/etc/alternatives	Symbolic links that choose defaults between certain programs

The /etc/default Directory

This directory contains files that set values to variables used by other scripts. Typically, any time a program or script needs to have values assigned to it that are specific to the installation, the variables are placed in a file in /etc/default and the script or program reads this file to determine its settings. This way, administrators don't have to edit the script itself to tweak the settings. (Actually, this is a different solution to the same problem that inspired Red Hat to use the "drop-in config directory" approach discussed throughout Chapter 4.)

For example, Linux 2.4 kernels support the iptables functionality, which allows administrators to create firewalls, among other things. (See Chapter 16 for an example of a Linux-based firewall using iptables.) Using iptables requires that some variables be set. So, the script provided by Debian that sets up iptables reads these values from /etc/default/iptables rather than requiring the administrator to modify the /etc/init.d/iptables script directly.

Since the only files in this directory will be placed there by individual packages, the contents of this directory will obviously vary by which packages are installed. Whenever you install a new Debian package, be sure to check /etc/default to see if is contains a file to modify. Of course, you should always read all the documentation for the software as well.

The /etc/network Directory

This directory is similar to /etc/default in that it contains configuration information for the networking system. However, the network-related files were placed here to keep them all in one place and to prevent them from getting mixed in with other files in a confusing bundle. This directory is analogous to /etc/sysconfig/network on Red Hat Linux systems, though its contents are different.

The /etc/network directory is installed by the ifupdown and netbase packages. Table 6-8 lists the typical contents of /etc/network.

Table 6-8. Contents of the /etc/network Directory

FILE OR DIRECTORY	PURPOSE
if-down.d	Holds scripts to run when a network interface is brought down
if-post-down.d	Holds scripts to run *after* an interface has been brought down
if-up.d	Holds scripts to run when an interface is brought online
if-pre-up.d	Holds scripts to be run *before* an interface is brought online
ifstate	Contains information on whether each network device is up or down
interfaces	Contains network configuration information for all interfaces
options	Enables or disables various optional networking features
spoof-protect	Enables or disables protection from network spoofing attacks

Generally, the files you're most likely to interact with will be interfaces and options. The interfaces file contains detailed network information (such as IP address, netmask, and gateway, or whether to use Dynamic Host Configuration Protocol [DHCP]) for each interface that the system is to use. By editing the contents of this file, you can control most aspects of your system's network configuration. The only other file you're likely to need to interact with is options, which enables or disables additional general networking options, such as whether to configure the kernel to act as a network router by forwarding IP packets. An excellent manual page for the /etc/network/interfaces file is provided; simply type man interfaces and you'll have all the information you need to configure your system's network interfaces.

The other files in /etc/network are for cases where administrators need more advanced capabilities. For example, the if-down.d, if-up.d, if-pre-up.d, and if-post-down.d directories provide administrators with a way to hook scripts into the process of activating and deactivating network interfaces, in order to log such events, for example. (These directories implement the common config.d configuration directory approach discussed throughout Chapter 4.) Similarly, the /etc/network/spoof-protect file allows administrators to set parameters that are used to detect network spoof attacks. (This file may actually no longer be needed by recent kernels.) Finally, the /etc/network/ifstate file is internal to the ifup and ifdown scripts and is used to indicate which interfaces are active and which are not. Again, generally you won't need to work with these files, but it's good to know they're there if you do need them someday.

The /etc/dpkg Directory

This directory contains files that configure the dpkg and dselect programs. The dpkg.cfg and dselect.cfg files can be used to set default options for dpkg and dselect, so that they don't have to be entered on the command line each time the programs are run. The origins directory contains files that describe where the particular distribution originated. (This is typically used by the various organizations that provide variants of the base Debian distribution.) The shlibs.default and shlibs.override files can be used to tweak the shared libraries used by dpkg (such as when upgrading core system libraries like glibc). This is a rather arcane area, and you shouldn't mess with it unless you know what you're doing!

Understanding the /etc/alternatives Directory

The /etc/alternatives directory, listed in Table 6-7, establishes default programs in cases where more than one program may be installed that fulfills a certain purpose.

For example, probably the most ubiquitous Unix text editor is the vi program. However, there are a number of free implementations of vi, such as Vi Improved (vim), nvi, and elvis. Typically, whenever one of these programs is installed, a symbolic link is created to run the vi clone every time a user types the command vi. (That is, /bin/vi is usually a symbolic link to one of those programs.) However, a given Debian installation could have several or all of these installed at the same time. When that's the case, how do you choose which vi clone gets to masquerade as the "real" vi? Obviously, you simply must choose one and make it the default.

This scenario happens fairly frequently. In addition to the vi example just mentioned, there are multiple implementations of the awk program (including gawk), the yacc program (including bison and byacc), and so on. In fact, this happens so frequently that the Debian Project created the /etc/alternatives and the "update-alternatives" system around it.

The purpose of the /etc/alternatives directory is simply to indicate which clone of a particular program is to be the "real thing" on the system. The real program in the filesystem is actually a symbolic link to the /etc/alternatives directory, and the file there is in turn a symbolic link to the clone. Going back to the vi example, suppose nvi and vim are installed, and that vim is to be configured as the real vi on the system. To implement this configuration, /etc/alternatives/vi is linked to point at /usr/bin/vim. The actual /usr/bin/vi file, meanwhile, is symbolically linked to point at /etc/alternatives/vi. The /usr/bin/vi file never changes; to switch to a different clone, you only change the /etc/alternatives/vi file.

The /etc/alternatives directory actually handles more than just the program itself; it also handles man pages. (After all, it doesn't do you any good to have vim as your vi clone but get nvi's manual page when you type man vi!) The mechanism for the manual pages is very similar to that of the programs; the "real" man pages in the /man and /usr/man directories are symbolically linked to point to /etc/alternatives, where they are in turn symbolically linked to the man page for a clone.

As you can probably tell, it would quickly get annoying to manage all these symbolic links. To address this, Debian GNU/Linux also includes the update-alternatives program, which manages the symbolic links in /etc/alternatives for you in much the same way that update-rc.d (and chkconfig on Red Hat Linux) manage the SysV init symbolic links. The update-alternatives program is easy to use, so check its manual page (man update-alternatives) for full details.

Configuring the X Display Manager

The X display manager is the program that allows users to log in directly to X via a graphical user interface. Several programs are available that act as X desktop managers; notably, KDE and GNOME each have one, named kdm and gdm. This section discusses how to configure Debian GNU/Linux to use kdm or gdm as the X display manager.

Red Hat Linux and Slackware Linux both start the X display manager from /etc/inittab. Specifically, Red Hat has a program known as prefdm that is invoked directly from /etc/inittab and is responsible for choosing the default desktop manager (usually gdm or kdm) to use; similarly, Slackware starts a very simple shell script (/etc/rc.d/rc.4) from /etc/inittab that selects the display manager dynamically and runs it. Debian does things a little differently, however.

CROSS-REFERENCE   *See Chapters 4 and 5 for details on Red Hat's and Slackware's techniques.*

Debian starts the display manager as a normal SysV service. Each package containing a display manager installs its own SysV script in /etc/init.d. For example, gdm and kdm install /etc/init.d/gdm and /etc/init.d/kdm, respectively. Debian is then able to treat these scripts as standard SysV init services, and doesn't need to have an entry in /etc/inittab for them.

A potential problem with this approach can arise if both gdm and kdm are installed; the system has to choose between them since they both can't run at the same time. To avoid such conflicts, both init scripts are written to check the file /etc/X11/default-display-manager, which contains the path of the official default display manager for the system. The gdm and kdm init scripts check this file to determine whether they should run; as a result, only one will run at a time.

So, to change the default display manager on Debian GNU/Linux, you must edit the /etc/X11/default-display-manager file. This file contains a single line, which is the path to a desktop manager program—for example, /usr/bin/gdm. Simply change this program name to something like /usr/bin/kdm.

Now that you know how to do this by hand, you should know about the tool that automates it. When you actually install two display managers on the system, Debian's package manager will prompt you to select which one you want. In order to change display managers, then, you can simply have dpkg reconfigure one of the packages; the command shown shortly demonstrates how to do this. When you run it, you'll be prompted to select your display manager again. Of course, all this program is doing is modifying the contents of /etc/X11/default-display-manager, so it's really a question of which method is faster. The command to have dpkg reconfigure the display manager is as follows:

```
$ dpkg-reconfigure gdm
```

Securing the System

As with Slackware Linux, Debian GNU/Linux leaves many services running in a default installation. It's very important to remove unneeded services, or else you risk letting your system be compromised by an attacker, especially if your system is connected to the open Internet. This section will discuss how to lock down your system.

Shutting Down Unneeded SysV Services

Typically, if you install a Debian package that is started by the SysV init system, it will be configured to start by default. As a result, depending on how carefully you selected your packages when you installed the system, you may have a number of services running that you don't need. Some of these, such as the portmap and NFS statd program, have a history of security vulnerabilities, so it makes sense to shut them off.

On Red Hat Linux, the chkconfig program can be used to easily view which SysV services are configured to run and which are not for each runlevel. Unfortunately, it doesn't seem to be quite that easy on Debian GNU/Linux. In order to tell if a service is configured for a given runlevel, you actually have to check the symbolic links in the appropriate runlevel directory. For example, to see what's configured to run in runlevel 2, you would have to issue the command ls /etc/rc2.d; any files that start with a "K" are configured to be stopped in that runlevel, and any that start with an "S" are configured to be started.

CROSS-REFERENCE   *For full details on how the SysV init system works, see the section "System Startup Scripts" in Chapter 4.*

Once you've seen what's running, you have to decide what needs to be running and what doesn't. Generally, if you don't need a service, you should shut it off, to prevent exposing yourself to a potential future vulnerability in a program you don't even need. To actually configure a service to not run, you can either modify the symbolic links by hand (as discussed in Chapter 4), or you can use the update-rc.d program as discussed earlier in this chapter.

Removing inetd Services

Debian uses a traditional implementation of inetd. (It's the same implementation used by Slackware Linux; contrast this with Red Hat Linux, which uses the alternative xinetd program instead.) Like Slackware, Debian's default inetd configuration comes with a number of services enabled by default. As always, it's a good idea to disable services you don't need.

Using the update-inetd Program

To disable services, you can use the exact same techniques discussed in the section "Configuring Inetd" in Chapter 5. However, Debian also provides an additional tool called update-inetd. This program is similar to Red Hat's chkconfig and Debian's update-rc.d, except that it works strictly on inetd services configured in the /etc/inetd.conf file. This program makes it fairly easy to add new entries to /etc/inetd.conf (such as when you install a new inetd service on the system; see Chapter 12 for an example of this) as well as enabling and disabling existing services. (For example, you may wish to disable the CVS service from running while you perform maintenance, but you don't want to remove the entry entirely.) The update-inetd program also allows you to delete entries from /etc/inetd.conf outright.

When update-inetd is run, it's simply taking the actions discussed in Chapter 5, so you don't have to do them manually. The update-inetd program will actually be discussed more in Chapter 12, so I won't discuss it here in much detail. However, to use it to disable inetd services for security purposes, follow this example, which disables the finger service:

```
$ update-inetd --disable finger
```

Just repeat this command for each service you wish to disable! If you find that you don't need any inetd services running at all, then you should disable the inetd SysV service entirely by using the technique mentioned in the previous section. (Note: To see which services are currently enabled, you will have to look at the contents of /etc/inetd.conf and find the lines defining services. See Chapter 5 for details.)

Derivatives of Debian GNU/Linux

A number of commercial distributions have been based on Debian. However, recently many of these have died away, leaving only Debian itself and a few others. The Debian Project actually maintains a list of derivatives on its web site at www.debian.org/misc/related_links.

This list is most likely not complete, and it may include some derivatives that have since been abandoned, but it does demonstrate that there is a lively community surrounding Debian, not only on the core distribution, but also on other related efforts.

Summary

Well, you've done it—you've slogged through your third distribution. This chapter covered Debian GNU/Linux, introducing you to the various aspects of the system. However, you have already seen two before this one, so much of it is likely starting to look familiar. In fact, you probably couldn't help but notice the same thing I did while writing this chapter: I found myself saying " . . . just like Red Hat Linux and Slackware Linux" quite a lot!

However, Debian GNU/Linux is clearly its own distribution, so you also read a good deal of material about Debian's unique features, tools, and ways of doing things. You should now feel fairly comfortable with a Debian system; you should know how to do the most common tasks, and you should have a good feel for where to start looking when you need to figure out how to do something not covered in this book.

In fact, you know all this for three distributions now. By extension, you should have quite a leg up on figuring out any distribution you come across. A lot of this material probably even applies to non-Linux systems! That, of course, was the goal of Part Two.

....

Learning a New Linux Distribution in Ten Easy Steps

A useful exercise at this point is to stop and think about what you've learned. Suppose you were handed a computer with a Linux distribution you had never seen before, and you had to use and manage it. How would you go about doing that? The list that follows is a short checklist that you might use, but before you read it, take a moment and think about how *you* would do it.

Here's a little recipe for learning a new Linux distribution, in ten easy steps:

1. Figure out what package manager it uses, if any. (Debian? RPM? Something similar to Slackware's?)

2. Check out the /etc/inittab file, and see what functionality is configured when the system boots. (Are there virtual consoles? Is X running?)

3. See whether the system uses the BSD or SysV model of init scripts.

4. Browse the filesystem, and look for directories whose purpose you don't recognize. (How closely does it follow the Filesystem Hierarchy Standard? Watch out for unique things like Red Hat's /etc/profile.d and Slackware's /var/log/packages.)

5. If it's a SysV system, look around for tools that might help you manage the scripts.

6. While you're at it, look around for other useful tools, such as Red Hat's Xconfigurator and Debian's update-alternatives.

7. If the system lets you view the list of installed packages, check out what versions of the software are installed, and look at the contents of any packages that look interesting or unfamiliar. (`rpm -qa` on Red Hat; `dpkg -1` on Debian; `cat /var/log/packages` on Slackware.)

8. Make sure the system isn't running unnecessary services, and disable any that are running.

9. If you have to install software of your own, figure out the best place for it, so that it fits well with the system. (Does the system use /opt for something else, or can you use it yourself?)

10. As you use the system, be on the lookout for patterns and generalities that define the "character" of the distribution; in the long run, you're much better off working with the distribution than fighting with it.

How closely does this match your own list? What would you do differently? As you think about these questions, take a moment to enjoy that feeling of accomplishment; you've learned a lot! Enjoy it. When you're ready, move on to Part Three, and start learning how to install software to customize your system.

Part Three

Installing Software

Welcome to Part Three of *Tuning and Customizing a Linux System*! Part One of this book covered the basics of Linux, and Part Two discussed three major distributions in detail. These two sections should have helped you attain a working knowledge of Linux systems, and now you're probably ready to actually get down to work and customize your system.

Part Three discusses how to install and configure software on a Linux system. Chapter 7 covers the basics of software installation and configuration and discusses some broad generalizations and techniques that may be useful. Chapters 8 through 13 provide detailed examinations of the installations of several example software packages. The example software packages were chosen to illustrate the general points raised in Chapter 7. Once you've finished reading these chapters, you'll be equipped to install and configure (or at least teach yourself how to install and configure) virtually any software you come across.

The following table summarizes the examples in these chapters and which techniques outlined in Chapter 7 the examples demonstrate.

Sample Software Installations

SOFTWARE PACKAGE COVERAGE	CHAPTER	TECHNIQUE DEMONSTRATED
OpenSSH secure shell	Chapter 8	Global configuration file
Pluggable Authentication Modules (PAM)	Chapter 9	Drop-in configuration directory
Dante SOCKS library	Chapter 10	Userspace software library
Apache Web server	Chapter 11	Flat directory installation
Concurrent Versions System (CVS)	Chapter 12	inetd service
Sun Microsystems' JDK	Chapter 13	Flat package with user environment variables

Each example software installation will include a summary of the software itself, a synopsis of the installation procedure, a list of potential pitfalls, and detailed lists of any commands, scripts, or other information required to accomplish an actual installation on each of the sample distributions. For example, this might include SysV-compatible scripts to hook the software into the bootup sequence on a Red Hat Linux system.

Another important thing to note is that some of the software in these examples may already be present on a given distribution, so check your system to see if the packages are installed or available for installation. If you attempt to install the software described in these chapters while packages provided by your vendor are already installed, neither installation may work. Make sure to check and remove any packages that are already installed before you attempt to install them yourself.

Finally, remember that these chapters are here to provide examples, and the packages were selected primarily to illustrate specific types of installations. Even if the packages are already installed—or if they're not installed and aren't needed—it will still be worth your time to read their sections in these chapters, just to get insight into that *class* of software installation. Beyond that, the last section of this book, Part Four, contains a set of case studies that demonstrate actual uses of a Linux system in a variety of configurations. Those chapters draw extensively on the material in Chapters 8 through 13. You are strongly encouraged to read or at least skim the chapters in Part Four before tackling the case studies.

#### CHAPTER 7

Installing and Configuring Software

Once you have a Linux system up and running and are acquainted with its operation and administration, you can begin customizing the system. This chapter covers the general problem of software installations. You'll learn about some of the most common, general installation and configuration techniques used by many different software packages. After reading this chapter, you'll have been exposed to a breadth of techniques that cover the majority of installations. The next six chapters provide more detail in the form of specific examples of the concepts discussed in this chapter.

Some of the information in this chapter is rather basic. Users who have installed some software on their own in the past may wish to skip much of the information found here. You can pick up much of the content with a little experience. However, some of the sections and sidebars contain useful information regardless of your level of experience, so you may want to pick and choose from the various topics covered here.

Getting Started

The process of installing software can't really begin until you've done your homework. Once a software package has been identified, a would-be user has to settle some basic logistics involving the software's license and its features and installation procedure.

Just because a software package fills a certain niche doesn't mean it meets a user's needs. The Apache web server, for example, is extremely robust and full-featured. However, Apache is not engineered to be ultra-high-performance; rather, its focus is on correctness and features. If a user's main requirement in a web server is speed, then Apache might not be the right choice. The real first step to installing software is simply to determine whether it meets the needs of the user.

Reading the Documentation

A user should do her homework and research the software through its documentation. The obvious starting points are the software's web site (if it has one), or the nearly ubiquitous "README" file. This documentation also usually includes installation instructions (often in a file called "INSTALL"), so it's a good idea to review those as well. Only after familiarizing herself with the software should a user begin the installation with the steps that follow; it's a real hassle to spend an hour installing and configuring software only to find out that it doesn't quite meet the needs. Unfortunately, sometimes there's no way to know that until after the fact. A few false starts are to be expected.

Accepting the License

Chapter 2 discussed open source software, which is fundamental to Linux and Linux-based systems. Additionally, Chapter 2 listed some example open source licenses, and briefly described some of the differences between them. Most of the software that users encounter for Linux systems is open source and falls under one of those licenses. However, other licenses exist, and of course there is commercial (non–open source) software for Linux. The first step—one that is sometimes overlooked—is for a user to find out if the desired software is legal to use and if the license is acceptable. For open source software, there is typically a file named "LICENSE" that contains everything the user needs to know; commercial software packages frequently have "click-through" license agreements to which a user is explicitly required to agree. In any case, the license must be reviewed prior to installation.

After the user has reviewed the documentation for the software, verified that it meets the needs at hand, and agreed to the license, it's time to actually install the software. The next section lists and describes the basic installation steps, and provides some tips and guidelines.

Software Installation in Six Easy Steps

Installing software on a Linux system is pretty easy, after a few tries and a little experience. However, in the long term the biggest challenge is keeping everything orderly and sane. It's easy to let things get out of control and wind up with one big ball of string instead of a functional system. This chapter outlines the following steps of installing software:

1. Choosing between a source or binary installation

2. Deciding on a destination

3. Building the software

4. Configuring the software's settings

5. Configuring the user environment

6. Hooking into the operating system

This chapter will describe each of these steps in detail. The steps don't provide detailed instructions on how to install software; for details like that, users should consult the documentation for the software or another, more introductory reference book. Like the rest of this book, rules of thumb, guidelines, and general patterns and techniques are emphasized. After reading these sections, users will have a broad understanding of exactly what is going on when they install software.

Choosing Between a Source and a Binary Installation

The first step to installing a new software package is, of course, to obtain the package. However, since the vast majority of software used on Linux systems is open source, source code is usually available. This means that your first decision is whether to install precompiled binaries of the software or build your own binaries from the source code. The appropriate option is going to vary from one situation to the next, depending on the hardware and particular distribution being used as well as the needs of the user. This section will discuss how to make this decision, based on factors such as platform architecture and software configuration needs.

Understanding Hardware Platforms and Processor Families

Most microprocessors have a "family" of related processors. As manufacturers develop newer and faster chips, they generally augment existing capabilities of older chips, and so the later processors from a particular manufacturer are related to—but not always 100% compatible with—other chips in the family. Two example microprocessor families are Intel's ubiquitous x86 family and Compaq's Alpha family of RISC processors. The later chips in these families are simply extensions of earlier chips; for example, Intel's Pentium 4 processor is backward compatible with the original 8086 processor, while Compaq's 21364 EV67 chip is backward compatible with earlier chips, such as the 21264 EV56.

However, each subsequent chip in a family generally introduces new extensions to the processor. For example, Intel introduced the Multimedia Extension (MMX) instructions to their Pentium line of processors. One of the jobs of the compiler is to take the source code and optimize it for use with the features of a particular processor. Obviously, code that was compiled to make use of instructions or optimizations available on a specific chip isn't going to run on a processor that doesn't have those features, even if the chips are in the same family.

The impact of these optimizations varies. In a case like the MMX instructions, the code simply might not run at all on processors that don't have the MMX instructions, and fail with an error. In a more subtle case, code that was optimized to run on an Alpha EV6 makes use of timing characteristics and instruction scheduling of the EV6 processor. Even though these instructions will physically run on an earlier EV5 processor, they might not run optimally since the EV5 might have different timing requirements.

What does this have to do with installing software? Well, if the only binary package available is compiled for a slightly different version of your own processor, it might run suboptimally, or it might not run at all. This varies by architecture; in the Intel world, it's generally not a big deal, but Alpha users frequently choose to build their own software to make certain they have the appropriate optimizations for their specific system. So, depending on your platform you may wish to build software yourself from source code rather than rely on someone else's prebuilt package.

Software Configuration Options

Sometimes it's not the compiler optimizations that the user is concerned with, but rather the software configuration options. That is, a given piece of software might support different features or behaviors that the user can request be activated or deactivated when the software is built from source code. These changes are independent of any optimizations the compiler might perform, and are called *compile-time* (or *build-time*) configurations.

The important thing to understand about compile-time settings is that they can't be changed later; if a user elects to disable a specific feature at compile-time, it cannot be added later without recompiling all or some of the software. For example, the Apache web server supports the ability to dynamically load modules that provide various capabilities; however, a user may wish to disable this behavior and build Apache as a single program, without support for modules. If an administrator chooses to do this and later wishes to use a dynamic library, Apache will have to be recompiled.

A given prebuilt software package will have been compiled with a specific set of features. If the user of this package wishes to use a different set of features, then she would need to build the software from source code. This issue is independent of packaging format; whether the binary software is shipped in RPM, Debian, or some other format, it still has been compiled with a certain set of compile-time options. When considering the installation of a binary software package, users should consult the documentation of whoever prepared the package to see what options are enabled. If the package's configuration is inadequate, the administrator will have to build her own copy from source code, after all.

Making the Decision

Unfortunately, there's no truly general rule of thumb for making the decision of installing from source or binary. The rule varies by platform (such as Alpha users who prefer to build from source) and by need. (A user may be more security conscious about a production server than about a workstation, and so may be more proactive about disabling unneeded features in software.) Obviously, of course, it is easier and simpler to install from binary packages when doing so is acceptable, and for most applications that policy will work perfectly well. Occasionally, though, you might need to install from source code; for such situations, "you'll know it when you see it," as the saying goes. The key is just to make sure you know what you need from your software before you install it—that will tell you whether to install from source or binary.

Deciding on a Destination

Once it's determined how the software is going to be installed, where it's going to be installed is next. This section will discuss the options and some guidelines for choosing an installation location. The location of a single software package on the computer's filesystem isn't really that important (provided it can be properly accessed by everyone who needs it), but it is a good idea to standardize on a policy of where software is installed, to prevent maintenance and upgrade headaches later.

The best location to install software is going to vary by the type of software and the distribution. Most Linux distributions closely follow the Linux Filesystem Hierarchy Standard (FHS) mentioned first in Chapter 3, so that document may be a good guide for making the decision. For most systems, though, there is a rule of thumb that can be applied: If the software comes as a prebuilt binary package or as a preconfigured source package (such as a source RPM file), let the packager install the software according to the package's defaults. If the software is being built from raw source (such as a ZIP file or tarball), it should be installed in a subdirectory of /usr/local or /opt.

Installing into /usr/local

A common place to install software is /usr/local. As discussed in Chapter 3, the FHS specifies that /usr is essentially a mirror of the root directory, in that they both have /etc, /lib, /bin, and other subdirectories. The /usr directory is intended to be used for general files, while the root directory is intended to be used only for files that are absolutely critical to the system during startup. The /usr/local directory, meanwhile, is intended to contain software that is specific to a particular system; /usr generally contains only general software.

On Linux systems, this essentially means that /usr and the root directory contain software managed by the native package manager (such as Red Hat's RPM or Debian's system), while /usr/local is intended to be used for files that are installed manually and bypass the native packager. The native packager typically handles conflicts between packages; however, it can't do anything for software it doesn't know about, and so it's useful to keep manually installed software in /usr/local, which most package managers seldom use.

Typically, software installed in /usr/local is placed into the standard directories. That is, /usr/local/etc contains configuration files, /usr/local/bin contains program executables, and so forth. The /opt directory, discussed in the next section, is usually a bit different.

Software Installation on Multiuser Systems

Sometimes you might encounter a system where you wish to install some custom software, but don't have root privileges. For example, many users used to Linux systems and the accompanying GNU tools frequently find it frustrating to use the less capable default tools found on commercial Unix systems. These users may wish to install the GNU tools for their own use.

The lack of root access prevents you from installing in the usual places, and you're stuck with installing to your home directory. An effective technique in such cases is to simply create a subdirectory of your home directory and create your own little mini /usr/local or /opt. For example, you could create a directory named "~/usr" and install all your software into it in the standard way, so that programs go in ~/usr/bin, libraries go in ~/usr/lib, and so on. With this technique, you can use all the tricks covered in this chapter, even if you don't have root access. If you're truly ambitious, you might even install your own copy of a package manager (such as RPM) in your home directory!

Installing into /opt

Like /usr/local, the /opt (for optional) directory is usually not used by the package managers. So, it's a good place to install software manually, since files placed there won't conflict with files managed by the system. However, /opt is usually used somewhat differently than /usr/local.

The /usr/local directory typically contains files from all packages mixed together. This makes it simple to configure (since, for example, you only have to add a single directory—/usr/local/bin—to the path). However, it also makes it somewhat tricky to upgrade a specific package. For example, if you installed version 1.0 of a software library called "my-software" into /usr/local and then wish to upgrade it to version 2.0, you'll have to overwrite what's already in there. Users who did not wish the library to be upgraded might be impacted by this.

Most systems that use an /opt directory use it to address these issues. Sun Microsystems' Solaris appears to have been the first to use /opt extensively, and since then many other systems have copied the style. Essentially, rather than mixing all the software into a set of shared directories, each package installs into its own subdirectory of /opt. For example, that software library could have been installed into /opt/my-software to keep it separate. Beyond that, it could have been installed into /opt/my-software-1.0; that would allow the new version to be placed in /opt/my-software-2.0. This allows for easier upgrades, and symbolic links can also be used (such as a link in /opt/my-software pointing to the current version) so that users don't have to reference specific versions' directories.

....

Tradeoffs: /usr/local vs. /opt

There are pros and cons to the use of both directories. On the one hand, /usr/local makes it simpler to configure the system, since only one directory needs to be added to the shells' path for all programs to be accessible. (Similarly, only one "lib" directory needs to be added to the library path, etc.) However, once you've mixed a large number of files, it can be hard to manage. The multiple-directories approach used in /opt makes it easier to keep track of which files belong to which packages. (It's a sort of poor man's package manager!) However, with /opt you have to hook in multiple directories—and multiple paths, library paths, and so on—into the system's configuration. This can also be a pain to manage. Which is better? It depends on the software, really; with a little experience, you'll work out your own rules of thumb.

....

Making the Decision

Choosing the location for the software is easy if it's being installed via the native package manager: Just let it be installed wherever it pleases, and let the manager deal with it. It's a bit trickier when you have to install it manually. A good way to choose between /usr/local and /opt is on the size or complexity of the software. If it's simply a small utility package, such as, say, an SSH (secure shell) client, then it's probably fine to place it in /usr/local. However, if it's a large package, such as the Apache web server or the KDE desktop, you might want to use /opt to make it easier to upgrade later. Additionally, if the users need multiple versions of a package installed, such as the Java programming language, where developers frequently need access to several versions, /opt is probably easier to use.

Building the Software

After an administrator has decided where to install the software and settled on a set of compile-time configuration parameters, he can actually build the software. Of course, this step only applies to software that is being installed from source code; installations of prebuilt binary packages omit this step. Generally, there are two stages to building software: specifying compile-time options and automating the build.

Specifying Compile-Time Options

Source code is turned into an actual program by a *compiler* (such as the *gcc*, the C language compiler from GNU). Typically, the compiler has to be invoked on each source code file. Most software projects consist of dozens or hundreds of files (or even more), and compilers are complex beasts, with hundreds of compilation options. This is clearly not something that administrators can do by hand—it's just too much typing. Almost every software project known to humankind uses some sort of scripting mechanism to automate the build process; almost universally, this is the *make* tool. This tool reads files (usually named, intuitively enough, Makefile) that specify compilation options and identifies files that need to be compiled. In most cases, building the software is as simple as running make from the top-level directory of the source code.

Before the software can be built, though, the compile-time options have to be specified somehow. It's all fine and well for the Makefile to script the compilation process, but how does it know what compilation options the user wants? There are, unfortunately, a lot of different ways of accomplishing this. Some software requires the user to edit a Makefile to set some options (such as installation directories or the locations of libraries that the software depends on). The vast majority of open source software, however, uses the GNU project's *autoconf* tools, which are described in more detail later in this chapter. In the end, the only way to find out how to configure an application's settings is by reading its documentation. That's why the first step, as mentioned previously, is to read the ReadMe, Install, and other documentation files. As they say, "RTFM," or Read The Fine Material (or something more explicit, if you're not in polite company!).

Performing the Compilation

The last step after building the software is installing it. Again, this is typically automated by the Makefile for the project. The make command lets the Makefile specify *targets*. One target (the default target) usually builds the target, and a second target (usually called "install") handles the installation. So, in most cases installing the software after it is built is as simple as typing make install. Again, though, this can vary and the software's own documentation is the last word.

Configuring the Software's Settings

The administrator's task isn't done, even after the software is built and installed! Frequently, there are additional configuration activities that must be accomplished after the software is installed. Configuration options that alter the behavior of software while it runs are called *run-time* options. This section will describe the most common ways of configuring a system at run-time.

A compile-time option typically enables or disables some feature in the software, or hard-codes a parameter such as the location of a required file. Since these options are literally compiled into the software, they can't be altered. (If you disable a feature at compile-time, it's simply not there to be activated later!) A run-time option, in contrast, sets a value or alters behavior for a specific execution of the program. There are a lot of ways this can be accomplished, and the remainder of this section describes some of the most common techniques.

Command-Line Parameters

The simplest and most direct run-time configuration mechanism is the *command-line parameter*, sometimes known as *command-line switches* or *flags*. This isn't really a full-blown configuration option like the others mentioned in this section, but its end result is similar. Even the greenest Unix user is intimately acquainted with this technique, and almost all the example commands in this book use command-line parameters.

On Unix-like systems, command-line parameters typically follow the command name and are delimited by dashes; for example, the ls file listing command takes several command-line options to alter the output. Most of these are single-character options and can be joined together with a single dash; for example, `ls -la` is equivalent to `ls -l -a`. The GNU project introduced a variant of this technique by using two dashes and a full word instead of a single dash and letter. This is intended to be a more intuitive and easy-to-remember syntax. As an example, GNU's version of ls has color highlighting that is enabled by the command line flag `--color=always`. (Typically, GNU programs also offer both traditional single-dash/single-letter forms in addition to the longer forms.)

There are other forms of command line options, too. Some programs, such as the Concurrent Version System (CVS) program, which is a software change management tool, take *sub commands*, which are simple words. The command `cvs checkout`, for example, fetches a module from a CVS repository. There are other variants as well, and they vary in complexity. The manual page (which can be accessed by the command "man cvs") or other documentation is the best bet, but it's useful to be aware of the patterns.

Application-Specific Tools and Wizards

Once the software has been configured for features, compiled, and installed in the appropriate directory, it might need to be configured for actual use. This differs from the first step—compile-time configuration—in which the software is configured before building it, to activate or deactivate features and behaviors. In this step, the software will be configured to actually run; this is known as *run-time configuration*. For example, the Apache web server can be configured to either activate or deactivate support for dynamic shared objects before compiling it, but in either case it must still be configured with values required to actually run correctly, such as the location of the HTML files it is to serve up, or the TCP/IP port number to use.

There are a number of different ways to configure software, and different packages will take different approaches. Generally, though, there are some traditional techniques used on Unix-like systems that most applications follow. The next five subsections will discuss the following most common ways of configuring software:

- Global configuration files

- Drop-in configuration file directories

- Flat files or directories

- Servers launched by inetd

- User libraries

Some are typical of all Unix-like systems, and some are more specific to Linux systems or particular distributions.

Global Configuration Files

The canonical way to configure software for a Unix-like system is to have the software read one or more specially-named configuration files in the /etc directory. For example, the file /etc/sendmail.cf is used to configure the sendmail SMTP server. Sometimes, applications that require more than one configuration file will use multiple files in a subdirectory of /etc. For instance, by default the OpenSSH package reads its client and server configuration files out of /etc/ssh. (These locations are frequently hard-coded at compile-time and can usually be altered by rebuilding the package.) This is probably the most common way of configuring software.

Drop-in Configuration File Directories

The drop-in file configuration directory is a technique used extensively by Red Hat's Linux distribution, and it's catching on in other systems as well. This technique is used when a single software package can have separate configurations for separate scenarios. The software then defines a single directory (typically as a subdirectory of /etc) and reads a separate configuration from that directory for each scenario. A scenario can be anything from a different user to a different software application—anything that requires its own unique configuration. For example, the xinetd package stores configuration files in /etc/xinetd.d and has a separate configuration file for each inetd service that it is to manage. The PAM (Pluggable Authentication Modules) package, meanwhile, reads configuration files out of /etc/pam.d and has a separate file for each service or program for which it manages authentication.

The advantage of this approach is that software can be customized for a given scenario by altering a file specific to that scenario, rather than by modifying the contents of a single file containing configuration for all of the scenarios. For example, a new inetd service can be configured with xinetd by adding a file to /etc/xinetd.d for that service. The alternative would be to have the service being installed modify a single shared configuration file, which is prone to error and might end up breaking another service's configuration. As mentioned previously, this technique is used extensively in Red Hat Linux, and it is discussed in more detail in Chapter 4.

....

Drop-in File Tip

The drop-in configuration file technique works best with software that is
providing some kind of service to other software. In such cases, the software
that provides the service doesn't know in advance how many other applications
need to use it. So, the service software simply provides a "hook" for other
programs to add their own configuration data to the mix. Look for uses of this
technique wherever a program doesn't know in advance how much it will be
used. It's becoming quite popular!

....

Flat Files or Directories

Some applications simply locate their configuration files in the same directory in
which they are installed. Normally, Unix applications place their configuration files
in the /etc directory, however, so this technique is most commonly seen in applications that are ported to Unix from another platform, or that have no global
configuration requirements at all (such as the OpenOffice productivity application).

Additionally, users sometimes install software in a specific directory that differs
from the default directory. For example, if the Apache web server is built from
source and placed in /usr/local/apache-2.0, its configuration files will be found in
/usr/local/apache-2.0/etc. (Normally, these would be found in simply /etc.)

Servers Launched by inetd

Some server applications are not stand-alone servers, but rather services
managed and launched on demand by the inetd superserver. Services such as
these do not have their own configuration files, but are instead passed whatever
information they require by inetd when they are launched. The inetd program, in
turn, provides a way to specify configuration information for each service. There
are several different implementations of the inetd server, and each has its own
method of configuring the services.

User Libraries

Some software is not intended to be used by itself, but is rather providing functionality other programs rely on (i.e., some software is shipped as libraries used by
other programs). This software may or may not have any configuration needs. For
example, the Dante library, which provides SOCKS5 functionality, requires a

configuration file defining which servers and addresses Dante uses, while the OpenSSL library, which provides various cryptographic algorithms, requires no run-time configuration at all. User libraries that require configuration information generally follow one of the other patterns (such as flat configuration files and the drop-in directory) discussed in the earlier subsections.

Configuring the User Environment

Sometimes software requires (or simply allows) that users set additional configuration values. Typically this is user-specific information such as home directory, location of various files, etc., and it is usually handled by setting shell variables. For the newly installed software to function correctly for a given user, the user may need to set some environment variables in her login shell.

Users can always do this themselves, and for software that's used only by a small number of users, that works fine. However, commonly used software demands that many users set the environment variables, and this quickly becomes an administrative burden. In these cases, it is necessary for the administrator to configure the software globally; however, how this is done varies from system to system.

CROSS-REFERENCE *The user environments for Red Hat Linux, Debian, and Slackware are described in Chapters 4, 5, and 6, respectively; the information in those chapters should be enough of a head start to figure out how to customize any Unix-like system's global user environment. In particular, see Red Hat's mechanism in Chapter 4. It appears to be catching on even among non–open source applications.*

Hooking into the Operating System

For end-user applications, installation is complete once the user environment is configured. However, server applications are obviously only useful when they are running, and so servers need to be hooked into the startup process of the computer. Each Unix system does this in its own way, but there are two general methods in common use.

One method is the set of startup scripts used by AT&T System V (SysV), and the other is the equivalent startup script mechanism used by BSD. These two systems serve the same purpose, but they are very different in practice. The SysV approach uses the "drop-in file configuration directory" technique described earlier in this chapter, while the BSD approach is simpler but relies on a single file. Red Hat Linux uses the SysV technique, while Debian and Slackware use the BSD technique. For more information on the SysV technique, see Chapter 4; for information on the BSD approach, see Chapter 5.

Software Installation Tools

This chapter has described a variety of tools and techniques for software installation. This section will describe the following tools and discuss the ones provided by most distributions:

- GNU autoconf

- Red Hat's RPM

- Slackware's tarballs

- Debian's dpkg format

After reading this material, users will be familiar with how software is built and installed on a variety of distributions. This section probably isn't quite a complete reference, but it can be viewed as a sort of "quick guide" for using these tools. The most common uses are covered, but readers who need more extensive information should consult the documentation for the specific tools.

Using GNU autoconf

Many open source packages use the GNU *autoconf* tools to configure the software's compile-time options. GNU autoconf works by generating standard Makefiles from templates produced by the developers of the software. The autoconf tools scan a system, looking for the presence or absence of specific features by compiling small test programs. The Makefiles that it generates are then used to automate the actual compilation of the software.

GNU autoconf can be somewhat arcane to write templates for; fortunately, only the software developers have to worry about that, and the tools are fairly straightforward for users who are only interested in building a package. Usually, there will be a program called "configure" in the top directory of the source code tree; users simply run ./configure and the program will examine the system and construct Makefiles, header files, and similar files used by the make tool and by the source code.

The ./configure program generally takes a number of arguments. The most common of these is the --prefix option, which sets the destination directory that the software will be installed into; for example, the command ./configure --prefix=/usr/local/my-software-1.0 will configure the software so that it is installed into /usr/local/my-software-1.0. Many packages support their own options via configure; users can check what options are available by executing the command ./configure --help. After the software has been configured in this way, users simply run make, which will build the software, and usually make install to complete the installation. A given package's documentation will explain the specific compile-time configuration options for that package, but Table 7-1 lists some common parameters used by GNU autoconf.

Table 7-1. Common Options for GNU autoconf's configure Program

OPTION	MEANING
--help	Displays the list of arguments and options supported by this package
--prefix=[path]	Causes the software to be installed in the directory [path]
--host=[name]	Specifies the architecture and platform of the computer building the software; for example, alphaev56-unknown-linux-gnu or i686-unknown-linux-gnu; used to specify that the software should be built for a different architecture than the default
--with-include-dir=[path], --with-lib-dir=[path]	Adds [path] to the list of directories containing header files or libraries for the build process
--enable-[option]	Activates the option named [option] in the software
--with-[package]=[path]	Instructs the build process to look for the package named [package] in the directory [path]; for example, --with-openssl=/usr/local/openssl-0.9.5a

Watch Out for the Prefix!

Normally, specifying an installation directory with the --prefix option to ./configure causes all files to be placed in subdirectories of the prefix. For example, --prefix=/usr/local will cause configuration files to be placed in /usr/local/etc, program binaries in /usr/local/bin, and so on.

However, some packages treat a prefix of /usr as a special case. These packages will place binaries and libraries in /usr/bin and /usr/lib, but will place configuration files in /etc (rather than /usr/etc as might be expected). Watch out for these programs! To override this behavior, you can probably add an option such as `--config-prefix=/usr/etc`.

GNU autoconf is an extremely powerful tool for writing *portable* software (that is, software that runs on multiple operating systems) since it can customize a Makefile for almost any Unix-like system. Because it's so powerful, it's also very widely used. These days, you'd be hard-pressed to find an open source software package that *didn't* use these tools! A working understanding of the autoconf tools is a huge benefit to any user or administrator of a Linux-based system.

Using Red Hat's Tools

The packaging system used by Red Hat Linux—the Red Hat Package Manager (RPM)—was described in Chapter 4. That chapter briefly mentioned the support RPM has for source packages. This section will describe that functionality in more detail.

RPMs and Architectures

Each RPM package has an "architecture" associated with it. Normally, this architecture denotes the hardware platform for which the package was compiled; for example, a .i386.rpm package is an RPM compiled for the Intel platform. A source RPM has the extension .src.rpm. Whereas a binary RPM is obviously only useful on platforms for which it was compiled, a source RPM can be built into a binary RPM and so is useful for a variety of tasks.

Construction of Source RPMs

Typically, a source RPM is constructed to match the configuration of a binary RPM. For example, along with the actual installation CDs, Red Hat also ships CDs containing source RPMs for each package included with the system. When built, these source RPMs will produce RPMs just like the ones included on the installation CDs. That is, rebuilding all the source RPMs will duplicate all the RPMs on the CDs. This is useful, for example, in building a copy of Red Hat Linux on a platform for which Red Hat does not deliver a distribution (though in practice it's seldom that simple).

Each source RPM is built with a specific configuration. That is, the contents of the source RPM are set up with a predetermined set of compile-time options.

How these options are specified varies by the software being packaged; the most common method, as mentioned earlier in this chapter, is through GNU autconf. These compile-time options are specified in *RPM specification files* with extensions of .spec. The .spec files can be customized to alter the configuration of an RPM.

RPM Commands

The RPM command can be used to build binary RPMs from source, and there are generally two ways to accomplish this. The quickest and simplest method is to rebuild a source RPM into a binary package with its default configuration. This can be accomplished with the command rpm --rebuild <filename>.

The rpm --rebuild command recompiles a source package with its default configuration. In cases where a source RPM's settings need to be customized, a somewhat lengthier process can be used. Each source RPM usually contains a tarball containing the software, the specification file for the RPM, and sometimes supporting files (such as patches to be applied to the software). Installing a source RPM (via the usual rpm --install command described in Chapter 4) causes these files to be extracted and installed, and then they can be customized.

Contents of the /usr/src/redhat Directory

Installing a source RPM on a Red Hat system causes its contents to be placed in the /usr/src/redhat directory. This directory contains several subdirectories; the uses of these directories are described in Table 7-2.

Table 7-2. Red Hat Linux /usr/src/redhat Contents

DIRECTORY	CONTENTS
BUILD	Separate, temporary scratch subdirectories for packages as they are built from source code
RPMS	Completed (i.e., compiled) binary RPM packages of source RPMs that were successfully built
SOURCES	Source code tarballs and patches used to build software extracted from source RPMs that are installed
SPECS	Specification files for building binary RPM packages from source code installed in SOURCES
SRPMS	Copies of source RPMs (SRPMS) that have been installed, for later reference

After a source RPM is installed, it can be customized by editing its .spec file, which will be placed in /usr/src/redhat/SPECS. After editing the RPM's .spec file, the `rpm -ba <filename>` command can be used to instruct RPM to build the package, including all stages. (There are several stages to an RPM build, from configuration to installation, and each phase can be specified independently, though usually this isn't necessary.) The .spec file will be examined and its contents (which are much like a script) will be executed to compile the package. During this process, it will attempt to locate the tarball for the source code in /usr/src/redhat/SOURCES, and when the process is complete, it will place the new binary RPM in /usr/src/redhat/RPMS.

In most cases, system administrators and users need to alter a few configuration options, such as disabling a compile-time feature or altering a path. These needs can be met by the preceding techniques. For more complicated tasks, though, users should consult Red Hat's extensive RPM documentation at `www.redhat.com`. (Alternatively, the *Maximum RPM* reference book is included in digital form on the documentation CD of recent Red Hat Linux distributions.)

Using Slackware's Tools

The Slackware Linux distribution was discussed in Chapter 5. Slackware's packaging mechanism is based on simple tarballs, which are standard compressed Unix tar (Tape Archive) files. Typically these files have extensions of .tar.gz or .tar.Z. Since it uses such a simple format, Slackware has limited capability to add extensive support for source code packages.

The typical method for installing a package from source code on a Slackware Linux system is therefore pretty simple. The administrator simply builds the package manually, by whatever mechanism is required, and then constructs a Slackware package from it and installs it via the standard tools. Typically, this involves running the ./configure script that is provided with most packages.

For example, you might install the hypothetical package my-software to the directory /opt/my-software-1.0 by following these instructions:

1. Download the source code tarball, and consult the documentation for compile-time options.

2. Extract the software source code into a convenient directory, such as /usr/src/my-software. Choose a temporary directory to "install" the software to, such as /tmp/my-software-tmp/opt/my-software-1.0. This will not be the permanent location, but is instead passed to the command that follows.

3. Run the ./configure program with the appropriate arguments, in particular the --prefix option (e.g., ./configure --prefix=/tmp/my-software-tmp/opt/my-software-1.0).

4. Build the software via the make command; when it completes, "install" it into the temporary directory via the make install command.

5. Enter the temporary directory—that is, cd /tmp/my-software-1.0.

6. Create a Slackware package from the temporary directory, via a command such as makepkg /tmp/my-software-1.0.tgz. This command will create the Slackware package (which is simply a standard tarball with some extra information).

7. Install the newly created package via the command installpkg /tmp/my-software-1.0.

Some readers may wonder why the software was built and installed into a temporary directory such as /tmp/my-software-1.0 in steps 3 and 4. The other alternative would have been to directly install the software in its ultimate location (such as /opt, /usr/local, or the root directory). However, if this approach is used, the software will be installed in its permanent location, without the knowledge of the packaging tools. This means that the tools won't be able to uninstall, upgrade, or otherwise manage the package. Instead, the software is installed in a temporary scratch directory, so that the makepkg tool can be run to locate and consolidate all the files. When the package is installed, the tools will know about it and therefore be able to manage it. (In reality, you could always just edit the contents of /var/log/packages directly, but that's a lot of work and defeats the purpose of the tools in the first place!)

One last thing to note about the installation process is the actual temporary directory chosen. In this example, it was /tmp/my-software-tmp/opt/my-software-1.0. The reason for this is to make sure that the software is installed into its temporary directory in such a way that the makepkg tool can properly create the package. The tool will include all files and subdirectories contained in the current directory in the resulting package; thus, by installing the software into the temporary /tmp/my-software-tmp/opt/my-software-1.0 and running the command from /tmp/my-software-tmp, the package will be created so that all files are stored in opt/my-software-1.0. Since installpkg will install the files relative to the root directory, this will cause the package contents to be placed in /opt/my-software-1.0—which was the original goal. Similarly, if the goal was to install into /usr/local, meanwhile, the scratch directory would have been /tmp/my-software-tmp/usr/local.

Slackware's tools are very simple, in keeping with the Slackware philosophy. This makes them easy to use but still leaves the administrator a bit more work to do. (Compare this example for Slackware with the shorter `rpm --rebuild` command used on Red Hat Linux systems.) On the other hand, even though Slackware's tools may require a bit more work when building software from source code, they're a lot easier to understand and don't require as much study as more sophisticated tools.

Using Debian's Tools

Building Debian packages is accomplished using the dpkg-deb program included with Debian GNU/Linux. This tool has similarities to the approaches of both RPM and Slackware's system. Specifically, Debian's system has a custom format for archives, but it generally builds such packages by simply processing and storing up the contents of a particular directory. The custom format makes Debian's system similar to RPM, in that you can perform operations like install, uninstall, and query on packages, and the system itself keeps track of dependencies for you. However, *creating* such packages involves just archiving the contents of the (specially prepared) current directory, which is similar to Slackware's approach.

 CROSS-REFERENCE   *Creating Debian packages is also discussed in the "Manipulating Debian Package Archives" section in Chapter 6.*

For example, suppose you wanted to create a Debian package for the hypothetical "my-software" package considered in the previous section on Slackware's tools. At a very high level, the step for building such a package for Debian is very similar to the seven steps outlined in the Slackware section. The main differences are that instead of using the `makepkg` command in step 6, you'd use the command `dpkg-deb --build /tmp/my-software-1.0.deb`. Similarly, once you've created the package, you would use the command `dpkg -i /tmp/my-software-.0.deb` to install it, rather than the `installpkg` command in step 7.

As you can see, creating Debian packages from source code is conceptually fairly similar to the equivalent process on Slackware Linux. On the other hand, once you have the file in hand, you can perform various queries on it (such as listing its contents, or fetching its description) as you could with an RPM. However, this story isn't quite complete, and there is another way in which Debian's system is similar to Red Hat's.

Specifically, the process just outlined omits a very important step—namely, the creation of the required files and directory for Debian archives. In order to run correctly, the dpkg-deb command expects to find a directory named "debian" as a subdirectory of the tree you wish to build into a Debian package. This directory contains several additional files, which are summarized in Table 7-3.

Table 7-3. Debian Archive Files

FILE	PURPOSE
control	Contains basic information about the software being packaged, such as its version, description, and dependencies
rules	A script used to prepare the directory's contents for packaging
changelog	Lists a history of changes made to the package
copyright	Identifies the copyright holder and related issues

You've probably realized by now that when taken together, the files outlined in Table 7-3 amount to the equivalent of Red Hat's ".spec" files for RPM packages. These files are used by the dpkg-deb command to prepare the directory and construct the Debian package from its contents. Thus, while mechanically the process has similarities to Red Hat (in that it builds an archive from the contents of the current directory), it also has strong similarities to Red Hat. Clearly, there's more than one way to skin this particular cat. (Most commercial Unix flavors usually each have yet another way of tackling this problem.)

Unless you're a software developer, you may not need to create Debian packages at all. As a user, all you probably *need* to know about this process is that it's not as easy to rebuild a Debian package from source code as it is an RPM, since there is no ready-packaged "source .deb" akin to a "source RPM." Since this isn't a book on software development or how to build Debian packages, if you need more detail than that you should consult the Debian Project's documentation, which you can find at www.debian.org/doc/manuals/programmer/index.html.

Summary

A system is customized through the software and software configurations installed on it. This chapter outlined some of the basic decisions that must be made and steps that must be taken in order to install a new software package on a Linux system. Chapter 8 describes in detail the installation procedures for several popular software packages. Now that you've read this chapter, you have the basic tools you need to perform almost any software installation, from the decision-making stage all the way to installation.

CHAPTER 8

OpenSSH
Secure Shell

Chapter 7 covered the basics of software installation. It also provided some rules
of thumb and general techniques that are useful in the installation of many types
of software. This chapter is the first of six that will go into detail on the installations of several common, real-world applications. These chapters can be used
as references. After reading them you'll be able to install almost any software you
come across, on almost any system.

OpenSSH is a subproject of the OpenBSD project. The OpenBSD project is
one of the free, open source offshoots of the original BSD Unix-like system. (See
Chapter 1 for a discussion of the lineage of Unix systems.) OpenBSD is focused on
security, and it makes extensive use of strong cryptography, rigorous code
auditing, and other security measures. OpenSSH is the implementation of the
Internet Engineering Task Force's (IETF) Secure Shell (SSH) protocol standard,
which is developed by the IETF's secsh working group. OpenSSH has been ported
to a variety of platforms, including Linux-based systems.

OpenSSH is composed of both a server and a suite of clients. The server
program, named sshd, provides encrypted, secure remote access to a server or
workstation. The clients remotely access servers running sshd (or another
compatible program) and provide functionality such as simple remote login (via
the ssh client program) and secure file transfers (via the scp, "secure copy," and
sftp, "secure FTP," programs). Since SSH is a standard protocol, the OpenSSH
clients and server interoperate with any other software that implements the SSH
protocol.

The OpenSSH package that is installed on Linux systems is not actually the
same version that ships with OpenBSD systems. OpenSSH comes in two flavors:
the core OpenBSD version and a slight variant of it, which is the "portable"
version. This portable version is maintained in parallel to the core OpenBSD
version and is what users actually download and install on non-BSD systems.

OpenSSH is fairly straightforward to install and configure. OpenSSH relies on
the OpenSSL generic cryptography library for some of its functionality. (OpenSSL
is provided by most distributions, so it is already present on most recent systems.
If it's not present on your system, you can install it in a fashion similar to that
described later in this chapter for the Dante library.) Once installed, it looks for

configuration files (for both client and server programs) in a specific directory, which is normally /etc/ssh. The configuration files in that directory control the run-time behavior of OpenSSH.

OpenSSH itself is provided by most distributions. Citing it as an example here might therefore be viewed as somewhat redundant. However, as this book aims to be useful beyond mere Linux systems, OpenSSH was selected as an example anyway. The material from this section can be applied to install OpenSSH not only on Linux systems that don't already have it (such as older distributions), but also on other Unix-like systems, such as commercial systems. An SSH implementation is a must-have, and OpenSSH is one of the best around. In addition, its utility as a classic example of an application configured from /etc contributed to OpenSSH's inclusion in this chapter.

Just the Facts: OpenSSH

Purpose: Free implementation of the SSH (Secure SHell) remote access protocol

Authors: The OpenBSD Project

Web site: www.openssh.org

Description: OpenSSH is a free (open source) implementation of the Internet Engineering Task Force's (IETF) standard SSH protocol. This protocol provides strongly encrypted, secure access to remote systems via a telnet-like interface.

Installing OpenSSH

The following sections describe the process of installing OpenSSH. They discuss not only the mechanics of installation, but also the details and decisions—for example, how to choose an installation directory. After reading this material, you'll be able to install OpenSSH on any system.

Compile-Time Options

Like all examples in this book, you will compile OpenSSH from source code. The first step in building software is, as discussed in Chapter 7, to decide on compile-time options. This section will discuss the compile-time options supported by OpenSSH and provide an actual detailed configuration appropriate for a real-world system.

Choosing an Installation Path

The first option that is relevant to almost every software package is the installation directory—that is, the directory where the compiled program is to be installed. Chapters 3 and 7 discussed some typical options for installation directories, namely the /opt and /usr/local directories. Chapter 7 provides complete details, but in general the /opt directory is appropriate for software that might need to be upgraded regularly or need more than one version installed, while /usr/local is more appropriate for software that is upgraded infrequently. Since OpenSSH is typically upgraded infrequently, this example will install it into /usr/local.

Selecting the Configuration Options

OpenSSH supports a wide variety of configuration options. Generally these configuration options relate to whether to enable various authentication mechanisms (such as Kerberos or "smart card" support) and a few other things, such as whether to support the new IPv6 Internet protocol standard. These options, meanwhile, generally boil down to whether or not the operating system supports them; for example, if the operating system doesn't have or use Kerberos libraries, then it doesn't make sense for OpenSSH to enable Kerberos support (and in fact the process will fail if you try). Since the ./configure program will automatically detect whether each of these options is available on the system and enable or disable the option appropriately, there's no need for you to worry about them.

That isn't a general rule, though: Many programs come with options that enable or disable actual features in the program. In such cases, there's no way for the program to do any autodetection; after all, how does a program automatically detect whether you want a certain feature disabled? In those cases, features can be explicitly disabled and enabled. (See the section later in Part Three on the Apache web server for an example of this type of installation.)

Additionally, even though most OpenSSH features get autodetected, under some circumstances you might actually not want this behavior. For example, you may not want OpenSSH to use Kerberos authentication, even if it's installed on the system. In such cases, you can consult the documentation and the ./configure --help command to find out how to disable the unneeded features.

In a nutshell, your OpenSSH installation probably needs no custom options, except to set the installation path. Use the following command to configure it. (This command will change if you choose to explicitly enable or disable one or more of the automatically detected features.)

```
$ ./configure --prefix=/usr/local
```

Note that the --prefix option indicates /usr/local as the installation directory. This means that the program binaries will be installed in /usr/local/bin, configuration files in /usr/local/etc, and so on. If the command completes without any errors, the software should be ready for compilation.

Installing from Source Code

Once the ./configure program has been run as discussed in the previous section, the software can actually be built. This is very simple; it consists of running the make command followed by the make install command, as shown here:

```
$ make
```

(Information on the build process will scroll by.)

```
$ make install
```

(Information on the installation process will scroll by.)

In addition to copying files, the make install command will also run a few scripts that set up cryptographic server keys and other basic details. If the make install command (and the make command before it) both complete successfully, then OpenSSH is installed! If either failed, it probably means that something went wrong in the configuration process; check to see if the ./configure command actually completed successfully and that the various options you may have passed to it are correct. (For example, watch for possible typos in path names.)

Configuring OpenSSH

With the installation path of /usr/local, the OpenSSH configuration files will be placed in /usr/local/etc. (This can be altered with the --sysconfdir= option, which is used to point to a different configuration path, such as /etc instead of /usr/local/etc. However, it's generally a good idea to leave the configuration files in the default location, unless there is a reason not to.)

There are a number of OpenSSH-related files in /usr/local/etc. Most of them contain the public and private keys for the server, for both the RSA and DSA systems. (RSA and DSA are public-key cryptographic algorithms. For information on these systems, consult a book on cryptography.) The public and private key files are ssh_host_dsa_key, ssh_host_rsa_key, ssh_host_dsa_key.pub, ssh_host_rsa_key.pub, ssh_host_key, and ssh_key_key.pub. Each of these files is in the /usr/local/etc directory. These files are automatically created when the software is installed, so you shouldn't have to do anything with them, unless you need to (such as if you're copying key files from another server). Another related file is /usr/local/etc/moduli, which is used as part of the cryptographic key exchange. Like the key files, you shouldn't need to do anything with this file.

The remaining files are /usr/local/etc/ssh_config and /usr/local/etc/sshd_config. These are the real "bread and butter" configuration files for OpenSSH. They configure the ssh client program and the sshd server program, respectively.

....

Upgrading OpenSSH

Eventually, an updated version of the OpenSSH package will be released, and you may wish to upgrade to it. In this case, you will need to upgrade the binary files without altering the configuration files. For example, you don't want to overwrite the private key files, or else your system's SSH identity will change, which can be very inconvenient to users. So, you need to be careful when upgrading to avoid losing the configuration files.

Most distributions include OpenSSH with the base installation and provide periodic upgrades if they are required. (For example, Red Hat Linux includes an RPM package for OpenSSH, and Red Hat periodically releases updated versions.) In these cases, the system's native packager will handle upgrading the binaries without altering the configuration files.

If you follow this book's example and install from source code, however, then you are relying on the source code package's installation scripts to copy the new binaries. Such scripts also install default copies of the configuration files. If the script isn't "smart" enough to see that copies are already installed, it may over-write them. Therefore, it's always a good policy to back up your configuration files before installing a new piece of software. In the case of OpenSSH, the scripts are in fact smart enough to avoid overwriting existing copies of the configuration files, but a good administrator is always wary.

....

Configuring the ssh Client

The configuration file for the ssh client program is /usr/local/etc/ssh_config. (This file is also used by the other client programs, such as the "secure copy" scp program and the "secure FTP" sftp program.) The file contains a number of lines, each of which sets a different option that controls the run-time behavior of the OpenSSH client. The file format is straightforward. First, a host is specified via a "Host" line, and then options for that host are listed. If additional hosts are required, another Host line can be included followed by options for that host. A Host line consisting of "Host *" will match any host and so is effectively the default host.

After installation, /usr/local/etc/ssh_config will contain a typical default configuration. This is a pretty generic setup optimized for maximum security; that is, it leaves only basic options set and disables the "riskiest" features. For example, by default /usr/local/etc/ssh_config disables SSH agent forwarding, since it can be a security vulnerability if not used carefully. The default options are pretty reasonable, so generally it doesn't need to be modified that much.

OpenSSH supports a fairly large number of options, and most of these are related to the nuances of the cryptographic systems and algorithms it supports. Covering all these options and their nuances is really a task best left to the OpenSSH documentation, such as the manual page (which is quite detailed). However, it is worthwhile to cover two common examples of how to change an option from its default.

Enabling SSH Agent Forwarding

Recall that OpenSSH by default disables SSH agent forwarding. An *SSH agent* is a special program (usually named ssh-agent) that runs in the background and manages private keys for a user. The SSH agent is given the name of a program it is to run, and it then manages keys for that program and all children spawned by that program. The most common way to use this is to start ssh-agent up to manage a login shell, such as via the command ssh-agent bash. Once the special program ssh-add is used to add a key for ssh-agent to manage, all programs spawned by that shell will be able to automatically make use of the key.

Essentially, this means that the user won't have to enter the secret passphrase to unlock the key whenever it's used; the ssh-agent program will handle that. An example of using ssh-agent follows. If the user has her keys set up correctly on the local and remote servers (as described by the SSH documentation), then the following commands will set up and make use of an SSH agent:

```
$ exec ssh-agent bash
$ ssh-add
```
(ssh-add will prompt the user for her passphrase)
```
$ ssh my.remote.host
```

(ssh will fetch the key from ssh-agent and log in automatically.)

After logging in to my.remote.host (which will happen automatically in the preceding example), the user may wish to log in to a second remote system, as if it were a relay or leapfrog. If SSH agent forwarding is enabled (and the remote server also allows it), then the agent that was initially set up on the local machine will again be used to log in to the second remote machine. If agent forwarding is disabled, then the user will have to type a passphrase or password.

If this seems confusing, then you now understand one reason why agent forwarding is disabled by default: It's simply too easy to get wrong. Another potential major issue is that enabling SSH agent forwarding exposes your account to additional weaknesses known as *man-in-the-middle* attacks, in which a trusted intermediate server (a "man in the middle") is compromised. The consequence of these weaknesses could be that a user accidentally puts his account in a state where an attacker could gain access to a remote system without even needing the user's password or SSH passphrase. Before you use SSH agents, you should carefully read and understand the OpenSSH documentation and configure your system and account properly.

If you do wish to use SSH agent forwarding, it will have to be enabled on your local system. To activate it, edit the following line in /usr/local/etc/ssh_config to be "yes" from the default "no." The change will take effect the next time a client program is run.

```
ForwardAgent no
```

Really, this is all a roundabout way of describing how to make a change in the ssh_config file. Each option has a value, and configuring the program is as simple as changing the values of options. However, OpenSSH is only as secure as its configuration, and it is very easy to configure OpenSSH in an insecure way. A wise administrator will read the OpenSSH documentation thoroughly before making any changes.

Disabling Strict Host Key Checking

Another option that is enabled in the default /usr/local/etc/ssh_config file is strict host key checking. OpenSSH implements the RSA and DSA public-key cryptosystems, meaning that both client and server have secret keys that allow them to unambiguously identify each other. However, if two computers have never "met" before (i.e., if they have not already exchanged their keys), then there is no way for them to verify each other's identities.

The OpenSSH clients have two options for handling this case. They can either abort connections to hosts with unknown keys or simply add the host's key to their list of known keys and issue a warning to the user. The first option is known as *strict host key checking* and can be enabled or disabled in the /usr/local/etc/ssh_config file. Using strict host key checking is more secure, since it helps prevent man-in-the-middle attacks similar to the one mentioned earlier; however, it's less convenient since it requires users to manually import keys from servers they trust (or it requires them to manually override the option on the command line). As always, it's a tradeoff between security and convenience, and you must carefully weigh your options. For more information on strict host key checking, consult the OpenSSH documentation at www.openssh.org.

If you decide to disable strict host key checking, the procedure is the same as for enabling SSH agent forwarding (discussed in the previous section). That is, locate the following line in /usr/local/etc/ssh_config and change the default "yes" value enabling strict key checking to "no."

```
StrictHostKeyChecking yes
```

Once this change has been made, the OpenSSH clients will start automatically adding the keys for remote servers to the user's list of known keys. A warning will be issued, but it becomes the responsibility of the user to be wary of untrustworthy remote hosts. (Note, however, that users can override this behavior in their own configurations. In general, ssh_config changes only the *default* options for clients.)

If disabling strict host key checking outright isn't palatable, there's also a third option, called "ask," that can be used as a compromise. When in this mode, the ssh clients will neither automatically add nor reject unknown keys. Instead, they'll prompt the user whenever an unknown key is encountered, asking whether it should be accepted. This requires user input, but it's less inconvenient than leaving strict host key checking on. To enable this option, simply use "ask" instead of "no" or "yes" in the preceding line.

Configurations in Binary Packages

The examples in this section on changing the default configurations of the OpenSSH clients and server demonstrate how to make such changes in general. The procedures will work on any installation of OpenSSH, whether it came from an installation from source code or from a binary installation such as an RPM file or a Slackware package. However, it's important to remember that these prepackaged binary installations are themselves set up with a specific configuration, which may not be the same as the default installation from the pristine OpenSSH source code. (For example, the OpenSSH installation that Red Hat ships with their distribution comes with strict host key checking already disabled, whereas it's enabled in the pristine installation.) So, always check to make sure a change you're making hasn't already been made, and don't be confused if you find that it has been. "Installer beware," so to speak.

Configuring the sshd Server

Configuring the sshd server is very similar to configuring the client programs. The /usr/local/etc/sshd_config file contains multiple lines, where each line sets the value of a particular option. As with ssh_config, sshd_config contains a reasonable set of default values. Changing the value of an SSH option is also as simple as editing the appropriate line in the file.

Again, OpenSSH can easily be rendered insecure by poor configuration options, so it is crucial to read and understand the OpenSSH documentation (such as the man page for sshd) before you make any configuration changes. However, one popular change is to enable X Window connection forwarding.

Enabling X Window Connection Forwarding

Frequently, a user will log in to a remote machine from an xterm or other shell that is running within an X Window environment. Usually, X programs that the user runs on the remote machine are intended to be displayed on the local machine physically present in front of the user. (After all, the program's not much use if the user can't see it.) Normally, the user would have to set a DISPLAY environment variable in order for the program to behave correctly; however, OpenSSH supports X connection forwarding to automatically handle this.

That is, the sshd server and ssh client can automatically establish a "tunnel" across which X programs on the remote machine can be run. When a client logs in, the sshd server on the remote system establishes a virtual or phantom X Window server that programs running on that system can connect to. This server simply relays any programs that connect to it back along the SSH connection to the user's own local system. Aside from the convenience of the automatically configured DISPLAY variable, the connection is also encrypted. Thus, X Window connection forwarding is a very useful and popular feature of OpenSSH.

However, under certain circumstances it can be a security hole (since it might prevent unwanted access to the user's X server, or even worse), so the default OpenSSH configuration has X connection forwarding disabled. To enable it, simply locate the following line in /usr/local/etc/sshd_config and change the default "no" to "yes":

```
X11Forwarding no
```

Note that this will enable X connection forwarding on your local machine, meaning that it will allow users who log into your system via SSH to make use of X connection forwarding. If you are a user who wishes to make use of X connection forwarding on a remote server, a similar change will have to be made on the remote server.

OpenSSH Configuration Summary

Once it's installed, configuring OpenSSH is generally pretty easy. It is, however, important to understand all the consequences of a configuration change before making it. OpenSSH is responsible for letting users log into a system, after all, and so a misconfiguration could potentially hand an attacker the keys to the system. However, the actual act of configuration is very easy: Just edit the appropriate line for the option that is to be updated.

Installing OpenSSH on Different Distributions

The previous section discussed the configuration of the OpenSSH client and server programs. Since OpenSSH has a server component, however, that server has to be hooked into the operating system's bootup process. The following sections describe how to accomplish that on each of the sample distributions.

Installing OpenSSH on Red Hat Linux

As discussed in the "System Startup Scripts" section of Chapter 4, Red Hat Linux uses the SysV model of system initialization scripts. In this model, a special directory contains many scripts, each of which manages a specific server or service. When the system starts up, it is configured to execute these scripts. This section describes how to configure the OpenSSH server for use with Red Hat's implementation of the SysV model. Actually, the OpenSSH source code distribution includes such a script ready-made; however, it's useful to see how one of these scripts works, so a less sophisticated and simpler version is presented.

To be compatible with the SysV model, a script minimally needs to support three arguments: stop, start, and restart. Installing OpenSSH on Red Hat Linux, then, involves writing a shell script that understands these three commands. The stop command shuts down the sshd daemon, the start command starts it up, and the restart command both shuts it down and starts it up again. The script in Listing 8-1 demonstrates a very basic SysV-compatible init script.

Listing 8-1. SysV-compatible Script for OpenSSH sshd

```
#!/bin/sh
# chkconfig: 345 25 25
# description: Manages the OpenSSH sshd server.
```

```
[ -x /usr/local/sbin/sshd ] || exit 0

RC=0

start () {
    echo $"Starting sshd."
    /usr/local/sbin/sshd
    return 0
}

stop () {
    echo $"Stopping sshd."
    [ -e /var/run/sshd.pid ] && kill -TERM `cat /var/run/sshd.pid`
    RC=$?
    return $RC
}

restart () {
    stop
    start
    RC=$?
    return $RC
}

# See how we were called.
case "$1" in
    start)
        start
        ;;
    stop)
        stop
        ;;
    restart)
        restart
        ;;
    *)
        echo $"Usage: $0 {start|stop|restart}"
        RETVAL=1
esac

exit $RETVAL
```

Particularly noteworthy in Listing 8-1 are the first two lines, which enable the script to be used with Red Hat's chkconfig and service tools. This means that the file can simply be placed (or a link to it created) in /etc/rc.d/init.d, and then chkconfig can be used to manage it. The following commands demonstrate how to install and use the sshd script in Listing 8-1:

```
$ cp listing-8x.sh /etc/rc.d/init.d/sshd
$ chkconfig --add sshd
$ service sshd start
```

Listing 8-1 is minimal: It doesn't include many niceties, but it does get the basic job done. A good script programmer will immediately spot additional ways in which the script could be more robust or useful. However, the objective of Listing 8-1 is to demonstrate how to construct a basic SysV-compatible script, not to teach advanced scripting, so it is very basic.

Recall that OpenSSH itself actually includes a vastly more robust version of Listing 8-1 in the contrib/redhat/sshd.init file of the source code package. This script is the one Red Hat uses in their RPM-packaged version of OpenSSH, and there is absolutely no reason not to use the official OpenSSH script instead of Listing 8-1. The goal of Listing 8-1 is to demonstrate a basic script. If someone gives you a better script, by all means use it.

Installing OpenSSH on Slackware Linux

As discussed in the "System Startup Scripts" section of Chapter 5, Slackware Linux uses the BSD model for its initialization scripts. In this model, there is essentially a single script that is responsible for most system startup tasks; however, Slackware's version of this system also includes very basic support for SysV-compatible scripts. This section discusses how to configure the OpenSSH sshd server to be started on bootup on a Slackware Linux system.

Recall that there are two ways to configure OpenSSH's server to run on Slackware Linux. One way is to modify the system's /etc/rc.d/rc.M or /etc/rc.d/rc.inet2 script and directly include script code similar to that in Listing 8-1. This would indeed cause the server to be started when the system boots up.

However, as mentioned in the previous section, OpenSSH actually includes a SysV-compatible script for starting and stopping the server. Since Slackware also provides basic support for SysV, it might also make sense to simply use the file provided for Red Hat Linux with Slackware's /etc/rc.d/rc.sysvinit mechanism. Unfortunately, the file provided with OpenSSH requires files specific to Red Hat Linux's implementation of the SysV model, so that file can't be used on Slackware Linux without modification.

However, Listing 8-1 is much simpler, and so it *could* be used on Slackware, without modification. Simply place Listing 8-1 into the appropriate subdirectory of /etc/rc.d and it will be handled automatically by Slackware's startup process.

 CROSS-REFERENCE *See Chapter 5 for more information on /etc/rc.d.*

Either option (directly editing /etc/rc.d/rc.M or /etc/rc.d/rc.inet2, or using the SysV approach) is a perfectly serviceable solution. Which one an administrator will prefer is really a matter of taste; for example, one administrator may prefer to keep all startup activities in /etc/rc.d/rc.M to avoid accidentally overlooking one, while another may prefer to recycle SysV scripts that have already been written in order to save labor. There's more than one way to do it, as is typical of Slackware Linux.

Installing OpenSSH on Debian GNU/Linux

Installing OpenSSH on Debian GNU/Linux is very similar to installing it on Red Hat Linux. Since Debian GNU/Linux uses the same initscripts model as Red Hat Linux—namely, the SysV model—then the material discussed previously that applies to Red Hat Linux also applies to Debian GNU/Linux.

Also as with Red Hat Linux, Debian GNU/Linux includes a package for OpenSSH with the base distribution. This means that you can probably just use the Debian package (with your own custom configurations as discussed throughout this Chapter, of course) as is, unless you need to upgrade it yourself.

About the only substantial difference between installing OpenSSH on Debian GNU/Linux and Red Hat Linux is that Debian doesn't include Red Hat's service and chkconfig tools; instead, you'll have to use Debian's own update-rc.d program, as discussed in the "Working with Debian's Tools" section of Chapter 6.

Summary

The OpenBSD project's OpenSSH program is a highly compatible, robust implementation of the standard IETF SSH protocol. Installing the portable form of OpenSSH suitable for Linux systems is quite straightforward, though many distributions provide a more convenient prepackaged form. Configuring OpenSSH is generally as simple as editing the appropriate file, depending on whether you are attempting to configure the client or server programs. However, it's important to be cautious since it's easy to misconfigure OpenSSH so that it is in an insecure state.

More generally, this chapter illustrated how to install a generic, stand-alone server or daemon program, and hook it into the operating system. By reading this chapter, you've gained insight into how other similar programs are installed, and you've also gained a little real-world experience into how to install and properly configure a fairly complicated program. The next chapter demonstrates a different software installation technique, using Pluggable Authentication Modules as an example.

CHAPTER 9

Pluggable Authentication Modules

The Pluggable Authentication Modules (PAM) system is a generalized API for system authentication. It was originally developed by Sun Microsystems, and a version of this system was developed for Linux systems. This chapter presents a brief overview of PAM and describes how to work with it.

The term *authentication* refers to the task of confirming that a given user is who he claims to be (i.e., whether the user's claim is "authentic"). This is generally a fancy-pants word for the notion of a username and password combination with which almost all computer users are acquainted. However, there are additional forms of *credentials* besides passwords that can be used for authentication, such as cryptographic keys or hardware devices such as smart cards or key tokens. Additionally, even the traditional username/password method of authentication has more sophisticated forms, such as the Network Information Services (NIS) or Kerberos systems.

Any program that needs to use a particular authentication mechanism needs to be written to support it. For example, in order to support Kerberos, a program would need to be coded to the Kerberos API. Similarly, any system on which such a program is to be installed needs to have Kerberos installed correctly. Since there are many different authentication schemes in common use, this quickly becomes a problem for both software developers and system administrators.

The purpose of PAM is to make the use and management of authentication schemes easier. PAM provides a software API that developers use when writing their applications. This API is generic and has no knowledge of the details of any particular authentication scheme. Additionally, PAM provides a mechanism for installing modules (called, intuitively enough, *PAMs*) that support a given scheme.

For example, there would be one PAM for the Kerberos system mentioned earlier and another for the traditional Unix username/password scheme. A program such as login that needs to perform authentication, however, is not written to use either system, but is instead written to use PAM. The same login program can then make use of either Kerberos or the basic username/password scheme, depending on which PAM or PAMs the system administrator has installed.

PAM is fairly straightforward in concept. The following sections discuss the nuances of the installation and configuration of PAM. There are essentially three such tasks: installing the PAM system itself, configuring the PAM system with specific PAM modules, and configuring user applications to make use of the installed PAM modules.

....

Just the Facts: Pluggable Authentication Modules

Purpose: The Linux Pluggable Authentication Modules (PAM) architecture provides for a modular, easily configurable solution for flexible system authentication.

Authors: Andrew Morgan, et al

Web site: www.kernel.org/pub/linux/libs/pam

Description: The PAM architecture provides two services. First, it allows software applications to be written with support for generic authentication. This allows client software to transparently make use of any authentication mechanism installed on the system without needing to know any details about the mechanism, which makes client software more flexible. Second, PAM allows system administrators to easily install modules for specific authentication mechanisms without having to recompile or reconfigure other applications. Example authentication back-ends supported by PAM include simple Unix username/password pairs, Kerberos, user credentials stored in LDAP, and many others.

....

Installing PAM

It's probably pretty clear that PAM is a low-level system. That is, PAM is used by many other programs, and so it's an important part of a distribution. PAM is really at the same level as the other core system libraries, such as the GNU Project's glibc libraries or XFree86.

For this reason, the installation of PAM really has to be done by the distribution vendor. To see why, consider what an administrator would have to do to install PAM. Obviously, the first step would be to install the PAM libraries themselves; however, after that any program that is to use PAM would have to be recompiled to do so. This means that a potentially significant number of applications would have to be reinstalled. This is quite a bit of effort, and so if PAM is to be used on a distribution, it has to be installed early in the process.

Therefore, this book will not describe the process of installing PAM itself. Really, it's a simple process, and it's similar to the installation of any other software package. However, it involves so much effort and low-level "hacking" of the

Linux distribution that it's a task best left to the vendor. If your distribution comes with PAM installed, then the following sections might be of interest. If it doesn't, then it's probably not worth trying to install it.

Of course, this is a chapter on installing software, right? If I'm not going to discuss the installation of PAM, why even mention it? The reason is that the installation of *other* programs frequently requires interaction with PAM. That is, you may need to do some PAM-related configuration when you install a program that needs to perform user authentication (such as OpenSSH or even the Apache web server if it has the appropriate modules loaded). The next section discusses this task.

Configuring PAM

This section focuses on configuring PAM to properly support and work with an application. This section has two goals. The first is obviously to explain how to configure and use PAM. The second goal is a bit deeper. The overall goal of this chapter is to demonstrate and discuss a variety of configuration techniques commonly used by programs. PAM uses a certain technique, and so it's a good example to add to the mix. After reading this section, you'll not only understand PAM, but you'll also have seen a distinctive configuration technique that may someday help you figure out a new program on your own.

Constructing the Configuration File

PAM can use two different configuration file mechanisms. The first is a simple "flat" configuration file in the /etc directory, and the second is the drop-in configuration file directory approach. The format of the file is similar in both cases.

 CROSS-REFERENCE *The drop-in configuration file directory approach is discussed extensively in Chapters 3 and 4. The flat file approach is discussed throughout this chapter.*

In the first case, all the rules governing PAM's behavior on a particular system are contained in the file /etc/pam.conf. In the second case, files containing PAM rules for a particular service are placed in the /etc/pam.d/ directory. If the /etc/pam.d directory is present, then it overrides the /etc/pam.conf file even if it exists; that is, PAM ignores /etc/pam.conf if the /etc/pam.d directory is present.

In both cases, PAM is configured by rules placed into the files, where each line defines a rule. As is traditional of configuration files, the pound (#) character denotes a comment in the file (meaning that any text after the # symbol is ignored). Each rule is bound to a particular service (such as login for the system login service or ftp for an FTP server).

A program that uses PAM identifies itself by a service name. PAM then goes to its configuration and fetches and executes any rules that are defined for that service. PAM also has a catchall service named "other" that is executed when a program identifies itself as a service that PAM doesn't recognize.

These rules are then executed in order to determine whether the application's use is properly authenticated or to perform other tasks such as account management or session management. The next section discusses how the rules work together and interact to accomplish these tasks; the remainder of this section describes the format of a rule line.

Each rule has the following format:

```
service    type    control    module    arguments
```

Each element is discussed in the following sections.

The service Element

The *service* is the name by which a program will identify itself. This name will be used to locate rules pertinent to the application. If the /etc/pam.conf file is being used, then the service element indicates which service the rule applies to.

If the /etc/pam.d directory is used in lieu of the single /etc/pam.conf file, however, then the rules for a given service are located in a file matching the service's name and the service element is not used. For example, the rules for the login service would be contained in a file named /etc/pam.d/login; since the name of the service is implicit in the file name, the service element can be omitted from the individual rules contained in the file. In contrast, if the /etc/pam.conf file is used, the services' rules are mixed together, and the service element is required to distinguish them.

The type Element

The *type* defines the property the rule acts upon. The type element must be one of these values:

- **auth**: The rule affects the authentication of the application's user.

- **session**: The rule affects the application's environment for the duration of the login session.

- **account**: The rule pertains to some permanent aspect of the user's account (other than the password), such as whether the account even exists.

- **password**: The rule pertains to checking, changing, or otherwise interacting with the user's account.

A type of *auth* is used to determine whether the user is authentic. Typically, auth rules are used to physically validate credentials. This might involve comparing a password to see if it matches the official password, validating a "token" generated by a keychain token system, or authenticating against some external system such as a Kerberos server. An auth rule can also perform other checks; for example, it's common to find auth rules that automatically grant access if the user is already root.

A type of *session* typically performs ancillary or miscellaneous work required by the functioning of a program. For example, programs that need to use X can have a session rule that configures an xauth entry for a newly authenticated user. A session rule alters the environment of the application.

A type of *account* indicates that the rule is related to management of the actual user account. Account rules pertain strictly to the account and check things such as whether the account exists, what times of the day or night a user is allowed to log in, and so on. A common use of an account rule is to check to see if the user's account has been disabled and notify the user (and reject access) if that is the case.

A type of *password* indicates that the rule is related to the management of the user's password in some way, such as expiring a password or checking to see if a password is null (i.e., empty). A common use is to include a password rule that checks whether the account's password has expired and can prompt the user to change the password or eventually reject access entirely.

The control Element

The *control* element defines the action to be taken by the rule, such as granting or rejecting access. The control element actually has two forms: a brief (also called *historical*) form, and a more complicated and powerful form. The longer form is quite a bit more powerful, but it is generally only used where very complicated rules are required. Since this is generally not the case on workstations and even servers, this book will only discuss the short form. Interested readers should consult the man page on PAM for information on the long form.

The short form of the control element must be one of the following four words:

- **required**: Indicates that the PAM must be successful for the stack to succeed.

- **requisite**: Just like required but terminates the PAM stack immediately (PAM stacks are discussed in the next section).

- **sufficient**: Indicates that the success of this single rule is enough for the stack to succeed, and no further rules in the stack need be executed.

- **optional**: Indicates that the success or failure of the rule isn't relevant (unless it's the only rule).

A *required* rule must be successful, or else the entire PAM stack will fail. A *requisite* rule is the same, but a failed requisite causes all subsequent rules to be ignored, while a required rule allows them to be executed even though the stack as a whole will fail. (See the next section for more information on PAM stacks.) Typically, it's better to use required than requisite, since the act of terminating a stack early itself can give information to an attacker. For example, if you never prompt for a password because the check to see if the account exists failed, then an attacker immediately knows to stop wasting time on that account.

A *sufficient* rule is able to "speak for" the entire stack—that is, the success of the rule is "sufficient" to approve the entire stack. An *optional* rule is always executed, but its success or failure isn't relevant to the stack. (However, if the optional rule is the only rule in the stack, then obviously it's the only rule that can apply, and so it isn't really "optional" and the stack is successful based on whether the single optional rule is successful.)

Generally, most auth rules in a stack will be marked as required in order to make sure that they are successful before granting access. Most session rules will be marked optional since typically they are only doing additional work for the sake of convenience. Rules marked as sufficient are typically auth rules, since they essentially bypass the rest of the stack.

The module Element

The *module* is a path to the PAM that is to be used to physically execute the rule. A PAM is actually a standard dynamic shared object that implements the PAM API. The main PAM library (which is called by the application) loads the shared library and then executes its contents. PAMs are usually located in the /lib/security directory. (Note that they are on the root partition rather than the /usr partition, since they are required by the system during the bootup process.)

PAMs can be installed by the system administrator in order to support some desired feature, and each PAM generally has a separate function. For example, there might be one PAM for handling standard Unix username/password authentication and another for handling Kerberos authentication. Additionally, there would also be PAMs handling session and account rules. The *module* element essentially defines the specific auth, session, or account action to be taken.

NOTE *It's possible for a given PAM to support multiple stack types; most actually do.*

The arguments Element

This element is used to pass additional arguments to the PAM specified in the rule. The format and meaning of any argument is specific to the PAM. Each PAM can define its own specific arguments, and the *arguments* element simply provides a way for PAMs to access their own custom parameters.

Understanding PAM Stacks

When an application attempts to authenticate a user, PAM looks up the rules for the pertinent service and type, and executes them in order. The set of rules that are applied to a given execution are referred to as a *stack* of PAM rules. This section discusses how PAM stacks are executed and how control flows through them. The next section discusses a sample file in detail.

A PAM stack is simply a list of rules. When all is normal, PAM simply processes each rule in turn, in the order in which it was defined. If each PAM executes successfully, then the stack as a whole is successful, and the application's call to PAM succeeds. However, when all is *not* normal, a variety of things can occur.

The most obvious case is when a rule marked required fails. For example, the user may enter an incorrect password for the account, which would cause that PAM to fail execution. In that case, any remaining rules will still execute, but the stack itself will fail regardless of whether the later rules succeed. This behavior is useful since you often don't want to override other rules simply because one failed; for example, one rule might be an account rule that must make an entry to a log, regardless of whether the login was successful.

A similar case occurs when a requisite rule fails. This type of rule works exactly like a required rule, but it terminates the stack immediately, and later rules are not executed. This "early return" notion is useful for cases where it's known that a failure of one PAM obviates the rest. For example, if a stack consists of multiple account rules and the first fails because the account doesn't exist, the rest are also guaranteed to fail and there may not be a reason to execute them. (However, in practice this is a bad idea, since the very act of terminating a stack early can give an attacker useful knowledge, as mentioned earlier.)

Rules that are sufficient are similar to requisite rules in that they terminate the stack; however, the meaning of a sufficient rule is precisely opposite of a requisite rule. A sufficient rule alone is enough for an entire stack to succeed, and so there's no reason to bother executing the rest. The most common use of sufficient rules is probably to immediately and unconditionally grant access to the root user (or to another user, such as the personal power user account on a personal workstation). After all, if you're *already* the most powerful account on the system, there's no reason to check to see if you can become more powerful.

An optional rule is a bit different, however. Most of the time, optional rules have no impact on the operation of a stack. An optional rule can fail and it won't matter to the overall success of the stack. There is, however, an exception to that behavior, which is when the optional rule is the only rule in the stack. In that case, PAM has no other rule to use to determine the success or failure of the stack, and so it has no choice but to use the optional rule.

The key to understanding and using PAM rule stacks is to understand the conditions that can cause them to deviate from the "normal" case. The general idea can be summarized as follows:

- PAM groups rules in /etc/pam.conf (or /etc/pam.d/*) into "stacks" by their service and type.

- PAM executes the appropriate stack each time an application requests a particular service.

- Each rule in the stack is executed, unless a requisite or sufficient rule interrupts the process.

This model used by PAM is actually fairly common, especially in security-related systems. For example, the Linux kernel (and in fact most firewall-capable systems) uses a roughly similar paradigm for running its iptables firewall scripts. Another example is the access control list functionality supported by many disk filesystems (such as the AFS network filesystem). This type of configuration can be notoriously subtle and tricky to get right, precisely because it's extremely powerful. The trick to working with this type of configuration is to understand the conditions that can cause a deviation from the norm and to think through all possibilities. Also, the fewer rules, the better, since fewer rules make for simplicity, and simplicity makes for robustness.

Dissecting a Sample File

Listing 9-1 is a copy of the /etc/pam.d/up2date file from Red Hat Linux 7.3. The up2date program is a system maintenance tool developed by Red Hat and is discussed in Chapter 4. Since up2date is a system maintenance tool, it requires root permissions to run, and so it has security needs that make for a good example of PAM. This file is a typical example of how PAM is used in practice. Each line in the file is described individually. Note, however, that the PAMs themselves are not discussed exhaustively.

Listing 9-1. Sample PAM Configuration File

```
#%PAM-1.0
auth        sufficient  /lib/security/pam_rootok.so
auth        required    /lib/security/pam_stack.so service=system-auth
session     required    /lib/security/pam_permit.so
session     optional    /lib/security/pam_xauth.so
account     required    /lib/security/pam_permit.so
```

The first line is simply a comment, and it includes information on the version of PAM required by the file. The remaining lines define three stacks: an auth stack, a session stack, and an account stack. Note that these lines *do not* include the service element; this is because Red Hat's distribution uses the /etc/pam.d mechanism. If Red Hat had chosen to use a single /etc/pam.conf instead, then each line would have to be prefixed by "up2date".

The auth stack first checks the pam_rootok.so PAM and then the pam_stack.so PAM. The first PAM checks to see if the user is already root and is immediately successful if so. The second PAM, however, causes a branch to a second stack, namely the "system-auth" service. This is a separate file (in /etc/pam.d/system-auth) that itself contains an entire PAM stack that simply fetches and authenticates a username and password (as well as performs a variety of checks for expired passwords and similar things). This technique allows stacks that are commonly used by many PAM services—such as the very common password verification in this example—to be stored in one single file and reused, rather than having to be copied into every file that needs them.

In this stack for up2date, the normal case is that the user must authenticate via a username and password, which is handled by the system-auth PAM stack, via the pam_stack.so line. However, before this rule can be executed, the first rule (marked sufficient) is given the chance to intercept. This rule simply checks to see if the root user is running the up2date program, in which case the stack succeeds immediately.

The session stack is a bit odd at first. Normally, the pam_permit.so PAM is executed, as well as the optional pam_xauth.so PAM. If the first fails, then the second will still execute, but the overall stack will fail. The optional rule attempts to handle xauth session authentication for X. The pam_permit.so PAM, however, is always successful; it cannot fail. The reason it's there is because the pam_xauth.so PAM can easily fail—for example, if the user is not using X. Since that is an optional rule, if it were the only rule in the stack it would cause the whole stack to fail unnecessarily. Thus, the pam_permit.so rule is there to ensure that the overall stack always succeeds. (Remember that the success or failure of an optional stack is ignored if there are other rules in the stack.)

The third stack is the account stack, which has a single rule. This rule again refers to the pam_permit.so module, which always succeeds. This rule is simply here as a placeholder, to make sure the account stack doesn't fail. (This rule is actually not doing much, since you don't necessarily need an account stack at all, but it's there for good measure.)

This is a pretty simple example of a PAM service configuration file. Other PAM files can get more complicated, but as long as you remember the basics of how PAM operates, they shouldn't be too difficult to figure out. In most cases, you won't have to write your own PAM configuration files, but occasionally you do, and knowledge of PAM is a good thing to have for those cases where you need to *read* a PAM file.

Don't Forget the *other* Service!

There is a special service named "other" that PAM defines to be the "default" service. That is, if an application specifies a service name that PAM doesn't recognize, then the other service kicks in. By configuring the other service, you can control the access rights granted to unknown programs.

It's a good idea when dealing with systems like PAM to be conservative and set your default rule to be extremely restrictive. First deny everything, and then approve only specific permissions for specific services; that way, you don't accidentally allow permissions you didn't mean to. (This rule also generally applies to things such as firewall rules and access controls on files.)

In the context of PAM, it's a good idea to make the rules for the other service highly restrictive. For example, the following rules are from Red Hat Linux's definition of the default other service. These rules constitute a reasonable default.

```
auth       required    /lib/security/pam_deny.so
account    required    /lib/security/pam_deny.so
password   required    /lib/security/pam_deny.so
session    required    /lib/security/pam_deny.so
```

Installing PAM on Different Distributions

Recall that PAM is generally too low level a mechanism to install "after market" on a system, at least without a significant amount of effort to recompile existing programs. Rather than describe how to install PAM, the following sections instead cover a few nuances of the PAM usage on the sample distributions.

Installing PAM on Red Hat Linux

PAM comes installed by default on Red Hat Linux 7.3. In keeping with Red Hat's extensive use of the drop-in configuration directory, Red Hat's PAM installation uses the /etc/pam.d approach for configuring the individual services.

Typically, each RPM that installs a service that makes use of PAM installs its own service configuration file into /etc/pam.d. This makes it possible for the rpm tool to install and uninstall additional PAM configuration files. Other programs that you install from source code might include a PAM configuration file for that program; in these cases, you need only to copy the file into /etc/pam.d.

Installing PAM on Slackware Linux

Slackware Linux 8.0 does not include PAM in the stock distribution. It is obviously possible to install PAM after the fact, but that's a tradeoff that can only be left to the administrator. There's a point of diminishing returns, and installing PAM on an existing distribution might be past that point.

Installing PAM on Debian GNU/Linux

Like Red Hat Linux, Debian GNU/Linux comes with an installation of PAM. In fact, Debian's configuration of PAM is very similar to Red Hat's: It also uses the /etc/pam.d directory and the drop-in configuration paradigm. In other words, all the notes for the previous section on using PAM with Red Hat Linux also apply to Debian GNU/Linux. In all likelihood, the only difference that you'll see is that the actual list of services reflected in /etc/pam.d is somewhat different on the two distributions and also obviously varies depending on which packages are installed. Additionally, the contents of the service files themselves will be substantially different.

Summary

In this chapter, you read about how PAM works with the operating system and how to configure it. You learned about the types of information PAM requires for its configuration and the way in which that information is structured in the files. At this point, you should be able to read and understand the functioning of any PAM configuration file you come across.

At this point, you've now seen two chapters' worth of configuration. You've seen two very different software applications, which provide two perspectives on similar problems. After you've read the next four chapters, you'll have seen examples of the most common ways of configuring software, and you'll be well prepared for any installation task set before you.

CHAPTER 10
Dante SOCKS Library

This chapter describes how to install the Dante SOCKS client library. Dante provides support for the SOCKS firewall-traversal protocol to client applications. A *firewall* is a network device frequently employed by businesses or even individuals to protect a network of computers from hostile attackers. Typically, all network traffic to and from the Internet is forced to pass through a single point. A firewall is installed at this point, and it blocks all access to the protected network, except perhaps for a set of specific, tightly controlled services. The potential downside of a firewall is that it usually works both ways: It also prevents users inside the firewall from accessing Internet resources directly.

Typically, a *proxy server* is employed to provide internal users access to the World Wide Web. However, proxy servers are only useful for the Web, and don't help with other applications. For example, because the SSH protocol doesn't work over the Web's HTTP protocol, it would be blocked, preventing users behind a firewall from using a program such as OpenSSH to access an Internet host. The SOCKS protocol fills this gap, by acting as a sort of generic proxy server for all services (not just the Web).

Network administrators can install a SOCKS server on the firewalled network. This server must "straddle" the firewall, in that it has access to both the internal network and the Internet. Client programs that speak the SOCKS protocol can be configured to connect to the SOCKS server, which acts as a relay. The client will request a connection to a particular resource, and the SOCKS server will act as an intermediary, relaying communications between the client and the Internet host. As far as the Internet host can tell, it will be communicating only with the SOCKS server, but the connection is otherwise transparent. The SOCKS protocol is therefore a "tunneling" protocol in that it allows a client program to "tunnel" through the firewall.

Because the SOCKS protocol allows hosts on the protected network behind the firewall to access arbitrary Internet services, it can be viewed as a security risk, albeit a greatly reduced risk since it only allows outgoing connections and not incoming ones. For this reason, not all networks with a firewall run a SOCKS server, so if you find yourself stuck behind a firewall, you'll have to ask your network administrator about SOCKS access. Even if a SOCKS server is running, it may be configured to restrict the types of connections it actually permits.

So what is Dante? Simply put, Dante is both a SOCKS server and a SOCKS client library. The Dante server program can be installed on a system and used to set up a SOCKS server that supports firewall traversal, as described previously. The client library, meanwhile, gives client programs a way to traverse a firewall. Since Part Three of this book contains several other examples of installing server software, and setting up the Dante SOCKS server is very similar to those installations, discussing the Dante SOCKS server would be redundant. As a result, this chapter focuses on demonstrating the installation of a client library, and the Dante server is not discussed. By reading this chapter, you'll see a very typical example of how software that functions as a shared library is configured. This isn't an especially common type of software, but you will still most likely run across it at some point so it's useful to see.

The Dante client library comes as a Unix shared object. (This is a similar creature to Windows' dynamic link libraries [DLLs].) Specifically, the Dante client libraries implement a SOCKS-aware version of the standard BSD sockets API. This API is the API used by the vast majority of networked Unix applications, and it's even used on some other operating systems. By replacing this library with a version that is able to transparently use SOCKS, Dante is able to make almost any program SOCKS-enabled.

....

Unix Shared Libraries and Dante

A *shared library* (sometimes called a *shared object* or *shlib*) is a file, usually named with an extension of ".so", that contains compiled software code that is shared by multiple running programs. The motivation for sharing code between programs is to reduce memory: Since each program shares the library, there's only one copy in memory, which reduces the memory footprint of running programs, and thus conserves RAM. Programs that use a dynamic shared object are said to be *dynamically linked* against that library. (Programs that link in their own copy of a library are said to be *statically linked*.)

Another benefit of shared objects is that they can be upgraded independently of applications that use them—within certain restrictions, of course. You can't completely change an API and expect old programs to be able to use it. Shared libraries are said to be *binary compatible* when they can be used without modification by programs that were compiled against a different version. The Dante SOCKS library takes advantage of this feature and provides a SOCKS-aware version of the BSD sockets API that is binary compatible with the standard (non-SOCKS) version. This makes it possible to SOCKS-enable almost any program that uses the network.

....

Some distributions include Dante with the standard installation; for example, Red Hat Linux has included the software as an optional package in previous versions (though this is not the case in 7.3). As always, check to see if a package is already installed on your system or is available for installation before bothering to do all the work discussed in this chapter. However, even if Dante is already installed, chances are it won't be properly configured. As you'll soon see, configuring Dante means knowing a good deal about your network's configuration, and so obviously the default configuration is probably going to be inadequate. For this reason, the "Configuring Dante" section of this chapter will still probably be useful to you, even if Dante is installed with your distribution.

Just the Facts: Dante SOCKS Library

Purpose: Provides support for the SOCKS firewall-traversal protocol

Authors: Inferno Nettverk A/S, Norway

Web site: http://www.inet.no/

Dependencies: None

Description: Dante is an implementation of the SOCKS firewall traversal protocol, supporting versions 4 and 5. The SOCKS protocol allows client programs that use it to access general Internet resources even while located behind a firewall. Dante provides a generic library that can make almost any program "socksified," providing transparent access to the Internet.

Installing Dante

As software packages goes, Dante is pretty "clean" in the sense that it doesn't have any dependencies and it doesn't have any obscure compile-time options. (Well, technically Dante requires various BSD-sockets headers and library files, but it would be an odd Unix system indeed that didn't already have these installed.) So, installing Dante is a textbook case of using the GNU autoconf system to configure and install a software package. The remainder of this section discusses this installation.

Setting the Installation Path

The only option that really needs to be set is the installation path. As discussed in the "Deciding on a Destination" section of Chapter 7, there are generally two good places to install custom-built software: either the /usr/local or /opt directory. Like OpenSSH (whose installation was discussed earlier), you probably don't expect to be upgrading Dante frequently or needing to have more than one version installed at a time. Therefore, /usr/local seems like a good place to install Dante.

One minor gotcha with Dante's configuration is that it doesn't automatically set the location of its configuration files to match its installation directory. Normally, if a program is installed in /usr/local, you would expect to find its configuration file in /usr/local/etc. However, Dante defaults to using a configuration directory of /etc. This can be altered by using the --with-socks-conf= option with the ./configure program, but it's not automatic, which is a bit unusual. For this example, since you're installing the program in /usr/local, you want the configuration file to be /usr/local/etc/socks.conf—this is demonstrated shortly.

NOTE *Because you aren't using the Dante SOCKS server, don't bother to set the server's configuration file via the* --with-sockd-conf= *option.*

The following command, when executed from the top-level directory of the Dante source code package, will configure the software with a path of /usr/local:

```
$ ./configure --prefix=/usr/local --with-socks-conf=/usr/local/etc/socks.conf
```

This command will configure *both* the client library and server components of Dante; however, as mentioned previously, you're only interested here in the Dante client library. It would be ideal to disable the server component so that it's not even compiled, but unfortunately Dante's autoconf scripts don't provide a way to do that. The server will never be run, though, so while it does waste disk space, it's not much of a security hole. If this is still a concern for you, you can modify the scripts yourself or build a package (such as an RPM or Debian package) to exclude the server files.

Compilation and Installation

After configuration, Dante is ready to be compiled and installed. Again, this is a textbook example of GNU autoconf installations, so the following commands are very straightforward. The first one compiles the software, and the second one actually installs it:

```
$ make
```

(Output related to the compilation process follows.)

```
$ make install
```

(Output related to the installation process follows.)

Installation Summary

Dante is a classic example of a package using the GNU autoconf mechanism. The canonical ./configure; make; make install sequence of commands applies, and there are no major dependencies or compile-time options of which administrators need to be aware. However, as easy as Dante is to install, it can be a bit subtle to configure, since that requires a certain degree of detailed knowledge of the network. The next section details the configuration of Dante.

Configuring Dante

The installation of Dante as described earlier in this chapter will include both the Dante SOCKS server and the Dante client libraries. However, the Dante SOCKS server is a fairly typical server installation, and its configuration is very similar to those of the other servers discussed in this chapter (such as Apache and the OpenSSH server). Consequently, this chapter focuses on the Dante client libraries, and this section focuses on configuring them.

Recall that the Dante client libraries are a binary-compatible replacement for the standard BSD sockets API. This is the API used by almost all Unix network programs. The Dante version of these libraries are "aware" of the SOCKS protocol, and so programs that use the Dante version will automatically have access to a SOCKS server, even though they have no idea that they're not using the standard BSD libraries. The Dante client libraries themselves use a configuration file to locate the SOCKS server and retrieve other required settings. This section discusses this configuration.

Locating the Configuration File

The standard Unix location for configuration files is a subdirectory of the installation path named "etc"; if you installed Dante from source code as described in the previous section, then the location of the Dante configuration file will be /usr/local/etc. (If you're using an installation of Dante that was included with your distribution, then the configuration directory can vary but is most likely simply /etc.) The standard name of the configuration file is socks.conf, though this can be changed via a compile-time option to the ./configure program. So, the name of the file in this example should be /usr/local/etc/socks.conf. Dante's default installation process, however, does not actually install a configuration file—not even a default copy—so one will have to be created from scratch.

Fortunately, Dante *does* include example configuration files; they're just not installed by default. They are located in the "examples" subdirectory of the Dante source code package. The configuration file for the client programs is named socks.conf, but there are other examples, such as socks-simple.conf. To use one of these files as a template for creating your own configuration file, simply copy it to /usr/local/etc/socks.conf. For example, the following command will use the simpler example file as a starting point:

```
$ cp examples/socks-simple.conf /usr/local/etc/socks.conf
```

You can also create a socks.conf file from scratch, though it's probably easier to start with one of the example templates. In either case, you can now alter the configuration simply by editing /usr/local/etc/socks.conf.

Obtaining Network Settings

Configuring Dante correctly requires a bit of knowledge of how the network is configured. For example, since the SOCKS protocol requires the presence of a SOCKS server, the host name and port number of the SOCKS server must be known. Additionally, the version of the SOCKS protocol supported by the server must be known. Table 10-1 lists the required data fields and briefly explains their meanings; typically, you'll have to ask your local network administrator for this information. However, this isn't a book on networking or the SOCKS protocol, so if you require more detail, please consult the documentation for Dante.

Table 10-1. Typical Dante Configuration Fields

OPTION	POSSIBLE VALUES	MEANING
SOCKS version	v4, v5, or msproxy	The version of the protocol to use; typically, SOCKS v4 or SOCKS v5 is used, or alternately the msproxy protocol.
Local network mask	A standard "dotted quad" IP mask	The range of IP addresses in use on the protected, local network (inside the firewall).
IP address of server	a standard IP address	The IP address (*not* host name) of the SOCKS server.
Server port number	Usually 1080	The port number on the server machine on which the SOCKS server process itself is actually running.

Conceptually, Dante's functioning is fairly simple. For each connection, it compares the destination IP address to see if it matches a pattern (the network mask), and if so it routes the connection through the SOCKS server (or not) depending on the configuration. For most networks, the network mask is the local network, and local requests are *not* routed through the SOCKS server, while nonlocal (i.e., Internet) connections are. So, once the relevant information is gathered on local network, server address and port, and so on, the configuration file can be modified.

Format of the Configuration File

Dante's configuration file is a bit more complex than many other software's, but it is still fairly straightforward. It consists of sections delimited by braces (that is, the { and } characters), where each section enables or disables a particular feature or defines a "route." Each line within each such "route block" configures a particular option for that route. There are also a set of optional one-line parameters that can be placed *outside* a block to configure things such as logging support and debugging support. The configuration file also permits comments in the file, which are for human consumption such as documentation purposes, and are ignored. Like most Unix config files, any line that starts with a pound (#) character is considered a comment and ignored.

Setting Global Options

Dante supports a few *global* options—that is, options that are general and exist outside any particular route. These global options configure where to print logging information, whether to enable debugging support, and the type of network nameserver in use. Typically, you won't want to turn on debugging support, and letting the software log to the standard location is just fine. So, these options can be left as the defaults (which means they are not present or are commented out); however, if they *are* required they can be enabled, as shown here:

```
debug: 1
logoutoutput: stdout
```

....

Watch Out for File Formats

Observant readers may notice the format for options in Dante's /usr/local/etc/socks.conf is "option: value"; for example, debugging is activated via debug: 1. (A value of 1 is common in configuration files to mean "true" or "enabled.") Compare this format with the OpenSSH format described earlier, where each line has a format of "option value" (such as StrictHostKeyChecking no). Unfortunately, there's no standard way of setting values in Unix configuration files, so you must be careful to get the format correct when working with a particular file. If you encounter a bug with your software that you think is related to the configuration, it's good to check the file to make sure the format is correct.

....

The remaining option is resolveprotocol, which tells Dante whether to use a TCP (stream-based), UDP (datagram-based), or no protocol for resolving host names. This is a somewhat arcane issue, and it varies according to the SOCKS server and network in use. Usually, SOCKS v5 servers should have resolveprotocol: tcp, SOCKS v4 servers should use resolveprotocol: udp, and configurations without a network nameserver at all should use resolveprotocol: fake. There are exceptions, though, so if you need more information, you'll have to consult the actual Dante documentation.

The three options of debug, logoutput, and resolveprotocol are all the global options. If they're not needed (as debug and logoutput usually are not), they can be omitted or commented in /usr/local/etc/socks.conf. The example in the next section shows an actual sample configuration, including these options.

Creating a Route Block

The most important parts of a Dante socks.conf configuration file are the route blocks. A *route block* consists of a number of lines enclosed between the lines route { and }. (The use of braces to indicate "blocks" of related lines is fairly common; later in this chapter, you'll see that the xinetd program uses a similar format.) Each line within a block configures a different option for that block. Table 10-2 summarizes the options that can be set within a block.

Table 10-2. Common Dante Route Block Options

OPTION NAME	MEANING
from	The IP pattern used to match the *origin* of a connection
to	The IP pattern used to match the *destination* of a connection
via	The IP address of a SOCKS server to be used to handle the connection
port	A TCP/IP port number; can be used with from, to, or via
proxyprotocol	The protocol to be used (such as SOCKS v4 or v5) for the route block

There are a few additional route block options that are somewhat less common than the ones in Table 10-2; however, they're not discussed here for the sake of simplicity. If you need more information, please consult the documentation for Dante, and especially the manual page for the socks.conf file (which can be obtained via the command man socks.conf) and the detailed example configuration file named example/socks.conf in the Dante source code package.

Recall that the basic gist of a route block is to tell Dante which SOCKS server (if any) to use for a given connection. The from and to options define the origin and destination, and the via option specifies the SOCKS server (if any) to use. The remaining options simply indicate which SOCKS protocol to use.

A Sample File

This section will present a sample socks.conf file to illustrate the points discussed previously. Other example configurations are included with the Dante source code package itself in the example subdirectory. You should also consult those samples, since this one doesn't cover all the nuances of Dante configuration. Instead, this example is intended to illustrate the configuration for a common network setup. Specifically, this example handles the following case:

- The local network is on the IP range 192.168.0.0, and all computers on the local network are behind the firewall.

- The firewall computer is on the IP address 192.168.0.1.

- The firewall runs a SOCKS v4 server on port 1080.

- All connections to the local network should be direct connections (i.e., bypassing the SOCKS server), and all other connections should go through the SOCKS server.

- Debugging should be disabled, and the log output can be left at the default.

Listing 10-1 is a sample socks.conf file that meets these criteria. This setup is actually fairly typical of a small home or office network that is protected by a firewall. (The 192.168.0.0 address range is frequently used by Network Address Translation [NAT] firewalls.)

Listing 10-1. Example socks.conf File

```
debug: 0
# logoutput: stdout
resolveprotocol: tcp

# all nameserver traffic (i.e. port=domain) should BYPASS the SOCKS server
route {
        from: 0.0.0.0 to: 192.168.0.9 port=domain via: direct
}

# all traffic to the local machine should BYPASS the SOCKS server
route {
        from: 0.0.0.0   to: 127.0.0.0/8  via: direct
}

# all traffic to the local LAN should BYPASS the SOCKS server
route {
        from: 0.0.0.0   to: 192.168.0.0/8  via: direct
}

# all other traffic should go through the proxy server
route {
        from: 0.0.0.0   to: 0.0.0.0   via: 192.168.0.1 port=1080
        proxyprotocol: socks_v4
}
```

For the example installation of Dante, you could place the contents of Listing 10-1 in the file /usr/local/etc/socks.conf. However, chances are that won't work, because it's unlikely your network exactly matches the one reflected in Listing 10-1. Be sure you have your network data correct before attempting to create any Dante configuration file, or you'll probably end up wasting a lot of time.

Installing Dante on Different Distributions

The following sections describe techniques and tasks for installing Dante on the three sample distributions. The previous material is generic; it is applicable to any distribution. The sections that follow tailor the general information and demonstrate real installations on real distributions.

Installing Dante on Red Hat Linux

Recall that Dante is a textbook example of an installation. However, the example installation from this chapter installs the software into /usr/local, and it is not known to the package manager, RPM. Consequently, RPM can't manage or protect the installed files. As always, it would be convenient to have an actual RPM package to install, rather than having to build one manually. Therefore, if you can find a prebuilt RPM package for Red Hat Linux, you may wish to use it. (A good source to check for such packages is `rpmfind.net`.) Otherwise, you can build Dante from source code and configure it as described in this chapter if you don't have a prebuilt binary RPM. Alternatively, you could create your own RPM package of Dante by creating an RPM specification (.spec) file for it. You should see the "Packaging Format" section of Chapter 4 for more information.

Installing Dante on Slackware Linux

Slackware's philosophy is to keep the system as simple as possible, and cases like this are where that philosophy really pays off. Installing Dante on a Slackware system is about as straightforward a task as you could hope for. The details in this chapter should be plainly applicable to a Slackware system.

The only potential exception is if you wish to install Dante such that it can be managed by Slackware's packaging tools, as discussed in Chapter 5. Fortunately, this is as simple as installing Dante to a different directory (via the `--prefix` argument to the ./configure script), and then using Slackware's tools for creating and installing packages. See the "Packaging Format" section of Chapter 5 for full details.

Installing Dante on Debian GNU/Linux

As with Red Hat Linux and Slackware Linux, installing Dante on Debian GNU/Linux is extremely easy. However, Debian actually includes a prebuilt binary installation of Dante that you can use, saving you the effort of building and installing Dante yourself. The package name is dante-client, and you can obtain it through the apt-get program in the usual way (as discussed in Chapter 6 in the section on "Using the apt-get Program"). If you also need the Dante SOCKS *server* (which isn't discussed in this book), you can likewise obtain in via apt-get by installing the dante-server package.

Summary

In this chapter, you read about how to install and configure software that comes in the form of client libraries. This technique is not as common as configuring a server or traditional client program, but you'll still encounter it from time to time, so it's useful to see. Essentially, it involves installing a shared library and creating a configuration file for it. This technique is somewhat similar to that used by other client library software, such as the core libraries of the KDE and GNOME desktops. A more pervasive example of this technique is the ubiquitous /etc/resolv.conf file, which is used by the core network libraries. In each of these cases, the client program itself has no knowledge that the configuration file (and sometimes not even the library) even exists.

The remaining chapters in Part Two continue to illustrate additional software installations. The next chapter discusses the Apache HTTP Server.

CHAPTER 11

The Apache HTTP Server

The Apache Software Foundation is a non-profit umbrella organization that develops a significant number of open-source software projects; the flagship product is the Apache HTTP Server. The Apache HTTP Server is arguably one of the most successful open source projects. It is certainly one of the most well known; many of the uninitiated frequently recognize only Linux and Apache as open source projects. This chapter describes how to install and configure the Apache HTTP Server (referred to throughout this chapter as simply "Apache").

Like OpenSSH, Apache is included in almost every Linux distribution out there. However, also like OpenSSH, Apache is such an important and useful part of many Linux systems (and is such a great example of a particular style of configuration) that I include it as an example.

The Apache web server began life as a variant of the original National Center for Supercomputing Applications (NCSA) httpd web server. It was a collection of patches against the core NCSA software, and so it was "a patchy" server (hence "Apache"). Eventually, the NCSA stopped maintaining their server, but by then the Apache developers had rewritten effectively all of the original NCSA code. Apache became a separate project, and active development continues on it today.

The objectives of the Apache server are reliability, flexibility, and robustness, rather than blazing speed. As a result, Apache is an incredibly sophisticated and feature-rich product. Apache can be used in a variety of capacities; in addition to basic web serving tasks, Apache can be integrated with various web development languages, such as Perl, PHP, and Java. Apache also provides an extensive API that allows developers to augment its capabilities so that it can do almost anything.

The Apache team is not focused on raw speed, though that's not to say that Apache isn't fast. In fact, it's quite speedy. However, since the Apache developers aren't interested in eking out every last ounce of performance they can, a number of products are faster than Apache. Very few are more stable or feature-rich, though.

The Apache HTTP Server is an extremely flexible and sophisticated piece of software. This chapter describes the process of installing Apache and getting it running. This chapter also discusses the basics of customizing Apache to meet the needs of a specific site. However, Apache is far too sophisticated to go into much detail. Instead, this chapter focuses on making generalizations about Apache that illustrate techniques that will be useful with other software.

Just the Facts: Apache Web Server

Purpose: The Apache HTTP Server is a robust, full-featured, extensible web server suitable for serving both static web pages and dynamic web applications written in a wide variety of languages.

Authors: The Apache Software Foundation

Web site: `httpd.apache.org`

Description: The Apache Software Foundation is the parent organization for a number of important software packages. Foremost among these is the eponymous Apache HTTP Server. This server is among the most robust web servers available, and it is the platform of choice for over half of the web sites on the Internet. Apache provides the basis for designing web sites using a wide variety of technologies.

Installing Apache

This section discusses the installation of the Apache HTTP Server from source code. Most Linux distributions contain a preconfigured version of Apache. However, Apache is a very sophisticated and complex product, and so it frequently happens that a user or an administrator needs a custom installation of Apache with options and functionality not included in the distribution's default configuration. In such cases, the administrator will have to build a custom Apache from source code, which is the topic of this section.

Apache really is a very complex product—so complex, in fact, that entire books have been written on it. There is no way that this section can pretend to be a comprehensive coverage of the Apache HTTP Server. Instead, this section has two less ambitious goals:

- Demonstrate a real-world installation of a highly complicated server

- Provide the *basics* of configuring Apache

Apache is one of the most sophisticated software packages around, and so in completing this chapter you will take a major step in your understanding of software installations.

Depending on your role and reason for reading this book, this chapter will probably be useful to you in one of two ways. Perhaps you're just an average user who doesn't have much more than a passing interest in Apache, or maybe you're a system administrator who may actually be responsible for a production deployment of Apache in a real web site. In the first case, reading this chapter will be a great academic tutorial on how to install a complex piece of software. In the second case, this chapter will be a good primer on Apache installation, but it probably isn't going to be comprehensive enough to bet your job on. If you need more information, you should definitely consult Apache's documentation at httpd.apache.org or get a copy of one of the excellent Apache reference books.

Compile-Time Options

Even though Apache is a very complex package, it is a straightforward GNU auto-conf installation. Part Three of this book has already covered several other examples of autoconf installations, so by now this should be old hat. As with all autoconf installations, though, the devil is in the compile-time options. This section covers compile-time options for the Apache HTTP Server.

At the risk of being repetitive, remember that Apache is a very complicated product. A quick ./configure --help command shows that it has a very long list of compile-time options, and many of these are interrelated and even mutually exclusive. In other words, figuring out Apache's compile-time options can be a bear.

However, remember that the Apache developers are not out to make life needlessly complicated, and so all the options are actually necessary. Because of this, unfortunately, there's no easy way out, and there's no magic trick to configuring Apache. To install Apache, you have to understand its compile-time options, and the only way to do so is to consult the documentation for the software. Fortunately, Apache's documentation is outstanding and comprehensive; the web site at httpd.apache.org contains all there is to know about installing (and running) Apache, and a copy of the manual is actually included with the source code and installations.

That said, you can draw a few generalizations about the types of options that Apache supports. The remainder of this section discusses the following compile-time options:

- Installation directory

- Support for Dynamically Loadable Objects

- Selection of a Multi-Processing Module (MPM)

- Other important options

With these options, you can create a basic, reasonable Apache configuration. Almost any production environment will have to customize these options, but they'll be a good starting point. (Actually, the configuration as discussed will be very similar to Apache's default configuration, but it's worthwhile to see it broken down a little.)

Choosing an Installation Directory

As you've probably come to expect by now, the first step in installing a software package is to decide where to install it. In Chapter 7, two general options were discussed: the /usr/local directory and the /opt directory. The /usr/local directory is a good place to put software needed by many users that is upgraded infrequently, while /opt is a good place to put software that needs to be self-contained or that needs to be frequently or systematically updated.

The other example software installations covered by this book include samples of both possibilities; the OpenSSH package, for instance, is needed by many users and was installed into /usr/local. The Java environment (which is discussed later in this book) was installed into /opt/java, since it can be a fairly complicated package and it helps to have it organized into its own location.

So, where should Apache be installed? Well, the answer to that depends on the type of system that Apache's being installed on. If the target is an actual production machine, then chances are the system is going to be very closely monitored and upgrades are going to be done infrequently at best; in this case, you'll probably never need more than one copy installed at once, and it's probably just fine to install Apache into /usr/local. Most distributions that include Apache typically assume that the machine is going to be more or less a production server, or perhaps just someone's personal web server, and that upgrades can be handled via the package mechanism (such as RPM). Thus, most distributions install Apache into /usr; therefore, if you're installing a custom Apache from source code for such a system, you should probably use /usr/local.

CROSS-REFERENCE   *See Chapters 3 and 7 for more information about /usr/local.*

There are other common use cases for Apache, though. For example, you might be a developer installing Apache on your desktop system. In this case, you might need to track the latest and greatest changes to Apache or have different copies installed, each with a different configuration. In this case, you probably want your Apache installation or installations to be more isolated, and so it's better to put them in a subdirectory of /opt; for example, /opt/apache. This is the case assumed by this book.

For the purposes of this chapter, then, the installation directory will be /opt/apache. To actually set this as a compile-time option via the ./configure program, you need to use the `--prefix` option; to wit, `--prefix=/opt/apache`.

(If you think you'll need to upgrade frequently, another option would be to include the version number in the path, such as `--prefix=/opt/apache-2.0.36` for Apache v2.0.36, and create `/opt/apache` as a symbolic link pointing to your version. This allows you to upgrade Apache more easily, by installing the new version separately and replacing the symbolic link after it's been tested.)

Installation Directory vs. Data File Location

This section advises that "production" installations of Apache be installed into `/usr/local` and that "development" installations be installed into `/opt`. That's a good rule of thumb, but there's an additional issue—namely, where to install the actual data files, such as the content on the site that you're using Apache to run. This might actually depend on (or even be dictated by) what language or tools you use to develop your site, but typically there's at least one file that contains your site's contents. By default, Apache will create a directory called htdocs that is supposed to contain such data files, though you can easily change this in the run-time configuration.

However, this htdocs directory will be alongside the other Apache files and directories; for example, it might end up being `/opt/apache/htdocs`. This means that your data files will be "mixed in" with your program binary and configuration files. This is okay, but it might be a better idea to place your data files on a separate partition, or even disk, that can be easily backed up and restored in case of a hardware failure on your server. This can be done after the installation, of course—check out the "Configuring Apache" section for more information. Just remember to plan ahead!

Enabling Loadable Module Support

Apache has a vast amount of functionality, and this means that if it's all enabled at compile-time, the resulting run-time memory footprint will be very large. Most installations, meanwhile, won't need all that functionality and so it's really a waste of memory. This section discusses how to enable the loadable modules that Apache supports to address this issue.

Apache uses *Dynamic Shared Objects* (DSOs), which are also referred to as *Apache modules* or just *modules*. Each module is a file on disk that contains some specific functionality for the Apache server. For example, there are separate DSO modules for monitoring server status and for spell checking.

Normally, if you want the functionality from a specific module, you have to compile that module into the Apache installation. (For example, you have to compile Apache to include the spell-checking module if you want that functionality.) However, if you later change your mind, you can't get rid of that spell-checking support without recompiling Apache. You can always just leave it in and not use it, of course, but in that case it's wasting memory and perhaps processing time, and it might even be a security risk if an attacker figures out a way to exploit it. For these reasons, you generally don't want Apache to include modules that aren't being used, even if they sit idle.

Apache addresses this issue by allowing each module to be loaded dynamically when the server starts up. This way, removing support for a given module is as easy as editing Apache's configuration file to remove the line that loads the module and then restarting the Apache server process. For example, disabling that spell-checking module is as easy as commenting out or deleting a line in a file, and then the spell-checking module will not only be idle, it won't even be present.

Another major benefit of loadable modules is the inverse case, which is *adding* a module to include support that you didn't think of or didn't exist when you built Apache. Without DSO support, for example, if you actually did want spell-checking support but forgot to compile it in, you'd have to recompile Apache to get it. If you enabled DSO support, though, you can easily add the module later and turn it on by restarting the server. This technique is also useful for making use of third-party modules that aren't included with Apache proper: You can simply compile such third-party modules as DSOs and load them into Apache at run-time. The alternative without dynamically loadable modules would be to somehow cause Apache to compile these third-party files along with the standard Apache files. Apache actually does support this but it's somewhat more cumbersome, as you'll see later.

Actually using modules (i.e., compiling them, installing them, activating them in the configuration file, and so on) is discussed later in this section. The beauty of DSOs, after all, is that once you've built the core of Apache, you can add and remove modules later at your leisure. For now, all you have to do is enable support for DSOs within Apache. This is accomplished with two options: the `--enable-mods-shared` and `--enable-so` options.

The `--enable-so` option simply activates support for DSOs within Apache; however, it does not actually cause any specific modules to be build as DSOs. The `--enable-mods-shared` option to ./configure is the one that allows you to add or enable specific modules. For example, if you wanted to add that spell-checking module as a DSO, you would use `--enable-mods-shared=mod_speling`. However, there's also a convenience form you can use—namely, `--enable-mods-share=all`— that saves you the trouble of having to type out all the individual modules explicitly. This is the option used by this book, and its result is that all modules that *can* be enabled as DSOs are so enabled.

DSOs and Security

It can be argued that enabling DSOs with Apache is a security risk, and therefore, it should not be used on actual production systems. An attacker can conceivably cause Apache to dynamically load a DSO module designed to compromise the Apache server or the system itself. If DSO support is disabled, this would obviously be impossible.

This is a risk. However, in practice the risk is probably rather remote, and it's largely irrelevant anyway. After all, if an attacker can gain access to the file system on which Apache is installed (in order to place his own hostile module for Apache to load), then he can almost certainly do much more damage than just loading a module into Apache.

So, as security risks go, enabling Apache DSOs is quite small. However, it *is* a risk, and users and administrators always need to compare the risks against the potential impacts. Forewarned is forearmed!

Choosing an MPM

Some Apache modules cannot be loaded as DSOs. These include the core module, which contains things such as the capability to actually load the DSO modules, and the *Multi-Processing Module* (MPM) to be used for the installation. This section discusses the MPM options available for Apache.

An MPM is a module that handles connections to clients and governs how Apache behaves while fulfilling those clients' requests. Each MPM can use a different technique for this "multiprocessing," and each has a different performance profile. By allowing the MPM to be customized, Apache can use a different technique for each operating system it runs on, allowing the best possible performance on each platform. MPM functionality was added in Apache's 2.0 release.

Because the MPM being used is the foundation for the rest of Apache, the MPM cannot be built as a dynamically loadable module; it has to be hard-compiled into the core Apache program. In other words, once Apache has been compiled and installed, changing to a different MPM requires that Apache itself be recompiled.

Generally, the ./configure program can detect which operating system Apache is being compiled on and it selects the most appropriate MPM for that platform. Some platforms, however, support multiple MPMs from which you can choose. In these cases, the ./configure program selects a reasonable default MPM, which is usually the most stable one.

Switching to a different MPM is not a small matter, since it has major performance implications. If you want to use an alternate MPM, you should consult the Apache documentation on the subject. This section is here just to advise you of the presence of MPMs in Apache; the actual configuration used simply accepted the default MPM that Apache selected for the system. No custom MPM-related options were passed to ./configure.

Other Options

As I've mentioned repeatedly, Apache supports a very wide variety of compile-time options. Exhaustively covering these options is beyond the scope of this section, and indeed, exploring the features offered by Apache is a diversion of several hours just by itself. If you'd truly like to master Apache, you should consult the Apache documentation or another book. However, there are a few fairly common options that users frequently need, some of which are outlined in Table 11-1.

Table 11-1. Some Common Apache Compile-Time Options

OPTION	DESCRIPTION
--enable-ssl	Activates SSL/TLS connection encryption support
--enable-proxy	Activates support for Apache to act as an HTTP proxy server
--enable-dav	Activates support for the WebDAV content management standard
--enable-speling	Includes URL spelling correction

Completing the Installation

Now that you've selected the compile-time options, you can install Apache. This is a very straightforward example of a GNU autoconf installation, meaning that it consists of essentially three commands: ./configure with the appropriate arguments, make, and make install. Here's the actual ./configure command used for this example:

```
./configure --prefix=/opt/apache --enable-so --enable-mods-shared=all
```

After the ./configure command and the make commands have completed, Apache will be installed in the /opt/apache directory.

If you've read the other software installation examples in this book, you should be starting to see some patterns. By reading this section on Apache, you'll have seen a real-world installation of a pretty complicated software server.

You'll be able to apply many of the same techniques and modes of thought to installing any other server program, such as the OpenLDAP directory server or Samba file- and print-sharing server. Installing these things is pretty easy—you just read the documentation to find out what options you need, then run ./configure, make, and make install, and voila! You've got your software installed. Of course, even then the work will only be half done—it also has to be configured. That's the topic of the next section.

Configuring Apache

This section will discuss configuring Apache, after it's been installed. The previous section discussed configuring Apache's compile-time options, which really boils down to enabling or disabling specific features. The run-time options, however, govern the actual behavior of Apache as it runs.

 CROSS-REFERENCE *For more information on compile-time versus run-time options, see the section "Software Configuration Options" in Chapter 7.*

Apache uses a typical server configuration; that is, it reads a configuration file that sets a variety of options and alters its behavior accordingly. Apache is a pretty complicated piece of software, however, so it comes with a lot of files. This section first summarizes the various files and directories relevant to Apache, and then discusses how to use these files to change the configuration.

Navigating the Installation Directory

The previous section installed Apache into the /opt/apache directory. A quick look in that directory will reveal a number of subdirectories. This section describes these directories, focusing on the important ones. After this "guided tour" of an Apache installation, the next section discusses how to configure the server. To get started, Table 11-2 contains a list of the standard Apache configuration directories.

Table 11-2. Apache Installation Subdirectories

DIRECTORY	CONTENTS
bin	Program binaries for the server and various utilities
build	Utility scripts and other files used for building and adding additional DSO modules
cgi-bin	Web scripts used to dynamically generate web content
conf	Configuration files for the server
error	Files containing text messages the server displays when various errors occur
htdocs	Actual content files served up by the HTTP Server
icons	Small graphical icons referred to by the server when printing certain dynamically generated pages (such as directory listings)
include	Files required to compile DSO modules and other programs
lib	Shared libraries (*not* DSO modules) required by the HTTP Server
logs	Files containing log information on various HTTP events
man	Standard Unix man pages for the server and utility programs
manual	The full Apache installation and usage manual in HTML format
modules	Dynamically loadable (DSO) module files

Some of the directories listed in Table 11-2 are covered individually in the following sections. Others are less important and are discussed as a group at the end of this section.

Programs in the bin Directory

As you probably expect from reading Chapter 3, the bin subdirectory of the top-level Apache installation directory contains binary programs. This includes both the actual Apache HTTP Server program (httpd) and several utility programs. Table 11-3 summarizes these programs.

Table 11-3. Programs in the Apache bin Directory

PROGRAM	PURPOSE
httpd	The Apache HTTP Server
ab	A developer's utility for benchmarking the performance of an HTTP Server (such as Apache)
apachectl	Provides a convenient way to start, stop, and manage the HTTP Server

Table 11-3. Programs in the Apache bin Directory (continued)

PROGRAM	PURPOSE
apxs	A developer's and administrator's utility used to compile and install new DSO modules to an existing Apache installation
checkgid	Used internally by the Apache programs
dbmmanage, htdigest, htpasswd	Programs used to manage Apache user accounts and passwords in several formats
logresolve	A convenient utility to resolve numeric IP addresses in Apache log files into actual human-readable hostnames
rotatelogs	"Rotates" the log files by renaming current log files and starting new log files

Server Programs

The httpd, ab, apachectl, and checkgid programs are all related to server management and performance testing. The httpd program is, of course, the Apache HTTP Server itself; this is the main event, so to speak. The apachectl program is actually a shell script, and it is used to start, stop, restart, and otherwise manage the httpd process. The apachectl program is similar to the service scripts used by the SysV init model on Red Hat Linux, as discussed in Chapters 3 and 4.

The checkgid and ab programs are less crucial. The checkgid program is simply a small utility program invoked by Apache; users and administrators don't need to worry about it (it doesn't even have a man page!). The ab program is the "Apache Bench" program, and it's used to benchmark the performance of an HTTP Server. (Even though ab is included with Apache, it can really work with many HTTP servers.) The ab program is used by administrators and developers to test performance-tuning configurations and the performance of web applications. Generally, most users won't need to worry about ab unless there's a problem with the installation.

Administration Programs

In addition to the most important server program and support programs, there are also a few convenience utilities that are included to make users' lives easier. The apxs program is the "Apache Extension" utility. This program is used to compile and install Apache DSO modules. (Recall from the previous section that DSOs are files that Apache can load when it starts up to include certain features into the server.) DSOs provide a way to add functionality to Apache without having to recompile the entire server. If you find yourself needing to install a new

Apache DSO module, apxs will be very useful. It's pretty simple to use, but if you have trouble, check out Apache's documentation on it.

The logresolve program is used to convert numeric IP addresses in Apache log files into host names. A typical Apache server gets a lot of hits from web browsers on the Internet. Each hit contains information about the client, including its IP address. Apache logs these hits (as well as other things, such as errors), but the log entries include only the IP address. This is because the process of looking up a client's host name from the Domain Nameservers (DNSs) can be very expensive and needlessly waste bandwidth. The logresolve program is included as an easy way to take Apache's log files (which contain only IP addresses) and "reformat" them with host names fetched from the DNS service. You can use logresolve any time you need or want to view your site's logs with more than just IP addresses.

The rotatelogs program manages Apache's log files. As the HTTP Server runs for a long time, it keeps logging various events (especially hits from web browsers) into its log files. These files can become very large as a result. The `rotatelogs` command "rotates" Apache's log files; essentially, it just renames the current log files and then starts Apache logging to fresh files. The user can then delete the old log files after reviewing them, in order to conserve disk space.

NOTE *The* `rotatelogs` *command isn't actually used from the command line; instead, it's inserted into Apache's logging mechanism via the configuration files. For more information, see the man page for rotatelogs included with the Apache installation.*

User Database Management Programs

A common feature required by web sites is the restriction of access to certain pages or sets of pages to specific users. (These pages and sets of pages are known as *realms*.) Apache supports this functionality by various directives in its configuration files. However, another key component in supporting user authentication is, of course, to have a database of users.

There is any number of ways to set up a database for users. Commercial web sites, with which most of you will be familiar, use some kind of high-capacity relational database or directory to store user account information. The authentication that Apache supports out of the box, however, is more modest. It supports user databases stored on local disks, in a few different formats. (There are, of course, third-party modules that you can use to provide support for Apache for high-capacity data stores; they're just not included with the standard Apache distribution.)

The three programs dbmmanage, htdigest, and htpasswd are utilities that manage these user databases. The nuances of which data format is best for a given application, and when you can use Apache's basic mechanism or switch to a high-capacity database are advanced topics and aren't really relevant to this book. If you need more information, please consult the manual pages for these programs (included with the Apache installation) or the documentation on the web site at httpd.apache.org.

Configuration Files in the conf Directory

The conf directory contains all configuration files for Apache. (In reality, the httpd program, which is the actual Apache HTTP Server program, can be told which configuration file to use as a command-line parameter, so the Apache configuration directory isn't hard-coded or forced to a specific value.) This section briefly discusses the contents of this directory.

The canonical name for Apache's configuration file is httpd.conf. (Again, however, this doesn't have to be the case; the httpd program can be passed an arbitrary file name.) A typical installation of Apache will have several sample httpd.conf files, such as a configuration tuned for maximum performance and one that enables SSL support, as well as a standard "vanilla" httpd.conf. As a result, there will usually be several files with a ".conf" extension in the conf subdirectory of the Apache installation; only one of these files actually needs to be there. Additionally, for each .conf file there is a -std.conf file. The -std files are copies of the original files; their purpose is to act as a backup in case a tinkering administrator really mucks up a .conf file. However, the -std files are also not required for Apache to run.

You can actually remove all the .conf and -std.conf files except for httpd.conf if you don't like them cluttering up the directory. That will leave the traditional Apache configuration file as a starting point to begin customizing the server. However, it *definitely* pays to take a look at the other sample files before removing them if you choose to do so; there's a lot of very valuable information and sample configurations in those files. Of course, there's still no substitute for reading the actual documentation. The sample configuration files are just that and are not comprehensive.

There are two other files in the conf subdirectory: mime.types and magic. MIME is the Multimedia Internet Mail Extension, and it is an industry standard for specifying the type of a file, such as "executable" or "plain text" or "HTML." (Don't be confused by the "Mail" in MIME—the MIME standard can be used just about anywhere!) Apache's mime.types file is just a mapping that assigns MIME types to file extensions. (For example, the extension ".txt" is mapped to a MIME type of "text/plain".) Usually, you won't have to modify this file, since it contains reasonable defaults. If you do, carefully read the Apache documentation on it, since altering mime.types can have subtle consequences. The magic file works similarly to mime.types, except that it is used to assign MIME types to files where the file extension may be unreliable, based on "magic numbers" contained in the file. This is frequently used for items such as audio files.

Log Files in the logs Directory

The logs subdirectory contains, intuitively enough, the log files for the Apache HTTP Server. Apache's logging mechanism is very flexible, and it can be configured to log a variety of events to any number of files in any format. Altering this configuration is seldom necessary, and so I don't cover it here. Fortunately, Apache has a default logging configuration that is almost always good enough. Table 11-4 summarizes the files involved in this default configuration.

Table 11-4. Default Apache Log Files

FILE NAME	CONTENTS
error_log	Errors related to the functioning of the server or to failed or erroneous requests from web browser clients; used for error debugging
access_log	Information on each request received from a client; used for gathering statistics on the web site and users' usage
httpd.pid	Contains the Unix process ID of the currently running httpd process

Technically, the httpd.pid file isn't really a log file; it just contains the process ID (PID) of Apache. This file makes it easy to quickly figure out the PID in order to restart or shut down Apache. Also, depending on what platform Apache is running on and what options are enabled, there may be more or fewer files in the logs directory than shown in Table 11-4.

Content Directories

The point of the Apache HTTP Server is, of course, to serve up documents such as HTML web pages. Apache also supports many different programming languages and environments that web developers can use to create and run dynamic, interactive web applications. The Apache installation uses the htdocs and cgi-bin directories to contain the files that actually make up the site's content.

The htdocs directory is the home of "static" HTML files. These are files that don't have any dynamically generated content, such as tables of contents, default home pages, standard header and footer HTML files, and so on. The htdocs directory also contains any other static files needed by the site, such as graphical image files, tarball (.tar.gz) files that are downloaded from the site, and so on. Literally, any file placed into the htdocs directory (and that the httpd process has permission to access) becomes available for download over the web site. In other words, don't put anything in htdocs that you don't want people to be able to download!

The cgi-bin directory contains scripts and programs that make use of the *Common Gateway Interface* (CGI) standard for dynamic web applications. CGI defines a standard, fixed way in which a web server (such as Apache) interacts with the programs used to generate content. Web developers write programs in a programming language such as Perl, Python, C, or some other language that understands the CGI standard, and this allows them to work within a web server that supports CGI, such as Apache. Apache's cgi-bin directory contains all the CGI programs used on the site. The directory is separate from the htdocs directory for security reasons and to make it easier to manage.

Note that the htdocs and cgi-bin directories are for the "standard" way of using Apache. Apache is extremely flexible and supports a wide variety of ways to serve up and dynamically generate content. For example, Apache can be used with web applications using Sun's Java Servlets technology, which defines a very different way that web application data is stored and served up. Java Servlet–based sites frequently don't use either htdocs or cgi-bin.

Documentation Directories

There are two directories with similar names in a standard Apache installation: manual and man. No, this wasn't a typo! These directories contain documentation for Apache, and for its related support utilities.

The *manual* directory contains a copy of the Apache user's manual, which is in HTML. You can use any web browser to browse this manual, which is a copy of the documentation on Apache's web site. These files are not required for Apache to run, however, so if you're low on disk space they're safe to delete (though they are definitely useful to have around!). Depending on the configuration, you may also need to remove the reference to the manual directory in the httpd.conf file; check that file for details. At any rate, you can access the manual from your server by accessing the URL `http://localhost/manual` with your favorite browser.

The *man* directory, meanwhile, contains Unix manual pages for the program binaries in the bin directory. This is where the manual pages for httpd, apachectl, and so on are located. However, if you've installed Apache into a directory such as /usr/local or /opt/apache, you may not be able to access these pages because the man program itself doesn't know to look in those directories for the pages. In order to access these manual pages, use a command similar to this one:

```
man -M /opt/apache/man <command name>
```

You'll have to substitute your actual installation directory for /opt/apache.

NOTE *The -M option to the man program is actually a useful thing to know, in general! The option lets you specify an alternate directory for it to search for manual pages. It's very handy when you install software into a location other than /usr.*

Using the MANPATH Variable

Using the -M parameter to the man command can be tedious if you check man pages frequently. Fortunately, the man program supports a shell environment variable named MANPATH. By setting this variable to a colon-separated list of paths containing man pages (such as /opt/apache/man), you can permanently add directories for the man program to search when it looks for manual pages. By adding this setting to the global user configuration scripts described in Chapters 4, 5, and 6 (for Red Hat Linux, Slackware Linux, and Debian GNU/Linux, respectively), you can make manual pages in nonstandard locations available to all users.

Other Directories

Several other directories are included in an Apache installation—namely, build, error, icons, include, lib, and modules. In most cases, these directories are used by Apache and the related tools, and users and administrators don't have to do anything in or with these directories. If you'd like more information on them, you can check the Apache web site and other documentation.

Customizing Apache

So far, I've discussed only the installation of Apache and very basic configuration tasks required to get it to run. Apache's purpose, however, is to run a web site, and so the next step is to discuss how to customize Apache to run *your* web site.

It's imperative to remember that Apache is a very sophisticated product, and it is capable of an amazingly wide range of behavior. The goal of this section is not to exhaustively describe how to customize Apache for every possible circumstance. Instead, the goal is to illustrate the *mechanics* of customizing Apache and also to demonstrate a particular methodology for configuring a server. After you read this section, you'll not only have a basic understanding of how to configure

Apache, but you'll also understand how to go about figuring out other servers' configurations.

Perhaps the most common customization you'll need to do to an Apache HTTP Server is configuring specific directories. Generally, a given web site has many directories, and sometimes each directory needs specific behaviors or features. For example, most directories might be publicly accessible, but one directory needs to be "locked down" in terms of security and to require a password. To support this functionality, Apache allows you to specify properties or enable features for individual directories, by using directives within "Directory" blocks in the httpd.conf file.

A *directive* is, in Apache's parlance, a statement in the httpd.conf file that instructs the server to take some action. For example, a line that enables SSL/TLS encryption support would be a directive, as would a line that turns off the ability to list the contents of a directory. Apache directives, in turn, are enclosed in various "blocks" that determine the scope of their effect.

There are many types of these enclosing blocks, but the simplest is the Directory block. A Directory block has a definite beginning (marked by a <Directory ...> line), and a definite ending (marked by a </Directory> line). And directives inside the block affect only that block (and any children of that block).

A typical Apache httpd.conf configuration file contains an entry for the top-level directory on the site. This entry contains some directives that are applied to the root directory. Since they also apply to any children of the root directory, this effectively sets up site-wide defaults. The following text is an example Directory block that might be used for the Apache installation discussed in this chapter:

```
<Directory "/opt/apache/htdocs">
    Options FollowSymLinks
    AllowOverride None
    Order allow,deny
    Allow from all
    DirectoryIndex index.html index.htm
<Directory>
```

The path of /opt/apache/htdocs in the preceding directory block points to the location in the installation where HTML content is to be placed, and the directives enclosed in the block will be applied to that directory. Since all of the content has to be located under that directory, meanwhile, this block also effectively serves as a site-wide default. (Describing what each of those directives does would take too much time and isn't really relevant—see the Apache documentation mentioned earlier for details.)

It is possible to override these defaults on a case-by-case basis, however. For example, perhaps you wish to add files named home.html to the DirectoryIndex directive, but only for the directory /opt/apache/htdocs/home. The following

Directory block will accomplish this; the DirectoryIndex directive will be updated for that specific directory, but all other directives will remain unchanged.

```
<Directory "/opt/apache/htdocs/home">
    DirectoryIndex index.html index.htm home.html
</Directory>
```

Most of the customization of an Apache site revolves around creating these Directory blocks (and other blocks) as appropriate, and then using the correct directives within each block. This model is actually very powerful, since it lets you customize the behavior of each individual area of the site. Unfortunately, this is as much detail as I can really go into here, since I just couldn't do justice to the full power of Apache's configuration system in the space I have. Read the Apache manual cited earlier for full details.

All this terminology about Directories and directives aside, what this really boils down to is that Apache provides you with a set of options (directives) and provides you with a mechanism (Directory blocks) to scope the options to different parts of the system. This is actually a very common model for configuration of server daemon software: Create scope blocks somehow, and then set options within each scope block.

In the Apache world, these scope blocks are created by pairs of `<Directory>` and `</Directory>` lines; in other programs, they might be set up through pairs of braces ({ and }) or simply through positioning of the lines in the file (as with the OpenSSH server). Even though these programs differ in their syntax, it's the same general idea in each case. When you find yourself trying to configure a new, unfamiliar program, try and identify cases where you establish "scopes" and create "options" within them.

Installing Apache on Different Distributions

This section discusses issues that arise when the Apache HTTP Server is installed on the three sample distributions. Generally, Apache's installation and startup processes are fairly self-contained (meaning that they don't rely much on other services being started first), so there isn't a great deal of variance across distributions. However, there are a few things that you should understand.

Installing Apache on Red Hat Linux

Installing Apache on Red Hat Linux is very straightforward using the techniques discussed in this chapter. There are, however, a couple things to be aware of relating to the Apache version and how to manage the software once it's installed.

Selecting the Correct Version

Red Hat Linux includes a package of the Apache HTTP Server. However, as of Red Hat Linux 7.3, this package is of an older version of Apache than the one discussed in this section. Generally, configuring the older Apache is largely the same (in the sense that it requires many of the same techniques), but there are some differences. If you choose to use Red Hat's standard distribution of Apache, be sure to consult and understand the Apache project's documentation for the older version.

Starting the Apache Server on Startup

One common need is to start up the Apache server automatically when the system boots up. As discussed in Chapter 4, this is accomplished on Red Hat Linux via the SysV model for system initialization scripts. This model is based on a "master" script that invokes a number of service-specific scripts, each of which adheres to a certain structure. These scripts are in turn responsible for starting, stopping, and restarting a particular service.

 CROSS-REFERENCE *See Chapter 4 for more information about the SysV model.*

The Apache HTTP Server includes a script program that automates the startup and shutdown of the server—it's the apachectl program mentioned earlier. This shell script can be passed the `stop`, `start`, and `restart` commands. These are the same commands used by SysV-compatible scripts, meaning that the apachectl program can be used to manage the Apache HTTP Server on a Red Hat Linux system.

To set this up, you need only create a symbolic link. The following command shows how this would be done if you've set up the server as discussed throughout this chapter:

```
# ln -s /opt/apache/bin/apachectl /etc/rc.d/init.d/apache
```

This command will configure Apache so that it can be started and stopped by the system—that is, the `service` command can be used as discussed in Chapter 4.

However, Chapter 4 also describes the special naming and ordering of symbolic links that actually determines whether and when a service gets started when the system boots up. Simply making the preceding symbolic link won't actually cause Apache to be started when the system boots.

 CROSS-REFERENCE *See Chapter 4 for more information about the use of symbolic links in the SysV init scripts model.*

There are two options to make Apache start on system boot. One is to manage the necessary symbolic links by hand (which is discussed in Chapter 4), and the other is to make the apachectl script compatible with Red Hat's chkconfig command, which can then be used to manage the script.

Making apachectl Compatible with chkconfig

In order to properly integrate Apache with the tools Red Hat provides for managing system services, the apachectl script needs to be integrated with Red Hat's service command (which was discussed in the previous section) as well as the chkconfig command. Both of these commands are discussed in detail in Chapter 4, and you must read that chapter to get the full details on the material discussed in this section.

Making a script compatible with chkconfig means adding a comment to the script that contains information used by chkconfig to configure the service. The following lines can be added to the apachectl script—they contain the required information:

```
# chkconfig: 345 99 99
# description: The Apache HTTP Server
```

Those lines will cause apachectl to be (by default) configured to run on runlevels 3 through 5, with priority 99 for both startup and shutdown (since Apache has no dependence on other services being run). Once you've made this change to the apachectl script, you can activate it by running the command chkconfig --add apache; after that, you'll be able to manage Apache's startup status normally, using the tools and techniques described in the section "System Startup Scripts" in Chapter 4.

Some administrators may not like the idea of modifying a script provided by Apache, for very good reason: If Apache is upgraded, this change will have to be made to the upgraded apachectl script as well. If this is a concern, it may be worthwhile to write a very simple shell script (similar to Listing 8-1 from Chapter 8) that contains the chkconfig information and simply calls the apachectl script. This way, the service command and other system tools will use the custom script, and the apachectl script won't have to be modified. Some administrators may prefer this option.

Installing Apache on Slackware Linux

As with Red Hat Linux, Apache is easy to set up on Slackware Linux. Slackware Linux 8.0 also contains a package for Apache, but again, like Red Hat it's an older version than the one discussed in this chapter. Configuring Apache to be started by Slackware Linux is very simple.

As discussed in the section "System Startup Scripts" in Chapter 5, Slackware Linux uses the BSD model of system startup scripts, but it also provides a minimal SysV-compatible "hook" for convenience. Configuring Apache to be started when Slackware Linux boots is as simple as creating a symbolic link in the appropriate directory, such as with the following command:

```
# ln -s /opt/apache/bin/apachectl /etc/rc.d
```

This command is very similar to the equivalent command provided for Red Hat in the previous section. However, again demonstrating Slackware's primary goal of simplicity, there's nothing more to it than that. With the preceding command, Apache will be started each time the system starts up.

Installing Apache on Debian GNU/Linux

Like Red Hat Linux and Slackware Linux, Debian GNU/Linux includes a prebuilt package for Apache, but again it's the older version of the software. If you choose to use the material discussed in this chapter to build and install your own installation, you'll find that most of the material earlier on Red Hat Linux also applies to Debian GNU/Linux.

That is, since the two distributions both use the SysV model for their init scripts, the process is very similar. However, you'll have to use Debian's tools for managing the init scripts for your system's runlevels, as discussed in the section "Working with Debian's Tools" in Chapter 6. Additionally, you'll probably want to create that separate script that simply invokes the apachectl script (as mentioned earlier in the context of Red Hat Linux).

Summary

Having read this chapter, you have now seen an example of how to install and configure the Apache HTTP Server. This is no mean feat: Apache is a very large and flexible (and therefore complicated) piece of software. While you probably can't add "Master Apache Administrator" to your resume just yet, you should be well on your way to mastery. Once you've worked through the installation of Apache on your own system with your own configuration, you'll be doing very well indeed. More than that, if you can successfully configure Apache, then most other software will start to seem easy.

The next chapter in Part Three continues the trend of illustrating software installations, by focusing on the Concurrent Versions System (CVS). Chapter 12 will illustrate the installation and configuration of an inetd service.

CHAPTER 12

Concurrent Versions System

The Concurrent Versions System (CVS) is a member of a class of tools known variously as *change management tools, software and configuration management (SCM) tools*, and a few other names. CVS acts as a repository that houses a master copy of a software project, and allows developers to "check out" their own copies (known as *sandboxes*) as one might check out a book from a library. Acting as the repository, CVS also records, tracks, and manages changes to the software as they are made by the developers.

CVS is a next-generation version of a more primitive class of similar tools. The original Unix tool in this space was called the Source Code Control System (SCCS). SCCS also acted as a repository and allowed developers to check out and commit changes, but it was rather more restrictive in what it allowed developers to do. For example, only one developer could edit a given file at a time, and the repository had to be located on a local disk. The GNU project implemented a functionally similar tool known as the Revision Control System (RCS). CVS is based on RCS and uses it at the core, but provides enhanced capabilities.

CVS' major claim to fame is its ability to handle asynchronous development. Recall that SCCS and RCS allow only one developer at a time to edit a file, such as a header file. If this header file is a common one shared by all aspects of the software, then it becomes hard for multiple developers to work on different parts of the software at the same time. The approach CVS takes is to keep each developer's sandbox completely dissociated from the master repository, until the developer commits a change. At that point, the sandbox is synchronized with the repository, and any discrepancies are merged. CVS can handle and merge most types of discrepancies, but for a small set of cases it requires human intervention to resolve conflicts. (Actually, it's generally good practice to review any merges that CVS does even automatically, since no software is perfect.)

In addition to the major productivity gains provided by CVS, it also offers a few extra conveniences. CVS operates in several different modes, including both a client-server mode (and in fact, several such modes), as well as the traditional local repository mode used by SCCS. These features make CVS extremely useful as a tool for coordinating the changes of a far-flung team of developers; thus, CVS is extremely popular with open source development projects, and is even becoming increasingly common within large global corporations as a way to share projects across the world.

CVS is most commonly used for software development, as a repository for source code. However, nothing about CVS is specific to programming languages or source code. In fact, CVS can be used to manage any type of project. It works best for projects that consist of text-based files, but it can also be used with binary files (such as images or photos), at the expense of some of its ability to merge changes. Thus CVS is commonly used to manage nonsource code items such as the HTML files for web sites, XML data, text configuration files, and so on.

CVS' main strengths are its decentralized model (since developers aren't bound to the repository, but rather insulated until they commit their changes) and its support for asynchronous development. However, explaining how to use CVS as part of a successful software project management methodology is a topic large enough for its own book. Interested readers should consult the excellent CVS reference manual by Per Cederqvist at `www.cvshome.org/docs/manual/cvs.html`.

Like many of the other examples in the preceding installation chapters, CVS is included with most distributions. However, they typically only install CVS in its client mode, rather than its server mode. This makes sense, because setting up a CVS server (or even just a simple CVS repository) is only useful to software developers.

This chapter will detail how to install CVS in its server capacity as an inetd service. By reading this chapter, you'll also gain good insight into how to install *any* inetd-based service, as well as being able to set up your own functioning CVS repository. CVS is a classic example of an inetd service, so even nondevelopers should consider reviewing this chapter.

Just the Facts: Concurrent Versions System

Purpose: The Concurrent Versions System is a tool that provides software developers with the ability to manage changes to their products.

Authors: Many!

Web site: `www.cvshome.org`

Description: CVS is a change management tool designed to aid software developers (or other teams that collectively produce a body of work) in organizing, tracking, and managing their work. CVS helps developers collaborate without getting in each other's way or destroying each other's work. CVS improves on a variety of older tools in the same area.

Installing CVS

To install CVS in its server mode, the client programs need to be installed. This is because CVS' server mode operates as an inetd service. The inetd "Internet super-server" was discussed in Chapter 4; in brief, inetd is a program that provides basic networking support for other programs, so that they don't have to manage their own networking support. The standard CVS client programs make use of this functionality to "transform" themselves into server software. This section will describe how to install the standard CVS programs, with appropriate support for server mode. The section "Configuring CVS" will describe how to configure the standard programs for the most popular server mode.

Compile-Time Options

Like most open source programs, CVS supports several compile-time options. As discussed in Chapter 7, a compile-time option is a parameter that hard-codes a particular property into the software at the time it is built. Typically, compile-time options are used to enable or disable particular bits of functionality.

The first option that needs to be set is the --prefix option. This option determines where the program binaries will ultimately be installed. Chapter 7 discussed the possible destinations for software—namely, /usr/local and /opt. Since the installation of CVS is a single installation consisting of pretty simple files that will only occasionally need to be updated (if ever), a good destination is /usr/local.

 CROSS-REFERENCE   *For more information on choosing between /usr/local and /opt, see the section in Chapter 7 on "Deciding on a Destination."*

CVS supports compile-time options that enable or disable features related to the behavior of the client and server modes. Table 12-1 summarizes the major features supported by CVS, and lists the options for enabling and disabling them. Additional information can be obtained from running the command ./configure --help in the CVS root directory. (The ./configure command is the GNU autoconf tool also discussed in Chapter 7; the --help option displays information on supported options, and Table 12-1 is largely a summary of this information.)

Table 12-1. CVS Compile-Time Options

FEATURE	ENABLING FLAG	DISABLING FLAG
Support for authentication via the Kerberos protocol*	--with-krb4=[path]	--without-krb4
Support for authentication via the GSSAPI protocol*	--with-gssapi=[path]	--without-gssapi
Support for encryption of data in client/server mode when Kerberos is in use	--enable-encryption	--disable-encryption
Support for client mode	--enable-client	--disable-client
Support for server mode	--enable-server	--disable-server

*   Note: Options with a value of [path] must include a path to an installation of the corresponding library—for example, the Kerberos library. See the CVS documentation.

Generally, the options boil down to enabling these three possibilities:

- Client and server modes (via the --enable-client and --enable-server options)

- Encryption of the data across the network (via the --enable-encryption option)

- Alternative authentication mechanism such as Kerberos or GSSAPI

The vast majority of CVS installations will have both client and server enabled, most will have encryption enabled, and some will have the authentication mechanisms enabled.

Networks (such as a corporate or university network) that already use Kerberos or GSSAPI would benefit from those options; enabling them would permit an alternative to the rather insecure password server (pserver) mode to be used. Additionally, if Kerberos is in use, encryption can also be enabled. This prevents potentially valuable and secret material from being intercepted across the network. (Actually, it can still be intercepted, but since it's encrypted it can't be read.)

Most installations will require both client and server modes. However, an administrator could configure the CVS on workstations to contain only client support, whereas CVS on servers would contain only server support. This would prevent users from running CVS servers on their workstations and prevent users who log in to a server from running the CVS client. This functionality may be used to enforce a set of CVS usage policies, though it's not covered explicitly in this chapter.

For this example, I will show you how to enable client and server modes. You don't explicitly want Kerberos or GSSAPI support; however, if the libraries are already installed, you might as well use them, so you'll simply let the ./configure program detect their presence. (By default, ./configure will always auto-detect any features you don't explicitly include.) The following command is the command used to configure the software:

```
% ./configure --prefix=/usr/local --enable-client --enable-server
```

Installing from Source Code

Once the compile-time options have been selected and the ./configure program has been run, the software can be compiled. This section describes how to build and install the software. For CVS, this is quite simple.

Essentially, all you have to do is type make, followed by make install, as shown here:

```
% make
% make install
```

Various build messages will scroll by as the software is compiled, and more messages will scroll by as CVS is copied to /usr/local.

If both commands complete without errors, CVS will now be installed! The section "Configuring CVS" later in this chapter will discuss how to configure CVS (via its run-time options) for actual use.

Selecting the Best CVS Mode

This book discusses how to install and configure CVS for pserver mode. However, CVS actually supports a number of different modes and even several different server modes. (For example, there are modes that use Kerberos authentication instead of passwords.) The pserver mode discussed in this book is probably the *least* secure way to use CVS.

However, pserver mode is the most popular, which is why this book discusses it. Administrators concerned about security (and especially administrators running a repository on a public network) should consult the CVS documentation on how to use the more secure modes.

Configuring CVS

This section will describe how to configure CVS for server mode, once the standard CVS client tools have been installed. Password server–mode CVS works as a service that's run from the inetd "superserver." Configuring CVS for server access is as simple—and as tricky!—as correctly configuring inetd. As has already been noted, pserver mode is a rather insecure way to run a CVS repository. However, this section is as much about demonstrating how to configure an inetd service as it is about installing CVS, and so the pserver mode is demonstrated.

Unfortunately, different distributions sometimes use different versions of inetd; for example, Red Hat Linux uses the xinetd program, whereas Slackware Linux uses a more traditional Unix implementation. Whichever inetd implementation is used, it still has to run the same CVS command. The next few sections describe the configuration options related to CVS that are common to all implementations of inetd. The section "Installing CVS on Different Distributions" later in this chapter describes how to hook CVS and its server-mode parameters into the implementations of inetd on the three sample distributions.

The various compile-time options supported by CVS were discussed earlier in this chapter; see Table 12-1 for a list of these features. Notably, several options deal with authentication in server mode, such as Kerberos and simple password. This section will only discuss configuring a CVS server in normal password, or pserver, mode. Many distributions might not support some of the other modes (by not having Kerberos installed, for example), and pserver mode is the most common. Additionally, pserver mode is the simplest and makes the best example inetd installation. Consult the CVS documentation for information on other configuration options.

An installation of CVS in pserver mode consists of a few separate steps, described in the next section. These steps really go beyond what's strictly required to install an inetd service. However, every inetd service is going to have some kind of specific configuration requirements, like these steps or others. It's therefore useful to track the overall configuration of CVS—not just the inetd-related steps—to gain insight into general configuration techniques.

Creating the Repository Directory

The first step in the installation of CVS in pserver (or any other) mode is to create a directory for the data files. Recall that CVS encompasses the notion of a repository; this must be an actual directory where files that are checked in are stored, as well as the history of those files and various control information.

This directory can be located wherever is convenient. One possibility might be a subdirectory of the /opt or /usr/local directories. However, the Filesystem Hierarchy Standard (FHS) actually specifies a directory for such things as these databases: the /var directory. A reasonable choice then is the directory /usr/local/var/cvs. (The /usr/local/var directory was chosen over /var because, as was discussed in Chapter 7, most native package managers typically ignore the contents of /usr/local, treating it as system-specific material.)

The following simple command can be used to create the directory:

```
% mkdir -p /usr/local/var/cvs
```

The -p argument to the mkdir command instructs it to create not only the cvs directory, but also any of its parent directories that don't already exist. For example, there is frequently no /usr/local/var directory by default, so the preceding command would fail; with the -p option, the /usr/local/var directory will be created along with its child directory /usr/local/var/cvs.

Mission-Critical CVS Repositories

Using /usr/local/var (or even /opt/var, depending on taste) to hold CVS data is a good choice for a personal installation or for limited use. However, more important uses of CVS, such as those for organizations that actually produce software, have additional requirements, such as regular data backups and possibly failure tolerance and "hot backup" servers. After all, a CVS repository represents the master copy of whatever it manages; if you put all your eggs in one basket, it'd better be an extremely safe basket! Such users of CVS would likely place the CVS repository on a separate volume, partition, disk, server, and so on, and mount it as something like /cvs. Such users would also be sure to regularly back up the /cvs repository directory, and would also probably use one of the more secure CVS modes to better protect the server from attack.

Creating the User Accounts

Once the directory that is to house the CVS repository and related data has been selected and created, at least one user account must be created to access it. You can use a variety of ways to accomplish this task, and they are outlined in this section.

Relying on the System Accounts

CVS, by default, will grant access to any user who has a valid account on the underlying system. For example, any user with a valid user ID and password will be able to log in to and access the contents of the CVS repository (though that user would also have to have the correct Unix filesystem permissions). Thus, the simplest way to manage access to CVS is simply to pass the buck and let the standard operating system services handle it.

However, in this case, users will actually be logged in as themselves, and so they will be accessing the filesystem with their normal permissions. This might become a management burden, since file permissions are a little trickier to manage. (Setting up the file permissions for this example is covered in a later section.) Additionally, using this approach means that users literally have to have an account on the machine, meaning they can log into it, as well as use CVS; this may be a security risk if the machine is intended to be strictly a CVS server.

The upside of letting the system manage accounts is that it's easy to manage the users (simply because you don't have to manage them at all). The downside is that it's harder to manage file permissions and requires every CVS user to have an account on the system. This technique is most useful when the CVS pserver is to be used by a small workgroup and run on a server (perhaps a development server) to which all members of the group have access. It's less useful for larger projects with a more extensive user base.

Sharing a Single User Account

CVS provides an alternative to administrators who don't wish to defer authentication to the operating system. Instead, a single account can be set up for CVS, and it can even be an inactive account (that is, an account that doesn't permit logins). The CVS repository directory can be created to be visible only to this single real user, and the administrator can create multiple "phantom" accounts that are visible only to CVS.

This is accomplished by using CVS' local passwd file. This file is similar to the standard Unix /etc/passwd file, but is only used by CVS. The file allows administrators to map phantom CVS accounts to physical accounts. Users can be added to CVS simply by adding them to CVS' passwd file and mapping the phantom accounts to the single real account.

The upside of this approach is that it is a little more secure, since there is only one account to maintain, and the account can be granted restricted permissions to reduce the potential damage in the event of a security break-in. Also, the permissions on the repository directory itself are easier to manage, since there's only one physical account that needs access to it. The downside is that the administrators have to manage a CVS-specific passwd file. This approach is probably more appropriate for larger projects with many developers, with at least one person designated as an official CVS administrator.

This approach is the one taken by this book for the remainder of the example. In reality, it's also possible to use both techniques simultaneously, in a sort of hybrid mode. Setting up the permissions for both techniques and the procedures for adding users to the phantom CVS passwd file is covered in the next section.

Setting Permissions

This section will describe how to configure the permissions for the repository directory and give some details on how to manage user accounts. Each of the two cases previously outlined is discussed. The case where CVS' authentication is deferred to the operating system has more complicated repository directory permissions but simpler user administration, whereas the opposite is true of the virtual CVS accounts case.

Settings for the System Authentication Case

In the first case, CVS is configured to simply rely on the underlying operating system to handle authentication. That is, whenever a user logs in, CVS essentially just asks the operating system whether the username and password are valid. If they are, the process running CVS switches to that user identity and attempts to perform whatever CVS command the user requested.

This means the CVS server is actually running with the Unix permissions of the user account that logged in. That, in turn, means that if a particular user account doesn't have permission to read or write the actual CVS repository directory, then the account won't be able to access the installation of CVS!

So, the file permissions on the directory must be specified. Typically, installations in this case have three major properties:

- The repository directory is owned by a CVS-specific group in the /etc/group file (or another mechanism, such as the Network Information Service [NIS]).

- All users on the system who need access to CVS are included as members of the CVS group.

- The repository directory has permissions of group-readable and group-writable, and has the sticky bit set.

The first property is easy to achieve. Most distributions come with tools for managing users and groups, and the chown or chgrp command can be used to set the group associated with a given directory. Once the group exists, a command like the following (which uses the example path of /usr/local/var/cvs) will change ownership of the directory to the group cvsusers:

```
% chgrp -R cvsusers /usr/local/var/cvs
```

The second property in the list is also easy to achieve. For standalone systems that use the /etc/passwd and /etc/group files for authentication, there are typically utilities (such as useradd and groupadd) for adding, deleting, and managing the contents of users and groups. This is a pretty basic task, so if you don't know how to do this, check the documentation for your distribution. Systems that are on a network may use another authentication scheme (such as NIS, Kerberos, or another PAM module) that has a different mechanism for managing groups and group members; if you think that this might be the case, you may have to contact your network administrators for assistance in creating a group in the appropriate manner.

The third property—setting the sticky bit on the directory—is likewise easy, but requires some explanation. You should be familiar with the traditional Unix file permissioning scheme: that is, there are three classes of access and four permissions that can be individually granted to each class. The classes are the account that owns the file (user), members of the group to which the file belongs (group), and everyone else (other). The chmod command is used to set permissions for each class, and the permissions are read, write, execute (which is used for executable programs and scripts, and to view the contents of a directory), and sticky.

The *sticky permission* (sometimes called *sticky bit*) denotes that the file is to retain the permissions set on it, no matter what happens. Usually, the sticky bit is used to indicate that an executable program is to be run as the user or group who owns the file, rather than the user who actually ran the program. (When used this way, the sticky bit is called the *setuid bit*.) When applied to a directory, however, the sticky bit means that all subdirectories and files that are created underneath the directory are to retain the same permissions as the directory itself. The correct permissions and the sticky bit can be set on the /usr/local/var/cvs directory via the following commands:

```
% mkdir -p /usr/local/var/cvs
% chgrp -R cvsusers /usr/local/var/cvs
% chmod -R ug+rwx /usr/local/var/cvs
% chmod -R ug+s /usr/local/var/cvs
```

The -R parameter to chgrp and chmod instructs them to be "recursive" and repeat the command on all files and subdirectories contained within.

The reason it's important to use the sticky bit on the CVS repository directory is because there are multiple users, and the CVS pserver program actually runs as the individual users. If a user adds a file to CVS, the file is actually created and owned by the user who checked it in and will adopt that user's default permissions. This means that it's possible for one user to check in a file that's not accessible by another user, which is inconvenient, to say the least. Setting the sticky bit on the CVS repository directory overrides this behavior and forces any new files to have the same permissions as the /usr/local/var/cvs directory itself, preventing this problem.

Which User Owns the Repository?

Astute readers may be wondering which user has to actually own the CVS repository directory (which is /usr/local/var/cvs in this example). That is, which user has to actually run the mkdir command to create the directory? Well, the beauty of the sticky bit technique is that it doesn't matter! The root user can create the directory, and as long as the sticky bits are set correctly, as in the example, then any user in the CVS group will have full access to the repository.

Once these basic conditions are met, the CVS repository directory is ready to be used (though of course the server itself is not quite configured yet; read on for the remaining steps). Remember, though, that deferring user authentication to the operating system is just one way that CVS can be managed; the next section covers the other case.

Settings for the Virtual Accounts Case

The second major authentication technique for a CVS pserver installation is to use a list of virtual users specific to CVS. In this case, only a single user needs to be created on the underlying operating system. Additionally, this user never needs a login shell, so the account can have an empty or otherwise disabled password, to prevent security risks from allowing in a remote user. Instead of having an account on the system, users of CVS have phantom or virtual accounts within CVS itself; the virtual accounts are mapped to the physical account on the system.

Setting up this scenario is quite simple. Since there's only one user, there doesn't need to be a separate user group, and there's no sticky bit silliness to manage. Instead, the repository is simply created and owned by the single real user account, and all the virtual CVS users are mapped to (and run with the permissions of) the physical account. So, setting up the repository directory is as simple as executing these commands:

```
% mkdir -p /usr/local/var/cvs
% chown -R cvs:cvs /usr/local/var/cvs
```

This example assumes that the physical CVS username is cvs, and that a group is created for it, also called cvs. Not all distributions have a separate group for each user account; check your distribution's documentation for how to manage users and groups.

Adding virtual users to CVS is a bit more complicated. Once the CVS server is up and running, there is a special module named CVSROOT that users can check out. This directory contains various files that control how CVS behaves; one of those files is CVSROOT/passwd. This file contains usernames and passwords for the virtual accounts, and an additional field specifying the physical account name to which each virtual account corresponds. In this example, all accounts are mapped to the physical cvs user.

Unfortunately, managing the contents of the CVSROOT/passwd file (and performing additional administrative tasks) is getting beyond this discussion, which is simply focused on installing CVS. If you are interested, consult the documentation on CVS found at www.cvshome.org, especially the Cederqvist manual. The remainder of this section will focus on installing CVS pserver via the inetd service.

Using Hybrid CVS Authentication

These examples describe two ways to set up user authentication with CVS: either by deferring authentication to the operating system entirely or by mapping phantom CVS user accounts to an actual physical system account. In reality, this isn't an either/or proposition: CVS can be configured to operate in both modes at once. That is, CVS will always check the list of virtual accounts first; however, if the user isn't found there, it will then check with the operating system. This means that some users can be mapped to a physical account, whereas others can be left alone to log in through the operating system. This adds an additional layer of flexibility.

Establishing the Run-Time Parameters

The previous sections described how to decide on the values of various parameters that CVS requires to operate. The next step is to pull these parameters and values together into an actual command to run. This will be the command that the inetd server is configured to run for CVS connections, and this section will discuss how to formulate the specific command.

Really, it's quite simple. If you were to type the command to run CVS directly on the command line, it would have this general format:

```
% cvs -f --allow-root=<path to CVS repository> pserver
```

The key is the list of parameters. The -f argument instructs CVS to disregard any settings that may be in the user's ~/.cvsrc configuration file. This is important, because such options might change the behavior of CVS when running in server mode. The --allow-root parameter specifies the directory (or directories, since there can be more than one such parameter) of the CVS repository (which is /usr/local/var/cvs in this book's example). The pserver argument has no value and simply instructs the program (which normally runs as a client) to switch to server mode, using password authentication.

So, substituting in the repository path for this example, the specific command you need is as follows:

```
% cvs -f --allow-root=/usr/local/var/cvs pserver
```

This is the command that needs to be entered into the configuration for inetd. The precise mechanics of doing this varies by implementation of inetd. The next few sections discuss how to accomplish this on the sample distributions.

Installing CVS on Different Distributions

The previous sections described how to select parameters for configuring inetd to run CVS in pserver mode, and produced the actual command that needs to be run. The following sections will describe how to configure the sample distributions to actually run that command from within inetd.

Installing on Red Hat Linux

As discussed in Chapter 4, Red Hat Linux uses the xinetd program as its implementation of inetd. This program is a modernized version of the classic inetd that uses newer techniques for making configuration simpler. Classic inetd implementations (which are covered in the section "Installing on Slackware Linux") use a single configuration file to drive all inetd services. In contrast, xinetd uses the "drop-in configuration" technique (also discussed throughout Chapter 4) to configure services.

Updating the /etc/services File

This section will describe how to update the /etc/services file, which contains information assigning names to network services, to include CVS. The /etc/services file is a part of the operating system, rather than specific to any particular distribution or implementation of inetd. Thus, even though it's presented under the Red Hat Linux–specific section, it will need to be applied to each distribution.

The /etc/services file assigns symbolic names to TCP/IP network ports. For example, the standard port number for telnet connections is 23; there is thus a line in /etc/services that assigns the name "telnet" to port 23, like so:

```
telnet       23/tcp
```

You can probably already discern the general format from that line. It's very simple: a service name followed by the port number and the port number type, either TCP (stream oriented) or UDP (datagram oriented). (Whether a program uses TCP or UDP is determined by how the program was written.)

Programs written to employ the network typically determine the port number to use by looking up the service name via the operating system. For example, a program that needs to know the port for telnet would look up "telnet" from the operating system, which in turn consults /etc/services and returns a port number of 23.

Standard port numbers are typically assigned by a standards body such as the Internet Engineering Task Force (IETF) or the International Association for Names and Addresses (IANA), or agreed upon by convention. Most Linux distributions come with a recent /etc/services file that includes the vast majority of ports and service names with which users interact. In fact, the stock /etc/services file on a recent Red Hat Linux system includes well over 400 predefined network services. This list is fairly complete and contains many services that are not strictly required, but are present for reference; for example, it contains an entry for the Quake multiplayer network game!

Since the list of standard ports is constantly evolving, older distributions may not have as recent a list, so whenever you add a service to /etc/services, always check to make sure that it's not already there under a different name. For example, the version of /etc/services that ships with Red Hat Linux 7.3 already has an entry for CVS in pserver mode, as you can see here:

```
cvspserver          2401/tcp
```

So, on Red Hat Linux 7.3 systems, you don't actually have to modify the /etc/services file. However, some older versions of Red Hat Linux and other distributions' copies may not include this line, or may include it under a different name (such as "cvs" instead of "cvspserver"). Regardless, however, the port will be 2401. Adding two names for the same service won't break anything, though; it is simply redundant. (In fact, you don't really even need to add this line to /etc/services at all, and can instead use the raw port number directly. However, adding the line to /etc/services makes things more "human readable.")

The /etc/xinetd.d Directory

The xinetd program uses the drop-in configuration directory technique to configure services. That is, when xinetd is started up, it examines a particular directory looking for files containing configuration, and then reads those files. Each file contains configuration information for a different service that xinetd is to manage. By default and as installed on Red Hat Linux systems, the directory that xinetd uses for configuration files is /etc/xinetd.d.

To configure a service to run with xinetd, the first step is simply to create a file in /etc/xinetd.d that contains configuration data for the service. By convention, each file in /etc/xinetd.d is named according to the service it configures (though this is not required); for example, /etc/xinetd.d/wu-ftpd is the configuration file for the wu-ftpd FTP server program. For CVS, the file should be named /etc/xinetd.d/cvs.

Constructing the Configuration File

The next step is to create the contents of the CVS configuration file. This file contains information such as whether the server is enabled (since xinetd allows for a particular service to be configured but not actually active), whether the service is stream or datagram oriented, which user the service is to run as, and so on. This file has the following general format:

```
service <service name>
{
        configuration parameter] = [value]
}
```

The <service name> parameter is the name of the service as specified in /etc/services. The configuration parameter lines each contain a parameter and a value, and specify the bulk of the actual configuration data used by xinetd. Table 12-2 summarizes the most common parameters.

Table 12-2. xinetd Configuration File Parameters

PARAMETER	MEANING
disable	"yes" or "no"; indicates whether the service is active or not.
socket_type	"stream" or "dgram"; indicates whether the service is stream or datagram-oriented.
wait	"yes" or "no"; indicates whether the service will wait for additional incoming connections, or exit after servicing just one.
user	Username under which the service is to run (usually root).
server	Path to the service program executable.
server_args	Any arguments that need to be passed to the program.nice. Can be used to determine a priority for the service; this can reduce (or increase) the priority of a particular service to give it a reduced (or increased) portion of CPU time.

Table 12-2 shows only a portion of the total available options that can be used in a configuration file for xinetd services. The full documentation can be obtained from the manual page for xinetd.conf—that is, via the command man xinetd.conf. Although Table 12-2 is a good starting point for configuring an xinetd service and may be adequate for most simple cases, more complicated inetd services may require some of the options listed in the manual page.

Recall that Red Hat Linux 7.3 already includes an entry in /etc/services for CVS—"cvspserver"—so that much is easy. (On a distribution that uses xinetd but does not already have an entry for CVS, the administrator would have to add the entry and reference it in the xinetd configuration file, or use the numeric port number.) The disable parameter obviously needs to be "no", or else xinetd will still not run the CVS server. The socket_type parameter must be "stream", and the wait parameter must be "no"; these are properties of the CVS pserver program, and cannot be altered. The nice argument is really optional in this case, but can be left at "10". That will keep the CVS server running at a reasonable priority with respect to other processes on the system. (That is, it won't monopolize the CPU, but also won't get totally ignored by the system. See the manual page for the `nice` command for more information.)

The remaining three options—user, `server`, and `server_args`—are the values that were decided on earlier in this section. In the example, the user under which CVS is to run is cvs. The program itself was compiled from source code and installed in /usr/local/bin, so the `server` argument must be `/usr/local/bin/cvs`. Finally, the `server_args` parameter must be the arguments described earlier: `-f --allow-root=/usr/local/var/cvs pserver`. Listing 12-1 shows a complete xinetd configuration file for CVS.

Listing 12-1. xinetd Configuration File for CVS pserver Mode

```
service cvspserver
{
        disable         = no
        socket_type     = stream
        wait            = no
        user            = cvs
        server          = /usr/local/bin/cvs
        server_args     = -f --allow-root=/usr/local/var/cvs pserver
        nice            = 10
        port            = 2401
}
```

Managing xinetd

Now that CVS has been configured for xinetd, xinetd will begin managing it. However, if xinetd is already running, then it will need to be restarted. Additionally, some installations of Red Hat Linux may have xinetd installed, but not running. In these cases, xinetd will need to be configured to run on system startup. This section will describe how to accomplish these tasks.

If it's already running, restarting xinetd will cause it to reload its configuration files; this will result in xinetd "noticing" the new configuration file for CVS and running the server. The kill command can be used to terminate the old process, and xinetd can then be restarted from the command line. However, there is an easier way to do this on Red Hat Linux systems: As discussed in Chapter 4, Red Hat includes a command called service that can be used to conveniently start, stop, and restart services. Thus, the command service xinetd restart is much simpler than using the kill command and restarting xinetd manually.

There's actually yet another way to cause xinetd to "notice" CVS. By sending the SIGUSR2 signal to xinetd, the administrator can instruct xinetd to reload its configuration file, without actually exiting, which is a bit more graceful than killing and restarting the process. This can be accomplished with the following command:

```
% kill -USR2 `pidof xinetd`
```

There are actually a few more special signals that xinetd can handle; for more information on these signals or the SIGUSR2 signal already mentioned, readers should consult the manual page for xinetd.

One other convenient utility provided by Red Hat is the chkconfig command. This command was mentioned in Chapter 4, and allows administrators to examine, enable, and disable specific services (not just xinetd services!) running on the system. The chkconfig command can enable or disable xinetd services, as well as standard servers. So, once the CVS pserver xinetd service has been configured, it can be turned on and off using the chkconfig tool. For example, you could disable the CVS pserver from this example through this command:

```
% chkconfig cvs off
```

CVS pserver can later be reenabled by a similar command, replacing "off" with "on".

Installing on Slackware Linux

Configuring CVS to be run in pserver mode on a Slackware system is similar in spirit to the installation on Red Hat Linux, as discussed in the previous section. However, Slackware uses a traditional implementation of the inetd superserver, in contrast to Red Hat's modernized version. This makes for a few differences in the details of how to install it.

Actually, hooking CVS into Slackware's inetd is quite simple. First, the /etc/services needs to be modified, in precisely the same way as for Red Hat Linux. Then, the /etc/inetd.conf file needs to include a line that adds the CVS pserver to the list of ports that inetd monitors. Again, Slackware's philosophy of simplicity pays off: This operation involves adding a single line, rather than having to deal with multiple files in a directory and a custom format for the configuration file itself.

The following code is typically enough to configure CVS for Slackware's inetd (or for most Unix-like systems' inetd servers, for that matter).

```
cvspserver   stream   tcp   nowait   root
      /usr/bin/cvs cvs -f --allow-root=/usr/local/var/cvs pserver
```

Note that the preceding two lines should be joined into a single line in your copy of /etc/inetd.conf.

CROSS-REFERENCE   *For full details on configuring applications to work with inetd, see Chapter 5.*

The only difficulty that might arise with this technique is that many traditional implementations of inetd only support up to five arguments for the program executed (and one of those arguments has to be the name of the program itself). If you're running a sizable CVS repository with multiple roots, you might encounter this limit through the need for multiple --allow-root arguments. In these cases, however, inetd can be configured to call a very simple shell script which itself invokes the required CVS command. Since the shell script will have no limit on the number of arguments, CVS will run normally.

Installing on Debian GNU/Linux

Debian GNU/Linux uses a traditional implementation of the inetd program, like Slackware Linux. (Contrast this with Red Hat Linux's use of the xinetd variant.) This obviously means that preparing a CVS pserver installation on Debian GNU/Linux is very similar to doing so on Slackware Linux; in fact, the processes are identical.

Debian, however, also offers an additional tool used to manage the services run by its inetd version. The tool is named update-inetd and is discussed in the section entitled "Using the update-inetd Program" in Chapter 6. You may wish to investigate this tool, instead of doing things manually as you would on Slackware Linux.

Summary

In this chapter, you read about how to install and configure the Concurrent Versions System. You learned about its dual nature as both a server and a client, and learned how to configure the server facet to function as an inetd service. Additionally, you learned about the tools available on each of the sample distributions to automate this configuration process. You should also find your new skills to be very useful in configuring and managing any inetd-based service you encounter.

The next and final chapter in Part Three discusses the Java 2 Software Development Kit (J2SDK) from Sun Microsystems. This application is crucial for developing software written in the extremely popular Java programming language. By demonstrating the J2SDK, this book will also teach you how to install and manage a fairly complicated suite of command-line tools—skills for which you will find wide applicability.

#### CHAPTER 13

Sun Microsystems'
Java Development Kit

The Java programming language was created by Sun Microsystems to facilitate the development of both client-based and server-based applications. The Java language can really be viewed as a whole platform, since it specifies not only a programming language and the associated syntax and APIs, but also a runtime environment known as a *virtual machine*. The Java Virtual Machine (JVM) specification describes a sort of generic computer—the Java Virtual Machine—that is essentially emulated on top of actual hardware. Sun's Java 2 Software Development Kit (J2SDK) consists of both a set of tools (such as a compiler) for the Java language and a JVM for running applications. Countless books have been written on the equally countless aspects of the Java platform, and so this book doesn't go there. Interested readers can look into any of the books on the market (such as *Java in a Nutshell* by David Flanagan, and *Learn Java with JBuilder 6* by John Zukowski).

Distinguishing between J2SDK and JDK

The Java 2 Software Development Kit—J2SDK—is a product of Sun Microsystems. However, other vendors (such as IBM) that produce similar software for running and developing Java software frequently call their products a Java Development Kit (JDK). Moreover, Sun itself also formerly called its J2SDK a JDK.

You can think of the term "JDK" as describing the class of software that is used for developing and running Java software, whereas "J2SDK" is simply the name of Sun's particular version of a JDK. This is the terminology used in this chapter.

The J2SDK is a proprietary product. That is, even though Sun makes the specifications for the Java programming language and Java Virtual Machine freely available, the actual product of the J2SDK is Sun's proprietary software. Source code for the J2SDK is available; however, don't confuse this with open source software, since the Sun Community Source License under which Sun provides the code is not an open source license! For many of you, of course, this doesn't matter, and this book itself takes a pragmatic approach: sometimes, proprietary software is simply a necessity. A great many professional developers need to use Sun's J2SDK on Linux systems, so this chapter is provided to show you how. The upshot for you, however, is that in order to install this software, you must agree to a proprietary (but no-cost) software license. Examine this license carefully before agreeing to it and performing any of the steps in this chapter.

 CROSS-REFERENCE *See Chapter 2 for more information about open source software.*

Java is a full-blown programming language, and so it may not by itself be of interest to readers who aren't software engineers or programmers. However, the inclusion of the J2SDK as an example is primarily to demonstrate the installation of a proprietary software package that requires extensive user environment customizations to function properly. It's a great illustration of some very useful techniques, so even nondevelopers may wish to read this section.

Just the Facts: Sun Microsystems' JDK

Purpose: Provides a runtime environment and development tools for the Java programming language.

Authors: Sun Microsystems, the Blackdown Project

Web sites: `java.sun.com/j2se` and `www.blackdown.org`

Description: The Java programming language is Sun's highly portable platform for developing many types of applications, including GUI client programs, enterprise server applications, and small web-based applets.

Installing the J2SDK

The first step is, as always, to download the software. It can be found under the Products and APIs section of Sun's Java home page: `java.sun.com`. You'll need to download the Java 2 SDK for Linux. Since this is a proprietary software product, an installation from source code is not available as an option. Therefore, it's important that you make sure that the software will run on your actual distribution; the download page lists requirements that the distribution must have (which typically boils down to whether the distribution has the required version of the GNU glibc library package). Note that even though the source code is available for a no-cost download, the license isn't an open source license and building the code is no mean feat; this isn't really an option for end users such as you.

At the time of this writing, the current J2SDK version was 1.4, so this example assumes you are installing that version. In practice, however, it's common for Java developers to switch between different versions of the J2SDK, and even switch between different JDKs. For example, they may need to support a specific version of the J2SDK (which may or may not be the latest and greatest from Sun). Also, developers sometimes need to switch to another vendor's JDK implementation; IBM also has a version, and sometimes it's useful in debugging Java software to switch between the IBM and Sun versions.

This requirement implies that at any given time a system may need more than one JDK installed on it. As discussed in the section "Deciding on a Destination" in Chapter 7, this situation makes it more appropriate to install the software in /opt, rather than /usr/local. For example, a system might have /opt/ibm-jdk-1.3 and /opt/sun-j2sdk-1.4 both installed simultaneously. However, there's more to Java than just the JDK; developers and users of Java software also need a wide variety of Java libraries (called *Java Archive files* or *JAR files*) in order to actually use most software. Thus, this example takes the /opt technique a step further: the software will be installed in /opt/java rather than simply /opt. This will be discussed in more detail as this section continues; for now, it's enough to say that the installation directory is /opt/java/sun-j2sdk-1.4.

The next step is to physically extract the JDK. The package is distributed as a shell script, actually. This may seem somewhat strange to those of you unfamiliar with it; security-conscious users may even be (justifiably!) suspicious of packages that must be executed in order to install them. However, this package is fairly innocuous. It is a *shell archive (shar) file*. This format is similar in concept to a Tape Archive (tar) file, ubiquitous on Unix systems and probably already familiar to you. However, a shar file is actually encoded into a shell script, unlike a tar file, which is simply a binary data file. There are generally two reasons for using a shar file instead of a tar file: One is that since it's a shell script, it's simply an ASCII text file, and so is easier to e-mail than a binary tar file would be.

The other reason for using a shar file—and the one that Sun is interested in—is that since the format is a shell script, the packager can include a script to be run when the package is extracted. In the case of the JDK, Sun uses this capability to display a copy of the software license to which you are required to agree before the shar file will continue with the extraction. Thus, when the JDK distribution is unpacked, the license will be displayed, and you must agree to it before continuing.

At any rate, the JDK distribution file can be extracted simply by executing the file. However, the shell script extracts the contents into the current directory, so it's important to move to the *parent* directory of the desired ultimate location! An additional potential nuisance is that the JDK will extract itself into a specifically named directory: j2sdk1.4. If there's already a directory by that name (which may be the case if more than one JDK is installed), then its contents will be over-written, so check carefully before proceeding! Thus, it may be advisable to perform the extraction in a directory other than the destination, such as /tmp. At any rate, here are the steps to extract the J2SDK (assuming that the J2SDK distribution has been downloaded into /tmp/[filename]):

```
% mkdir /tmp/jdk; cd /tmp/jdk
% sh /tmp/[filename]

% mkdir -p /opt/java
% mv j2sdk1.4 /opt/java/sun-j2sdk-1.4
```

After performing the second step, you must read and agree to the license, and then the contents will be extracted.

The -p parameter to the mkdir command causes it to silently return, rather than fail with an error, if the directory already exists; consult the manual page for mkdir for more information.

At this point, the Sun Java 2 SDK version 1.4 will be installed in /opt/java/sun-j2sdk-1.4. The reason that the name was changed from the default name of j2sdk1.4 is because more than one version of the J2SDK may need to be installed on the system at the same time. This name change makes it easier to manage the versions installed. For example, version 1.3 of IBM's JDK implementation could be installed alongside the Sun version in the directory /opt/java/ibm-jdk-1.3. This naming scheme makes it easier to keep track of which vendor's software is installed in which directory.

Configuring the J2SDK

Extracting the J2SDK is the easy part; it's somewhat more complicated to get it working correctly. This section will discuss techniques for configuring the J2SDK for actual use. There are two main goals: It should be possible to install multiple versions of the JDK on the system at the same time without conflict, and it should be quick and easy to install and use Java applications.

The /opt/java Directory

In the previous section, the JDK package was installed into /opt/java/sun-jdk-1.4. This is a bit of a deviation from the normal practice of installing software directly into /opt. (For example, in Chapter 11 the Apache HTTP Server was installed directly as a subdirectory of /opt.) The reason for creating an entire separate subdirectory for Java software is because there's more to Java than just the J2SDK. The J2SDK is just the beginning: Once it's installed, actual programs that are written in Java will need to be installed, and Java support libraries also need to be installed.

In this sense, the J2SDK (or any JDK) is really its own little operating system, with programs and libraries that need to be installed on top of it. This would quickly clutter up the /opt directory, so the /opt/java subdirectory was created. It works just like /opt, except that it contains only Java-related files. The /opt/java directory as used by this book contains the following files and directories:

- /opt/java/[directory]: Separate subdirectories for each JDK to be installed

- /opt/java/packages: A directory containing Java support libraries; JAR and ZIP files

- /opt/java/jdk: A symbolic link that points to the "primary" or default JDK installation

The use of the /opt/java directory is clearly optional, and it won't be found in any standard or specification (such as the Filesystem Hierarchy Standard mentioned in the "Filesystem Layout" section of Chapter 3). It's a technique that the author developed over time to support a large group of Java developers using Linux workstations, at a major corporation. The /opt/java directory simply makes it convenient to manage installations of vendors' JDKs, applications, and support files. Other administrators may prefer another solution (such as placing all files directly in /opt); in the end, it's a matter of taste. The purpose of this book is to provide examples and best practices; you should take this material and run with it, developing your own custom solutions.

Installing Multiple JDKs

Recall that one of the goals of this example Java installation is to make it quick and easy to actually use Java and Java applications. This means that individual users shouldn't have to make extensive configuration changes, edit many (if any!) shell scripts, and so on. However, this is (as it always is) at odds with the need for flexibility: If you install multiple vendors' JDKs, then obviously the user has to choose between them.

The compromise in this case is the /opt/java/jdk symbolic link (or *symlink*). This link points to one particular JDK installation that is designated to be the default JDK. For example, a given system might have three JDKs installed: the latest production-quality J2SDK from Sun, a JDK from IBM that is optimized for speed, and the absolute latest beta-quality J2SDK from Sun for testing. Most of the time, the developer will only want to use the latest release JDK, so the /opt/java/jdk link should point to that installation. In this example, there's only one JDK installed (namely, Sun's J2SDK), so the /opt/java/jdk link must point to it, which can be accomplished by issuing this command:

```
% ln -s /opt/java/sun-j2sdk-1.4 /opt/java/jdk
```

When a JDK is upgraded (perhaps when that beta-quality J2SDK is replaced by the next production release), it can simply be installed alongside the others, and the default JDK can be switched simply by updating the /opt/java/jdk symbolic link. However, it's crucial to remember that this only works if the users' environments actually point to /opt/java/jdk; obviously, if users have specific installations directly hard-coded into their environments, then changing /opt/java/jdk won't work. For this reason, all the user environment details described in the following sections are created to refer to /opt/java/jdk instead of a specific installation directory.

Installing JAR Files

The Java platform provides the ability to add support libraries for applications' use. These libraries are packaged either as ZIP-compressed files (which have an extension of .zip) or as Java Archive files. These libraries are similar in concept to the Unix dynamic libraries discussed in Chapter 7 and the Apache dynamically loadable modules discussed in Chapter 11.

These JAR files, however, must be explicitly made available to the Java Virtual Machine. Depending on the implementation of the JVM, there are typically a couple ways of doing this: most commonly, you'll either place the JARs in a specific directory known to the JVM, or add the names of JAR files to an environment variable (called the CLASSPATH variable.) Either way, there can quickly be an explosion of JAR files, with conflicting versions. This confusion of files is error-prone and can sometimes be very difficult to debug.

This is the motivation for the existence of the /opt/java/packages directory. Administrators place system-wide JAR and ZIP files in this directory, and the user environment will automatically set up the users' CLASSPATH variables to include the files. Adding a new file to /opt/java/packages will be picked up by the users' environments the next time they log in.

One issue with this approach, however, is that /opt/java must be owned by root; this means that average users can't place their own custom files in that directory. They'd have to manage their CLASSPATH on their own, which defeats the purpose of having a common /opt/java/package directory. To address this, the user environment scripts contained in the next section support not only the /opt/java/packages directory, but also a java/packages directory in the user's home directory. The scripts work identically on both of these directories, and they are complementary to each other. See the next section for more information.

Configuring the User Environment

The subdirectories of /opt/java work fine for organizing files, but they're useless unless the users' login environments are set up correctly. This section will present and discuss the necessary changes and scripts for configuring the users' environments for accessing the Java installation in /opt/java. Generally, there are only three things that need to be done: setting the users' CLASSPATH, adding the Java programs to the users' PATH, and setting the JAVA_HOME environment variable.

Setting the CLASSPATH

The CLASSPATH is an environment variable that instructs the Java Virtual Machine where to find JAR files. (Java is an object-oriented programming language, meaning that it operates on the notions of *classes* as a model of the software system. These classes are what is stored inside JAR and ZIP files, and so the path containing these libraries is known as the CLASSPATH.) The CLASSPATH is simply an environment variable whose value is a list of directories, ZIP files, and JAR files that contain Java classes, with each entry separated by colons.

In the earlier section, "Installing JAR Files," the directory /opt/java/packages was created as repository of JAR and ZIP files. Each file in this directory, then, must individually be added to the CLASSPATH variable. Additionally, whenever a new JAR file is added to (or removed from!) the directory, the CLASSPATH should be automatically adjusted, so that the administrator doesn't have to do it manually. By now, this problem should be familiar: It's the drop-in configuration problem, described extensively in Chapter 4!

The spirit of Unix is to never reinvent the wheel, so the easiest way to solve this problem is just to use the same techniques employed by Red Hat as described throughout Chapter 4. In fact, this problem is very simple to solve; the following shell script snippet in sh syntax (rather than csh syntax) will configure the CLASSPATH variable correctly:

```
set CLASSPATH=.
for jar in /opt/java/packages/*; do
    set CLASSPATH=${CLASSPATH}:${jar}
done
export CLASSPATH
```

The preceding fragment simply locates each JAR file in the /opt/java/packages directory and adds it to the CLASSPATH. The CLASSPATH starts out as a single dot("."). A path of ".", remember, is Unix shorthand for the current working directory, and so the fragment includes the current working directory as the first entry in the CLASSPATH. This is useful because it allows Java programs run from the command line to find classes that may be in the directory from which they were executed; this permits so-called anonymous Java classes to be located. (Don't worry if this doesn't make sense—it's not important to know how Java works. Just be sure to understand how the variable's getting set.) One final thing to note is that the code fragment adds any file *or* subdirectory in /opt/java/packages to the CLASSPATH; thus, Java libraries that are set up as flat directories rather than JAR or ZIP files will also work with the technique.

Recall that setting the CLASSPATH to include files in /opt/java/packages is only half the problem: Users will still need to modify their CLASSPATH to include specific files that they need themselves. However, the following similar example works for adding files from the users' own personal directories:

```
set CLASSPATH=.
if [ -d ${HOME}/java/packages ]; then
    for jar in ${HOME}/java/packages; do
        set CLASSPATH=${CLASSPATH}:${jar}
    done
fi
export CLASSPATH
```

This code snippet is almost identical to the previous case, except that it checks to make sure the user actually *has* a ~/java/packages directory before trying to add files from it. (The script can simply assume that /opt/java/packages is present, since it's global and managed by the system administrator.) Another thing to note is that the first line again globally resets the value of CLASSPATH; if you combine the two scripts, be sure to remove that line!

Setting the PATH and JAVA_HOME

The PATH variable is used by the shell to locate programs to execute; the JAVA_HOME variable simply needs to point to the directory where the J2SDK is installed. These are very simply variables to set; however, as was mentioned earlier, if they are set to point directly to a particular installation of a JDK (such as /opt/java/sun-jdk-1.4), then the script will have to be modified each time a JDK is upgraded.

One solution is quite simple: Just set these variables to point to the /opt/java/jdk symbolic link, rather than to a specific installation. Although this will work just fine, users who need to switch to a different JDK (other than the one indicated by /opt/java/jdk) will have to manually reset their PATHs. A more flexible solution is to allow the user a chance to override the default selection, by pointing to a specific installation. The following script fragment demonstrates this:

```
if "X${JAVA_HOME}" == "X"; then
    set JAVA_HOME=/opt/java/jdk
fi

set PATH=${PATH}:${JAVA HOME}/bin
export PATH JAVA_HOME
```

This fragment simply sets the JAVA_HOME variable to the default /opt/java/jdk—but only if it's not already set!—and then adds an entry to the PATH relative to JAVA_HOME. To switch to a specific version of the J2SDK (or to another JDK), the user simply sets the JAVA_HOME variable and reexecutes the preceding script. It will pick up the custom JAVA_HOME and configure the environment appropriately.

....

Understanding JDKs

The example installation of a Java Development Kit in this section is based on an important assumption. The examples (especially the shell scripts) assume that the JDK being used works the same as Sun's reference J2SDK. The most common JDKs (such as IBM's version) do behave the same as Sun's; however, it's possible that some do not. Watch out for differences in behavior, and be prepared to tailor this example to the specific JDK being installed.

....

Pulling It All Together

The script fragments presented in this chapter accomplish 90% of what needs to be done; the rest is just integration. Listing 13-1 is a complete, fully functioning version of the script fragments. This listing could be copied to a file and included in the shell environment configuration for users. (The next section describes how to actually accomplish this on each of the sample distributions.) This file is again in the sh shell syntax; check the web site at www.apress.com for an equivalent file in csh syntax for users of the csh and tcsh shells.

Listing 13-1. J2SDK User Environment Configuration Script

```sh
#!/bin/sh

# set the JAVA_HOME to the default, unless it's already set
if [[ "X"${JAVA_HOME} == "X" ]]; then
    JAVA_HOME=/opt/java/jdk
fi


# add the JDK's bin directory to the PATH
PATH=${JAVA_HOME}/bin:${PATH}


# set the CLASSPATH; initialize to just "." (current working directory)
CLASSPATH=.
for jar in /opt/java/packages/*; do
    if [[ "${jar}" == "/opt/java/packages/*" ]]; then
        break;
    fi
    CLASSPATH=${CLASSPATH}:${jar}
done


# also add any JARs in the user's own java packages directory
if [ -d ${HOME}/java/packages ]; then
    for jar in ${HOME}/java/packages/*; do
        if [[ "${jar}" == "${HOME}/java/packages/*" ]]; then
            break;
        fi
        CLASSPATH=${CLASSPATH}:${jar}
    done
fi


export PATH JAVA_HOME CLASSPATH
```

Installing the J2SDK on Different Distributions

This section will discuss how to tailor the generic example shown in the preceding section to specific distributions. Since generally installing the J2SDK consists of extracting the files and modifying the users' login environments, tailoring the installation for a distribution is as simple (or as complicated!) as hooking Listing 13-1 into the global user login scripts.

Installing on Red Hat Linux

As discussed in Chapter 4, Red Hat Linux makes extensive use of the drop-in configuration file directory technique. The drop-in directory for user shell environment customization is /etc/profile.d. Recall that the top-level login scripts simply invoke files in /etc/profile.d—the bash shell invokes files that end in .sh, and the tcsh shell invokes files that end in .csh.

CROSS-REFERENCE *See the section "User Environment" in Chapter 4 for details on Red Hat Linux's user environment configuration.*

Customizing the J2SDK installation on Red Hat Linux, then, is as easy as placing the shell script in Listing 13-1 into the /etc/profile.d directory; a good choice might be to name the file /etc/profile.d/java.sh. For tcsh users, the version of Listing 13-1 in csh syntax could be placed in /etc/profile.d/java.csh. (This version of Listing 13-1 can be found on the book's web site.)

One important caveat, however, is how users individually override the default JDK location. The script in Listing 13-1 checks to see if the user already has a JAVA_HOME variable set and only sets it to the default if the user doesn't already have one. However, since this script will be invoked from the global login process *before* the user's personal scripts are, the user will have no opportunity to reset the JAVA_HOME variable. Fortunately, all the user has to do is simply log in, set the JAVA_HOME variable manually, and then re-source /etc/profile.d/java.sh to reconfigure the shell (using the command such as . /etc/java.sh for users of bash).

Installing on Slackware Linux

As discussed in the section "Customizing the User Environment" in Chapter 5, Slackware Linux has a fairly simple mechanism for handling login scripts. On the one hand, this makes it easy to customize manually, but on the other hand makes it more difficult to customize automatically. That is, adding Listing 13-1 to the login process on Slackware Linux isn't as easy as just dropping a file into a directory (as is true of Red Hat Linux mentioned earlier).

Instead, the administrator will have to modify the global login scripts to add support for Java to the users' environments. The first solution to suggest itself is to simply copy the script in Listing 13-1 and paste it directly into the /etc/bashrc file (after removing the first line—#!/bin/sh). This would work fine, but then the global script is that much longer. A better solution might be to copy the contents of Listing 13-1 into the /etc directory (such as a file named /etc/javarc.sh), and then add a reference to it from /etc/bashrc, as this example shows:

```
if [ -f /etc/javarc.sh ]; then
    . /etc/javarc.sh
fi
```

The disadvantage of this approach is that if there are many such files being installed (in addition to just the one file for the J2SDK), then the /etc directory may become cluttered. So, it's a trade-off: a single monolithic shell script, or multiple files that may add clutter. It really comes down to a matter of preference on the administrator's part.

Installing on Debian GNU/Linux

The users' login shell environment on Debian GNU/Linux is set up in a similar fashion to that of Slackware Linux. That is, the files /etc/profile, /etc/bashrc, /etc/csh.cshrc, and /etc/csh.login are used to configure the users' various shells. These scripts on Debian GNU/Linux are similar to but have different contents from their counterparts on Slackware Linux. As a result, connecting the J2SDK installation described in this chapter is very similar to the process described in the previous section on Slackware Linux, though there will be some minor differences. By now you should have no trouble with this.

Summary

You've now seen how to install the J2SDK from Sun Microsystems. This has taught you three things. First, you've obviously learned how to install a JDK, allowing you to develop Java software (if that's your cup of tea). Second, you've learned in a more general sense how to configure a software "suite" similar to the J2SDK; this essentially boils down to managing environment variables and software installations. Third, you've also learned how to apply techniques you already knew to solve a new problem. I'm specifically talking about how the /opt/java directory helps you manage your Java software installations by mimicking the standard /opt directory, with which you were already acquainted.

Hopefully you're now starting to see how all these small tricks and techniques that this book has been discussing come together to help you solve actual problems. Now armed with knowledge of a variety of software installations, you should be able to apply these little tricks and techniques to any new problem you come across—just as you applied and tailored the principles of /opt for the new /opt/java directory. This chapter concludes Part Three of this book, which is about installing software. Part Four will discuss several case studies of real-world Linux systems. Part Four will draw on the material in the other parts, and especially on Part Three. If you've finished reading this entire part (from Chapter 7 to this chapter), congratulations—you're now ready to see some actual case studies!

Part Four

Case Studies

The next part of this book is a set of case studies. These three chapters describe actual real-world systems. As you'll see, though the systems start from the same stock distribution, they turn out quite differently. Once you've read these chapters, you'll be able to build such systems yourself. Even more than that, though, this is the last push of this book—it's the coup de grace, and after reading these chapters, you'll have gone end to end, from basics to application.

The three case studies are of different configurations of systems that I use. These aren't just theoretical examples, they're actual configurations used on a daily basis. The first is a desktop system that is suitable for home use. It includes software such as a good desktop environment, movie players, games, and so on. The second configuration is a corporate workstation used for software development in several languages. This system is part of a large network, and it includes a variety of technically oriented software. The third and final configuration is a firewall that I use on my home network.

Each case study system is built from a stock installation of Red Hat Linux 7.3. The studies take you through the process of installing (and in some cases removing) software packages and configuring the system for a specific goal.

You don't really need to read these chapters in any particular order, so if you're only interested in one or two cases, you can come back and read the others later. However, these chapters *do* draw extensively on the material covered in Parts One through Three. This means that the case studies focus on telling you *what* to do and refer to previous chapters to tell you *how*. In other words, be sure you're familiar with the other parts of this book before you read these chapters.

#### CHAPTER 14

Building a Desktop System

This chapter shows you how to install and configure a system suitable for personal use. As with all the case studies, this system starts with a stock Red Hat Linux 7.3 distribution, and additional software is installed as needed. First some background outlines the goals and applications of the configuration, and then the actual construction process is described in detail.

Getting Started

This section outlines the goals and motivations of this case study. It describes the type of user who will most likely be interested in this environment and defines some basic terms. You can skim through this section if you'd like, but do make sure you at least skim it, as you'll find the information useful when you read the actual case study.

Who This Example Is For

The goal of this chapter is to demonstrate how a Linux system can meet a typical user's everyday needs. There really isn't anything in this chapter that you don't already know how to do—no magic installation tricks or configuration voodoo. All the software can be installed and configured by techniques similar to those discussed in Chapters 7 through 13; sometimes the process will be as simple as installing the appropriate Red Hat Package Manager (RPM), and other times you may have to install applications from source code or other packaging format.

You can view this chapter as a sort of potpourri of useful applications. This chapter won't go into detail on the nuances of installing or configuring the software, since you already know how to do that. Instead, it focuses on pointing you in the right direction in selecting and installing the software you need to meet your goals.

The final objective, really, is to produce a feature-complete desktop. You will frequently hear technology "experts" claim that Linux systems are not good desktop systems. Well, after this chapter you'll be able to decide that for yourself. The system described in this chapter has everything I need; if your needs are similar to mine, then you—like me—may never need to use a non-Linux operating system again.

Of course, maybe your needs *are* different. Perhaps you'll read this chapter, experiment with some of the applications yourself, and decide that in the end, Linux *isn't* viable as a desktop system for you. That's really the ultimate goal: to educate you enough so that you can make that determination yourself, and not take some "expert's" word for it.

Defining a Desktop

Any problem can be easily solved, if you define the problem narrowly enough. So, you need to define the notion of a desktop system precisely enough so that you can create one. For the purposes of this example, a desktop system is simply a computer used for routine, everyday computing tasks. The tasks this chapter focuses on appear in the list that follows; if a system can support these basic, common tasks, then consider it a desktop system.

- Office productivity (word processing, spreadsheets, and so on)

- Web browsing

- Hardware support (USB devices, storage devices, and so on)

- Multimedia and entertainment (digital photography, games, and so on)

- Connectivity (accessing your desktop remotely, accessing other systems)

These items are great, but to what is this desktop system being compared? Well, there are three other general classes of computer system:

- Embedded devices, such as personal digital assistants (PDAs)

- Servers

- Workstations

This book doesn't discuss embedded Linux, so you don't need to consider that. Additionally, a server is pretty straightforward: It's a machine dedicated to providing some specific feature or functionality (that is, a service) to other machines on a network. This leaves us with a workstation, which is a bit fuzzier.

Many people use the terms "desktop" and "workstation" interchangeably, but it's useful to draw a distinction between them. I've just defined a desktop. A workstation is usually a high-performance personal computer used for a *specific* task, rather than a general set of tasks. For example, the machine an architect or engineer uses to do computer-aided design work would be a workstation; similarly, the system a software engineer uses to develop applications would be a workstation, as would a computer used by a research scientist to run a "number-crunching" program.

Each of these examples is of a computer being used for a specific, highly demanding task. Building such a workstation is the subject of the case study you'll find in Chapter 15; this chapter focuses on configurations that you're more likely to find in a home or office rather than an engineering department.

Contents of This Chapter

Now that I've defined the goals and outlined what I'll be covering, it's time to talk about how the approach for meeting these goals. This section describes the kind of information you'll find in this chapter.

Recall that this chapter assumes that you're already familiar with the material in Part Three, which discussed the mechanics of installing and configuring software. This chapter points you in the right directions, to give you some idea of how to apply the mechanics you've already learned.

To that end, this chapter focuses on software. Several categories of software are discussed, and each category cites popular, functional software packages that fulfill the goals of the category. The software packages themselves are described briefly, their applicability is discussed, and alternatives are mentioned where appropriate. You'll also find information on any peculiar quirks of these packages, such as potential configuration pitfalls, licensing restrictions, and so on. Finally, I'll choose a package for the case study and explain the reason for my choice.

Once you've read the section on a given category of software, you'll have a general understanding of the options available to you in that category, some of their limitations, and a bit of insight into any difficulties you might encounter. In other words, you'll have a sense of the state of the art within that category. This understanding will allow you to apply the skills you've gained in Parts One through Three. You'll be able to either take the selections presented in this chapter verbatim to duplicate the configuration, or you'll be able to make an educated choice of an alternative.

To get started, the next section will describe the basics of the desktop system case study. You'll learn what the goals and requirements of the system are, and then read how the basic Red Hat Linux 7.3 system was installed as the core of that system.

Building the System

Obviously, the first step in constructing any system, including this case study, is to install the base distribution. Like all the case studies, this one starts with a stock Red Hat Linux 7.3 installation. This section describes a few basic details of how the system was initially configured.

This section focuses on the installation of the *stock* Red Hat Linux distribution. It doesn't focus on explaining the entirety of the system in detail; that is, after all, the focus of the rest of the chapter. In other words, if you want to duplicate this case study, you can start the Red Hat Linux installation after reading this section, but it's a good idea to read the entire chapter first, so that you get a comprehensive feel for how to duplicate the system.

Selecting the Packages

As discussed in Chapter 4, Red Hat Linux has several installation classes from which the user can select when installing the system. These classes are really just lists of RPM packages that together make up a typical configuration for a particular use. For example, the Server configuration contains packages such as the Apache HTTP server, Network Filesystem software, and so on.

The installation class selected for this case study was the KDE Workstation. As you'll read later in this chapter, KDE was selected over GNOME for this case study, though nothing prevents you from making a different choice. The package list was not further customized at installation, though parts of the rest of this chapter discuss additions to the basic configuration.

Details of the Configuration

During the installation process, the Red Hat installer (called *anaconda*) prompts you for a variety of configuration information. Nothing out of the ordinary was done for this case study; the defaults were configured as you would expect them to be for a workstation. For example, the network was configured to use Dynamic Host Configuration Protocol (DHCP), and the disk was partitioned along fairly typical lines, with /boot, /usr, and /home on different partitions.

CROSS-REFERENCE *See Part Two, or consult your favorite Red Hat reference for more information about configuring the system during installation.*

After the configuration, nothing was changed, except for the basic security procedures discussed in Chapter 4 (such as disabling unwanted inetd services). Notably, the firewall included with Red Hat Linux was left enabled, with the security level set to High. Only the port for the Secured Shell (SSH) protocol was left exposed, so that OpenSSH can be used for remote access (which is explored later in the section "Accessing the Desktop Remotely Using SSH"). This is important for security (even if your network has a separate firewall such as the one discussed in Chapter 16), and it is referred to occasionally throughout the rest of this chapter.

As you can see, there isn't much to configuring the base Red Hat Linux installation used for this case study. That, of course, was the point of choosing Red Hat in the first place: It does much or most of the work for you. In the rest of this chapter, you'll read about the reasons why each decision was made, and about any caveats or pitfalls that you may encounter if you reproduce this case study. The next section goes into a bit more depth, and starts to outline additional software that was installed.

Using Desktop and Productivity Applications

The first thing you'll encounter when you use any operating system is the user interface. On Linux-based systems, the user interface is usually the X Window system (typically embodied as XFree86), and a desktop or window manager. After the desktop environment, many users consider the "office productivity" environment and similar tools to be the next most crucial software. This section describes the X desktop manager and a set of major productivity tools for the case study system.

Desktop Environment

The desktop environment is probably the most immediate and therefore comprehensive part of an operating system with which the user interacts. Thus, choosing the desktop environment for this case study defines the character of that environment.

On the other hand, choosing a desktop environment typically doesn't define the software you can and cannot use on your system. For example, choosing the KDE system does not prevent you from using programs written to work with the GNOME environment. From this perspective, then, the selection of a desktop environment does not greatly affect the selection of software you can use.

In other words, your choice of desktop environment is largely a matter of taste. It can have some impact on the way you work, but it usually doesn't *prevent* you from using a particular program. The worst case is probably excessive memory consumption. For example, if you normally use GNOME but run a KDE program, that program may need to load a variety of KDE-related shared libraries that will only be used by that one program; normally these libraries would be shared among many KDE programs, but they aren't used by GNOME programs.

The Selection: KDE

Observe the following details about the K desktop environment:

- **Location**: www.kde.org

- **Version**: 3.0

- **Package**: Many packages; included with Red Hat 7.3

- **Description**: A complete, full-featured, open-source X desktop environment, and related productivity tools

This case study was configured to use KDE. KDE was installed during the Red Hat Linux distribution installation (rather than after the fact) simply by selecting the KDE high-level package set. With few exceptions, each of the other programs mentioned in this chapter will work just fine with KDE, even if they're intended for a different environment.

In a nutshell, use whatever desktop environment you wish to. If you find yourself using many programs from another environment (such as using many GNOME programs if you're a KDE user), then you may wish to consider switching, but in the end it doesn't matter a great deal. Excellent documentation exists online for each of the major environments, so it's really quite hard to go wrong.

The Alternatives: GNOME, GNUStep, Sawfish, BlackBox, and FVWM

Perhaps the most popular competitor to KDE is GNOME. Both KDE and GNOME have been mentioned in this book several times, and are well-documented elsewhere. However, there is actually a substantial number of other desktop environments and window managers that are less well known than these two "giants." Table 14-1 lists several such environments, and provides URLs to information on them. Some of these environments are quite intriguing, so you may wish to check them out when making your own decision.

Table 14-1. Desktop Environments and Window Managers

ENVIRONMENT	DESCRIPTION	URL TO INFORMATION
GNUStep	Open source implementation of OpenStep	`www.gnustep.org`
Sawfish	Scriptable via the LISP language	`sawmill.sourceforge.net`
BlackBox	A minimalist window manager	`blackbox.alug.org`
FVWM	A popular, classic window manager	`www.fvwm.org`

Table 14-1 is *by no means* comprehensive. A simple search in your favorite web search engine will reveal several metric tons of X Window managers. You should take a look around and see if anything catches your eye.

At any rate, if you feel like this section has glossed over the desktop environment topic, you may be right. This book is about the distribution, tuning, and customizing of your system. These days, every distribution worth its salt includes packages of several window managers, and selecting a window manager is as simple as whipping out your package management tool (such as RPM or apt-get) and installing the correct files. Spending much time on something that's so old hat seems like a bit of a waste, especially when it doesn't matter a great deal. So, just choose what you like and move on!

Office Productivity

Many users swear by their office suites, and indeed such software has become a staple of modern computing. Several such suites are available for Linux systems. This section describes some of them.

The Selection: OpenOffice

I choose the OpenOffice suite for this case study primarily for its extensive support for importing and exporting files to other office suite formats. This ability becomes crucial when you need to interact with other people who may not use the same suite you do—such as when you're writing a book on tuning and customizing a Linux system! However, if this is not relevant to you, you may be able to use one of the alternatives listed later. Here are the details for OpenOffice:

- **Location**: www.openoffice.org

- **Version**: 1.0

- **Package**: OOo_1.0.0_LinuxIntel_install.tar.gz

- **Description**: A complete, open-source office productivity suite

Installing OpenOffice

OpenOffice is distributed from OpenOffice.org as a tarball—a .tar.gz file. Since it's not an RPM, you won't be able to use that tool to install and manage the program. Moreover, this means you have to install the software yourself manually. OpenOffice is a pretty large software package, and so the tarball includes an installation script, even for binary distributions.

Ultimately, you can treat OpenOffice the same way you treated Sun's Java Development Kit, as discussed in Chapter 13. That is, both are prebuilt distributions of large software projects in .tar.gz format. Essentially you just extract them, although in the case of OpenOffice you then have to run an installation script. Most of the techniques you read about in Chapter 13 also apply to OpenOffice, in terms of the need to update PATH variables, and so on.

However, there's one thing you'll need to keep in mind when installing OpenOffice, which is that unfortunately the installation is not really multiuser. Specifically, the user who runs OpenOffice has to own the installation files. This makes it impractical to install a single copy—such as in /usr/local or /opt—for all users to share. Each user must have her own copy, which can become quite a waste of disk space. (It is very likely that support for such multiuser installations will be added in a future version, however.)

Once you get past these difficulties, though, OpenOffice is a very capable application. You should check out the OpenOffice site at www.openoffice.org for more information.

The Alternatives: Koffice, Abiword, HancomOffice, Applixware, and Wordperfect Office

OpenOffice is not the only game in town. Table 14-2 lists several other office suites and productivity programs (though of course even Table 14-2 isn't an exclusive list). Some of them have RPM packages that can be installed (making configuration easy), whereas others use other packaging formats. Really, there's not much more to say than that; installing these packages will vary from simply installing the RPMs to more complicated procedures similar to those described in Chapters 8 through 13. You can also obtain source code packages for some, as well, and build the programs yourself.

Table 14-2. Office Productivity Applications

APPLICATION	URL	NOTES
KOffice	www.koffice.org	The KDE office suite; included with Red Hat Linux
Abiword	www.abisource.com	Another open-source word processor
HancomOffice	en.hancom.com/index.html	A commercial office suite
Applixware	www.vistasource.com/products/axware/	Another commercial office suite
Wordperfect Office	linux.corel.com	Another commercial office suite

Personal Finance

Personal finance software helps its user manage income, checking accounts, investment accounts, and so on. Such software is very popular among computer users, and competition in the area is fierce—at least, in the Windows world. Today, a few open-source personal finance software packages are available, though not quite as many as in the Windows world.

The Selection: GNUCash

GNUCash is the personal finance software chosen for this case study. GNUCash is a fairly straightforward and functional personal finance program, and should be easy to learn for anyone who's used such software before. Notably, GNUCash also supports several standard formats for personal financial data, giving it a degree of interoperation with electronic and web banking. Red Hat Linux 7.3 includes an RPM package for GNUCash, making installation trivial. Here are some details about GNUCash:

- **Location**: www.gnucash.org

- **Version**: 1.6.6

- **Package**: gnucash-1.6.6-3.i386.rpm

- **Description**: A personal finance manager

One thing to be aware of is that GNUCash uses the GTK+ X widget set. This means that while it works fine with KDE, the two aren't really integrated. Probably the biggest concern this raises is that GNUCash might consume more memory than it would if you were using GNOME (which is also based on GTK+), since they'd be able to share memory for the widget sets. This is unlikely to be a problem unless you have limited memory, though.

For documentation, users' manuals, and so on, see the GNUCash home page at www.gnucash.org.

The Alternatives: Kapital

GNUCash appears to be the only release-quality open-source personal finance application. However, there is another alternative: the Kapital application produced by TheKompany. Kapital is not open source, and in fact is not even no-cost; you'll have to purchase a license from TheKompany. Many users do find it superior to GNUCash, though, so it may be worth checking out if you're dissatisfied with GNUCash.

You can find information about Kapital at www.thekompany.com/products/kapital/.

Once you've selected a personal finance manager (if you want or need one), you can read on to choose a web browser.

Web Browsing

One of the most fundamental applications on a computer these days is the web browser. Many people don't view an operating system as complete if it doesn't contain a good browser. This section discusses the web browsers evaluated and chosen for the case study.

The Selection: Konqueror and Mozilla

This case study actually includes two browsers: the Konqueror browser that comes with KDE and the Mozilla browser. Both browsers are modern, fast, and very capable. Here are some details about Konqueror:

- **Location**: www.konqueror.org/

- **Version**: 3.0

- **Package**: Included with KDE

- **Description**: KDE's integrated, componentized media browser

And now some details about Mozilla:

- **Location**: www.mozilla.org/

- **Version**: 1.0

- **Package**: Several! See the web site.

- **Description**: A very high-quality, full-featured open source web browser, editor, and email client.

Konqueror is the built-in browser included with KDE. Konqueror is more than just a web browser; it is also the filesystem browser and manager, and can view a very wide variety of file types such as HTML, PDF, text, and so on. Konqueror really is just a framework that uses KDE components—one for each file type—to display files within the browser. For this reason, Konqueror is very closely integrated with KDE, and is easy to use within that desktop environment. This was the primary motivation for choosing Konqueror as a browser (though Konqueror is also quite fast and robust), so if you're using another environment such as GNOME, you will probably choose another browser.

The Mozilla browser is a full-featured open-source web browser. This is a traditional web browser suite, meaning that it includes an email reader, HTML page editor, and other applications in addition to the browser itself. (Contrast this with Konqueror, which is really just a generic browser and allows other KDE programs to perform the other tasks.) Mozilla is also the core on which Netscape's latest browsers in the 6.*x* series are based; the Netscape products include some functionality not present in Mozilla, but otherwise the two are functionally very similar. Mozilla is not really integrated with either KDE or GNOME, though it does use the GTK+ widget also used by GNOME. This means that Mozilla will work well within either environment.

The reason *both* browsers are used in the case study is because occasionally some web pages work better with one than with the other. One reason for this is that sometimes the developers of web sites foolishly choose to use nonstandard content for their pages; for example, they may assume that viewers of the site are using a specific browser. Konqueror and Mozilla both have good support for the various web standards, but their "emulation" of some of these nonstandard quirks and features commonly used by web developers varies. Consequently, Mozilla works on some pages where Konqueror doesn't do a good job (or even locks up or crashes), and vice versa.

Recent versions of both browsers are improved enough that this is becoming less and less common, so you may find that you need only one or the other. Additionally, if you choose an alternative browser, your situation and experience may be completely different.

The Alternatives: Galeon and Opera

There is a quite a selection of web browsers to choose from. Table 14-3 lists many of the most popular browsers available on Linux systems. If you're interested, you should take a look at these browsers and choose the one that best fits your own taste.

Table 14-3. Web Browsers

BROWSER	LOCATION	NOTES
Galeon	galeon.sourceforge.net	A streamlined, simple browser based on the same core as Mozilla
Opera	www.opera.com	A very functional, commercial browser

Browser Plug-Ins

Perhaps just as important as the browser itself is the support the browser has for plug-ins. A *plug-in* is third-party functionality that is typically distributed in the form of a shared library (or dynamic link library) and is loaded into the browser via some application programming interface (API). Several browser plug-ins are in common use on the web; users without these plug-ins may find many pages inaccessible to them. This section outlines some popular plug-ins available for Red Hat Linux, and installed on the case study system.

Using Plug-ins with the Browsers

A plug-in is only useful if it can be installed and used in a browser. This means that the browser has to implement an API to allow plug-ins a way to be executed. Each browser could potentially implement its own API; however, in this case the makers of plug-ins would have to support a wide variety of APIs.

To avoid this, many browsers—especially browsers on Unix systems—have adopted the Netscape plug-in API. This was the API that Netscape Corporation developed for their Netscape Navigator product. Netscape Navigator was a very popular browser for many years, and so there are a large number of plug-ins available using the Netscape plug-in API. When other browsers implement the Netscape plug-in API, they can take advantage of those plug-ins.

KDE's Konqueror web browser implements the Netscape plug-in API, and in fact uses the same installation directory as Netscape Navigator. So, any plug-ins that get installed for Netscape Navigator can also be used by Konqueror. Additionally, the Mozilla browser is a descendent (at least in spirit if not actual implementation) of Netscape Communicator, and so Mozilla also supports these plug-ins. Many of the alternative browsers do, as well.

The following sections discuss two specific plug-ins that are available and work with Konqueror and Mozilla, but in general any plug-in that uses the Netscape plug-in API should work, with varying degrees of success. These plug-ins are Macromedia Flash and Java.

 NOTE *Sometimes bugs or idiosyncrasies can cause plug-ins to crash or even not work at all.*

The Macromedia Flash Plug-In

Macromedia's Flash format is a way to produce games, animations, or interactive utilities, and publish them on the web so that they are available to users. Users access these applications through their web browser, rather than by downloading and installing them. The applications are executed by a plug-in that runs in the users' browsers. Flash applications are typically fairly lightweight, and are usually used for short animations or simple games or to spice up a web site.

Flash is extremely popular, but it's not an entirely open standard, which is a concern to many people. Whether you like or dislike Flash, though, it's a reality of the web. Red Hat Linux includes Flash in the package netscape-common. If you have that package installed already, you have support for Flash.

If you don't have that package and don't care to install it (perhaps because you don't use the now-dated Netscape Communicator), then you may need to visit Macromedia's site at www.macromedia.com and download and install the Flash plug-in yourself. You would also need to do this if you wish to upgrade to a later version of the plug-in. Installation is quite easy and generally involves extracting the contents of the .tar.gz file from Macromedia into a directory—usually ~/.netscape/plug-ins—and then instructing Konqueror (or other browser) to refresh its list of installed plug-ins. Macromedia's distribution file contains full documentation.

The Java Plug-In

Chapter 13 discussed the installation of the Java Development Kit (JDK). Part of the Java API includes an applet API. An *applet* is simply a program written in Java that is intended to be run from within a web browser. Just as with Flash, support for Java applets requires a browser plug-in.

With recent versions of the Java platform, a plug-in is available that connects the installation of Java to the browser. This plug-in is not included with the installations of KDE or Mozilla (since Java isn't, either), but it is included with the JDK. Installing the plug-in is pretty easy, and instructions are available from Sun Microsystems' web site at java.sun.com.

Installation is quite simple with Konqueror. The JDK already contains everything you need—you simply need to set up your browser. If you create a symbolic link from your ~/.netscape/plugins directory to the plug-in library (which happens to be /opt/java/jdk/jre/plugin/i386/ns4/javaplugin.so) and then refresh Konqueror's list of installed plug-ins, you'll be all set! It's as easy as this command:

```
$ ln -s /opt/java/jdk/jre/plugin/i386/ns4/javaplugin.so ~/.netscape/plugins
```

The only caveat to remember when installing this plug-in is to use the correct path to the JDK. Chapter 13 installed the JDK in such a way that it can be upgraded easily. Specifically, the JDK was installed in a subdirectory of /usr/local/java— for example, /usr/local/java/sun-jdk-1.3.1 for JDK version 1.3.1—to permit multiple JDKs to be installed. A symbolic link was created in /opt/java/jdk pointing to the JDK installation that is to be the default for the system.

However, only one Java plug-in can be enabled at a time, so be sure you're installing the correct plug-in. Also, make sure you remember to upgrade your plug-in installations if you upgrade the JDK.

Just as important as functional core software is functional hardware (and implicitly the low-level software that drives the hardware). The next section discusses how to configure and use some common hardware devices with Red Hat Linux.

Support for Hardware

Computers have the ability to do a very wide range of things for you, but frequently only if you have the appropriate hardware installed. This section discusses some custom hardware devices installed on the case study system, and the support available for them.

This case study is based on Red Hat Linux 7.3, and some of the information in this section is specific to that distribution. However, hardware support for any Linux system really boils down to what the *kernel* itself supports. Since all distributions have the same kernel, much of this material is *not* distribution specific, and would be applicable to the other distributions covered in this book, and even others that are not covered. Things that are kernel specific and things that are Red Hat Linux specific are pointed out.

Using a ZIP Drive

Iomega's ZIP drive is an extremely popular product. ZIP disks are 3.5-inch cartridges, roughly the same dimensions as floppy disks, that can store several hundred megabytes of data. ZIP drives are available in a number of interface formats; some are attached externally via the system's parallel port or a SCSI or USB interface, whereas others are internal and use the very common ATAPI IDE standard.

The Linux kernel supports ZIP drives in each of these formats. However, since each drive interface is quite different, the support for them varies. For example, if the ZIP drive uses a SCSI interface, then it appears literally identical to any other SCSI device. However, if the ZIP drive is an internal ATAPI drive, then it is supported as a standard IDE drive, just as would an IDE hard disk. USB ZIP drives are supported by a special USB device driver and exposed as SCSI devices. Finally, just to complicate things, ZIP drives on the parallel port are supported by a ZIP drive-specific device driver kernel module (called "ppa" or "imm" depending on the particular ZIP drive version), but are exposed to the system as SCSI devices.

Configuring a ZIP Drive

There are four types of ZIP drive—parallel port, SCSI, USB, and IDE—and therefore four cases for configuring a ZIP drive. Each of these methods is fairly different at a low level, but in the end they all have the save result: a device file pointing to the disk that can be used to mount it. The three following sections discuss how ZIP drives are handled for SCSI, parallel port, and IDE cases; USB drives are discussed later in this chapter.

Configuring SCSI ZIP Drives

A SCSI ZIP drive is supported transparently as a SCSI disk by Linux's SCSI framework. This means that the ZIP drive will be exposed to the system as a standard SCSI device, having a name such as /dev/sda. The "/dev/sd" part denotes a SCSI disk; the "a" indicates that it is the *first* SCSI disk on the system. If you have a SCSI ZIP drive, then it may or may not be the first SCSI device, so you'll have to change "a" to another letter. For example, if your ZIP drive is the fourth SCSI device, it will be /dev/sdd.

The Linux kernel driver for SCSI devices is sd_mod (for "SCSI Disk") and is usually included as a kernel module on Red Hat Linux systems (and included in the initial ramdisk on systems that need it, as discussed in Chapter 4). The ZIP drive will appear as a simple disk on whatever SCSI host controller to which it is connected.

Configuring Parallel Port ZIP Drives

A parallel port ZIP drive contains special hardware that is actually a SCSI controller. The Linux kernel includes a device driver that can communicate with this hardware over the parallel port and expose the ZIP drive as a standard SCSI device. This takes the form of a second SCSI host controller; that is, if the system already has a SCSI controller card, these kernel drivers will appear as a *second* SCSI controller.

There are two versions of this parallel port/SCSI hardware, known as PPA and IMM. Linux includes drivers (named simply "ppa" and "imm", respectively) for both variants. The drivers themselves create a separate SCSI host controller for the device, and the ZIP drive will appear as the sole device attached to that controller. As with normal SCSI devices, parallel port ZIP drives will appear as /dev/hda, /dev/hdd, and so on.

Configuring IDE ZIP Drives

An IDE ZIP drive is treated as an IDE floppy device. Linux includes a device driver that supports IDE floppy disk drives. IDE ZIP drives perhaps have more in common with IDE CD-ROM drives than IDE floppy drives, but they are treated as floppy drives nonetheless. That is, they are supported by the same device driver.

The IDE floppy disk device driver is named ide-floppy. Normally, Red Hat Linux has this driver built into the kernel (and not as a loadable module), so you shouldn't have to do anything, and the kernel should detect your ZIP drive on bootup. The device will appear as a normal IDE device, such as /dev/hda for the first IDE device, or /dev/hdd for the fourth. (The naming convention is similar to that of SCSI devices, mentioned earlier, except that "hd" is used instead of "sd".)

IDE ZIP Drives on Other Distributions

Red Hat Linux includes the ide-floppy device driver, which supports IDE ZIP drives as a built-in feature, rather than a loadable module. This makes it easy to detect ZIP drives (and, of course, other IDE floppy drives) on bootup. However, not all distributions do it this way, and some include ide-floppy as a kernel module.

On these systems, you may run into a scenario that may be confusing at first, especially if you're using the ide-scsi SCSI emulation module, which is mentioned in the section "Using a CD Writer" later in this chapter. Specifically, if that module is used and ide-floppy is compiled as a kernel module, then it's possible that the ide-scsi module can load *before* the ide-floppy module.

In this case, the ZIP drive might be managed by the ide-scsi module (rather than the ide-floppy module) and would be exposed to the system as a SCSI device instead of an IDE device. For example, it might be /dev/sdb instead of /dev/hdd. If you are using another distribution, or even simply a custom kernel on Red Hat Linux, you might run into this issue and should be aware of it. All that will change is the device name of the ZIP drive.

Mounting the ZIP Drive

Once you have the appropriate kernel modules loaded, the ZIP drive will appear as a standard block disk device, so you can interact with it as you would with any such device. If you aren't yet sure what device name your ZIP drive is exposed as, you'll have to check your system's configuration. You can check by using the dmesg command or /var/log/messages to see how the kernel named the drive, or by looking at /etc/fstab to see how kudzu set up the mount points for the device.

There is a minor idiosyncracy to be aware of when using ZIP drives, and that is which partition you use. If you buy a ZIP disk, it will probably come preformatted with the FAT (File Allocation Table) filesystem. Normally you would expect this partition to be the first partition—for example, /dev/sda1 (if your ZIP drive is /dev/sda). However, this isn't the case, and by default new ZIP disks have the filesystem on the fourth partition—/dev/sda4 in the same example. You can alter this if you repartition the ZIP disk with the fdisk program, but it's something to be aware of when you use new disks, or if you wish to reformat a disk without repartitioning it (such as reformatting a ZIP disk with the standard Linux ext2 filesystem, which is definitely possible).

ZIP Disk Partitions and Linux

ZIP disks are factory partitioned to use the fourth partition as the actual data partition (such as /dev/sda4 or /dev/hdc4). On a related note, some ZIP drive manufacturers have a hardware setting that is intended to make this behavior invisible to the operating system, by hiding the partition table on ZIP disks inserted into it. Unfortunately, this behavior breaks Linux. If you have such a ZIP drive (and it works under Windows or another operating system, but not Linux), then there is probably a jumper on the device that you can change to disable the behavior.

Of course, you may never actually have to do this, because Red Hat Linux does it for you. When kudzu detects a ZIP drive, it not only configures the device drivers for it, but it also creates a mount point for the drive. Specifically, the directory /mnt/zip100.0 is created for 100MB ZIP drives, and a corresponding entry is created in /etc/fstab. (The fstab file is pretty simple, and is common to almost all Unix-like systems; you should check the manual page for fstab for details.)

So, to mount your ZIP drive, you probably don't have to do anything more than just type `mount /zip100.0` and it will work. If you use a desktop environment such as KDE, icons for the drive will also be created for you automatically, in which case you can use them as well. However, should you need to do something with the drive or disk directly, it's useful to know how to find it, which was the purpose of this section.

Using USB Devices

The Universal Serial Bus (USB) is a standard for connecting a variety of hardware devices to a computer. Any number of nifty gadgets employ USB, such as MP3 players that use it to manage the playlist, PDAs that use USB to synchronize data with the computer, digital cameras that use USB to transfer images to the computer, and so on. USB support on Linux systems is primarily provided by the Linux kernel, meaning that the distribution doesn't have a great deal to do with it. This section discusses several example uses of USB with the case study system.

Generally, there isn't much you'll have to do to get USB working—at least, at the core. Chances are Red Hat Linux will detect your USB host controller hardware correctly and configure it for you. After that, all you have to do is plug in a USB device, and see whether it's recognized by the kernel (which is to say, whether the device is supported and has a kernel module available for it).

It's important to keep in mind that even once your device's driver is loaded, all that's happened is that access to it is exposed by the kernel to userspace programs. Another way to put it is that each USB device driver really just exposes a small API for interacting with the device. The userspace programs themselves are responsible for knowing how to *use* this mini-API. The API may take different forms, depending on the driver. Sometimes these are quite standard (such as USB storage devices, described later in this section), and sometimes they are quite complex (such as a USB MP3 player, also described later in this section).

Some example USB devices that I use with the case study system are presented in upcoming sections, along with information on how to configure them. The goal of these examples is to illustrate how the specific USB driver exposes access to the USB device in a way specific to that device, rather than provide a tutorial on how to use such devices. (By now, you should be able to work out the mechanics yourself, once you get some pointers.)

Before delving into the details, it helps to have an understanding of how the USB architecture in Linux generally works. There is ample documentation on Linux's USB architecture included with the kernel source code, so this is really just a brief introduction. In general USB support within Linux exists on four levels, as described next.

Core Framework

The first level is the core framework. This is the kernel module that implements the general USB system calls within the kernel, as well as an abstraction layer that applications interact with. That is, applications don't work directly with the USB controller hardware, but instead work with the core USB framework provided by the kernel. This level can be viewed as analogous to the general, high-level network APIs such as TCP/IP that run the same regardless of which hardware is being used.

USB Host Controller Driver

The second level is the USB host controller driver. This takes the form of a device driver customly written for a specific piece of hardware. Referring to the analogy to the networking system, the USB host controller would be equivalent to an Ethernet card driver. However, USB manufacturers agreed on two standards for USB controller hardware: the Universal Host Controller Interface (UHCI) and the Open Host Controller Interface (OHCI).

USB controller manufacturers implement one or the other of these hardware specifications, meaning that there isn't as wide a variety of USB drivers as there is of Ethernet controllers, because many manufacturers' devices use the same drivers. In fact, only three common drivers exist for USB controllers: the usb-ohci driver for controllers that use the OHCI standard, and the usb-uhci and uhci drivers for UHCI cards. (The two drivers for UHCI have slightly different support for different hardware; if one driver doesn't work well with your configuration, you may wish to try the other.)

Device-Specific Drivers

The third level of USB support is device-specific drivers. These are drivers that actually work with a specific USB device, such as a digital camera or MP3 player. You can think of the first two levels as simply providing USB connectivity, in that they merely allow the kernel and system to "see" USB devices. However, each device is different, so even if you already "see" the device, you still have to "speak its language" in order to use it. A number of drivers at this level implement support for various specific USB devices at the kernel level.

Kernel Hotplug

The final level of USB support is the kernel's "hotplug" mechanism, which is used for devices that are plugged in to a running system. When the kernel detects such an event, it invokes a program (specifically, /sbin/hotplug) that is responsible for identifying the device and loading the appropriate driver for it. Devices are identified by comparing their identifying string (which can be obtained from the device itself) to a list of supported identifiers that are mapped to kernel modules; the corresponding module is then loaded. The related files (containing these mappings and related scripts) live in the directory /etc/hotplug. The hotplug mechanism works for more than just USB—it also works with PCI and other similar hardware busses.

Using a Digital Camera

Digital photography is becoming increasingly popular as digital cameras become cheaper. This section will discuss how to connect such hardware to a Red Hat Linux system. The section "Working with Digital Cameras" later in this chapter discusses the application software you need to complete the circle. Many such digital cameras use USB (rather than the much slower RS-232 serial port or parallel port) to transfer images from the camera to the desktop computer for storage. Some of these cameras have USB drivers available for Linux.

The camera model used in this case study is a Kodak DC-280, though the model isn't really relevant; the same general information applies to any supported USB digital camera. Once the camera is plugged into the system's USB port, the usb-core driver will detect it, and the kernel will invoke the hotplug mechanism, which will load the camera-specific driver—in this case, dc2xx.

Once the driver is loaded, a new set of system calls is available to userspace applications. (The details of this API are only of interest to developers, so I won't go into them here.) The job still isn't quite complete, though. You still need a program to make use of these syscalls. Probably the most popular such program is the gphoto program discussed later in this chapter. Once you have gphoto running, you'll be able to use your digital camera just as you would with any other operating system.

Using a Flash Card Reader

Many devices, such as digital cameras, PDAs, MP3 players, and more, employ common and inexpensive flash cards for storage. Generally these cards use either the Compact Flash (CF) standard, or the SmartMedia (SM) standard, or some other format. In the case of CF and SM cards, you can also purchase widely available, inexpensive readers for the cards. Typically these readers are simply a small plastic port into which the flash cards are inserted, and that connect to the computer via USB.

Many of these readers adhere to a hardware specification standard for USB mass storage devices. In fact, this standard supports many things other than just flash card readers; it also includes such nifty gizmos as some keychain storage devices, USB ZIP drives, USB CD writers, and so on. The Linux kernel includes a driver for USB mass storage devices, named usb-storage. If you have a reader (or other device) that obeys the USB mass storage standard, the hotplug mechanism can detect it and load the usb-storage driver automatically.

Unlike the digital camera drivers just described, the usb-storage driver doesn't require any special software, because it doesn't use any custom system calls. Instead, the usb-storage driver simply exposes any devices it detects as standard SCSI disks. For example, if you already have two SCSI disks connected to your system and then connect a flash card reader, it will appear as the third SCSI disk: /dev/sdc. You can then mount, format, or even partition these devices, exactly as you would with any other SCSI storage device.

Using an MP3 Player

Another popular device is the portable MP3 player, which allows a user to store and play large amounts of music in the high-quality MPEG-2 Layer 3 (MP3) standard format. These devices are frequently connected to the computer via USB.

Some of the devices may actually use the usb-storage mechanism just discussed to allow you to copy files directly to and from them. However, many use some other scheme—that is, a custom API over USB. For some of these devices for which adequate technical information is available from the manufacturer (or that can be reverse-engineered independently), Linux USB drivers are available. For example, many Rio devices produced by SonicBlue are supported by the rio500 USB driver. As with the digital camera, connecting a Rio-500 (for example) to the system will cause the kernel to load the correct driver by invoking the hotplug mechanism. At that point, a set of system calls will be available—this time, for managing the contents of the Rio-500.

Again, as with the digital camera, you'll need a special program that is written to use these system calls. One such program is the Rio 500 project at rio500.sourceforge.net. This is actually the home of the Linux kernel USB driver module that provides connectivity to the Rio, but this URL also gives you access to userspace programs you can use to manage the device's contents. The tools allow you to store MP3s to the Rio, remove them, create playlists, and so on. Graphical tools are also available.

Using Other USB Devices

Linux has drivers for many other USB devices, and the list is growing. There is support for USB joysticks and gamepads, some USB network adapters, USB web cameras, and so on. This book obviously cannot discuss all of these, but now that you've seen some examples of using USB devices with Linux, you should be able to figure out how to add others.

Generally, just remember the basic procedure: When you plug in a device, the driver for the USB host controller will detect it, and the kernel will invoke the hotplug program to attempt to locate and load a driver for it. After that, you'll need a program that understands how to use the driver (as with the digital cameras and MP3 players), or you'll have to interact with the device (as with the SCSI devices exposed by the usb-storage driver).

Linux's support for USB has its warts; sometimes devices aren't detected by the drivers (especially when the devices are *newer* than the driver), and sometimes support for devices is spotty or slow, but overall it works pretty well. In some cases—especially with USB input devices such as keyboards, mice, and joysticks—

you may have to do a bit more work to get them working correctly, but by now this shouldn't be difficult. Just remember how the system works, and know where to start. USB on Linux really isn't that hard.

Using a CD Writer

Using writable CDs has become a very affordable way to store data, whether it's a backup of your operating system, a copy of important data, an album of photos from your latest family reunion, or a mix of tracks from your favorite music CD. Red Hat Linux makes it fairly painless to use these devices.

Understanding SCSI Emulation

Red Hat Linux tries to take a unified approach. Generally, Red Hat Linux tries to treat devices as SCSI devices as much as possible. Linux includes a kernel module known as ide-scsi that emulates the SCSI protocol on behalf of IDE devices. This allows IDE devices to be exposed as SCSI devices, and Red Hat Linux can use this module.

When the ide-scsi module is loaded (via a command such as modprobe or insmod), the driver scans the IDE bus (or busses), locates all IDE drives, and then begins treating them as SCSI devices, translating SCSI calls to IDE calls. Thus, if an IDE ZIP drive is present on the system, after the ide-scsi module is loaded it will be available as a SCSI disk, indistinguishable from other SCSI devices.

This ability to treat any disk as a SCSI disk is extremely useful, and really pretty slick if you think about it. It's used repeatedly within Red Hat Linux, as you've seen before and will continue to see in the rest of this chapter. Many of the sections that follow refer to this notion of SCSI emulation.

Red Hat Linux and SCSI

When Red Hat Linux boots, it will load the ide-scsi module if necessary (that is, if any devices—such as CD writers or ZIP drives—are present and require it).

Generally, whenever you connect a ZIP drive to the system, Red Hat Linux will detect it by using the kudzu program invoked from /etc/rc.d/rc.sysinit on system bootup, as discussed in Chapter 4. Because of Red Hat's use of the ide-scsi module, kudzu usually only has to worry about detecting SCSI devices, rather than both IDE and SCSI. Once the disk is detected, kudzu will prepare the device for use.

Configuring Your Writer

If your CD writer is a SCSI drive, then you're all set, and you don't need to do anything else. However, if it's an IDE writer, then the ide-scsi module is required, so that the IDE device is exposed as a SCSI device for the CD-writing software to use. Fortunately, Red Hat Linux 7.3 detects IDE CD writers, and automatically configures the ide-scsi module for you, for that device.

You can accomplish this by passing a parameter to the kernel from the boot loader (which is usually GRUB). The argument that needs to be passed is [IDE device]=ide-scsi; for example, if your CD writer is normally the third IDE device, it would appear as /dev/hdc. In this case, you'd need to pass the kernel argument hdc=ide-scsi. Red Hat Linux does this for you when you install it.

This means that you probably won't have to do anything in order to get your CD writer working, if it was present when you installed the system. However, if you add it *after* the system was installed, you'll have to add the line to the boot loader's configuration yourself. (Actually, the kudzu program discussed in Chapter 4 may also do this for you, when you reboot the system. Again, though, it's useful to know what's going on.)

CROSS-REFERENCE *See the section "Using the GRUB Boot Loader" in Chapter 4 for more information and references to the GRUB boot loader.*

Once the system is set up to expose the CD writer as a SCSI device, you need only use the appropriate program to burn a CD. Two popular programs, cdrecord and xcdroast, are discussed later in this chapter, in the section "Media and Entertainment."

Using 3D Graphics Cards

Modern computers usually have some kind of hardware 3D acceleration in the video card. This acceleration is used by games, and some kinds of technical and engineering software (such as CAD tools and medical imaging). Since this is hardware, these cards have to be supported under Linux with a device driver.

As you read in Chapter 3, the vast majority of Linux systems use XFree86 teamed with some kind of desktop or window manager as the graphical interface. As a result, XFree86 has to support 3D hardware on Linux systems. This generally means that XFree86 has to have a driver for the video card so it can run within the X server. Additionally, many applications that use 3D do so by using the OpenGL programming API, and so practically speaking, support for 3D under Linux also requires an implementation of OpenGL.

It can definitely be argued that 3D support on Linux systems is weak, though this situation is improving rapidly, especially with recent versions of XFree86. The main difficulties are that many vendors' 3D cards do not have drivers and that there is no hardware-accelerated OpenGL implementation for that hardware.

Some vendors release adequate programming information for their hardware, and so XFree86 itself supports 3D acceleration on these cards. Other vendors instead provide downloadable drivers for XFree86 that provide hardware acceleration. In this case, the drivers are frequently not free software or open source, even though source code may be available for them. You'll frequently have to install the driver in a directory and modify the XFree86 configuration to load the driver, which is distributed as a dynamically loadable library.

CROSS-REFERENCE *See "The Origins of Linux" and "GNU and Linux: The Operating System of Champions" in Chapter 1, and "Open Source vs. Free Software" in Chapter 2 for details on the distinction between free software and open source.*

However, even if hardware acceleration is enabled, software still needs to be able to access that acceleration. The OpenGL specification is widely used, but it's not technically a standard. An open source package known as Mesa is intended to be source-code compatible with OpenGL (meaning that it implements the same API), but even this library is only able to provide hardware acceleration for chips whose API it understands.

Consequently, many times the vendors who release their own proprietary drivers for XFree86 also include an implementation of OpenGL, so that software can actually take advantage of the accelerations. The plus side of this approach is that you get good hardware acceleration supported by the vendor, but the downside is that you'll have to install the drivers manually, since they aren't included with the distribution.

The video card in the case study is an NVidia TNT2 M64. NVidia is of the latter type of vendor—that is, it supplies its own drivers for XFree86 to provide hardware acceleration under Linux. Unfortunately, NVidia's drivers will obviously only work with its cards.

The bottom line is that if 3D acceleration on your video card isn't supported by XFree86, your card's manufacturer will have to provide that support. Each vendor can do things different ways, so there is no general rule of thumb. The only thing you can do is visit your card manufacturer's web site to see what support it provides, and then follow the instructions the manufacturer gives for installing the drivers. Fortunately, this usually isn't too complicated a task.

So far, you've read about the core desktop and productivity software, as well as the hardware used on the case study system. Now you'll read about the extra, less essential (but no less useful) software used on the case study system, starting with media and entertainment software.

Exploring Media and Entertainment Options

Many people use their computers to create and manage various types of content (such as images from a digital camera, art work, home movies, and so on), as well as for entertainment (such as computer games and digital video). This section will describe how the case study system is used for these types of activities and detail the software required to do so.

Working with Digital Cameras

If you have a digital camera, then there's a chance that you will be interested in this crazy notion of transferring the photographs stored in it to your computer's storage. If that sounds like you, this section will be of interest, since it describes how to retrieve images from a digital camera using the gphoto program.

Digital cameras invariably come with software to manage the photographs in the camera. Typically the software allows you to view small "thumbnail" versions of the photos, copy some or all to your computer's disk, delete photographs, and so on. However, few (if any) camera manufacturers have Linux versions of their software. That's great, since you can use the open source gphoto program instead!

The current version of gphoto is at the 2.0 level; however, the 2.0 version is very different from the previous versions (which were a sort of alpha version, in the 0.4x and 0.5x series). The main difference between the two versions is that the older versions provided a full-fledged graphical program and environment very similar to the software produced by the manufacturers for other operating systems. The newer 2.0 version has no graphical interface, and is instead focused on providing the ability to manage cameras from the command line, as well as a set of libraries that *other* programs can use to build custom interfaces.

Meanwhile, KDE 3.0 (which is included with Red Hat Linux 7.3) comes with a software program called Kamera, which uses the gphoto libraries to provide integrated support for digital cameras within the Konqueror browser. (Konqueror is KDE's standard browser for the web, filesystems, and so on.) This was another (albeit minor) reason for the selection of KDE for the case study. Instructions for using this functionality are included with the documentation for KDE, which is easily available within the system, but generally it's as simple as using KDE's tools to configure the gphoto libraries, and then entering the URL gphoto:/ into Konqueror.

Manipulating Photographs with the GIMP

Once you've downloaded the digital photographs from the camera to the computer, you'll want to manipulate them—that is, to do things such as cropping them, resizing them, changing the color and brightness, and so on. There is a wide variety of software available that does this, and most digital cameras come with at least a minimal program for editing photos. Again, this software seldom works with Linux systems. Fortunately, the GNU Image Manipulation Program (GIMP) was created to address just this issue.

The GIMP is not nearly as crippled as its name might imply. In fact, most users seem to agree that the GIMP is at least as functional as its commercial competitors, and many feel that the GIMP is superior in some ways. The GIMP is fairly easy to get started with, but it is a very complicated piece of software (as truly powerful programs usually are).

An RPM package of the GIMP is included with Red Hat Linux 7.3, and is probably installed by default on your system, unless you explicitly unselected it. Running the GIMP should be no problem, but mastering it is another matter! You can get started by visiting the user's manual at the GIMP's site, www.gimp.org.

Creating Compact Discs

The section "Using a CD Writer" earlier in this chapter discussed how to configure your CD writer hardware for use with Linux. (In brief, the kernel treats it as a SCSI device through the ide-scsi emulation kernel module.) However, that only gets the hardware working; you now need to access the hardware.

As with digital cameras, CD writers usually come with software for using the drive, but typically there is no Linux version of this software. Fortunately, a number of open source programs exist that let you use your CD writing hardware. The programs used on the case study system are mkisofs, cdrecord, and xcdroast.

The two most common types of CDs are music CDs and data discs that use the standard ISO-9660 CD filesystem format (perhaps with extensions). The mkisofs program creates ISO-9660 filesystems, and the cdrecord program burns them to actual media. The xcdroast program is a front-end to these other tools, and provides a graphical interface similar to programs you would find on Windows systems.

Using the mkisofs Program

If you're creating a data CD, the first step is to generate an ISO-9660 *filesystem image* for it. This is a normal file on your hard drive which itself contains a filesystem that can be burned to a CD. The mkisofs program, included with Red Hat Linux 7.3, is used for this, and it's a fairly straightforward program. It should be installed on most desktop configurations, but if it's not you can install it through the usual means.

Using mkisofs is usually quite simple, though it has a lot of options. In the simplest form, you just invoke it with the name of a directory that mkisofs is to place into the ISO-9660 image. Don't be overwhelmed by the large number of command-line options, since you won't use most of them. The most common options are -J and -R, which respectively instruct mkisofs to create the ISO-9660 image with "Joliet" and "Rock Ridge" extensions to the standard; and the -o <filename> argument, which instructs mkisofs to generate the ISO-9660 image in the indicated file. People frequently give ISO-9660 image files an extension of .iso, but this is not a formal standard of any sort.

When you run it, mkisofs will copy all the files in the directory you specified (as well as all its subdirectories) into the image file you specified. Once it's finished, you can burn the image to CD, or test it by using the -o loop argument to mount, which causes mount to mount a file as a volume via the loopback kernel module. For example, the following commands will create an ISO-9660 image in /tmp/foo.iso from the contents of the directory /home/foo and mount it (to test it) on the directory /mnt/foo:

```
$ mkisofs -R -J -o /tmp/foo.iso /home/foo
$ mount -o loop -t iso9660 -r /tmp/foo.iso /mnt/foo
```

The -o loop argument to mount requires that the loopback block device driver, which is a kernel module named "loop", be available to the kernel; this is the case with the default kernel from Red Hat Linux 7.3.

Using the cdrecord Program

The cdrecord program is used to burn data onto actual CD media, and is capable of creating both music CDs (that you would be able to play in most recent standard CD players) and data CDs (such as from an ISO-9660 image file created with mkisofs). Like mkisofs, cdrecord should be included with most desktop installations of Red Hat Linux.

Invoking cdrecord involves giving it a file or list of files that it is to burn to a CD, specifying which CD writer device hardware to use and giving the format of the CD (such as data or audio). Again, cdrecord has many options, but generally you won't need most of them. For example, to burn the image created in the previous example onto a CD, you might use a command such as this one:

```
$ cdrecord dev=1,1,0 -data /tmp/foo.iso
```

The only tricky issue with this command is the dev= argument. This argument tells cdrecord which device on the SCSI bus to use to create the CD. This is obviously not in the format you're used to (such as, for example, /dev/sda), but fortunately cdrecord can lookup all SCSI devices for you. Just run the command cdrecord -scanbus, and it will locate all available SCSI devices and display their human-readable identifiers. You should be able to easily identify your CD writer in the list, and use its descriptor in the dev= argument to cdrecord.

Using the xcdroast Program

As you've probably noticed, cdrecord and mkisofs can be pretty complicated programs. You should now be able to figure them out without too much trouble, of course, but you may prefer a graphical user interface. If that's you, then you'll want to try xcdroast.

The xcdroast program is a graphical front end to mkisofs and cdrecord, and it lets you create and burn both data and audio CDs by gathering the options it needs to pass to those programs, and then executing them for you. Again, xcdroast is included with Red Hat Linux 7.3. If you prefer a graphical environment, then you should check out this program; it really can make the process of authoring CDs quite painless.

Playing Digital Audio Files

Many users enjoy listening to music while they work, and one of the most popular formats is the MP3 standard. A similar standard is the Ogg Vorbis format; the Xiphophorous company has a project named "Ogg" that produces (among other things) a compressed digital audio format named "Vorbis." The Ogg Vorbis standard is a fully open project, whereas certain aspects of the MP3 standard are encumbered by various companies' patents. (For more information, see Xiphophorous' web site at www.xiph.org.) This section will discuss programs that can play Ogg Vorbis and MP3 files.

The mpg321 Program

Red Hat Linux includes the mpg321 program for playing MP3 files. (The RPM package is mpg321.) You can play back any MP3 files you have simply by running the command mpg321 <filename>. You can also specify a list of files, and command-line options are also available to randomize the order songs are played, and so on.

Commands such as mpg321 -z *.mp3 work very well for playing MP3s, but the mpg321 package contains no program to encode MP3 files. If you wish to encode MP3 files, you'll have to use another program. Unfortunately, the process of encoding MP3 files is the aspect of MP3s for which some companies hold patents, so free MP3 encoders can be hard to come by. The LAME project is an MP3 encoder, but a package for it is not included with Red Hat Linux 7.3. However, you can still install it yourself (using the techniques in Chapters 8 through 13), and you can find it at www.mp3dev.org/mp3/.

The ogg123 Program

Recall that the Ogg Project produces an audio coder/decoder (codec) specification known as Vorbis. The Ogg Vorbis codec is roughly similar to MP3, but is based on different algorithms and technologies, and so is not encumbered by the patents that encumber MP3.

There are three relevant RPM packages for Vorbis: libvorbis, libvorbis-devel, and simply vorbis. The first two contain the shared libraries that allow other programs (such as XMMS, discussed later) encode and decode Vorbis files. The vorbis package contains command-line playback and encoding tools.

The command to play Ogg Vorbis files is ogg123. This program is very similar to mpg321 in its command-line syntax, as was intended, since many users were already familiar with mpg321 (and the program that mpg321 itself was inspired by, mpg123, which is not discussed in this book). The command ogg123 -z *.ogg plays all Vorbis files in the current directory in a random order, and is similar to the mpg321 command.

Unlike mpg321, the Ogg Vorbis package also includes a program to encode Vorbis files from the standard .WAV format for uncompressed digital audio. The program is named oggenc, and, as a typical command-line program, its workings should be very familiar by now.

The library packages (libvorbis and libvorbis-devel) are used by other applications to integrate support for the Ogg Vorbis codec. For example, the XMMS program (discussed in the next section) makes use of these libraries to enable it to play back Vorbis files as well as MP3 files. (These RPMs are also used by the vorbis package itself.)

If you like encoding your music CDs to a more portable format, then you may wish to investigate Ogg Vorbis as an alternative to MP3. Vorbis' advantages are that it is at least as high quality as MP3 (and better in some opinions), and that it is a fully open standard, as well as open source. If this is important to you, you should look into the Ogg Project and its tools.

The X Multimedia System

The X Multimedia System (or XMMS for short) is a graphical interface used to play a variety of files. It's similar in appearance to the popular WinAMP music player available for Windows systems, and supports many file formats. Notably, it supports both MP3 and Ogg Vorbis, the two formats discussed earlier. XMMS also provides some interesting "eye candy" features to visualize the music as it's played.

If you prefer to use a graphical program to manage playlists of music files, or wish to mix MP3 and Vorbis files together into a single playlist, then you should consider XMMS. Other graphical programs that accomplish the same task are available for Linux systems, but XMMS has the virtue of being included with Red Hat Linux. For this case study, XMMS is more than adequate and is in fact quite nice.

Watching Digital Video Files

Just as many users enjoy listening to digital audio files, many enjoy watching digital video files. There's a lot of activity in this area currently, and several options to choose from among open source players and commercial versions. First, this section will discuss the actual players used by the case study system, and then point out a few other options.

The avifile Media Player

Some video codec standards are open standards, such as MPEG (Motion Picture Expert Group), whereas others are controlled tightly by their owners to dictate who can and can't use them. Unfortunately, it seems that most codecs fall in to the latter category, and because they are not open, it's difficult at best to write software to play them. Fortunately, that's where the avifile program comes in.

The avifile project produces a media player program that actually reads binary dynamic link library (DLL) files from Microsoft's Windows operating systems, and accesses the codec implementations contained in the libraries. This is an interesting approach, because it means that avifile can play back video files encoded to a certain format without actually having to implement the codec directly.

However, this isn't a foolproof approach, and obviously it only works for codecs for which DLLs are available and whose licenses permit them to be used in this manner.

Despite its limitations, avifile is quite functional, and is therefore used on the case study system. It's not included in Red Hat Linux (though it is included in some other distributions such as Debian GNU/Linux and Mandrake Linux), but it isn't too difficult to install. The only caveat is that when you build the program, you have to specify the name of a directory where the Windows DLL files will be installed, so it's important to make this decision upfront.

A major disadvantage of avifile is that it can be rather difficult to build. It also doesn't play MPEG files, meaning you need a separate program for that purpose. However, avifile is functional, if you can get past the difficulties in using it on a Red Hat System.

The smpeg Program

One minor disadvantage of avifile is that it doesn't play MPEG files. Thus, a separate program is required for these files. Fortunately, Red Hat Linux *does* include a capable MPEG player, in the form of the smpeg package, which installs a program named plaympeg.

The smpeg package is actually a part of the SDL project, which is a multimedia library mentioned in a bit more detail in the next section. You won't have any trouble at all using the plaympeg program once you have the package installed.

Other Programs

The two programs just mentioned are, obviously, two different programs. This means that you have to pay attention to which type of video file you're currently trying to play, and select the right program to play it. Additionally, many current media players can "stream" video data from servers and play them live. This can be difficult or sometimes impossible with either avifile or smpeg. For this reason, users who view video files frequently may find these programs to be unsatisfactory.

Other solutions are available, but generally they aren't free. For example, CodeWeavers, Inc. has a product known as CrossOver Plugin, which is a plug-in to the Mozilla and Netscape 6.*x* browsers. This plug-in is a sort of meta–plug-in that allows plug-ins for Windows browsers to function within Mozilla and Netscape on Linux systems. This includes, among other things, Microsoft's Windows Media Player. This product is not free, but it may be worth the cost for some users. The product can be found at www.codeweavers.com/products/crossover/.

There are many other applications available as well. KDE, for example, has a built-in media player, but it generally isn't as capable as avifile. Similarly, the Xine program has a very attractive user interface and can play both MPEG files and AVI files, but it can't play some of the newer codecs. You may wish to spend a little quality time with your favorite search engine looking into the other options that exist. There is a lot of activity in this area, and you might find something that works for you.

Playing Games

One of the final indicators that an operating system has entered the desktop mainstream is when commercial games are widely available for it. Linux can be used as a desktop system (as this chapter demonstrates), but it's probably too soon to say that it's become mainstream in that capacity. As a result, there are commercial games for Linux, but honestly not that many.

Some game companies' strategies include Linux, and they have produced profitable games on this platform. Of note are id Software's so-called "First Person Shooter" (FPS) games, such as Doom, the Quake Series, and so on. These games run well on Linux, and even have support for 3D hardware acceleration. Nor is id Software alone; many other companies have had their games ported to Linux. Unfortunately, these games can be sometimes hairy to install, to say the least. For example, supporting 3D graphics hardware was mentioned earlier in this chapter; that is frequently but one of many obstacles to overcome before you can get most games running on Linux systems. In a nutshell, commercial games on Linux aren't quite to the point where installation is painless. (Of course, since you've read Chapters 8 through 13, that should be easy for you, but it's usually not as easy as just installing an RPM!)

However, that's generally true of mainstream *commercial* games. If you're not an avid gamer interested in the latest and greatest games, you may actually be surprised by the number of desktop-type games available for Linux. You can find a vast array of card games, puzzle games, simple arcade games, and so on available for KDE and GNOME. Additionally, there are several efforts to produce commercially viable open-source multimedia engines for Linux. Notably, the Simple DirectMedia Layer (SDL) found at www.libsdl.org is a set of libraries for developing multimedia-intensive applications such as media players and games, on a variety of operating systems; Red Hat Linux includes RPM packages for these libraries. Many free games, and even some commercial games, are being developed on this API.

The bottom line is that if you're a hardcore gamer, you might be disappointed by the state of gaming on Linux. If you are really just looking for some casual diversions, though, there's probably more than enough for you. If you're interested in learning more, a great site to visit is the Linux gaming forum at www.linuxgames.com. For this case study, it so happens that I get my gaming fix from some of the old classics like NetTrek, so many of these issues don't come into play.

In the next section, we move from play to work. You'll read about some interesting tricks and immensely useful techniques that you can take advantage of, now that you've set up your Linux system.

Implementing Connectivity and Remote Access

As a final topic, this book will discuss some ways that the case study system provides enhanced connectivity and accessibility. You may not need any of this information, so feel free to skim it. However, even if you don't use it, you may wish to read through this section anyway, since it provides some interesting ideas that may lead you to some of your own.

Accessing the Desktop Remotely

The case study system is connected to the Internet at all times via a cable modem connection. This provides the ability to access the system remotely using SSH. This isn't a commonly used feature, but every now and then it comes in very handy, so it's something to consider if you have a similar high-speed, "always on" connection. (This would be quite painful to use over a dial-up connection.)

As it happens, the configuration of OpenSSH for the desktop system is nothing more than the installation discussed in Chapter 8. Everything in that chapter applies to this case study; however, the case study installation is based on the standard RPM packages of OpenSSH provided by Red Hat, so the system wasn't built from source code. Otherwise, you can read Chapter 8 for more information.

The ability to provide secure, encrypted access to the system can be very convenient. For example, if you're traveling, you can log in to the system to check your email (either using a command-line program, or by using SSH's ability to forward X Window connections automatically if you use a graphical client). Perhaps more importantly, running OpenSSH allows the files on the system to be accessed remotely, with the scp (secure copy) and sftp (secure FTP) utilities. This can be extremely useful if you forgot a file at home that you need at work, or while on the road. Just remember to keep the system up to date, to avoid exposing yourself to needless security vulnerabilities.

Providing Other Services

Another, perhaps more novel feature provided by the desktop is a personal web proxy server. Many businesses use a firewall to protect the corporate network, which in turn requires users to use a proxy server. Frequently these proxy servers perform various filtering techniques to restrict user access to some material on the web. This is sometimes done to protect the company's good name. For example, it might cast the company in a bad light if its employees are observed visiting questionable sites while on the job! Of course, sometimes the corporate proxy server is just too slow, or even down.

NOTE   *Before using **any** of the techniques in this section, check with your network administrators to make sure it's permitted! Not all employers may permit these types of connections.*

It's possible to run a proxy server such as tinyproxy (available at `tinyproxy.sourceforge.net`) on your home desktop system connected directly to the Internet, as with the case study system. By then logging into your home system from your desktop system using OpenSSH and setting up SSH port forwarding, you can access your proxy server at *home* from your computer at *work*. (Generally you simply set your web browser to use "localhost" as the proxy server, and set up SSH port forwarding to redirect those requests across the SSH link to be serviced by your personal proxy server running outside the firewall.)

This means that all your web requests will appear to originate from your own personal desktop computer, outside the company's firewall. Since you run that proxy server, you are not restricted in the sites you can visit. This can be a great feature for you at work, if the corporate proxy is blocking access to sites you need, or is malfunctioning or bogged down.

However, you shouldn't just go off and set this up! Many companies would not approve of this behavior, and you might be violating a company policy if you do this. This configuration is easy to set up, but before you do it's important to check with your network administrators for approval. Your employer may prefer or require that you not do this. This technique is presented here simply to demonstrate some of the creative things you can do with a Linux system, once you've mastered it. Don't blame us if you use this technique (or one like it) and something unfortunate happens!

Summary

You've now read a case study of a desktop system running Red Hat Linux. Parts One through Three introduced you to a distribution and covered three in detail and provided you with the basic skills required to install software and customize your system. This case study pointed out some neat things you can do with your system and demonstrated the ways in which a stock Red Hat Linux installation can be tweaked and customized to meet your needs. Hopefully what you've taken away from this chapter is that Linux is a very viable desktop operating system.

CHAPTER 15

A Corporate Software Development Environment

This chapter presents the second case study in Part Four, which is a development workstation. In real life, I'm a computer scientist and software engineer, and this case study is based on the system I built to meet those needs.

Once you've read this chapter, you'll know how to duplicate that configuration. Just as important, you'll have a basis for tweaking it to customize it for your own network and needs. If you've also read the previous case study of a desktop system, then after also reading this chapter you'll have an appreciation for how simply tweaking a few details can produce a very different system.

Getting Started

The first step to building any system is to understand the details. This section describes the goals and requirements that drove the development of the development workstation configuration presented in this case study. You should read this section and then compare it to your own needs and goals.

Who This Example Is For

This example is aimed at software developers, but a lot of it is more generally applicable. Chapter 14 detailed a configuration that is useful for simple, everyday desktop use; that configuration might work fine in some corporate environments, but typically such environments are a lot more complex than your average home desktop. So, even if all you need is a desktop configuration at work, you may need much of the information presented in this chapter, especially the material in the sections "Network and Management Tools," "Corporate Interoperation," and "Security Issues." If you actually are a software developer, of course, you'll need all the content in this chapter.

What the System Is Used For

The system presented in this case study is used for development for a variety of purposes in several languages. For example, this same configuration with surprisingly minor changes has been used to develop Java 2 Enterprise Edition (J2EE) applications, as well as hard real-time control software for electrical distribution equipment. This chapter, however, focuses only on the first case, since it's actually the more complex case in terms of system configuration. Many of the elements in this chapter set up the environment for developing software.

However, as much if not more of the content in this chapter focuses on configuring the system to work correctly with a corporate network. Such networks usually have an extensive authentication and file distribution mechanism (such as NIS+ and NFS, as discussed in this chapter), and so the workstation obviously has to live peacefully with these services. Additionally, the realities of modern business dictate additional functionality that the system needs to support, such as the ability to work with office documents, use standard company software that may only exist for other operating systems, and so on.

These dual (and sometimes competing) goals are what you'll find in this case study. What you *won't* find is extensive detail on how to install a lot of the software in this section; this chapter assumes you've already read Chapters 7 through 13 and refers to them extensively. Additionally, this case study is largely a superset of the desktop case study, so it may help to read Chapter 14 as well.

As with Chapter 14, this chapter starts out with the basics. In the next section, you'll read about how to start with a stock Red Hat Linux 7.3 system and use it to reconstruct this case study.

Building the System

This section describes how to build the basics of the development workstation. As with all the case studies, this example starts from a stock Red Hat Linux 7.3 system and customizes the list of installed packages and configuration of the stock system to meet the established goals.

Starting with the Desktop

A development workstation is mostly a superset of a desktop system. Since you've probably already read about such a system in Chapter 14, there's no need to rehash it all here. So, the first step in installing a corporate desktop is to install a desktop installation.

Of course, not everything from Chapter 14 is relevant. For example, you probably don't have much of a need to manage a portable MP3 player from your office workstation (though you may still need USB support). So, you don't really need *everything* from Chapter 14; you only need the basics.

Specifically, you're interested in items such as the following:

- KDE as the desktop environment

- OpenOffice for productivity

- Konqueror and Mozilla for web browsing

- Connectivity and remote access

- Support for hardware (such as a ZIP drive or CD writer, if not that MP3 player)

In other words, start with the desktop system in Chapter 14 and install the features relevant to your situation. This case study itself uses the preceding list, but of course your own list may vary.

Selecting Packages

The rest of this chapter is a list of software packages to install and, where necessary, pointers on how to configure them. Consequently, it might be a good idea to skim the rest of these sections *before* you install the base system to get an idea of what packages you'll need to select during the process. For the most part, however, you can get the majority of what you need by selecting a few of the high-level package options Red Hat provides you during the installation.

Selecting a few of the high-level categories will get you 85% of what you need. (Some of the software in this chapter isn't included with Red Hat Linux, such as OpenOffice.) For the rest, you can install them individually from the CD or using the up2date command (which is discussed in Chapter 4) and then configure them as you need to, using the information in this chapter as a guide. Another alternative is to simply select "Install Everything"; however, remember that this installs lots of needless software, which may have security implications.

Details of the Configuration

There isn't a great deal of change needed to the default Red Hat Linux configuration. Of course, a lot of the rest of this chapter involves configuring individual packages that are installed, but there isn't much you have to do to the stock system.

Perhaps the only thing to consider is whether you wish to leave the default firewall enabled. This, however, depends on your environment and policies; see the section "Security Issues" later in this chapter.

In the next section, you'll read about some important software that lets your new workstation connect to a network. You'll read about the information you need to gather to set up the system, and then you'll learn what and how you must configure.

Network and Management Tools

This section discusses several common tools and systems for managing various parts of a computer's environment. These are tools commonly employed by corporate networks for the ease of manageability that they can provide. Some of these tools will seem familiar from the desktop case study in Chapter 14, while others may be new to you. As always, since this is a case study of an actual system, your environment may not be identical to this one.

Understanding the Local Network

The first step in configuring your new workstation is to understand exactly what you're going to have to do to it. After all, you can't configure something if you don't know you're supposed to. This section outlines the realities of the network on which this case study resides. It's pretty typical for a corporate environment, so you may find your own environment to be very similar to it; just watch out for potential subtle differences.

The network used in this case study functions like this:

- Workstations obtain IP addresses via Dynamic Host Configuration Protocol (DHCP).

- Authentication to the system is handled by the standard Network Information Services (NIS+). The NIS domain name is "universal".

- Users' home directories and common project-related files are shared across workstations (and servers) using the Network Filesystem (NFS) standard.

- The organization's Information Technology Management Services (ITMS) group tracks the status of the system with Tangram Enterprise Solutions' Asset Insight software.

- The network support group requires root access to all Unix-like systems on the network via an OpenSSH key.

Not surprisingly, these issues are the topics of the remainder of this section. Each of the subsections that follows provides information on how to configure these aspects of the system, but not how to install them; I assume that by now you can do that, after reading Chapters 7 through 13.

Using DHCP on the System

The Dynamic Host Configuration Protocol (DHCP) is used by desktop, workstation, and sometimes server computers to connect to the Internet. You've already seen DHCP come up a few times; notably, the case study of the desktop system in Chapter 14 also uses DHCP. As you've no doubt concluded from this, DHCP is a very useful system. (In fact, even the case study of a network firewall in the next chapter uses DHCP. Not only that, it includes a DHCP server!)

Configuring DHCP is as easy as using Red Hat's netconfig program and activating DHCP. If you prefer to perform that task manually, you can edit the file /etc/sysconfig/network-scripts/ifcfg-eth0 (replacing "eth0" with the actual Ethernet device your system uses, if necessary). This file simply sets three variables: DEVICE, ONBOOT, and BOOTPROTO. The values should be "eth0" (or the identifier of your actual Ethernet device), "yes", and "dhcp", respectively. This should be familiar to you by now.

The first variable sets the Ethernet device and should match the file name (for example, don't use DEVICE=eth1 in the file ifcfg-eth0). The second variable determines whether the card is to be activated when the system boots up or only when the ifup command is used manually (such as with ifup eth0). The BOOTPROTO variable sets the protocol to use, which is DHCP in this (and probably almost every) case. Creating the /etc/sysconfig/network-scripts/ifcfg-eth0 file is really all Red Hat's netconfig program does (though it also modifies a few other files).

Installing the portmap Service

The portmapper service (known as portmap) is a fairly old form of a programming technique known as a *remote procedure call* (RPC). RPC is the term for when a program running on one machine accesses a function that resides on another machine, as if the "remote procedure" were actually part of the local program. The portmap service as an RPC mechanism is largely unused these days, but a few popular programs still need it. Notably, the NIS+ and NFS services discussed in this chapter require portmap in order to function. Therefore, you'll have to install portmap to use those services. Red Hat Linux 7.3 includes an installation of portmap for you, in the package portmap RPM. After installing it, you'll have to enable it using the chkconfig program; see Chapter 4 for details.

It's worth making a quick security-related note. The portmap program has a long history of having security weaknesses. For this reason, it's not unreasonable to suppose that there are additional existing security vulnerabilities that might be exploited in the future. To avoid exposure, you absolutely should not run the portmap service (or any service) unless you really need it. In other words, don't install portmap unless you really do need the NIS and NFS support discussed in this chapter.

Using Network Information Services

The first step to using a system is to log into it. This section describes how the case study system is configured to use the Network Information Services (NIS, or NIS+) for user authentication.

Normally, Unix systems store user information such as home directory, default shell, and password in the file /etc/passwd. However, if one user needs to log into several systems, that information has to be replicated in each system's /etc/passwd file. Having multiple copies of the same information on multiple systems is a management headache. NIS is a solution to this problem.

NIS is a fairly simple scheme, conceptually. Essentially, NIS is just a way of distributing files across a network. This is most useful for configuration files, such as /etc/passwd. In other words, NIS simply shares files across multiple systems, so that the central copy can be maintained, instead of maintaining many copies on many systems. One such file is a passwd file, which is used instead of a local passwd file.

Obviously, there is an overlap between some of these files. For example, if a user account is present in both places, which takes precedence: the system's local /etc/passwd file or the version found in NIS? The file /etc/nsswitch.conf defines this priority. For example, Red Hat Linux's default /etc/nsswitch.conf file has this line, which defines the order for passwords:

```
passwd:    files nisplus nis
```

The three words after "passwd:" each refer to a different source for that file. That the "files" identifier is first means that the system should consult the local /etc/passwd file before the copies stored in NIS+ ("nisplus") or the older NIS ("nis"). The defaults should work just fine in the majority if cases, but you *can* alter the order for a given file if you need to. (For example, you could change the order so that NIS account information takes priority over /etc/passwd.) If you look in /etc/nsswitch.conf, you'll actually see a number of other subsystems that can also load information from NIS. You should check the manual page on nsswitch.conf for more information.

In order for this scheme to work, the system's libraries have to be compiled to use NIS as part of the authentication process. (This is also true of any other systems that use files from NIS, such as those listed in /etc/nsswitch.conf.) This is why it's difficult to install support for NIS after the system has been installed, just as it would be difficult to retrofit PAM into the system, as discussed in Chapter 9.

Actually configuring your workstation to use NIS is fairly simple with Red Hat Linux, since it already includes all of the files you need. To get started, you need to install two packages: yp-tools, and ypbind. (NIS was formerly known as "yellow pages" and changed due to a trademark dispute, so some of the files still use the "yp" abbreviation.)

Once you install these packages, you must configure NIS to be able to locate servers. This is generally accomplished by two configuration files: /etc/sysconfig/network and /etc/yp.conf. The /etc/sysconfig/network file should already exist on your system; /etc/yp.conf will be installed by the ypbind package.

Modifying the /etc/sysconfig/network File

As you'll recall from Chapter 4, the /etc/sysconfig/network file contains values for important variables used by the network configuration scripts. For example, the HOSTNAME variable sets the network host name of the system. The relevant variable for NIS is NISDOMAIN, which sets the NIS domain name.

The NIS domain is simply a logical name for a particular configuration of NIS. A given network can have multiple NIS servers running, each serving a different set of users. These configurations are referred to as *domains,* and a client has to bind to a specific domain on the network. This is the domain being specified in the NISDOMAIN variable.

Your network administrator will have to tell you the name of the NIS domain you should use. On the case study system, the name of this domain is "universal", and so the line in /etc/sysconfig/network is simply `NISDOMAIN=universal`.

Modifying the /etc/yp.conf File

This file typically has just a single line, which tells the NIS client software where to locate the NIS server. There are three possible ways to create this line, and all three are documented in comments in the /etc/yp.conf file. One way is to simply specify an NIS host name to use as the server for a given domain. Another way is to have the client broadcast over the network to locate an NIS server for the domain. The third way is to hard-code an NIS server, regardless of domain.

You'll therefore need two pieces of information from your network administrator: the NIS domain (which you already have from the previous section) and possibly the host name of the NIS server itself. That, actually, leads to a rather odd subtlety of configuring NIS.

The issue is that the format you use in /etc/yp.conf can vary based on how your network is configured. For example, the case study system has this line:

```
domain universal server nis01
```

However, the case study system is actually one of several identical configurations on the network. Or rather, *nearly* identical. These other systems differ only in their /etc/yp.conf files. Many of them have this line, instead of the preceding line:

```
domain universal broadcast
```

The reason for the difference seems to be the router configurations of the network. These systems are located in various parts of the building and are therefore on various subnets of the LAN. This means that the NIS server is accessible via broadcast from some workstations, but it is not accessible from others. When a new system is added, frequently the /etc/yp.conf file will have to be created by trial and error. You may not encounter this problem on your network, but then again you might. Just be sure to try all the possibilities when you attempt to configure your system.

After you've configured the NIS system to be able to communicate with the NIS server, you'll be all set. The NIS system will usually automatically load whatever configuration files are available (such as the passwd user information file) from the NIS server.

Using Network Filesystem Services

NIS provides centralized authentication. The analog of this is the Network Filesystem (NFS) service, which provides centralized data storage. Typically, users' home directories are stored on NFS servers, which are mounted by other computers when users log in. Thus, users' data "follows" them around the network. Sometimes, project-specific shared directories are created to allow users to work on common files more easily. This section describes how NFS is configured for the case study.

Generally, NFS is fairly closely linked to NIS. That is, probably the most convenient way to distribute NFS configuration information is via NIS. (There's a reason why NIS is called "Network Information Services" and not just "User Information Services.") The core NFS functionality on Linux systems is found in the kernel modules that implement NFS. There are two such modules: one is an NFS server and the other is the client. The server module isn't used on the case study (since it isn't an NFS server).

The client kernel module is very straightforward: It's simply a filesystem driver. That is, it implements a filesystem using the standard Linux Virtual Filesystem (VFS) framework, in precisely the same way as the standard Linux ext3 and CD-ROM Iso9660 filesystems are implemented. You can mount and unmount NFS filesystems the same way as you would any other filesystem, using "nfs" as the type for the -t option to mount.

In other words, the NIS client authenticates a user using information fetched from the NIS server, and it also obtains information about the user's account, such as the location of the home directory. After that, the kernel simply mounts the user's NFS directory as a normal filesystem.

NOTE   *The implementation of NFS used by Linux is notoriously finicky and has been known to have strange issues with some vendors' NFS implementations (sometimes due to bugs in the vendors' products rather than Linux). If you encounter strange problems that seem to be related to NFS, check your distribution's bug or errata documentation, because you may not be the only victim. Red Hat Linux has been struck by such issues as recently as version 7.3.*

Setting Up the Support Services

The core NFS support is contained in the kernel. However, there are a couple support daemons that are required to use NFS in practice. The first is the portmap service, which I've already discussed. However, there are two additional services that are NFS-specific (and use portmap): the NFS locking daemon and the NFS Network Service Monitor (NSM).

The NFS file-locking daemon is an RPC service using the portmap service. It is used to handle distributed file locking for NFS. *File locking* prevents two users from accessing a file at the same time, since only one user can "lock" a file at a time. The NFS locking daemon implements this for NFS clients. (As it happens, the problem of distributed file locking is not an easy problem to solve, and this daemon has its limitations. However, it works reasonably well most of the time, at least for desktop systems.) The actual relevant program is /sbin/rpc.lockd, which is contained in the nfs-utils RPM package.

The NFS NSM is implemented by a program known as /sbin/rpc.statd. This program, like the locking daemon, is also an RPC program that relies on portmap. This program is used to monitor the status of the NFS servers, essentially watching for reboots. It's used by the locking daemon to keep everything in sync with the servers. This program is also included in the nfs-utils package.

These two daemons are generally paired; that is, you'll most likely never need one without the other. Thus, the nfs-utils package manages them both from a *single* SysV service named nfslock. To install this, simply install the nfs-utils package and then use the chkconfig command (discussed in Chapter 4) to enable the newly installed nfslock service for your runlevel (usually 3 or 5). That single service will manage both of the NFS support daemons.

Understanding the Automounter

The real question is how directories get mounted. After all, the kernel module may be a filesystem driver, but at some point, a program has to actually mount the user's home directory. Which program handles that?

The answer is the automounter, or autofs service. This is a daemon program that mounts NFS (or other) directories on demand, when they are actually accessed. This is both convenient and efficient. It's convenient because users (and administrators) don't have to manually mount home directories, shared project drives, and so on. It's efficient because mounting these directories on demand means that they don't have to be mounted up front, when the system boots, wasting resources when they're not in use.

In the case of this sample system, the autofs service takes its cue from the information picked up by NIS. (See the "automount" entry in nsswitch.conf.) When a user logs in, for example, the user's home directory will be referenced (such as when the shell attempts to change directories to the user's home directory upon login). The automounter will detect that the directory was referenced and automatically mount it.

There is one more relevant service of which you should be aware: the netfs service. This is a simple SysV init script that Red Hat Linux provides to enable all network filesystems. (This includes not only NFS, but also other protocols, such as SMB and NCP.) This service will mount any configured NFS file systems, but it will not cause any automounted file systems to be mounted. (In this case study, all the NFS filesystems are automounted, so the netfs service doesn't do much, but it's important to know about if your scenario differs—which is quite possible.)

Installing NFS and NIS is frequently very easy, especially with recent versions of Red Hat Linux. However, it's not 100% foolproof, and sometimes things go wrong, especially with more sophisticated cases or with less centralized administration. Additionally, there are quirks in the Linux implementations of NFS in particular that can cause headaches, so always make sure you're using the correct version. (Linux kernels in the 2.4 series include support for NFS versions 2 and 3; make sure you're using the correct version for your network by using the lsmod and modprobe commands.)

The upshot of all this is that configuring NFS is usually very easy once you have NIS properly configured. Essentially, you simply need to install the netfs and autofs services and configure them to start when the system boots, using the chkconfig command described in Chapter 4. However, NFS and NIS are quite complicated systems, and this book doesn't have space to discuss them completely. This section has simply outlined one particular configuration: the one used by the case study system. There are many, many other ways to configure these services. Check with your network administrator for information and assistance.

....

Customizing the Automounter

The configuration of NIS and NFS in this chapter is optimized for the particular network on which the case study system resides. In this case, the NFS and autofs configurations are stored via NIS. However, your environment may use a simpler technique, and you may have to manually configure NFS by modifying the files /etc/auto.master and /etc/fstab.

The /etc/auto.master file is the real configuration for autofs and can be used to automatically mount other devices (such as floppy drives and ZIP drives) through the automounter. (Essentially, a version of the /etc/auto.master file is what is stored in NIS on the case study system.) The /etc/fstab file can be used to configure specific NFS directories to be mounted. For more information, see the manual page for autofs, the Automount how-tos, and the NIS/NIS+ documentation at the Linux Documentation Project's site (www.linuxdoc.org) and Red Hat's site (www.redhat.com).

....

Managing Assets

One problem administrators have with a large network is simply tracking systems. Frequently, users will upgrade, remove, or add systems to a network, sometimes without the knowledge of the support organization. The support group, of course, can't support what they don't know about, and so this can present a problem.

To help resolve this, many network administrators make use of so-called asset management software. These are programs installed on workstations and sometimes servers that simply provide a way for administrators to track which machines are on a network and what the specifications of those machines are.

These programs are typically commercial software, so source code usually isn't available. Additionally, such programs usually were first written for other operating systems, and they have only recently begun being ported to Linux. Consequently, they sometimes suffer from annoying quirks, such as restrictions on where they can be installed.

If your network support group uses such software, you may or may not have much input on where it is to be installed. However, if you do have input, you should remember that it's just another piece of software like any other. Ideally, you would be provided with an RPM to install, but if that isn't possible, a good installation would be /opt or /usr/local.

The case study system uses a tool known as Asset Insight (produced by Tangram Enterprise Solutions at www.tangram.com) as asset-tracking software. The Linux version of this software is a fairly lightweight daemon process that tracks certain aspects of the system, such as system specifications.

Providing Remote Root Access

The administrators of a network are responsible for keeping that network, as well as the machines on it, running smoothly. They obviously can't accomplish this if they don't have the ability to manage the individual systems on the network. Therefore, the case study system is configured to provide remote root access to the network support group via the SSH server.

The first step, obviously, is to install the OpenSSH server. This has been discussed several times already in this book; a complete discussion is provided in Chapter 8. The case study system uses the OpenSSH packages provided by Red Hat Linux 7.3.

The next step is to add the appropriate key to the ~root/.ssh/authorized_keys file on the case study system. The network support group maintains an SSH key pair. The public key in this pair is installed on all the Unix systems on the network, permitting secure access to those systems to those who have access to the corresponding private key. That private key is controlled by the network support group.

Providing remote root access, therefore, is as easy as copying the public key provided by the support group into the .ssh/authorized_keys file in the root user's home directory; specifically, the file will be /root/.ssh/authorized_keys since /root is the root user's home directory.

Once the key is installed, it's a good idea to verify the key with the support group using some "out of band" technique, such as a simple phone call. This ensures that you're not installing a compromised key sent by an attacker. After you've installed and verified the key, the network support group will have secure administrative access to your workstation.

Now that you've installed some basic tools to allow your workstation to exist peacefully on the network, it's time to start installing the software you need to actually do your work. The next section outlines how to install the development environment used by this case study.

Development Environment

Once the basics of getting the system up and running on the network are out of the way, it's time to go about the business of setting up the software for which the machine is actually intended to be used. That's the topic of this section.

Installing the Core Development Tools

As I mentioned at the beginning of this chapter, this case study system is primarily intended to be used as a platform for developing Java 2 Enterprise Edition (J2EE) applications. However, some additional tools that aren't strictly Java-related are still pretty useful to have around.

Table 15-1 lists several common programs, their purposes, and the RPM package that includes them. Generally, these tools will be extremely familiar to software developers (whose jobs revolve around them) and familiar to system administrators (who frequently have to use them to install software, as discussed in Chapters 8 through 13).

Table 15-1. Core Software Development Tools

TOOL	RPM PACKAGE	DESCRIPTION
gcc	gcc-2.96-110.i386.rpm	GNU compiler collection; includes compilers for common languages such as C, C++, Fortran, and so on
libstdc++	libstdc++-2.96-110.i386.rpm	Core libraries for C++ programs and the compiler
make	make- 3.79.1-8.i386.rpm	A build automation tool
flex	flex-2.5.4a-23.i386.rpm	The GNU Project's version of the lex lexical analyzer
bison	bison-1.35-1.i386.rpm	The GNU Project's version of the yacc compiler generator
strace	strace-4.4-4.i386.rpm	A program for debugging system calls
ltrace	ltrace-0.3.10-7.i386.rpm	A program for debugging calls to shared libraries

Configuring the Java Environment

Installing the Java environment is obviously the most important part of building a Java development workstation. This section describes the basics of the environment on the case study system. The next sections describe additional software that is installed, based on the basic environment.

The basic environment is precisely that detailed in Chapter 13. To review, that chapter discussed how to create an environment in such a way that multiple Java Development Kits (possibly even from multiple vendors) can be installed "side by side." The separate installations are easy to switch between, and the environment also includes a mechanism for automatically setting environment variables (in particular the CLASSPATH variable) in users' shells. This environment is the core of this chapter's case study, so you absolutely should be familiar with Chapter 13.

Installing Additional Tools

Much of the power of the Java programming language comes from the wide variety of tools and libraries that are available. Developers use these libraries to boost their productivity and to share technologies and code. This section discusses some of these tools and describes how to add them to the basic Java environment framework set up in Chapter 13.

Automating Builds with ant

Earlier in this chapter in the section "Installing the Core Development Tools," the make tool was mentioned as one of the core development tools. Indeed, make is a venerable, extremely useful program. However, for a variety of reasons, it doesn't work seamlessly with Java programs. A popular alternative in the Java community is the ant tool, available from jakarta.apache.org/ant/index.html.

The ant tool is very similar to make, at a high level. The most immediate difference is that the format of its build files is in the Extensible Markup Language (XML), as opposed to make's use of a custom file format. Once you dig a bit deeper, you find additional advantages in ant that make is useful for Java applications; notably, it is extremely programmable, meaning that developers can extend it and embed it in their own Java applications.

Of course, this is a book on Linux systems, not Java programming tools, so I can't go into more detail than that. If you do need ant, you'll need how to install it. Fortunately, this is fairly straightforward. You should start by downloading a binary distribution of ant from jakarta.apache.org/ant/index.html. (You can download and build your own installation from source code, but with Java applications such as ant this is usually pointless, since Java binaries are designed to run on all machines.)

You'll quickly find that the ant distribution is a tarball (i.e., a .tar.gz file). To install it, you need simply extract the file with a command such as tar zxf jakarta-ant-1.4.1.tar.gz. The tarball contains the ant files in their own subdirectory, so when you extract the archive, its contents will be placed in a jakarta-ant-1.4.1 subdirectory of your current working directory. All this is easy and familiar; the real challenge is deciding *where* to install it.

In this case study, all paths lead to /opt/java. You'll recall from Chapter 3 that the /opt directory is intended for custom or system-specific installations of complete software packages. In this case, you're using /opt/java to contain all Java-related software. One goal is to keep similar software in the same location, to make it easier and more logical to manage as well as use. Another goal is to allow the ability to upgrade packages piecemeal, without having to remove older versions. (For various reasons, Java developers frequently need multiple versions of the JDK at once.) All this, of course, would be impossible if the contents of these software packages were mixed together in the /usr/local directory. For more details on all this, see Chapters 3 and 7.

Consequently, on the case study system the ant tool is installed in /opt/java/ant. This is the logical choice, since the JDK is installed in /opt/java/jdk.

(Or more accurately, /opt/java/jdk is a symbolic link to the "default" JDK among potentially several JDKs that are installed at once; see Chapter 13 for details.) Since the ant tool itself includes shell scripts and other files that are executed, the /opt/java/ant/bin directory needs to be included in users' PATH environment variables. This means that the java.sh script discussed in Chapter 13 needs to be augmented for this case study. The augmented version of this file is presented as Listing 15-1 in a code sample later in this chapter in the section "Updating the Environment Scripts."

That's really all there is to installing ant. Using it, of course, isn't quite so easy, but then this isn't a book on Java programming! Hopefully, though, the installation process is pretty straightforward to you by now.

Developing Java Software with JBuilder

The basic Java environment as described in Chapter 13 is quite functional. The Java Development Kits installed include all the tools that are technically required to install software. However, many developers prefer to use enhanced tools known as *integrated development environments* (IDEs), which provide various productivity aids. One popular tool used on the case study system is Borland's JBuilder. This section discusses how to install this software, which you can find at www.borland.com/jbuilder/.

JBuilder is commercial software, so there is no source code distribution. Additionally, JBuilder includes a program that installs the software, rather than an RPM package or tarball. (In other words, JBuilder is a typical commercial software application.) Typically, JBuilder is installed from a CD or a program that is downloaded. JBuilder provides full details on the mechanics of this process, which is similar to the installation processes of OpenOffice that was discussed in Chapter 14.

As with ant and discussed earlier in this chapter, the real question from an administrative standpoint is where JBuilder should be installed. Fortunately, the answer is just as easy as with ant: /opt/java/jbuilder. However, there's one extra tweak: It may be a good idea to install JBuilder in a directory whose name includes the version, such as /opt/java/jbuilder6 for version 6. This is because tools like JBuilder, as with the JDKs, sometimes need to have multiple versions installed at the same time. (You might also do the same thing with ant; however, on the case study system this didn't prove to be necessary.)

Once JBuilder is installed, it has to be configured. As with ant, JBuilder includes scripts to launch the application that need to be included in the users' PATH environment variables. The listing under the "Updating the Environment Scripts" section later in this chapter contains an updated java.sh file that includes support for ant and also includes support for JBuilder.

Installing Additional Java Libraries

One of the staples of Java developers are the standard Java Archive (JAR) files that contain libraries of code that developers can use in their applications. Some of these JAR files contain open source software, while others are commercial, but in either case they operate the same way. JAR files need to be added to a CLASSPATH environment variable so that they can be located by Java applications that require them. The Java environment constructed in Chapter 13 already fully supports a mechanism to automatically make use of these JAR files; essentially any JAR files that exist in /opt/java/packages are automatically added to the CLASSPATH variable by the login scripts.

This is generally pretty adequate. However, it bears another mention, in the context of installing additional JAR files. If you download a JAR file from the web (or perhaps build one yourself), all you need to do is place it in the /opt/java/packages directory and it will be automatically included in users' environments. Generally, this is all that's required to install Java JAR libraries—and of course, that was the point in constructing the script.

Updating the Environment Scripts

Listing 13-1 from Chapter 13 is a script that configures users' login environments to take advantage of the Java installation on the system. As I mentioned earlier in this section, this script needs to be updated to support the additional software.

Listing 15-1 is an updated version of /etc/profile.d/java.sh. (As with Listing 13-1, translating the script to other shell languages should be very easy, so it isn't covered here.) The only significant difference is the addition of two blocks toward the end of the listing that add ant and JBuilder to the users' PATH variables.

Listing 15-1. Updated /etc/profile.d/java.sh

```sh
#!/bin/sh

# set the JAVA_HOME to the default, unless it's already set
if [[ "X"${JAVA_HOME} == "X" ]]; then
    JAVA_HOME=/opt/java/jdk
fi

# add the JDK's bin directory to the PATH
PATH=${JAVA_HOME}/bin:${PATH}

# set the CLASSPATH; initialize to just "." (current working directory)
CLASSPATH=.
```

```
            for jar in /opt/java/packages/*; do
                if [[ "${jar}" == "/opt/java/packages/*" ]]; then
                    break;
                fi
                CLASSPATH=${CLASSPATH}:${jar}
        done

        # also add any JARs in the user's own java packages directory
        if [ -d ${HOME}/java/packages ]; then
            for jar in ${HOME}/java/packages/*; do
                if [[ "${jar}" == "${HOME}/java/packages/*" ]]; then
                    break;
                fi
                CLASSPATH=${CLASSPATH}:${jar}
            done
        fi

        # add JBuilder and ant to the PATH if they are installed
        if [ -d /opt/java/jbuilder ]; then
            PATH=${PATH}:/opt/java/jbuilder/bin
        fi
        if [ -d /opt/java/ant ]; then
            PATH=${PATH}:/opt/java/ant/bin
        fi

        export PATH JAVA_HOME CLASSPATH
```

Caveats and Enhancements

The information you just read works pretty well for most circumstances. However, there are occasions where you might run into some problems. This section points out a few snags you might encounter.

Using Many JAR Files

The script in Listing 15-1 adds JAR files to users' CLASSPATH environment variables automatically. Due to the way the Java Classpath mechanism works, these JAR files have to be specified with their full path names, even if they reside in the same directory. For example, the following CLASSPATH sets two JAR files, foo.jar and bar.jar:

```
export CLASSPATH=/opt/java/packages/foo.jar:/opt/java/packages/bar.jar
```

The problem with this scheme is that if too many JAR files are placed in /opt/java/packages (or the user's personal ~/java/packages directory), the value of the CLASSPATH variable can be very long. If it becomes too long, it will exceed the maximum limit that the shell (such as /bin/bash) allows for environment variables. If this happens, you may need to use a different technique.

Sun's Java Virtual Machine (JVM) also supports a mechanism known as the *optional packages* or *standard extensions* system. Essentially, this involves specifying one or more directories containing JAR files via a command-line option (which is the -Djava.ext.dirs option) to the java program. Here's an example of this:

```
$ java -Djava.ext.dirs=/opt/java/packages:${HOME}/java/packages <classname>
```

Unfortunately, this mechanism can only be used from the command line. That means that there's no easy way to configure the users' login environment to automatically use the Java extension mechanism. However, you *can* write an executable script to accomplish the task. This script should be placed in a directory which is in the users' PATH variables *before* the /opt/java/jdk/bin directory, so that the script is located first. (Otherwise the standard JDK's java program will be executed first.) One possibility might be to place the script in /usr/local/java. Listing 15-2 contains an example /usr/local/java script. The script simply sets the -Djava.ext.dirs argument and then executes the normal JDK java program.

Listing 15-2. Optional Replacement Java Script

```
#!/bin/sh

# Install this as /usr/local/java

# set the JAVA_HOME variable if it's not already
if [ "X$JAVA_HOME" == "X" ]; then
    export JAVA_HOME=/opt/java/jdk
fi

# The JDK's ${JAVA_HOME}/jre/lib at a minimum is required by -Djava.ext.dir
EXTDIR=${JAVA_HOME}/jre/lib@

# Add /opt/java/packages if there is one
if [ -d /opt/java/packages ]; then
    EXTDIR=/opt/java/packages@
fi

# Add ~/java/packages if there is one
```

```
if [ -d ${HOME}/java/packages ]; then
    EXTDIR=${EXTDIR}${HOME}/java/packages
fi

# this causes the "@" to become a " ", and then " " to become a ":"
# this is done to eliminate any spurious ":" at the end of the value
EXTDIR=`echo ${EXTDIR} | sed 's/@/ /g'`
EXTDIR=`echo ${EXTDIR} | sed 's/ /:/g'`

# finally, execute the real bin/java
exec ${JAVA_HOME}/bin/java -Djava.ext.dirs=${EXTDIR} $*
```

Managing Ownership and Permissions

One thing you might find while using this case study is that it can sometimes become a pain to administrate. Java programmers are sometimes "high maintenance," meaning that they frequently need to install or upgrade new JDKs, add or remove packages, install additional tools, and so on. In other words, individual developers frequently need to install and remove things from /opt/java.

Such constant requests for installations and removals can become quite a burden on the administrator (or yourself, if you're administrating your own system). If the developers are self-sufficient, you may wish to allow them to manage their own Java installation.

There are generally two ways to do this. Obviously, the users could simply replicate the /opt/java configuration themselves, except in their own home directory. If you have multiple users, however, this wastes space in the form of each developer having her own copy of the relevant JAR files and software installations.

Another alternative is to assign the group ownership of the /opt/java directory to be a group containing all your Java users and then make the directory group writable. If you go this route, you'll also have to set the "sticky bit" on the group (using the chmod g+s command, as discussed in Chapter 12). The downside of this approach, however, is that your users now have write privileges to at least one directory in the /opt directory, which may be unpalatable to some administrators.

Both solutions to these problems have their own pros and cons. You'll have to choose the best compromise for your situation. You may find that the basic installation is adequate, or you might find that you need to use one of these optional techniques. It's up to you!

Using the Apache HTTP Server

This case study is intended for use in developing J2EE applications. Typically, this means building web applications. Frequently, developers doing this type of work use the Apache HTTP Server as their web server. In fact, this case study is one such system. This section describes the Apache configuration.

Actually, there isn't much to describe. The configuration used in the case study system is identical to the one described in Chapter 11. (That chapter discusses how to install Apache from source code.) The only addition to the configuration in that chapter is that the Tomcat Servlet engine plug-in was installed using the apxs command. (See Chapter 11 for more information on the apxs tool.)

Running J2EE Applications with Tomcat

Developing J2EE applications requires appropriate J2EE server software. However, Apache is only an HTTP server, so additional software is required to develop and run J2EE applications. Typically these servers will be linked with the Apache HTTP Server through Apache plug-ins.

This case study system is primarily used for developing Servlet and Java ServerPages (JSP) applications. Another common type is Enterprise JavaBean (EJB) applications; however, this particular configuration was not used for that purpose. The Servlet engine chosen was Tomcat, which is produced by the Jakarta project and is available from jakarta.apache.org/tomcat/index.html. (If you do need an EJB server, you may wish to check out Sun's J2EE reference implementation, which is available at java.sun.com/j2ee/download.html.)

Tomcat actually includes its own built-in HTTP server. This HTTP server is perfectly adequate—you may not even need Apache. However, the case study uses Apache nonetheless, to better mimic the production environment into which the applications are deployed.

Installing Tomcat is fairly straightforward. There are two components: a stand-alone server written in Java, and a plug-in for Apache that connects the HTTP server to the stand-alone Java server. You should be well equipped to handle both of these installations. Installing the Apache plug-in is accomplished using the standard apxs tool included with Apache and discussed in Chapter 11 (see Chapter 11 for details).

Installing the separate server program is also fairly straightforward. Essentially, it amounts to extracting the distribution into a directory of your choice and then modifying a configuration file for the server. (This makes the server portion of Tomcat similar to the flat-file server configuration similar to OpenSSH and discussed in Chapter 8.) In keeping with the standard used throughout this case study, Tomcat was installed into the directory /opt/java/jakarta-tomcat.

Installing Tomcat is easy—once you know how to install a similar server such as OpenSSH. The details are different (especially when it comes to the configuration file), but once you understand the general paradigm, the configuration file is easy. Tomcat's documentation should cover the rest of what you need to know.

So far, you've read about how to get your workstation on the network and how to configure a useful software development environment. However, there are additional realities to working in the business world. In the next section, you'll read about some useful software and techniques that will help you navigate the seas of business.

Corporate Interoperation

There are many realities in the modern business world, and unfortunately many of them involve Microsoft's Windows product. For example, many businesses create and distribute documents in the formats used by Microsoft Office, and many businesses rely on software that exists only on Microsoft's Windows platform. Whatever you may think of these realities, they are still realities and a successful workstation must be able to handle them. This section discusses two very useful tools for working successfully in a corporate environment: OpenOffice and VMware.

Using OpenOffice for Business Documents

The OpenOffice suite of office productivity tools is an extremely capable system. It can read, modify, and write files in other suites' formats. For example, it can produce text documents in the format used by Microsoft Word. Sometimes this isn't a 100% effective translation, and small details will sometimes come out incorrectly. Notably, fonts frequently don't quite make the transition. (Linux and Windows use different dots per inch [dpi] values in their displays, and so sometimes font sizes come out poorly, especially in slides in presentations where font size is part of the display.) However, OpenOffice is still an incredibly useful tool, and it is more than capable for viewing Microsoft Office files. In fact, if your entire organization were to standardize on OpenOffice, you would most likely find nothing lacking.

OpenOffice is installed on the case study system. OpenOffice is also installed on the home desktop system discussed in Chapter 14, and this case study uses the same techniques. (See Chapter 14 for details.)

There is one difference, though, which is *where* OpenOffice is installed. This workstation exists on a corporate network, and the users' home directories are actually located on central NFS servers and mounted over the network. This allows for great flexibility, but adversely impacts performance, because read and write operations over a network are much slower than the same operations to a local disk drive. This is fine for data, but it can produce noticeable delays for large programs such as OpenOffice.

To avoid this, there is a directory created on the local system disk and assigned to the primary user of the workstation. In the case study, this directory is /opt/morrill. The user then can install local data and software (such as OpenOffice) into this directory and take advantage of performance from local disks. This requirement only exists on systems where the users' home directories (which is where you would normally install such a thing) are not located on a local disk. Other than this minor change, OpenOffice is installed precisely as in Chapter 14.

Running VMware

VMware, Inc., has a commercial product known as VMware. VMware is a hardware emulator or hardware virtualizer. That is, VMware creates a "virtual machine" (VM) in software that actually runs on top of a host operating system. This virtual computer is completely indistinguishable from a normal, independent machine. This means that you can install a complete operating system within this virtual machine. Of course, before you can install and use VMware, you will have to purchase a license for it, and download the software; you can accomplish both of these tasks at the VMware web site (www.vmware.com).

VMware has a version that runs on Linux host operating systems. By installing VMware and then installing a version of Microsoft Windows within the virtual machine, you can literally run Windows on your computer at the same time as Linux. This allows you to start up Windows (or another operating system) whenever you need to use some software required by your company that only exists on another operating system. (You could also use this solution instead of OpenOffice by simply using Microsoft Office within Windows. However, using OpenOffice is a lighter-weight solution. In the end it's largely a matter of personal preference, though.)

VMware is packaged in several forms, including an RPM. This is probably the easiest way to install the software. The RPM also includes a configuration script (called vmware-config.pl) that configures the global properties of the installation, such as whether to enable networking for the virtual machine, whether to expose the host operating system's filesystem to the virtual machine, and so on. After that, each separate virtual machine has its own configuration, which is generated through a dialog box within the VMware graphical environment. (This configuration file, however, is a text file and can be edited by hand if desired.)

VMware isn't all fun and games, though. There are a variety of obstacles you may run into. For example, VMware requires a variety of kernel modules; these modules are supported by VMware for a certain set of kernel versions. If you're using a custom kernel or a newer upgraded kernel than the ones supported by VMware, you may have to rebuild the VMware kernel modules, which might not work. Additionally, VMware has significant hardware requirements, and some lower-end video hardware (such as the built-in graphics hardware in some motherboards) may be inadequate. For problems like these, you'll have to consult VMware's site for support.

That's really all there is to using VMware. Of course, since you'll have an actual, separate operating system running "within" VMware, you'll have to be capable of securing and administrating *that* system as well. (For example, if you're using Windows within VMware, then that installation will be vulnerable to Windows viruses and other security issues.)

At this point, you've got a fully functional workstation. However, it would be a shame to let all that hard work (not to mention potentially valuable data) be lost to a hostile attack on your system. In the next section, you'll learn how to make sure your new workstation is reasonably secure.

Security Issues

No computer system is more important than the data it processes and stores, and so it's just as important to protect that data from theft as from damage. This section outlines some security-related issues related to this case study system. As you read this section, it's important that you keep in mind your own situation, because unless your environment is exactly like this one, you'll have to adapt the details to your own situation.

Understanding the Local Network's Security

Securing a computer workstation that is a part of a complex network such as the case study system is rather different than securing an individual, home desktop system (such as the case study discussed in Chapter 14). After all, when the system relies so much on the configurations and correctness of other systems and software, it becomes vulnerable to the weaknesses in those programs and systems.

This case study uses the Network Filesystem (NFS) to store users' data and the Network Information Services (NIS) to authenticate users and log them into the system. Each of these tools is extremely valuable, but the tradeoff is that they can reduce the security of the system.

In the case of NIS, the workstation is essentially a slave to the NIS server. This means that if an attacker compromises the NIS domain servers, that attacker will have access to any and all servers and workstations that are configured to authenticate with NIS. In the industry jargon, this is a "single point of failure," and it is to be feared much. However, it is a necessary evil.

NFS can also be a single point of failure; if the file server on which the users' data is stored is compromised, then all the users' data is available to the attacker. However, even if the NFS server itself is completely secure, the NFS clients can still be made vulnerable. For example, being an NFS client (such as this workstation case study) requires the portmap and nfs.statd services. These services have a history of security vulnerabilities, and so running them exposes the workstations themselves to attack, possibly even in cases where the server itself is secure.

Unfortunately, there isn't much the workstations can do about these situations. The value of NIS and NFS (that is, the value of centralized management and data storage) outweigh the security risks. Additionally, most such networks are protected by a firewall. The firewall will prevent casual attacks from the Internet, but it will not protect against a determined intruder who gains access some other way, such as through a wireless network or simple deception. (For more information on this topic, you may wish to read the next chapter, Chapter 16, which presents a firewall case study.)

In other words, in the case study's network environment, the workstations are only as secure as the servers and the software they run. Unfortunately, there isn't much else you as the administrator of a single workstation can do. If your own environment uses different software (such as Kerberos instead of NIS and AFS instead of NFS), then your security issues will also be different. This isn't a book on security, so there isn't room to say more than this: Know your network, and even if you can't secure it entirely, know what you can and can't secure.

Securing the Workstation

Given the constraints imposed by the network environment, the individual workstation in this case study can only be secured to a degree. However, it still pays to take some rudimentary precautions, which this section outlines. The main objective in securing your workstation is just this: Make sure *your* workstation isn't the one that lets an attacker compromise the network. Two basic tasks will go a long way toward keeping your workstation secure: Keep your software up-to-date, and don't disable the firewall.

The primary mode of attack against systems is exploits against known bugs in software. The only defense against this is to make sure that the software you run isn't the same version that the attackers are trying to exploit. That means that keeping your system secure is an ongoing process, and you have to follow the updates released for your distribution to make sure you upgrade to a bug-free version as soon as exploits are discovered and repaired.

One way to help reduce your system's vulnerability to attacks—even if exploits are discovered—is to keep the system's local firewall running. (Red Hat Linux 7.3, for example, includes a configuration that applies a "personal firewall" to the system.) However, depending on your environment, a local firewall may not be practical. (For example, it may block access to a required service, such as portmap.) You can always tweak the firewall configuration (by modifying the /etc/sysconfig/ipchains file), but this may not be worth the effort in some cases. (As it happens, the actual case study workstation does *not* run the standard Red Hat firewall.)

In the end, though, there's only so much you can do when you're not in charge of the entire network. (Of course, if you *are* in charge of the entire network, there are a lot more options open to you!) You may find yourself in the position of having to delegate security responsibility to the network administrator. This is largely the case with the case study system.

That's it! You can develop software, exactly the same way I do. Of course, that's not going to be especially useful to you if you have different needs. The next section points out some ways in which you could tweak this case study to adapt it to differing needs. These ideas may provide you with the seeds you need to cultivate your own custom workstation.

Alternate Configurations

This chapter has described a real workstation used for developing a certain type of web application. Your own needs may differ; this section briefly discusses some other software that may be useful.

Using an Alternate Application Server

The case study system is used to develop J2EE applications that use the Servlet and JSP systems. The specific software used for this is the Tomcat Servlet engine, as discussed earlier in this chapter. However, the realm of Java application servers is very competitive (to say the least) and you may find that you need a different server.

Table 15-2 lists several popular open source servers for developing J2EE applications. Of course, a number of proprietary solutions are available as well. However, these commercial offerings are usually extremely heavyweight and can be overkill to use for development.

Table 15-2. J2EE Application Servers

SERVER	URL	NOTES
JBoss	www.jboss.org	An EJB container; embeds Tomcat for Servlet and JSP support
Orion	www.orion.org	A full J2EE server
J2EE RI	java.sun.com/j2ee	The full J2EE reference implementation; no cost, but not open source

Installing these application servers is a little different in each case, but there's nothing you'll be unprepared for, especially after reading Chapters 7 through 13. When you do install these, you should still probably install them as subdirectories of the /opt/java directory to keep all your Java-related software in the same place.

Using Other Web Languages

You may need to develop web applications, but not in the Java programming language. For example, you may need to use the Perl or PHP languages. If you do a little research, you'll find that by using Apache as a core, you can build web applications in a wide variety of languages.

There's no way to describe a universal process for installing these languages, since they're so different. For example, Perl programs use the Common Gateway Interface (CGI) and are frequently run from a subprocess separate from the main Apache server, or within the Apache process itself. Contrast this with the approach that Tomcat uses, which is to run a completely separate server process that communicates with the Apache web server over the network via a dynamically loadable Apache module.

However, generally all languages will start with an Apache module. This module will be installed using the apxs program included with Apache, as with Tomcat. What happens after that is up to the system you're installing, but again, you shouldn't encounter anything truly unexpected. Developing applications in these languages, of course, is another matter entirely!

Developing Traditional Software

You may need a development workstation, but not for web applications. That is, you may simply be developing traditional desktop applications. In this case, you'll need some, but not all, of the material in this chapter. You'll also most likely need to install additional software related to your needs.

Every developer has his own favorite tools and environments for developing software. There's no way that this book could even begin to cover them all, but fortunately, if you need such a thing you probably already know what you need. (For example, KDE developers may—or may not—prefer to use the KDevelop program for building KDE applications.)

Unfortunately, there isn't much this book can say on this subject. Here again, though, you should be well equipped to handle any eventuality.

Summary

This chapter discussed a development workstation. The system exists on a large corporate network, and so it must be configured to behave properly on that network, according to the policies of the network administrators. Once the system basic system is configured, the development environment can be configured. This environment varies by need, but for this case study it involved a suite of Java software and related development tools.

If you've read this entire chapter, you've actually gained two separate skills. First is the ability to configure a system on a corporate network. This process isn't related in any way to a software development workstation and can be applied to any system (server or workstation) that needs to be connected to the network. The second area is, of course, the configuration of a Java environment.

Now that you've finished the second case study, you should be able to compare two distinct installations: the home desktop from Chapter 14 and the corporate workstation from this chapter. The differences and insights you've gained should help you customize your system for any environment you run into. The next chapter is a case study of a network firewall, which will give you a third, very distinctive insight into the customization of a Linux system.

#### CHAPTER 16

Building a
Network Firewall

This chapter presents an approach for building a basic but functional network firewall. As with all the case studies presented up until now, the objective of this chapter is not to make you an expert in building firewalls. Indeed, this chapter really only scratches the surface of network security; meddle not in the rules of firewalls, for they are subtle and quick to kill the network! Instead, the purpose is to demonstrate a complete customization of a Linux system.

In other words, the focus of this chapter is not to explain the nuances and subtlety of firewall rules, but rather to demonstrate how the underlying Linux *distribution* is tweaked in order to support a firewall. (If you want the nitty gritty details on Linux-based firewalls, see Ziegler's excellent book *Linux Firewalls,* cited in the bibliography at the end of this chapter.) That said, the contents of this chapter should nevertheless provide a solid basis for building your own basic firewall based on Red Hat Linux. After reading this chapter, you'll have seen a third case study, and learned about several software programs and configuration techniques that will help you in setting up a firewall or any other kind of server.

One important thing to note is that this chapter assumes a fair amount of knowledge of TCP/IP networking. You're not expected to be a master of all things Ethernet, but you should at least know the basics; you should know what a host is, what a port is, how the routing table works, and so on. If you don't know this material, parts of this chapter might be inaccessible to you. For a good primer on network-related topics, see *Linux Networking HOWTO,* cited in the bibliography at the end of this chapter.)

Getting Started

This section introduces the concept of a firewall, discusses who might be interested in such a configuration, and paints in broad strokes the general steps that are taken to build one. If you are already familiar with firewalls in general, you may wish to skim this section.

What Is a Firewall?

You can think of a *firewall* as a layer of insulation between two networks. The term "firewall" goes back several hundred years, referring to the fire-resistant masonry walls that were erected between the mostly wooden structures in old European cities, such as London, to prevent local fires from spreading and destroying large parts of the city. The term was later adapted by other fields, such as the automotive industry (where it refers to the metal plate that protects the driver and passengers in the cabin from the heat of the engine), and of course the computing industry.

In computing terms, then, a *firewall* resembles a "brick wall" erected between two networks that isolates them from each others' woes. Commonly, firewalls are used to protect private networks (such as at a large company or your own home) from the "wild, wild mess" of the Internet. Generally the primary reason for this is to prevent hostile network crackers on the Internet from compromising private systems.

A firewall is just a concept; it can take several different forms in reality. Traditionally, a firewall is an actual computer that sits on the network at the point where the internal network is connected to the Internet, and all traffic between the two networks goes through the firewall server. The server performs a variety of tasks (which you'll learn about later) to protect the networks.

However, the past couple years have seen the advent of so-called *personal firewalls,* which are software programs that run at the operating system level on desktop, laptop, and other individual machines. These programs perform the same types of protections as actual firewall servers do, but on behalf of the individual workstation itself rather than on behalf of an entire network.

Another recent type of firewall is the *broadband router* commonly used by home and small office users to link multiple computers to the same broadband connection (such as DSL or cable modem); such routers frequently include firewall features, functioning as the first type of firewall just mentioned in addition to fulfilling router and other duties.

In each of these cases, the notion of a firewall is the same: It's simply a layer of insulation.

Practicing Safe Computing

Firewalls are a major part of modern network security. However, if a hostile attacker somehow gets access to the protected network or computer inside the firewall (which is sometimes easier than you might think!), then he can still compromise the now-unprotected systems. So, it's important to view firewalls as tools, and not treat them as "black box" solutions that you never have to think about once they're installed.

Most security experts advise a policy of "security in depth," meaning that you should never rely on a single security technique, but rather create layers using multiple solutions. For example, it's not enough for a bank to simply lock its doors, because if someone gets past that lock, they have free run of the place. Banks rely on locks, alarm systems, surveillance cameras, armed guards, and so on.

You too should follow this policy. Specifically, don't blindly set up a firewall as discussed in this chapter and assume you'll be secure. Always stay on top of your systems' configurations, and keep an eye on security. For example, Chapters 4 through 6 discussed Red Hat Linux, Slackware Linux, and Debian GNU/Linux, and this material included tips on keeping these distributions secure; even if you make use of a firewall on your network, follow those tips anyway. Then, even if your firewall is compromised (or if you accidentally misconfigure it and disable its protections, which is quite easy to do), your protected systems still won't be completely bare to the world.

This is not just an academic or theoretical exercise, either. Some statistics show that in some circumstances the "life span" of an unsecured Linux system on the Internet is *15 minutes* until the system is compromised by an attacker. At that rate, if you casually connect a Linux system to the Internet, the question is not whether you'll be cracked, but *when*. I personally know several people who have had Linux systems cracked and exploited, and it's not pretty when it happens. At best it costs you time and emotional stress, and at worst it can cost you something more if data is lost or stolen.

So, take security seriously. Even if you have a firewall, secure your internal systems. Shut off those unneeded inetd services, and leave that local firewall running. If you're running other operating systems, find out how to secure those as well. It may be a little work up front and some time to maintain, but you won't like the alternative.

Who This Case Study Is For

This chapter discusses how to create a firewall server and gateway from a Red Hat Linux system. The goal is to create a reasonably secure, functional firewall for a small network, rather than a super-secure, fully monitored, high-availability system. In other words, this chapter will show you how to build a firewall suitable for a Small Office/Home Office (SOHO) network, rather than a full firewall that would be appropriate for a large, complicated network with many users.

Earlier in this chapter, under "What Is a Firewall?" I mentioned the "broadband router" firewall that you can purchase off the shelf. This chapter shows you how to build a system very similar to those creatures. Typically, these routers are small boxes and come with a variety of features in addition to the firewall, such as a built-in Ethernet switch and perhaps a Wireless Access Point (WAP) that lets you use 802.11b wireless Ethernet. These boxes are pretty inexpensive; you can find them for around $150 at the time of this writing if you look around.

Perhaps you may be wondering why you should bother reading this chapter, if you can accomplish the same thing with inexpensive off-the-shelf equipment. (In fact, some of these devices may actually be based on Linux, so the similarity is greater than you might think!) Well, there are two answers to that question.

The first is that you have greater control over your firewall if you build it yourself. You can set up whatever rules you like, and configure the system however you want, if you build your own firewall. You can also add whatever exotic features you want to your firewall, such as configuring a virtual private network (VPN) to another site, adding a modem to accept dial-in connections to your private network while you're on the road, and so on. Some of the off-the-shelf firewall units support some of these features; others don't. If you build it yourself, though, you're guaranteed it can support any features you need it to, no matter how offbeat. For example, if there's a specific network game you need to support, this might be easier with your own homegrown firewall than a "canned" system without the same level of configurability.

The second reason is to reuse existing investments. Perhaps you already have a wireless Ethernet network set up, and have all the switches and other equipment you need. All you need is a firewall, but you don't want to buy one of the off-the-shelf systems because you already have most of its bells and whistles. Meanwhile, you may have an old 486-based computer collecting dust, and you would like to brush it off and use it as a firewall. In such a case as that, this chapter will be of interest to you.

Of course, the main reason to read this chapter is just curiosity. If you have a do-it-yourself attitude, you may prefer to build your own firewall, just for the fun of it. Or, even if you do go buy one of the off-the-shelf units, you may want to know how it works behind the scenes. (Even if it's not based on Linux, it will be doing many of the same things.) If you read on, you'll learn about many techniques that may be useful to you in the future; for example, many are applicable to setting up *any* server, not just a firewall.

Replacing the Default Firewall

As discussed in Chapter 4, Red Hat Linux includes a basic local firewall installed with the system. It is installed by default unless it is explicitly disabled. (This firewall is actually an example of the "personal firewall" mentioned earlier in this chapter under "What Is a Firewall?"; recent versions of Microsoft's Windows system have similar functionality.)

It's worth noting that the default Red Hat firewall is not adequate for the purposes of this case study, which is why later on in the section "Creating the

Startup Scripts" you'll disable that built-in firewall. The reason for this is Red Hat's firewall is suitable for protecting only a single machine, whereas you're interested in protecting an entire (small) network. That means that you need your firewall to act as a router as well as a firewall, so your firewall needs to be more sophisticated than Red Hat's. Keep this in mind as you read on.

Now that you have a sense of what a firewall is and of the type of firewall you'll be learning to build, you can get right into it. First, you'll read an overview of what needs to be done; then you'll read about how to do it.

The Elements of a Linux Firewall

This section details the following primary goals of a firewall, and the next section describes how to customize a Red Hat Linux system to meet these goals and act as a firewall:

- Minimizing exposure

- Locking out the bad guys

- Masquerading

- Servicing the network

Minimizing Exposure

The first priority of a firewall must be to protect itself. After all, if your firewall is compromised, your entire network is exposed. Thus, a good firewall always has minimal exposure to attack.

Being "exposed" to an attack means the machine is running software that has a vulnerability that can be exploited to compromise the system. Typically, an all-too-common bug in software known as a *buffer overflow* allows an attacker to overload the program with carefully created input that causes the program to give the attacker a command line shell. If the program was running as the root user, then this command shell will be running with root privileges, meaning that the attacker has full permissions to the system! (Other types of attacks exist, such as denial-of-service attacks, for which there is little defense without the cooperation of your ISP, and even simple bugs that allow attackers to gain access they're not supposed to have.) If a program with a buffer overflow vulnerability is a network program, then it may also be vulnerable to a *remote exploit*. If the program is a server program such as an FTP or web server, then a buffer overflow bug can be exploited by a user on a remote system, making the exploit a remote exploit. Remote exploits are the holy grail of system crackers, since they allow attackers to compromise a system without ever even seeing it.

All programs have bugs, and so any server program can have a remote buffer overflow exploit. Even if none exist for a given program, that may not mean that none exist, it simply means that none are *known*—yet! In other words, any time you have a program running on a system, you are exposing the system to any remote exploits that may exist in that program. It's a risk vs. reward tradeoff: You tolerate the risk of running a program because its usefulness outweighs the risk.

Thus, any server system should run as few services as possible, since unused services are adding risk but no value. This is especially true of a firewall system, since the potential impact of having the system compromised is so great; it makes the risk less acceptable. Thus, a firewall should have as few services running as possible. The firewall as presented in this book runs *no services* whatsoever that are accessible to the outside network, and runs only a few that are required for the inside network. If you probe this configuration from the outside with a port scanning program (such as the nmap program mentioned later in this chapter), then you won't find anything, and in fact the system may appear to not even be running!

Taking this thought to its logical conclusion, you should uninstall any software you don't use. This way it doesn't take up disk space, and you're guaranteed it isn't running! Additionally, the smaller the installation footprint the better, because tools such as Tripwire (mentioned later in this chapter) are easier to manage with smaller installations. For this case study, you should instruct the system to install only the packages you actually *need* and omit the ones you do not; there are more details on this later in the section on "Slimming Down the Package List."

Locking Out the Bad Guys

If the firewall's first job is to protect itself, then it's second job (and ultimate goal!) is to protect the network. This essentially means preventing external users from accessing the internal network, at the Internet Protocol (IP) packet level. That is, the firewall simply rejects unauthorized packets bound for the internal network.

This is typically accomplished by configuring the firewall with a set of rules that are consulted for each incoming packet. Each rule consists of a pattern used to identify a packet, and an action to take when a packet matches that pattern. Usually, the pattern can contain things like the source or destination IP addresses, the Transmission Control Protocol (TCP) or User Datagram Protocol (UDP) port of the packet, the state of the TCP/IP connection, and so on; almost any aspect of the TCP/IP headers can be used in the pattern. The actions typically include accepting the packet, rejecting the packet (by sending an appropriate rejection packet back to the sender), or ignoring the packet entirely. A firewall's configuration is simply a set of rules that implement the policy defined by the network administrators (in this case, by you)!

Clearly, these *rulesets* are where the real work gets done in a firewall. If there is a mistake in the ruleset, then the network could be exposed. Additionally, sometimes patterns and actions can be pretty subtle, making them tricky to work with. However, there is a general rule of thumb most security experts use: First deny everything, then allow only what you explicitly want.

Really, this is just common sense: If your house has 200 doors but you only use 2, then you really want to just lock *all* the doors, and only unlock the ones you need when you need to. In the case of your network, the ports, IP addresses, and so on are the doors, so you should create a default firewall rule that rejects all access to the network, and then only allow specific access to the specific ports and IP addresses you need. The configuration script in Listing 16-1 presented later in the section "Creating the Startup Scripts" has more details.

This will all become clearer later as you read about the script that configures the actual firewall ruleset, discussed in the section "Presenting an iptables Script."

Masquerading

Unfortunately, we're not talking about a Victorian-era costume party; no "paper faces on parade" here. *Masquerading* is a term sometimes used in the Linux community to refer to a special case of *Network Address Translation* (NAT). NAT is used to make firewalls, well, usable.

The problem with firewalls is that usually they work in both directions: They shut down internal users' access to the outside network just as effectively as they shut down external access to the internal network. This means that legitimate internal users have a hard time accessing Internet resources, such as web sites, File Transfer Protocol (FTP) sites, remote servers via the SSH protocol, and so on. NAT and the special case of masquerading are a way to restore most of the users' ability to access the network, while still retaining the security features provided by a firewall. You should view firewalls and NAT as separate concepts, even though they are implemented in Linux by the same functionality (known as the *netfilter* or *iptables* code.)

Masquerading runs on the firewall, and simply takes all frames from internal machines and "mangles" them (which is actually the technical term) so that they appear to have originated from the firewall itself. That is, the firewall masquerades as the originator of the packet. The packet is then relayed to the destination, and any replies to it are unmangled before being returned to the original computer.

From the perspective of the destination machine on the Internet, masqueraded packets appear to have originated from the firewall machine, whereas in reality they originated from one of a number of machines *behind* the firewall.

NAT is more sophisticated than simple masquerading. Essentially, NAT is full-featured packet mangling. Masquerading mangles a specific part of the packet for a specific purpose: It mangles the source IP address in order to avoid revealing the existence of the original PC. NAT, however, supports a wider variety of patterns that it can operate on and rules that it can take.

With NAT, you can do things like forward connections to port 80 (the HTTP port) to another internal web server, even though the firewall itself runs no such server. (This is sort of the opposite of Masquerading; this particular form of NAT is known as Destination NAT or DNAT.) Doing so allows the web server to remain safely behind the firewall, exposing only port 80. From outside the firewall, the firewall server itself appears to be the web server, even though that's not the case. Figure 16-1 compares the functioning of masquerading and the reverse or destination NAT just described.

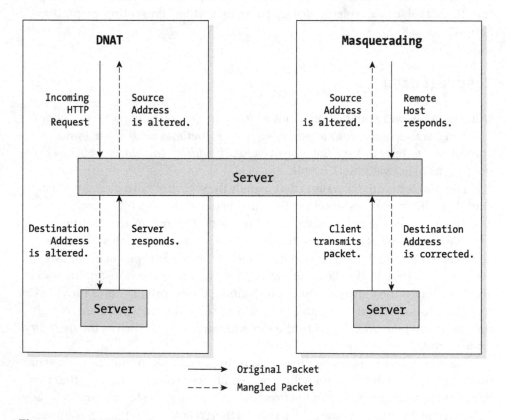

Figure 16-1. DNAT vs. masquerading

In Figure 16-1, two boxes depict network packet transformations that are performed by the firewall. The lefthand box depicts Destination NAT (DNAT), in which incoming requests to a server on the protected network are actually received by the firewall, and forwarded transparently to the actual server. In this box, the solid lines represent actual packets as transmitted from hosts, whereas dotted lines represent packets after they have been transformed by the firewall. What this figure really boils down to is that each host—both inside and outside the firewall—"believes" that it is talking only to the firewall, rather than talking to each other through a middleman. The firewall handles all appropriate transformations to complete that illusion, with the hosts being none the wiser. All software on both hosts runs normally.

The righthand box depicts masquerading, also roughly known as *Source NAT*. This figure is the analog of the lefthand box, and depicts a client on the protected network attempting to access a server out on the Internet. In this case, the client actually believes that it *really is* communicating with the real Internet server, and has no idea that the firewall is even present. The firewall, meanwhile, transforms the client's original packets (shown as solid lines) to appear to have come from the firewall itself, so that the remote Internet server believes that it is talking to the firewall. (The transformed packets are depicted as dashed lines.) The server's return packets are then transformed again, this time to tweak the destination address so that they eventually make it back to the client that originally requested them.

Just remember this summary: in the DNAT case, both hosts think that they're talking directly to the firewall, and have no idea that the firewall is merely acting as a middleman. With masquerading, though, the internal protected client believes it is talking directly to the server, whereas the server believes it is talking to the firewall. In both cases, the firewall handles all the transformations that need to occur. Keep this notion in mind as you read the rest of this chapter; it helps to come back to it if the various firewall concepts get blurred in your mind.

The Linux kernel supports firewalls and NAT. Each of the major versions of the kernel has its own mechanism, though. In the 2.0 series, the kernel really only supported IP masquerading and limited firewalling. In the 2.2 series, an enhanced system known as *ipchains* was developed, and in 2.4 the ipchains functionality was further expanded and called *iptables* (also known as *netfilter*).

Red Hat Linux 7.3 uses kernels from the 2.4 series, and so this book describes the use of iptables rather than the earlier versions. However, Debian GNU/Linux and Slackware Linux use the older 2.2 series kernels by default; if you're using those systems, you'll have to read up on ipchains in order to adapt the content in this chapter. Fortunately, the differences are not huge, so by now this should not be too difficult for you. (If you do need information on ipchains, a good starting point would be *Linux IPCHAINS-HOWTO* at www.tldp.org/HOWTO/IPCHAINS-HOWTO.html.)

Servicing the Network

The final task of a firewall is to provide some basic services to the other machines on the network. Generally, this involves running a Dynamic Host Configuration Protocol (DHCP) server so that other machines can obtain IP addresses, and a Domain Name Service (DNS) server so that the other machines have access to domain name lookups. Later in this chapter, you'll find discussions about how to set up these services on your firewall.

Some people might argue that services such as DNS and DHCP are not appropriate to install on the firewall computer itself, as doing so would both bog down the firewall with needless computation and make the firewall vulnerable to exploits that exist in the DNS and DHCP server software. Indeed, for many networks it might be more appropriate to have dedicated DHCP and DNS servers. However, this chapter is describing a firewall configuration for a network of modest size, and so it's probably not a big deal to run these services directly on the firewall.

Now that you understand the basics of a firewall and what one has to accomplish, the next section discusses the details of how to build a firewall from a Red Hat Linux 7.3 system.

Building the Firewall

This section describes the process of building a firewall from a stock Red Hat Linux 7.3 system. Given the somewhat more complex hardware and security requirements of a firewall, you have to take a bit more care in its installation. The following sections start by explaining how to handle the need for multiple Ethernet cards in your firewall, and then move on to the tasks of selecting packages to install and configuring the actual firewall itself.

Required Hardware: Ethernet Cards

A firewall, if you think about it, doesn't have to do a greal deal. All it has to do is boot up, start a few services for the internal network, and then set up and start running firewall rules. From this, you might rightfully conclude that you don't need much in the way of hardware to run a firewall. At least, for your purposes, you might find that you need quite a bit more horsepower to build a firewall for a large corporate network than you do for the humble SOHO firewall in this example!

The firewall described in this section was implemented on an old spare system with a 166-MHz AMD processor and 128MB of memory. Even that fairly modest configuration is overkill: You can most likely get away with an old 486-class processor and perhaps 16MB of memory. Clearly, it doesn't take much to build a firewall, and you probably need even less power than that. Have you got any "ancient" systems you're using as doorstops?

Abusing Ether

The only remarkable thing, hardware-wise, about the firewall itself is that it has to have two Ethernet cards. After all, you're straddling two networks. Under Linux, though, this can be a bit tricky to manage. When the kernel starts up, it detects Ethernet cards and assigns them interface names in the order in which it detects them. However, it's difficult to predict the order in which the kernel will detect the devices, especially if the devices are run by the same driver (that is, if they are the same model card).

Meanwhile, the firewall rules obviously require that you know the interface names. (How can you tell it to, say, enable masquerading for the external interface if you don't know which interface is the external one?) So, it's clear that you need to control the order in which the Ethernet devices get detected, or at least know which is which.

Naming the Ethernet Devices

There are two ways to get your Ethernet devices named correctly. The first way is actually not to bother renaming them at all. Instead, just figure out which one is going to be external, and which one internal. (Either eth0 is external and eth1 is internal, or vice versa.) Then you can just edit the /etc/sysconfig/firewall settings file that appears later in this chapter in the section "Touring the Script" to set the extiface and intiface variables correctly.

If you prefer to force the eth0 device to be external and eth1 to be internal and you are using two different types of Ethernet cards, then you may have to reverse them. Fortunately Red Hat makes this fairly painless. Red Hat Linux loads the actual device drivers for the Ethernet cards in the order of how they're named; that is, the driver for the card that is supposed to be eth0 is loaded first, and the driver for eth1 is loaded second. It's able to do this because the modules are aliased with names of "eth0" and "eth1" in the file /etc/modules.conf. If your eth0 and eth1 came out switched, just edit /etc/modules.conf, and change the line "alias eth0 <device driver name>" to be "eth1" (and vice versa for the other device). Then you'll either have to unload the modules with the rmmod command (don't forget to first shut down the devices with the ifdown command, since they may already be up), or simply reboot the system.

If you're using two cards of the same model, then life is a little harder for you. Since cards of the same model will both be managed by the same device driver, you can't play the little name-swapping game just described. Your only real alternative is to figure out which card is eth0 and which is eth1, and then modify the /etc/sysconfig/firewall file as shown in Listing 16-2, provided later in this chapter. If you're feeling ambitious, depending on the driver you're using you may be able to pass parameters to the kernel via the bootloader (usually LILO or GRUB, on i386-based systems). If you are really interested, you can look into this, but it's probably quicker just to figure them out by trial and error.

To avoid confusion, the remainder of this chapter assumes that the external Ethernet device is named "eth0", and the internal device is named "eth1". Just keep this in mind, and adjust for it if your configuration is different.

Using the Firewall with a Dial-up Connection

This chapter assumes that your firewall's connection to the outside world uses an Ethernet network. This is typically the case for common broadband connections like DSL and cable modems, and for other permanent connections like T1 lines or ISDN. However, if your connection is a dial-up phone link via an acoustic modem, you'll need to do some extra work.

In that case, your ISP is probably using the Point-to-Point Protocol (PPP) and your external interface will most likely be ppp0. You internal device will therefore probably be eth0. The scripts presented in this chapter can handle this case; however, you'll have to set up the PPP link yourself. Fortunately this is decribed in detail in the *PPP HOWTO* at www.linuxdoc.org/HOWTO/PPP-HOWTO/index.html.

Configuring the Interfaces

Once you've got you Ethernet devices named in the right order, it's time to set them up. Generally, you'll use Red Hat's /usr/sbin/netconfig command to configure them. This is a text-based program that prompts you for all the information required to configure the device. If you prefer, you can also edit the files /etc/sysconfig/network-scripts/ifcfg-<device-name> and edit the contents manually. It's probably easier to just use netconfig; you can pass it the -d argument to specify which interface to use; for example, netconfig -d eth1 will configure the eth1 device.

You'll need to configure the external interface (which is eth0 in this example), however your Internet service provider (ISP) instructs you to; typically this will either be a static IP address or the DHCP protocol. Configure the external device just as you would if you were connecting a standalone workstation to your ISP connection.

You'll need to configure the internal interface statically. Your firewall will be the router for your internal network, so it always has to have the same IP address. Typically this will mean you'll assign it an IP address of something like 192.168.0.1, a netmask of 255.255.255.0, and leave the gateway and default nameserver fields blank. (The firewall will itself be acting as a gateway and name server for your other computers.) To know which IP address you should use, see the section later in this chapter entitled "Presenting an iptables Script."

To help you visualize all this, Figure 16-2 depicts the network configuration just described. It also includes some additional network components such as an Ethernet switch and optional Wireless Access Point, which is discussed later on in the section "Integrating a Wireless LAN."

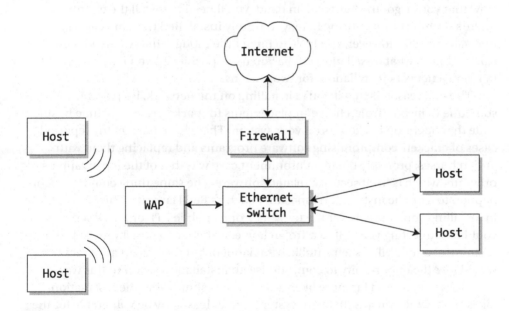

Figure 16-2. Example Network Topology

In Figure 16-2, the network firewall server is included, along with the Ethernet switch and a WAP, as part of the network's infrastructure. The infrastructure is collectively the technology that allows the four hosts depicted to communicate with each other, and ultimately with the Internet. The firewall also handles the additional task of keeping the hosts secure and isolated from the untrusted Internet. Of the four hosts, two are depicted as using traditional Ethernet (with wires), whereas the other two are depicted as using the newer 802.11 wireless Ethernet technology. The firewall is not aware of this distinction, and serves all hosts equally well.

Now that you understand the basics of the network configuration you need, it's time to consider how to actually install the system. The next few subsections walk you through this task; the next section makes some comments on sources you can use for the installation media.

Choosing Installation Media

Now that you've got the hardware in hand, you'll need to install the distribution. There's nothing too surprising here; you simply install Red Hat Linux as you normally would. However, you have to put a little thought into where you install from—that is, what installation media you use. Specifically, you may not want to perform a network installation, for two reasons.

The first reason is that if you're installing off the network, it's possible for someone to insert "Trojan horse" replacements for packages that include hostile code that opens up backdoors on your system. There have been many reported cases of crackers compromising software programs and replacing them with Trojan horses; probably the most prominent case was that of the tcp_wrappers program, which is itself security-related software! The same thing could, in theory, happen to a public installation repository such as Red Hat's site. This means that in installing your system over the network from a public FTP or HTTP server, you could be subjecting yourself to a Trojan horse. Is this a real possibility, or just a theoretical one? Well, it seems unlikely to happen, but then again any cracker would *love* the opportunity to compromise an installation server in this way.

The second—and far more likely—scenario is simply that the installation takes time, which means that your system is or at least may be vulnerable for the small window of time it takes to complete its configuration. For example, in this case study there are many tasks that have to be completed *after* you've installed the base Red Hat Linux system. In the time it takes you to complete them, an attacker could compromise your shiny new firewall. In these days of large-scale automated port scanning and a "lifetime" of 15 minutes, it's a very real possibility that someone could notice your new firewall on the network and compromise it before you can fully secure it.

These are real possibilities, though they may be remote. It's therefore probably a good idea to avoid network installations as much as possible, and install from reliable media such as CDs. If you absolutely must install from the network, then just keep these issues in mind. The safest firewall installation is one that occurs with the Ethernet cables unplugged.

Slimming Down the Package List

Recall that it's best to keep the list of installed packages on your server as small as possible. For example, don't even install any packages related to the X Window system, since it's a really bad idea to let users log in and work on the firewall computer. In general, the following types of applications are not necessary to a firewall and don't really need to be installed:

- User desktop software (XFree86, GNOME, KDE, multimedia software, and so on)

- Development tools (gcc, the GNU debugger, the Perl language, and the like)

- Server software (such as web servers and inetd)

- General user programs (FTP clients, text editors, printing tools, etc.)

By keeping the package list small, you'll not only keep the system lean and mean, you'll also save space (allowing you to install on older, smaller disk drives), and programs like Tripwire will be easier to manage. (Tripwire is discussed toward the end of this chapter in the section "Using the Tripwire Intrusion Detection System.")

Table 16-1 is the list of packages installed on the firewall system used to create this case study. Your list may vary, depending on what you need; just make sure that you have a legitimate reason for every package that's installed!

Table 16-1. A Sample Firewall Package List

anacron	ed	kernel	openssh-server	sh-utils
apmd	file	kernel-headers	openssl	slang
ash	filesystem	ksymoops	pam	slocate
at	fileutils	kudzu	parted	statserial
basesystem	findutils	less	passwd	sysklogd
bash	ftp	libstdc++	pciutils	SysVinit
bdflush	gawk	libtermcap	popt	tar
bind	gdbm	logrotate	procps	tcl
bind-utils	glib	losetup	psmisc	telnet
bzip2	glibc	mailcap	pump	termcap
bzip2-libs	glibc-common	MAKEDEV	pwdb	textutils
chkconfig	gmp	man	python	time
console-tools	gnupg	man-pages	python-popt	tmpwatch
cpio	gpm	mingetty	python-xmlrpc	traceroute
cracklib	grep	mkinitrd	rdate	up2date
cracklib-dicts	groff	mktemp	readline	utempter
crontabs	grub	modutils	redhat-logos	util-linux
db1	gzip	mount	redhat-release	vim-common
db2	hdparm	ncompress	rhn_register	vim-minimal
db3	hotplug	ncurses	rootfiles	vixie-cron
db3-utils	info	netconfig	rpm	wget
dev	initscripts	net-tools	rpm-python	which
dhcp	iproute	newt	sed	whois
diffstat	iptables	nmap	setserial	words
diffutils	iptables-ipv6	openssh	setup	zlib
e2fsprogs	iputils	openssh-clients	shadow-utils	

NOTE   *The list in Table 16-1 contains only RPM package names such as "openssh-clients" with no version, since the specific versions will vary from distribution to distribution, and from version to version. You can compare this list to yours, but just remember that the actual package name as installed on your system will include the version.*

Adding Security Packages

Once you've installed the basic distribution, it's time to start customizing it. Perhaps the first thing you'll wish to do is install a few popular security-related tools on it. This section briefly discusses one of these tools, the nmap network mapper.

The nmap program is a tool for discovering network topology. Most readers will be acquainted with the common network diagnostic tools of ping, traceroute, and telnet. (For those of you who aren't, it's worth it to take a quick read through their manual pages, because they are truly very useful tools.) The nmap program is used to map out network topology and is a great addition to this arsenal.

Essentially, nmap addresses weaknesses in each of those other programs. The ping program, for example, can be used to check whether a host is up and running and on the network, but it can only check one host at a time. The telnet program, meanwhile, allows you to test arbitrary TCP ports to see if a host has any servers listening on them; however, it can only test one port at a time. The nmap program is capable of scanning ranges of IP addresses and can test for the presence of a variety of servers in a variety of ways.

Since nmap is a port-scanner, it is an extremely popular tool among the cracker crowd. That means that an attacker might very well use nmap to probe your network or your firewall for potential vulnerabilities. Fortunately, nmap is available to you, too, so you can use it to test your own network for the same vulnerabilities.

Red Hat Linux also includes a package of nmap, but again it's not installed by default. Once you've got it installed, it's fairly easy to use, and its manual page and command-line help are quite good. The online documentation at www.insecure.org is also a great resource. However, the command that you as a network administrator securing your network are most likely to use frequently is this:

```
$ nmap -sT -p 1-1024 <hostname>
```

This command scans the machine <hostname> (which can also be a range of IP addresses, if you want to test your whole network at once) using the standard TCP scan method for open services on ports 1 through 1024. Most of the historically vulnerable Unix services reside on these low 1024 ports; you should probably also scan the higher ports as well, since occasionally crackers will install backdoor programs that open ports on compromised hosts.

As you assemble your firewall, run that command periodically, and watch as the output changes. When you're done, your system should appear to be almost invisible to nmap—or any other tool—except for the ports that you want to be open. Throughout the remainder of this section, the text will refer to nmap and describe the output that you should expect to see.

Setting Up User Accounts

During the system installation of Red Hat Linux, you'll be prompted to create at least one user account. Generally, it's a good idea to use the root account only for maintenance of a system, since this minimizes the potential damage you can do if you make a mistake. However, things are a bit different on a firewall.

Earlier in this chapter under "Minimizing Exposure," you read about remote exploits. These are vulnerabilities in server programs (usually through a common programming bug known as a buffer overflow) that allow attackers to gain unauthorized access to a system. However, nonserver programs can also have vulnerabilities. This type of weakness might still allow an attacker to gain root access, but only if she already has a normal user account.

Thus, having user accounts on a firewall system opens you up to another class of vulnerabilities. It's sort of like letting the crackers open a second front on your war against them. Moreover, normal users don't have any use for the firewall, anyway; this is a machine that does one task only. For these reasons, it's a good idea to not even create any local user accounts. If you use a centralized user authentication scheme such as Network Information Services (NIS), Kerberos, or Lightweight Directory Access Protocol (LDAP), you should not connect your firewall to these systems.

Configuring a New Kernel

As you know by now, the kernel is the core of the operating system. On a firewall system, all of the real action—that is, processing the firewall rules—occurs in the kernel. From this perspective, then, the kernel *is* the firewall. It's just as important to keep the kernel secure as it is the rest of the system.

The Linux kernel has the ability to use dynamically loadable modules for things like device drivers and additional features. (For example, the netfilter functionality itself is loaded as a kernel module.) This is a great convenience; however, it also means that you can alter the behavior of the kernel while the system is running.

Because of this, some people argue that crucial, secure systems such as firewalls should not be built with support dynamic modules. This prevents attackers from loading hostile modules and causing even more damage. However, it's also true that if the attackers can load modules at all, then they must by definition have root access to the system, and so they can replace the kernel anyway if they are determined enough. Of course, that would still require rebooting the firewall, but at least you're more likely to notice a firewall reboot (since it would temporarily shut down access to the outside network) than you are someone tinkering with the firewall. At any rate, it's an idea to consider. (For another alternative, see the section "Booting from Read-Only Media" later in this chapter.)

Creating the Startup Scripts

The best firewall setup in the world is useless if it isn't running. This section will discuss how to configure the system to start up the firewall on bootup. This section also goes into detail on the exact firewall rules. This is probably the most important section in this chapter; so far you've learned about concepts, but now you'll learn the details.

Selecting the Startup Services

As discussed in Chapter 4, Red Hat Linux uses the SysV model for its init scripts. Red Hat also provides a couple of tools—namely, chkconfig and service—that make it easy to manage these scripts. You will use these tools to set up the system. Specifically, you need to disable the default firewall configuration (if you had it running) to replace it with the custom system developed in this chapter.

Disabling the Default Firewall

Red Hat Linux's firewall configuration is contained in the SysV service ipchains. This means that the actual script file itself is /etc/init.d/ipchains. (This script functions by reading actual rules from the file /etc/sysconfig/ipchains, so if you're curious as to what Red Hat's default firewall looks like, that's the file to read.) In order to disable this script, you have to modify the symbolic links in the rc.d directories—for example, /etc/rc5.d for runlevel 5—or use the chkconfig tool.

In addition to disabling the ipchains script, you should also disable the iptables script. (The iptables and ipchains scripts are mutually exclusive; only one system can be used at a time. Normally, ipchains is enabled and iptables is not unless you altered the default, but you might as well disable both.) The following commands will shut down and permanently disable both scripts:

```
$ chkconfig --del ipchains
$ chkconfig --del iptables
$ service ipchains stop
$ service iptables stop
```

Executing the preceding commands will disable the default Red Hat firewall on your system. This may leave you temporarily exposed to attack. If you selected your package list appropriately and disabled all the services, then you shouldn't have any trouble. However, you may wish to proceed with the system disconnected from the external network until you finish configuring the iptables script anyway.

Running a Scan

At this point, it's worthwhile to run a quick port scan to see where you stand. If you run the nmap command introduced earlier in this chapter under "Adding Security Packages," you should see results indicating that the host is up, but with no ports open. If nmap reports any open ports, you probably have some services still running. Use the command netstat -a -p to determine which processes are running, and then use the service and chkconfig commands to shut them off.

....

ipchains vs. iptables

You probably noticed that even though Red Hat Linux uses a 2.4-series kernel, the default firewall configuration is based on the older, 2.2-series ipchains functionality.

For this reason, and because a few security issues have been uncovered (and fixed), you may wish to consider using the older, tried-and-true ipchains support (which is still available with 2.4-series kernels). In order to do this, though, you'll have to convert this chapter's content to the older system. The netfilter code should be just fine, however, as long as you keep your kernel up to date.

....

Presenting an iptables Script

Now that you've disabled the default firewall configuration, it's time to install the "new and improved" firewall. This is, of course, simply a script (like the /etc/init.d/ipchains and /etc/init.d/iptables scripts) that runs as a SysV service. The script you use, named simply "firewall", is presented in Listing 16-1. To install this script, simply copy it into the /etc/init.d directory as /etc/init.d/firewall, and then run the command chkconfig --add firewall. The next sections decompose the script and discuss its features.

Listing 16-1. A Firewall Configuration Script

```sh
#!/bin/sh
#
# firewall        Set and activate firewall rules and IPmasq
#
# chkconfig: 2345 70 25
# description: Activate/Deactivates firewall rules and masquerading.

PATH=/sbin:/bin:/usr/sbin:/usr/bin
. /etc/rc.d/init.d/functions
. /etc/sysconfig/network
[ ${NETWORKING} = "no" ] && exit 0

if [ -x /etc/sysconfig/firewall ]; then
    . /etc/sysconfig/firewall
else
    action "Firewall setup: No /etc/sysconfig/firewall" /bin/false
    exit 1
fi

case "$1" in
  start)
        # enable reverse path filtering (prevents IP spoofing across interfaces;
        # e.g. prevents someone outside from pretending to be inside)
        for iface in $extiface $intiface lo; do
            echo 1 > /proc/sys/net/ipv4/conf/$iface/rp_filter
        done

        # flush table & set default policies: DROP everything except what we
        # explicitly allow
        iptables -F
        iptables -t nat -F
        iptables -P INPUT DROP
        iptables -P OUTPUT DROP
        iptables -P FORWARD DROP

        # localhost is friendly
        iptables -A INPUT -i lo -j ACCEPT
        iptables -A OUTPUT -o lo -j ACCEPT

        # DO accept input related to legitimate connections
        iptables -A INPUT -m state --state ESTABLISHED,RELATED -j ACCEPT
```

```
# DO allow traffic originating from this machine to go out
iptables -A OUTPUT -s $extip -j ACCEPT

# specifically allow forwarding of internal iface to external iface,
# and activate MASQUERADING (AKA SNAT with auto-remangling)
iptables -A INPUT -i $intiface -j ACCEPT
iptables -A FORWARD -i $intiface -o $extiface -j ACCEPT
iptables -A FORWARD -m state -i $extiface -o $intiface \
        --state ESTABLISHED,RELATED -j ACCEPT
iptables -t nat -A POSTROUTING -o $extiface -j MASQUERADE

# set up DNAT redirections, to relay ssh, web, etc. to internal server
for port in $redir_ports; do
    # first allow the packets into the system...
    iptables -A FORWARD -i $extiface -o $intiface -p tcp \
            --dport $port -j ACCEPT
    # ...and then send them where they belong
    iptables -t nat -A PREROUTING -p tcp -i $extiface --dport $port \
            -j DNAT --to $intserver
done

# enable ssh connections to this machine from internal net ONLY
iptables -A INPUT -i $intiface -p tcp --dport ssh -j ACCEPT

# allow traffic generated on this machine to the internal network
iptables -A OUTPUT -o $intiface -j ACCEPT

# drop reserved/private IP packets that come in from outside
# these get dropped by the default policies anyway, but dropping them
# here keeps them from getting logged below, which reduces log spam
iptables -A INPUT -i $extiface -s 192.168.0.0/16 -j DROP
iptables -A INPUT -i $extiface -s 10.0.0.0/8 -j DROP
iptables -A INPUT -i $extiface -s 172.16.0.0/16 -j DROP

# log everything else that's about to get dropped -- i.e. log anomalies
iptables -A INPUT -m limit --limit 5/second -j LOG
iptables -A OUTPUT -m limit --limit 5/second -j LOG
iptables -A FORWARD -m limit --limit 5/second -j LOG

# Finally, enable IP forwarding now that everything is safe
echo "1" > /proc/sys/net/ipv4/ip_forward
```

```
        action "Firewall startup" /bin/true
        ;;
    stop)
        iptables -F
        iptables -X
        iptables -P INPUT ACCEPT
        iptables -P OUTPUT ACCEPT
        iptables -P FORWARD ACCEPT
        echo "0" > /proc/sys/net/ipv4/ip_forward
        action "Firewall shutdown [WARNING: system is unprotected]" /bin/true
        ;;
    status)
        [ 0 != `cat /proc/sys/net/ipv4/ip_forward` ] && \
                echo "Forwarding enabled."
        echo "Firewall rules:"
        echo "**************"
        iptables -L
        echo
        echo "NAT rules:"
        echo "*********"
        iptables -t nat -L
        ;;
    restart)
        $0 stop
        $0 start
        ;;
esac
```

Touring the Script

The firewall script is a Bourne shell (/bin/sh) script, and the first few lines are shell comments. Of particular note are these two lines, which permit the script to be used with Red Hat's chkconfig tool:

```
# chkconfig: 2345 15 85
# description: Activate/Deactivates firewall rules and masquerading.
```

These lines configure the firewall script to be run on runlevels 2 through 5 (which are all the runlevels under which networking is enabled on Red Hat Linux). The service is also run with priority of 20; this places it *after* the network is activated, but *before* most other services are started. In other words, the firewall is started as soon as possible in the bootup process.

CROSS-REFERENCE *For more information on using chkconfig and creating chkconfig-aware scripts, see Chapter 4.*

The next few lines set up some basic environment variables, and load some common scripts used by all SysV scripts on Red Hat Linux:

```
PATH=/sbin:/bin:/usr/sbin:/usr/bin
. /etc/rc.d/init.d/functions
. /etc/sysconfig/network
[ ${NETWORKING} = "no" ] && exit 0
```

Specifically, the /etc/rc.d/init.d/functions file contains some useful functions for writing SysV scripts, and the /etc/sysconfig/network file contains values for various network parameters. There is also a check for whether networking is enabled; obviously no firewall is required if the network is down.

Creating the /etc/sysconfig/firewall File

The next few lines check for the presence of an /etc/sysconfig/firewall file, which contains values for several variables important to the script:

```
if [ -x /etc/sysconfig/firewall ]; then
    . /etc/sysconfig/firewall
else
    action "Firewall setup: No /etc/sysconfig/firewall" /bin/false
    exit 1
fi
```

If the file isn't present, the script generates an error message and terminates.

As you'll recall from Chapter 4, Red Hat Linux uses the /etc/sysconfig directory to store files containing data required by other scripts and programs. For example, the /etc/sysconfig/mouse file contains settings used to configure the system mouse. Files in /etc/sysconfig are expected to be volatile, meaning that their contents change from system to system. This makes it easier to manage RPM packages, since all the volatile files are in one place; for a full discussion, see Chapter 4. Listing 16-2 contains a sample /etc/sysconfig/firewall with typical values.

Handling a Potential File Conflict

The /etc/sysconfig/firewall script presented in this chapter may conflict with another file installed by a standard Red Hat Linux package. Namely, the "firewall-config" RPM package installs a file named /etc/sysconfig/firewall. This means that if you have this package installed, you'll have a conflict. However, the firewall-config package is actually an X Window program. Since you're building a firewall here and you won't have X installed, you can't have firewall-config installed, and therefore the conflict shouldn't arise.

If you're building your system to do double duty as a desktop machine, though, you may run into this conflict, so it's useful to be aware of it. (If you need both installed, to avoid the conflict you can rename the firewall configuration file to something other than /etc/sysconfig/firewall. Just remember to change your copy of Listing 16-1 to match.) The firewall-config program is always optional, in any case.

Listing 16-2. Sample /etc/sysconfig/firewall Configuration

```
# variables read by the firewall startup script
extiface=eth0
intiface=eth1
intip=192.168.0.1
extip=`/sbin/ifconfig $extiface 2> /dev/null | sed -n \
    's/^.*inet addr:\(\([0-9]*\.\)*[0-9]*\) *.*$/\1/p'`
redir_ports="ssh http https"
intserver=192.168.0.3
```

Essentially, the /etc/sysconfig/firewall file simply has to assign six variables. These variables are listed in Table 16-2 along with their meanings. The extip variable deserves particular attention: The line defining it in Listing 16-2 is actually a shell command that extracts the IP address of the external interface from the output of the ifconfig command. This technique is useful for cases where the IP address of the firewall itself varies, as is typical of the cable modem and DSL connections popular with many SOHO environments, and on dial-up connections that use the Point-to-Point Protocol. If your particular situation permits you a static IP address, you should replace the definition of extip with your hardcoded IP address.

Table 16-2. Firewall Configuration Variables

VARIABLE	TYPICAL VALUES	MEANING
extiface	eth0, ppp0	The name of the external network interface connecting the firewall to the Internet
intiface	eth1	The name of the network interface connected to the internal protected network
extip	Assigned by ISP	The IP address of the firewall on the Internet
intip	192.168.x.x	The IP address of the firewall on the internal protected network; usually one of the reserved unroutable IP addresses
redir_ports	Varies	A list of ports separated by spaces that are to be transparently forwarded to an internal server
intserver	IP Address	The IP address of a server on the internal network that handles requests on the ports in redir_port

The values that you should place in /etc/sysconfig/firewall vary according to your particular situation. For starters, the extiface variable will depend on how you connect your firewall to the Internet. If you're using a cable modem or DSL, chances are this will be an Ethernet device such as "eth0". If you're using a dial-up connection, though, you might be using PPP, and the device might be "ppp0".

For the internal interface variable intiface, you'll most likely be using an Ethernet device such as "eth1". Ethernet devices are named according to the order in which the kernel detects them; the first device is "eth0", the second is "eth1", and so on. As a result, your particular system might boot in such a way that your internal network card is actually detected first, making it eth0 and making the external interface eth1. In this case, you'll have to ensure that your extiface and intiface variables are set correctly. (You'll encounter a similar situation if you use a PPP dial-up connection to connect to the Internet: Your extiface might be "ppp0", but your intiface will probably be "eth0".)

Using the Firewall Script with PPP Connections

If you're using your internal network and firewall to share a PPP dial-up connection among several computers, then you won't be able to run the script in Listing 16-1 as a SysV script. This is because dial-up connections are only active when the modem is in use, so until you dial in, you have no external IP address (or PPP network interface) for the script to use!

Instead of running it as a SysV service, you'll have to run Listing 16-1 *after* you've dialed in. Additionally, you'll have to use Listing 16-1 to shut down the firewall rules after you hang up and the PPP connection goes down. For more information on how to do this, check the manual page on pppd (the PPP daemon) for more information.

Another alternative is to use the "demand-dialing" feature of pppd, which will enable the PPP device (for example, ppp0) but not physically dial in. This allows you to continue to use Listing 16-1 as a SysV service. Again, consult the manual page for more information.

Once you've correctly identified your network interfaces, determining their IP addresses is easy. For the external interface, your IP address will probably be assigned to you by your ISP, in which case it will be automatically detected in Listing 16-2. However, now you must choose an IP address for the internal network.

For most SOHO environments, your internal network will probably be pretty small. You'll therefore only need a single Ethernet subnet—that is, you won't need any extensive routing. For this case, you can assign your internal network IP addresses on the 192.168.0.x network. For example, your firewall might have address 192.168.0.1, and other machines might have addresses starting at 192.168.0.2.

Choosing an IP Address Range

The Internet Assigned Numbers Authority (IANA) standards body at www.iana.org assigns IP address ranges to organizations that require them. IANA, however, reserves three address ranges for testing, research, and other purposes. (There are three "classes" of IP networks—A, B, and C—of varying sizes. Class A is the largest, and C is the smallest.) These IP ranges are considered "nonroutable," meaning that they'll generally be ignored by routers and similar equipment. However, because they're reserved, they're free for anyone to use without restriction. Additionally, since the firewall being constructed in this chapter performs Network Address Translation, the IP addresses of the internal protected network are invisible to observers on the Internet. For this reason these unroutable network ranges are useful (and safe to use!) for this basic SOHO case.

You can really use any of the unroutable network ranges; I simply chose the 192.168.x.x range because it's the Class C range, and it would be very unusual for a SOHO environment to need more than that. However, you can choose any range you want. The ranges are 10.x.x.x for Class A addresses, 172.16.x.x (or any network range up to 172.31.x.x) for Class B addresses, and 192.168.x.x for Class C addresses.

Setting the DNAT Variables

The remaining variables in /etc/sysconfig/firewall are redir_ports and intserver. These variables are used to configure the DNAT rules that allow public access to servers (such as a web server) running behind your firewall. When activated, these rules instruct the kernel to forward any incoming connections on the indicated ports to another machine inside the firewall. The protected machine is otherwise invisible; to an outside observer, it will appear as though the firewall *itself* is accepting the connections.

Two variables in /etc/sysconfig/network activate this functionality: One is a list of ports to forward to an internal server, and the other is the IP address of the internal server. The IP address is simple: Just enter the IP address of the computer you're using as a server as the value of the intserver variable. (Read the section "Installing DHCP for Internal Machines" for more information.) The list of ports, meanwhile, is stored in the variable redir_ports, and is a list of ports (or the symbolic names of ports from the /etc/services file) separated by whitespace.

NOTE   *Remember to include the list of ports in quotes, since it has to be a single variable!*

Once you've set these variables, the script will automatically configure rules setting up DNAT redirections for each listed port to the IP address specified. The example in Listing 16-2 configures three ports: HTTP, secure HTTP (HTTPS), and SSH. Read the next section for more details on how DNAT actually works and is configured.

Understanding the Firewall Rules

Now that you've seen the /etc/sysconfig/firewall (with an example in Listing 16-2), you can return to Listing 16-1. Since Listing 16-1 is a SysV init script, it supports these four targets, or commands:

- start
- stop
- restart
- status

This isn't a book on shell programming, so there won't be an extensive discussion of the structure of the shell script. Specifically, you won't be reading about how the "framework" of the script works, and how each individual target is executed. If Listing 16-1 isn't clear to you, you should consult your favorite shell scripting reference.

You should keep in mind that this chapter will **not** necessarily make you an expert in building firewalls. It's important to remember that the focus of this chapter is to illustrate an example of how to take a stock installation of a Linux distribution and extensively customize it for your own needs, rather than to delve deeply into the very complicated world of computer security and firewall design. (If you *are* interested in those topics, Ziegler's *Linux Firewalls, Second ed.* is an excellent reference.) Remember this as you read the rest of this section. Hopefully you'll find enough detail to understand what's going on, but the goal is not a mastery of firewall design.

Starting the Firewall

The start case in the */etc/init.d/firewall* script starts up the firewall by configuring a variety of netfilter rules via the iptables command, and executing a few other commands.

The first step in starting up the firewall is to enable reverse path filtering. This is a feature provided by the Linux kernel that drops packets whose "reverse path" doesn't match the IP address. For example, your firewall will only expect to "see" IP addresses in the range 192.168.x.x coming from *inside* the firewall—that is, from the eth1 device. If the kernel ever sees a packet coming from a 192.168.x.x address coming in over eth0 device, it can reasonably assume that the packet is either mistaken or an indicator of a hostile attack known as an *IP spoof*. The kernel will have to be compiled to include reverse path filtering support.

These lines enable reverse path filtering on both the internal and external network interfaces (as well as the local loopback device, just for safety's sake):

```
for iface in $extiface $intiface lo; do
    echo 1 > /proc/sys/net/ipv4/conf/$iface/rp_filter
done
```

The next block of commands establishes the default policies for the firewall. These are the "catch-all" policies; the kernel uses them to decide the fates of packets that don't trigger any of the other rules. Good firewall design says that you should always deny everything by default, and explicitly accept only the packets you want to allow.

The following lines first flush the kernel of any preexisting rules, and then set default policies:

```
iptables -F
iptables -t nat -F
iptables -P INPUT DROP
iptables -P OUTPUT ACCEPT
iptables -P FORWARD DROP
```

Note that the OUTPUT chain is set to accept packets by default; this is because any packets that originate from the firewall (or are allowed to pass through it) are almost certainly safe. The other chains—INPUT and FORWARD—are set to drop all packets by default.

Next, the script starts executing rules that allow desired packets. The first such rules essentially give unrestricted access to the local loopback device, named "lo". This is the "phantom" network device that always has IP address 127.0.0.1. Since the loopback device is by definition local to the machine, it can be fully trusted. These lines accept packets on the loopback device:

```
iptables -A INPUT -i lo -j ACCEPT
iptables -A OUTPUT -o lo -j ACCEPT
```

The next few lines in the /etc/init.d/firewall script are noteworthy because they are *not* used—they're disabled as comments:

```
# iptables -A INPUT -i $intiface -j ACCEPT
# iptables -A OUTPUT -o $intiface -j ACCEPT
```

What these rules would do if they were enabled is to implicitly trust the internal network device—that is, eth1—in the same way that the loopback device is trusted. The rationale for this would be that machines inside the firewall should be friendly, right? Well, perhaps on first blush, but if you think about it, there's no real reason that even internal machines need full access to the firewall. Suppose, for example, that you set up a wireless Ethernet network and connect it to your firewall. It would be possible for an attacker to "hijack" an IP address on this wireless network and attack your firewall from the inside. To avoid this kind of risk, these rules are commented out, protecting the firewall even from hostile attackers on the inside.

At this point, the firewall is configured to reject everything that comes in over the Ethernet devices; only the local loopback device is permitted to do anything. The firewall server might as well not even *have* network cards! The subsequent sets of commands are the ones that really start to establish the behavior of the firewall.

The next rule instructs the firewall to accept any packets that are known to be associated with legitimate connections requested by a user on the firewall system itself or behind the firewall:

```
iptables -A INPUT -m state --state ESTABLISHED,RELATED -j ACCEPT
```

This is a crucial step: Without this rule, computers on your network could send communications to whatever hosts on the Internet that they desire—but they'd never get a response back! Of course, this rule only applies to incoming packets associated with known connections; any incoming packets that weren't solicited by a computer inside the firewall are still ignored.

The next set of rules turns on the IP masquerading functionality, discussed earlier in this chapter in the section "Masquerading." The term "masquerading" is specific to the Linux community; the same process is frequently referred to as Network Address Translation by other operating systems. Actually, even within Linux, masquerading is just a special case of what is called *Source NAT (SNAT)*. Network Address Translation in general refers to when a firewall modifies the header of an IP packet to make it appear to have either a different source or destination; SNAT specifies the former type of modification, and DNAT indicates the latter.

However, IP masquerading obviously can't do anything if the packets get rejected before they even get in the door! Thus, the first two commands that follow allow packets from the internal interface into the kernel, and allow them to be forwarded to the external interface. This allows IP masquerading to be performed on them. Note that setting up forwarding has to have two rules—one for outgoing packets, and one for incoming responses; the incoming rule is further restricted to only relay packets related to known connections.

The following lines from /etc/init.d/firewall enable input and forwarding from the internal interface, and set up IP masquerading:

```
iptables -A INPUT -i $intiface -j ACCEPT
iptables -A FORWARD -i $intiface -o $extiface -j ACCEPT
iptables -A FORWARD -m state -i $extiface -o $intiface \
        --state ESTABLISHED,RELATED -j ACCEPT
iptables -t nat -A POSTROUTING -o $extiface -j MASQUERADE
```

In the section "Setting the DNAT Variables," you read about the redir_ports and intserver variables specified in /etc/sysconfig/firewall. The next rules in Listing 16-1 actually make use of those variables. For each port specified in the redir_ports variable, two rules are created. One rule allows packets on that port that come in from the Internet over the external interface (eth0) to actually enter the system and be forwarded, and the second causes them to be redirected to the internal server.

This allows you to configure a server system running a service such as the Apache HTTP server, place it behind the firewall where it's protected, and still have it be accessible from the public Internet. In other words, this exposes your protected server's ports to the Internet. The following lines accomplish this task:

```
for port in $redir_ports; do
    # first allow the packets into the system...
    iptables -A FORWARD -i $extiface -o $intiface -p tcp \
        --dport $port -j ACCEPT
    # ...and then send them where they belong
    iptables -t nat -A PREROUTING -p tcp -i $extiface \
        --dport $port -j DNAT --to $intserver
done
```

Exposing Ports

It's probably obvious, but it's still important to remember that if you set up DNAT port redirection as discussed in this section, then those ports on your server are actually exposed to the Internet! For example, if you expose an SMTP mail server such as sendmail, then your server will be vulnerable to any security exploits that exist in sendmail. This still puts your server system at risk, so use DNAT with caution, and don't expose ports unless you really need to.

Chances are you'll periodically have to perform routine maintenance on your firewall. However, you might want your firewall to be placed somewhere out of the way, such as in a quiet corner or a closet, and so you might not have a monitor and keyboard connected to it. For this reason, it's useful to be able to access the firewall remotely, via the Secure Shell (SSH) protocol. (The OpenSSH server can be configured on the firewall as discussed in Chapter 8.)

The following command accepts SSH connections to the firewall—but only from the internal interface, eth1!

```
iptables -A INPUT -i $intiface -p tcp --dport ssh -j ACCEPT
```

By restricting OpenSSH to only listen on the internal interface, you ensure that it is still not accessible to the outside world, even if the firewall script is temporarily disabled.

The last relevant line in the "startup" component of the /etc/init.d/firewall script enables IP forwarding:

```
echo "1" > /proc/sys/net/ipv4/ip_forward
```

Essentially, this instructs the kernel to start behaving as a network router. Until this command is executed, the firewall won't actually do anything useful, since the kernel will simply ignore any packets not destined for it. Enabling IP forwarding allows packets to actually make it into the netfilter rules.

Stopping the Firewall

Deactivating the firewall is much easier than starting it up. All that needs to be done is to flush out and clear that the kernel's list of packet filtering rules, reset the default policies, and disable IP forwarding. The following lines accomplish exactly that, and shut down the firewall. (This will also leave the firewall exposed, so don't keep it connected to the Internet if you shut down the firewall service.)

```
iptables -F
iptables -X
iptables -P INPUT ACCEPT
iptables -P OUTPUT ACCEPT
iptables -P FORWARD ACCEPT
echo "0" > /proc/sys/net/ipv4/ip_forward
```

One interesting feature of this /etc/init.d/firewall script is that the start command also begins with the command iptables -F. This means that in a certain sense, the start command also implicitly shuts down the firewall first, before re-creating it. In other words, you don't actually need to run service firewall stop before calling service firewall start.

Checking the Status of the Firewall

There isn't a good way to check to see if the firewall is running or not, since it's not a daemon program that you can simply look for in the list of running processes. Rather, the firewall is a set of kernel rules, and the only way to check on its status is to list all current rules.

That's exactly what the status command to /etc/init.d/firewall does, by executing the following commands:

```
[ 0 != `cat /proc/sys/net/ipv4/ip_forward` ] && \
        echo "Forwarding enabled."
echo "Firewall rules:"
echo "**************"
iptables -L
echo
echo "NAT rules:"
echo "*********"
iptables -t nat -L
```

The script also reports on whether IP forwarding is enabled.

Restarting the Firewall

The final command, restart, is the simplest of all. It literally just recalls the script with the stop command, and then calls it again with the start command. (Of course, this is redundant since, as mentioned previously, you don't technically need to call stop before start.) These lines are all it takes to implement restart:

```
$0 stop
$0 start
```

Validating the Installation

Now that you have the basic system installed, and the firewall rules running, it's a good time to do another quick port scan of your system using the nmap program introduced earlier in this chapter in the section "Adding Security Packages." However, you'll quickly find that this isn't as easy as it was before, because your firewall will have a different port scan depending on where you scan it from!

For example, if you connect your machine to the Internet and scan it from a remote host with nmap, it won't even appear to be on the network, except for the ports you list in the redir_ports list. If you scan it from *inside* the firewall, you'll get different results, and if you scan it from localhost, you'll yet again get different results! This, of course, is the point.

When scanned from outside, the firewall should have all ports filtered except the ones you put in the redir_list, which are 22 for SSH, 80 for HTTP, and 443 for HTTPS in this example. (These ports will appear to be either closed or open, depending on whether your internal server is actually running at the moment.)

When scanned from the internal network, all ports should appear closed except port 22 for SSH. When scanned from localhost, you might see SSH depending on how you configured OpenSSH.

Summary and Limitations

This section described the /etc/init.d/firewall script that sets up the kernel's network packet filtering rules. You should now have a good grasp of what the script does, and how it accomplishes its goal as a firewall. However, this isn't the whole story, and this script has limitations.

For example, consider the rules that set up DNAT. These rules cause a list of ports on the firewall to be redirected to an internal server. However, the way the script is written, all the ports get redirected to the same server. What do you do if you want to have HTTP requests sent to one internal server, but SSH requests to another? It's not hard to modify Listing 16-1 to accomplish that, but that support isn't included by default.

You've also probably noticed that there wasn't much detail into how the kernel netfilter framework and the iptables command work. Unfortunately, that's because this isn't a book about firewalls. It'd be great to provide more detail, but entire books have been written on this subject. Additionally, even once you understand what the netfilter and iptables code is doing, constructing good firewall rules is still a bit of an art.

In other words, if you want or need more detail, you're going to have to consult other references focused on those topics. Ziegler's book, *Linux Firewalls*, *Second edition* (referenced in the bibliography at the end of this chapter), is an excellent place to start, as is the *Linux iptables HOWTO* (also referenced in the bibliography). The best way to master the nuances of firewall rules, however, is to ask the experts; many of them can be reached at the Bugtraq mailing list (again, referenced in the bibliography). This book focuses on describing how to turn the overall Linux system into a firewall, rather than the nuances of the firewall rules. If you just want to create an installation of this material, you should be fine, but if you choose to modify it, it's imperative to make sure you understand it thoroughly first!

Supporting Internal Machines

Now that your firewall is up and running, you'll want to start connecting other computers to your newly protected internal network. This section will discuss how to set up two important aspects: a DNS nameserver and a DHCP server.

If you have a broadband connection such as a cable modem or DSL, your ISP provides various services to your computers, perhaps most importantly DHCP and DNS. The Dynamic Host Configuration Protocol (DHCP) is used to assign IP addresses to computers on a network, and many broadband ISPs use this to configure users' machines. (However, there are other possibilities, such as the Point-to-Point Protocol over Ethernet, or PPPoE and simply using static assigned IP addresses.) The Domain Name Service, meanwhile, is the standard way to resolve human-readable host names into IP addresses.

The computers on your internal network will need access to both of these services. However, since you've just installed a firewall, you've cut off their access to these services! You'll therefore need to configure your firewall to provide these services directly.

Installing DHCP for Internal Machines

The first step toward getting your internal computers active on the network is to assign them IP addresses. You could simply assign each system its own IP address, configure them all statically, and be done, but this can sometimes be a pain; for example, adding a new computer to the network can be tedious, and you might forget which IP addresses are already assigned and which are not. If you're configuring a laptop that also has to be able to access another network (such as your office network), it can be inconvenient to reset its network settings each time. DHCP addresses these issues and makes life generally easier. Almost every client you are likely to want to connect to your network will be capable of acting as a DHCP client, so all you need to do in order to get DHCP up and running on your internal network is install a DHCP server program on your firewall.

Installing the ISC DHCP Daemon

The Internet Software Consortium (ISC) provides an implementation of a DHCP server. This software can be obtained from their web site at www.isc.org. If you choose to build this software from source code, you'll find it to be a very typical server daemon, similar to OpenSSH or Apache as discussed in Chapters 8 and 11. However, Red Hat Linux includes an RPM package for the ISC's DHCP daemon, and there's little reason not to use it unless you have very specific needs.

To install the server (which is called "dhcpd",) simply install the RPM from CD, or use Red Hat's up2date program to obtain the latest available version. The package on the Red Hat Linux installation CDs is dhcp-2.0pl5-8.i386.rpm.

The package will also install a SysV init scripts service for the DHCP daemon, named dhcpd. Thus, to start or stop the DHCP server once you have it installed, just use the service command; use service dhcpd start and service dhcpd stop to start and stop it, respectively.

NOTE *The ISC DHCP Server program binary is called "dhcpd", but Red Hat's package of it is named "dhcp".*

Configuring the DHCP Daemon

After you've installed the ISC's DHCP server, you'll need to configure it. The configuration file for dhcpd is /etc/dhcpd.conf. This file could become quite complicated for large networks, but for this example it remains simple; Listing 16-3 is a sample /etc/dhcpd.conf file. The contents of this file are discussed next, but only as they pertain to high-level configuration details; for complete information on the syntax of this file, you should consult the manual page for dhcpcd.conf.

Listing 16-3. A dhcpd Configuration File

```
option domain-name-servers 192.168.0.1;
option routers 192.168.0.1;
# option domain-name "tacals.net";

# host wap.tacals.net {
#       hardware ethernet 00:00:00:00:00:02;
#       fixed-address 192.168.0.2;
#       option host-name "wap";
# }

host server {
    hardware ethernet 00:00:00:00:00:03;
    fixed-address 192.168.0.3;
    option host-name "server";
}

shared-network INTERNAL {
    default-lease-time 3600;
    max-lease-time 3600;
    subnet 192.168.0.0 netmask 255.255.255.0 {
        range 192.168.0.4 192.168.0.20;
    }
}
```

The format of /etc/dhcpd.conf is fairly straightforward. In a nutshell, you can set a number of parameters and options, and you can bind them to various scopes. For example, you can set options for specific host on the network, you can create groups of hosts and set options for them collectively (while setting different options for different hosts), or you can set global options that affect all hosts. (Compare this to the hierarchical configuration format of the Apache HTTP server configuration, as discussed in Chapter 11; though the syntax of /etc/dhcpd.conf is very different, the notion is similar.)

Several different scopes are present in Listing 16-3. The first three lines are in the global scope, since they affect all hosts. The next block, enclosed in braces ({}), defines a host, and sets options specific to that host. The last block defines a subnet and sets options for how DHCP leases are assigned to hosts.

Understanding DHCP Leases

When a DHCP server assigns an IP address, it assigns it as a *lease*, meaning that the client may only use that address for a certain amount of time. When that time is elapsed, the lease is said to be expired, and the client host must re-request an IP address. Frequently the client will be assigned the same IP address it had last time, which just renews the lease, but this is not guaranteed to be the case.

The global options being specified by the first two lines are setting the values of several useful options that the DHCP server sends along to clients. As you probably know, simply getting an IP address is not enough for a computer to join a network; the computer also needs routing information such as the IP address of a gateway router computer that connects it to the rest of the network and the Internet. It also needs the IP address of a DNS server, so that it can perform lookups of the IP addresses of network and Internet hosts.

In this example, both the router and the DNS server are set to be the IP address of the firewall computer—192.168.0.1. (The next section discusses configuring the firewall to also function as a DNS forwarder.) These lines are used to set up routing information on the clients; you should be able to connect any client computer (such as a laptop or desktop system) configured to use DHCP, and this information will be enough for the machine to become active on the network.

The third line sets another global parameter, which is the domain name of the local network. This line is commented out (by prepending the line with the "#" character in the manner of many Unix configuration files), because it's important not to just choose a fictional domain name out of thin air and expect it to work.

If you have your own domain name and your DNS servers are configured correctly, then you can enable this line; however, in the typical SOHO network targeted by this example, you probably don't have such a setup. So, you should leave this line commented out. The down side of this, though, is that you must refer to your internal machines by their numeric IP addresses, which can be inconvenient. It is possible to configure the ISC's DHCP server to function with the bind program discussed in the next section, but this is a more complicated situation and is not relevant to the goal of this chapter's example. If you're interested, you should consult the ISC's documentation on their web site at www.isc.org.

The next few lines are a "host" block, and contain options that are set only for a specific host. This block is actually quite simple: It just assigns a specific, fixed IP address to a particular computer on the network. It does this via the "hardware ethernet" option line. This line causes DHCP to look for the particular Ethernet Media Access Control (MAC) address to see if it matches the address listed. If it does, it assigns the fixed IP address listed, and instructs the client to adopt the indicated hostname. The key to this is the MAC address: Since no two Ethernet cards have the same MAC address, the server can use the address to uniquely identify a host; it then simply assigns the same IP address to that host each time it requests an IP address.

From the client machine's perspective, this appears to be a normal DHCP transaction, and it has no idea that it is effectively using a static IP address. However, this is useful for the firewall rules. The firewall configuration script discussed earlier in this chapter includes commands that configure Destination NAT rules to redirect certain types of traffic (such as SSH and web traffic) to some other machine on the internal network. However, the network uses DHCP, so IP addresses are subject to change, which obviously renders the DNAT firewall rules useless when the server's IP address changes. By entering the Ethernet MAC address of your server computer in this host rule, you can ensure that it always receives the same IP address, keeping the firewall rules consistent with the topology of the internal network. In this example, the server is designated to have the IP address 192.168.0.3; however, you should be sure to enter your own server's MAC address in the "hardware ethernet" line.

Listing 16-3 contains a similar host block that has been commented out. This block does the same thing as the one just discussed; however, it uses the IP address of 192.168.0.2, and assigns the hostname "wap". This refers to a Wireless Access Point, which is a device for connection computers using the 802.11b wireless Ethernet standard to your primary, wired Ethernet. Some such WAPs can be configured over the network (typically via the Simple Network Management Protocol, or SNMP). If your network has such a WAP, you may wish to uncomment these lines and set the Ethernet MAC address accordingly, so that your WAP, like your server computer, always has the same IP address.

The final block sets options for a shared internal network, named "INTERNAL". This is where you set the parameters to be used for the rest of the computers that join your network. The lines "default-lease-time" and "max-lease-time" are both set to 3600 seconds, indicating that the leases assigned by the DHCP server always be 1 hour in duration. (The units of these lines are seconds; 3600 seconds is 1 hour.) After this time has elapsed, the DHCP clients will have to send a new request to the DHCP server to renew their leases. This is how the server detects clients that are no longer on the network: It requires them to check in periodically.

The "shared-network" block also contains a subblock that configures actual network settings for the network. The first line of this subblock indicates that the network in question is the 192.168.0.0 network with the usual netmask for such networks (255.255.255.0). The addresses included this network start at 192.168.0.1 and run to 192.168.0.254. (192.168.0.255 will be the broadcast address to which *all* computers on the network will respond.) However, the "subnet" block further restricts the DHCP server so that it will only physically assign IP addresses up to 192.168.0.20; in addition, it will only *start* assigning IP addresses at 192.168.0.4. (Remember that 192.168.0.1 is the firewall, 192.168.0.3 is your server, and 192.168.0.2 might be used by a WAP.) There's no real reason for the upper limit of 192.168.0.20; it doesn't add security because hostile clients that get access to your network can simply start using a static IP address, which the DHCP server can't do anything about.

Once you install Listing 16-3 as /etc/dhcpd.conf, you will have to start the server via the command `service dhcpd start`. Once it starts successfully, other devices on your network will be able to obtain IP addresses, so you can now start up your server computer, power up that WAP if you have one, and boot up your desktop system. These devices will now be able to access the network; however, they will only be able to do so by using numeric IP addresses, since your firewall has cut off access to the DNS servers they would normally use to look up human-readable host names. The next section discusses how to configure a DNS forwarder to rectify this limitation.

Installing a Local Nameserver

A DNS server (also know as a *nameserver*) is simply a software program that runs as a daemon, and converts human-readable hostnames into IP addresses. Since the firewall rules from the previous section cut off access to your ISP's nameserver, you'll have to install one of your own on the firewall, to provide DNS services for your internal network.

The most commonly used Unix program for this is the bind program, which, like the DHCP server discussed in the previous section, is written by the Internet Software Consortium (ISC). (The name "bind" stands for "Berkeley Internet Name Domain.") The bind program can operate in a number of different ways: It can function as a full-fledged domain server to manage your own domain name zone, or it can merely act as a forwarder or relay to another server. The first case is a very substantial task, but fortunately the second case is much simpler and is all you need for the firewall you're building.

Configuring bind as a forwarder is pretty straightforward: You simply need to install the software, and then create its configuration file (which is /etc/named.conf) correctly.

Installing the bind Nameserver

As it happens, Red Hat Linux includes an RPM package for bind with the distribution. The package is bind-9.1.3-4.i386.rpm (for systems with Intel processors—see Table 4-1 in Chapter 4 if you use another architecture). You can either install this package from the CD media, or use the up2date program to get the latest copy from Red Hat.

You can also choose to download the source code for bind from the ISC (at www.isc.org) and install it yourself. In this case, the installation would be roughly similar to that of OpenSSH, as discussed in Chapter 8. However, here the package provided by Red Hat should work fine.

Configuring bind

The bind nameserver needs to be configured as a forwarder. A DNS forwarder is bind's term for a second DNS server to which bind defers. In this case, you're not going to be using bind to run your own domain, but rather to provide DNS services to your internal computers. To accomplish this, all you really need is for your local installation of bind to forward all queries submitted to it to the official DNS servers you might otherwise use.

There are three options that need to be set in /etc/named.conf to configure bind as a DNS forwarder. One instructs bind to function solely as a forwarder, one lists the IP addresses of the other DNS servers to which bind is to forward queries, and the third restricts the clients that bind will serve. Listing 16-4 is a complete /etc/named.conf that configures bind as a DNS forwarder.

Listing 16-4. A bind Configuration File

```
options {
        directory "/var/named";
        forward only;
        listen-on { 127.0.0.1; 192.168/16; };
        forwarders { 1.2.3.4; 5.6.7.8; };
};

include "/etc/rndc.key";
```

Listing 16-4 is quite simple. It consists of an "options" block that sets the three relevant properties, and also contains two other lines that specify installation options. First I'll discuss the installation-specific options to get them out of the way.

The first line in the "options" block specifies a directory where bind is to look when searching for additional configuration files. (This directory, however, should actually be empty since you are using bind merely as a forwarder.) The last line in the file, meanwhile, includes a separate file that contains a secret key used to authenticate clients and other servers; again, though, this configuration will not make use of that key.

The remaining three lines set the three properties mentioned earlier. The "forward only;" line instructs bind to behave only as a forwarder (that is, never to service queries itself but rather forward them to another server.) The "listen-on" line instructs bind to only respond to queries from trusted machines—specifically, the local machine 127.0.0.1, and machines on the 192.168.x.x subnet. (If you're using a different IP address range on your network, you'll have to enter the correct information here; see the manual page on named.conf for more information.)

The last line in the "options" block sets the IP addresses of DNS servers to which queries should be relayed. The IP addresses you enter in the "forwarders" block must be real, functional DNS servers. Typically, these will be the DNS servers provided by your ISP, though they can technically point anywhere. If you don't already know the IP addresses of your ISP's DNS servers, you'll have to contact them to find out. You should not, of course, use the example values in Listing 16-4 of "1.2.3.4" and "5.6.7.8".

Once you've installed Listing 16-4 as /etc/named.conf, you must start the bind service running via the command `service named start`. (If it's already running, you may need to use `service named restart`.) Once this succeeds, your DNS forwarder is running, and the internal machines will have access to DNS services!

What You've Accomplished So Far

If you've read the entire chapter and been building your firewall along the way, at this point, you've accomplished the following tasks:

- Gained a *rudimentary* understanding of firewalls and how they provide security to a network

- Started with a base Red Hat Linux system and pared it down to the minimum you need

- Configured a set of network filtering rules to implement a simple yet very functional firewall suitable for a small network for home or office

- Configured Network Address Translation and installed DHCP and DNS servers to provide completely transparent access to computers on your network

This is quite a feat, if you think about it! You've now got a fully functional firewall and internal network, which goes a very long way indeed toward maintaining your privacy and system integrity against hostile crackers on the Internet. Best of all, you built it yourself!

Hopefully you see how assembling a firewall really isn't so very different from configuring any other computer; it's simply a matter of installing what you need, and understanding how to properly configure what you install. Assembling a firewall does, however, require a certain expertise in assembling networks and creating a secure set of firewall rules, and this brief introduction certainly can't make you an expert in those areas. However, you *should* be capable of appropriately tuning and customizing the Linux system itself! If you find yourself interested in those more arcane topics, then you should check the bibliography at the end of this chapter for some excellent resources.

So, you now have a firewall. What do you do with it? Well, for one thing, you have to monitor it. No firewall will ever be 100% secure, and so you need to be aware of security exploits that may be discovered in software you've installed, and you need to monitor the system so that you know what's happening to it. These topics are discussed in the next section.

Monitoring and Maintaining the System

Even after you've installed your firewall, you can't just forget about it. There's a certain amount of maintenance that you have to perform, and you should always keep an eye on the system, watching for potential attacks and even compromises. This section discusses some common techniques that you might wish to make use of.

Configuring the System Logger

Perhaps the most important thing you can do to keep your firewall system (or any system) secure and running is to check its log files periodically. However, since you probably aren't going to be logging into the firewall computer a great deal, it would be nice to be able to view the firewall's logs from another computer you use more regularly. This can be done by configuring the firewall to use a remote syslog.

The basic idea is that you will configure a server computer to accept log messages, and then configure the firewall to send its log messages to the internal server, rather than log them to its local disk. The changes in both cases are quite easy to make.

To make these changes, though, you have to know the IP address of the internal server. In the example in this book, the IP address of the server is 192.168.0.3. (In the forthcoming section "Configuring a DHCP Server," this address was fixed, and does not change.) If your server is located at a different address, be sure you account for it.

Configuring the Internal Logging Server

Red Hat Linux includes an RPM package called "syslogd" that implements a system logger. This package includes a typical implementation of the Unix syslog facility. To configure the internal server to act as a network logger and accept remote messages from the firewall, you simply have to enable that behavior via a runtime flag passed to the syslog daemon when it starts up.

NOTE   *This section obviously assumes that your internal server is also running Red Hat Linux. If this is not the case, these instructions may not apply, and you may have to configure syslog some other way.*

You can probably guess which file you're going to have to modify: /etc/sysconfig/syslog, on the server to which the firewall will be sending its log messages. (Is this becoming old hat yet? Good!) In that file, locate the following line:

```
SYSLOGD_OPTIONS="-m 0"
```

You need to change this line by adding the -r flag to the variable containing flags that get passed to syslogd when it is started from the script in /etc/rc.d/init.d/syslog. (This flag instructs the syslog server to accept remote connections.) The line should now look like this:

```
SYSLOGD_OPTIONS="-m 0 -r"
```

You should now restart syslog on that server using the command service syslog restart.

Punching Through the Firewall

At this point, syslog on your logging server will happily accept connections from the firewall. However, if you have the **local** firewall enabled on the logging server itself (which you should), then the firewall will still be preventing the logging server from ever actually seeing the packets. There are two steps required to correct this.

First, edit the file /etc/sysconfig/ipchains on the logging server, which is the configuration file containing actual rules (in the older ipchains syntax) for the local firewall. You need to add this line to the file:

```
-A input -s 192.168.0.1 syslog -p udp -i eth0 -j ACCEPT
```

This line adds a rule to the firewall that permits syslog packets into the system. (As you can see, this ipchains syntax looks very similar to iptables.)

The second change you'll need to make to the logging server is to correct an idiosyncracy in Red Hat's /etc/sysconfig/network-scripts/ifup-post file. Among other things, this file creates iptables rules that explicitly allow DNS packets from the DNS servers specified by the DHCP server. This has to be done dynamically, rather than stored with all the other local firewall rules in /etc/sysconfig/ipchains, because the DNS servers could potentially change every time the DHCP server renews the lease. The ifup-post has code to check to see if a rule for the name-server already exists, and if one does, then ifup-post takes no action. Unfortunately, in this case study, the firewall is also the nameserver, and so the rule you just added to the /etc/sysconfig/ipchains file refers to the nameserver. This will prevent ifup-post from correctly allowing access to the DNS. In other words, you'll have no nameserver support!

Fortunately, the fix is simple and requires a simple change to the /etc/sysconfig/network-scripts/ifup-post file. To make the change, find this line:

```
if ! ipchains -L input -n | grep -q $nameserver ; then
```

Change the line to this:

```
if ! ipchains -L input -n | grep "\<53\>" | grep -q $nameserver ; then
```

(You're adding the command grep "<\53\>" to the line.) Once you've made these two changes, the local firewall on your server will allow access to both DNS and syslog. Red Hat has been alerted to this issue, and may—or may not—fix it in a later release.

Now that you've configured the relevant files and corrected the ifup-post script, you can restart everything that needs to be restarted with the service command. Specifically, you need to restart the ipchains local firewall, the syslog service (so that it listens to connections from the network firewall server), and the network. That is, run these commands:

```
$ service ipchains restart
$ service syslog restart
$ ifdown eth0; ifup eth0
```

After that, your internal server computer should accept syslog connections from the firewall server, and record its log for you! In the next section, you'll configure the network firewall server to start sending its log messages to your newly prepared logging server.

Configuring syslog on the Firewall

Once you have syslog on the internal server set to accept log messages from the network, you have to configure the firewall to actually send its log messages to the server. You can accomplish this by editing the file /etc/syslog.conf. This file contains rules and patterns that the syslog server uses to determine what messages get logged where. These rules are stored directly in /etc/syslog.conf instead of a file like /etc/sysconfig/syslog because they are generally not volatile; it's unusual to change the logging rules from the defaults, though you are in this case. For the purposes of your firewall, you really just want to send all messages to the internal server.

It's very simple to configure syslog to send its messages over the network to a separate logging server. First, comment out all lines in /etc/syslog.conf that aren't already commented, by adding a "#" at the start of these lines. This disables all the rules that would normally cause log messages to be placed in files such as /var/log/messages and /var/log/secure.

Once you've commented out the default rules, just add this rule; don't forget to change the IP address if your server is not at 192.168.0.3:

```
*.*         @192.168.0.3
```

This rule unconditionally sends all system log messages to the host 192.168.0.3 over the network, which means that syslog will *not* log any messages to disk. If you prefer to only have some messages sent to the internal logging server, or if you wish to have it log to both the network and disk, and so on, you can add additional rules to /etc/syslog.conf as appropriate. The format is not complicated, and by now you've seen enough different examples of configurations that you shouldn't have any trouble adding these rules yourself. Just check the manual page for syslog.conf!

Once you've made these changes, all the log messages for your firewall will appear in the log file of your server (or whatever host you instructed the firewall to log to). You can then view these log messages along with your server's log messages, and you won't have to log in to the firewall to check on its status.

However, you should keep a couple things in mind if you choose to use this approach. First, if your internal server is down, any log messages generated by your firewall will be *lost*! For this reason, you may wish to leave the firewall configured to store its log files on its local disk. Second, all the log messages from the firewall will be mixed in with the messages on the server, which can be a bit of a jumble; keep that in mind when viewing the logs.

Monitoring Firewall Traffic

The firewall rules discussed earlier in the chapter in the section "Presenting an iptables Script" include rules that log incoming packets to the syslog system logging facility. Meanwhile, the previous section just showed you how to configure the firewall's system log to be transmitted to a second server, which is where you'll view the log files. Shortly after you firewall is up and running, you'll undoubtedly start seeing many log messages reported by the kernel about packets that are dropped. It's a good idea to know how to interpret those lines.

The goal in logging any packets that get dropped by the firewall is to keep you advised of the goings-on that affect your firewall. Since the firewall rules were constructed to allow only legitimate traffic and nothing more, anything that gets dropped must not have been legitimate. This is usually for one of two reasons: Either a computer or network somewhere on the Internet is misconfigured and sending you erroneous packets, or you're being probed or attacked by a hostile host.

Unfortunately, there's no good way to tell the difference. Various vendors produce software that alleges to identify port scans—finding the needle in the haystack, as it were—with varying degrees of success. In the end, the most reliable tool is human judgment. So, when you look at your logs at dropped packets, it's up to you to decide whether it's innocuous or dangerous.

A typical log entry generated in response to a dropped packet looks something like this (except all on one line):

```
Mar 25 23:06:04 192.168.0.1 kernel: IN=eth0 OUT=
MAC=xx:xx:xx:xx:xx:xx:xx:xx:xx:xx:xx:xx:xx:xx
SRC=xxx.xxx.xxx.xxxDST=xxx.xxx.xxx.xxx LEN=60 TOS=0x00 PREC=0x00 TTL=51 ID=31194 DF
PROTO=TCP SPT=3780 DPT=500 WINDOW=65535 RES=0x00 SYN URGP=0
```

This line contains all relevant files for the packet. The ones you're most likely to focus on are the "SRC=" value, which is the IP address of the host that sent the packet; the "DST=" value, which is the packet's destination; and the "SPT=" and "DPT=" values, which are the source and destination ports, respectively. Most of the other fields indicate which TCP flags were set and other low-level information like the time to live (TTL) and packet size settings. This information can be used to identify attacks; for example, one attack might have the TCP/IP SYN and RST flags set, so any packets that meet that description are probably hostile packets.

This example is of a simple TCP port scan of port 500. Since you probably don't have anything running on port 500, you can probably assume it was a person or program scanning your machine for vulnerabilities. The fact that it got logged, however, means that it also got dropped, so the attacker got completely stonewalled. From his perspective, it will appear as though your computer doesn't even exist on the network!

Dropping vs. Rejecting Packets

The firewall in this chapter is configured to drop all packets that aren't explicitly accepted. This means that the packet is simply ignored, and no response of any type is sent. Because of this, the host sending the packet has no way of knowing that the firewall system even exists (unless, of course, it sends a packet to a port that *is* accepted). This is typical behavior for a firewall, and provides the greatest security.

However, there is another alternative. Rather than drop the packets, you can "reject" them. Rejected packets are not "silent" as are dropped packets; rejected packets actually send a response in the form of an Internet Control Message Protocol (ICMP) packet to the host that sent the packet, whereas dropped packets are simply discarded without notifying the remote computer (that is, dropped packets are silent). This may (or may not) reduce security a little, but it is sometimes required behavior for more sophisticated firewalls. For the SOHO application discussed in this book, it's adequate to simply drop packets instead of rejecting them, but it's a good thing to keep in mind.

Packets are rejected by using `-j REJECT` instead of `-j DROP` in the `iptables` commands. For more information, see Ziegler's book, *Linux Firewalls, Second Edition,* referenced in the bibliography at the end of this chapter.

Classifying Packets

Identifying attacks from the mess of data you get is not easy. As an end user, you may not even really care; your objective in watching the logs is just to keep an eye out for anomalies. Identifying hostile attack patterns from the normal flow is a huge topic, and a matter of big business in some cases. Unfortunately, there really isn't room to address it properly here; the best you can do is to watch your logs for a while to get a "feel" for what your normal traffic looks like, and then watch for deviations from that pattern. For more information on this topic, your best bet is again probably Ziegler's text, or the various online resources such as those mentioned in the bibliography at the end of this chapter..

What is the appropriate way to respond to these cases? Well, that's a difficult question, and is a matter of personal preference. If it bothers you, you can chase down the probe or attack and try to get action taken against the perpetrator by her Internet service provider. Or, you can just adopt a low profile and only worry about the big attacks. This is a very gray area, and it's a decision you have to make for yourself. For more information, you should check out the sites and documents listed in the bibliography at the end of this chapter.

Care and Feeding of Your Firewall

In many ways managing a firewall (or really any computer, even your desktop PC) is a lot like maintaining a car; periodically you have to change the oil and rotate the tires. This section lists some of the things you should do periodically to keep your firewall system secure.

The automotive maintenance analogy really only goes so far. The reason you need to maintain a car is because over time normal wear and tear will reduce its performance—to dangerous levels, if left unaddressed. However, your firewall will never "wear out" through normal usage; the computer will just keep doing what you told it to do, until you tell it to stop or its hardware fails!

The main reason you need to maintain a computer isn't because it wears out, it's because if you leave it alone, the world will pass you by. Exploits that were not known when you installed your firewall may become widespread later. For example, there have been several vulnerabilities identified in the Linux kernel's netfilter code since it's release. Once these weaknesses are known, they can be used against your machine. So, it's important to know as much as you can about what your enemies (that is, hostile crackers) know, and defend yourself.

In other words, knowledge is power. The remainder of this section describes some useful sources of knowledge. You should consider availing yourself of these sources, in order to practice safe computing.

The Bugtraq Mailing List

The Bugtraq mailing list, well, tracks bugs. The list is run by the SecurityFocus web site at `www.securityfocus.com`, and is a forum for individuals and organizations to report security and other major issues in popular software. The list includes information on most Unix-like systems as well as the Microsoft operating systems. The Bugtraq lists are highly regarded in the industry, and you should seriously consider subscribing to the relevant lists for each operating system you have installed on your network.

The Bugtraq mailing lists can be found at `online.securityfocus.com/cgi-bin/subscribe.pl`.

Vendors' Lists

Another valuable resource can be services provided by your operating system vendor. For example, Red Hat, Inc. tracks errata in its distribution, releasing critical updates for bug fixes and security. (Red Hat's up2date service makes it easy to download and install these errata. If you happen to be modifying this case study for use on a Debian system, you might use apt-get instead.)

Every operating system or distribution will provide updates and bug fixes periodically. It always pays to keep your system current unless you have an explicit reason not to. URLs to the vendors' support pages for Red Hat Linux, Slackware Linux, and Debian GNU/Linux are provided in Table 16-3.

NOTE *The URL for Slackware Linux is a link to Slackware's mailing lists page; you'll have to subscribe to the "slackware-security" list for security information.*

Table 16-3. Linux Distribution Update Pages

DISTRIBUTION	URL FOR UPDATE INFORMATION
Red Hat Linux	www.redhat.com/apps/support/errata/index.html
Slackware Linux	www.slackware.com/lists/
Debian GNU/Linux	www.debian.org/security/

Other Sources

As you follow these sites and lists and delve into the community a bit, you'll find that there are many more similar sites out there. Most sites have a certain slant on security-related issues, so it's definitely a good idea to look around and find the sites you like best. Generally, they all have the same information, so don't try and subscribe to them all—eventually any given bit of information gets around.

It doesn't take a great deal of time to stay on top of your system's security. Taking a few minutes out of each day to make sure that you're not vulnerable to any well-known exploits is a responsibility of any Internet user. After all, if *your* system is compromised, it can be used to attack *mine*, and that's not the way I like to be introduced to my readers!

Security in Depth

Your firewall is not Athena's Aegis, unfortunately; you're not invincible just because you have a firewall. If you install the firewall as described in this chapter, you'll have gone a long way toward shutting out casual attackers—the so-called "script kiddies." However, almost no system is guaranteed to keep out a determined attacker, and it's possible that a later exploit might be uncovered that even makes your firewall vulnerable. For these reasons, don't just install the firewall and stick your head in the sand. There is a principle known as *security in depth,* or *security in layers,* that you should follow.

Simply put, security in depth means that you don't rely on any single source for your security. For example, if you rely solely on a firewall and your firewall is compromised, your entire network is laid bare and unprotected. To avoid this, you must secure each system, not just the firewall.

For example, if you're running a Red Hat Linux system inside the firewall, don't disable the local firewall on it; there's really no need to, and if in the unlikely event that the external firewall is compromised, you'll still have the internal system's built-in protection. Later versions of Microsoft Windows also include a basic internal firewall; don't disable these, for the same reasons.

You should also keep internal systems up to date on security patches, as well. Again, if that external firewall is somehow compromised, an attacker still can't do anything to your internal systems if they aren't vulnerable to any exploits.

It all boils down to that old saw, "Don't put all your eggs in one basket." It may be easy to dismiss this as paranoia, or as a "managed risk" you're willing to take. However, systems are cracked *all the time*, and when it happens to you, you'll wish you had been more careful. Don't learn that the hard way.

Once you've got basic security in hand and are keeping up with the latest information relevant to your system, you can start to think about some more advanced issues. The next section describes some of these.

Investigating Advanced Security Techniques

You've now got a firewall, and you have a basic understanding of how to manage and maintain it. You've also got a network set up, with a few computers connected. You've realized a boost in productivity, and you've got a little more piece of mind about the security of your systems.

So, what now? This section will describe some interesting, more advanced techniques that you should now be quite capable of implementing, if you desire. With some diligence and research, you should be able to put any of these together.

Using the Tripwire Intrusion Detection System

Tripwire is an *Intrusion Detection System* (IDS). An IDS does just what its name suggests: It detects intrusions. This is a useful tool to have on a firewall, since it provides notification when a system is compromised and early notification is crucial to minimizing damage.

The task of intrusion detection is obviously not an easy problem to solve, and there are a variety of ways of approaching it. Some IDSs run on a separate computer on the network and monitor (or "sniff") network traffic. They watch for certain patterns in the flow of traffic that might signal an attack, using a variety of statistical and analytical methods. They can typically be configured to notify network administrators when attacks are detected. This type of system is probably most useful on larger networks.

Another approach to intrusion detection is to watch for changed files. The one thing that you're essentially guaranteed when a system is compromised is that the attacker will change files; after all, if he doesn't change any files, he can't do anything with the system he's just cracked. IDSs such as Tripwire monitor individual systems for files that change, and notify administrators when they do. Since a firewall is a server that exists for one purpose only, you don't expect its files to change very much; this means that it's a good candidate for using Tripwire effectively. Tripwire (and other similar IDSs) can't protect you from attacks, but they might help you quickly learn of compromises and minimize the damage if your system *is* somehow cracked.

The problem with a naive IDS is that it will notify you when any file changes on the system. You might be surprised at how many files change on a system, even a firewall server—for example, log files in /var/log, the random seed state for the random number generator in /var/lib/random-seed, the record of user logins (wtmp and utmp), and so on. As a result, a too-simple IDS will overwhelm the administrator with false alarms.

Tripwire, though, is not a naive tool, and has extensive features that allow you to stipulate which files should change, which should not, and even identify the specific *ways* in which a file may change (such as change in length but not ownership, as with a log file). Of course, this flexibility comes at a price: A typical Tripwire configuration is nontrivial, to say the least. Really, Tripwire requires extensive knowledge of a distribution, and to an extent knowledge of the particulars of the given installation. In other words, configuring Tripwire from scratch is too large a task to cover in this book.

Fortunately, Tripwire is an optional package included with Red Hat Linux. You can install it in the usual ways—either by installing it from scratch or by using the up2date utility. Obviously, Red Hat also includes a good default configuration for Tripwire, which goes a long way toward helping you set up this particular IDS.

If you want an IDS installed on your firewall, then Red Hat's Tripwire configuration is a good place to start. To activate Tripwire, you should install the "tripwire" package, and then consult the documentation. The package itself contains some documentation (use the `rpm -qi tripwire` command to see a list), and full online documentation is available at `www.tripwire.org`.

Probably the only problem you'll run into as a result of the content in this chapter is that you'll need to have sendmail installed; otherwise, Tripwire won't be able to send you email notifications. If you followed the details of this chapter, then you'll have removed sendmail and will have to add it back. If you reinstall the sendmail package, don't forget to use chkconfig to disable the sendmail server!

Tripwire (or any IDS) can be a very valuable addition to your firewall, and a boon to security. As with all such tools, though, it's not infallible or universal, so don't rely solely on it.

Integrating a Wireless LAN

A very popular feature that many people are adding to their networks is a wireless LAN based on the IEEE 802.11b standard. Typically, this involves adding a Wireless Access Point (WAP) to an existing Ethernet network. The real relevance here is to make sure that the new wireless segment of the network works properly with the firewall.

When you constructed the DHCP server configuration earlier in this chapter, you reserved an IP address for a Wireless Access Point. In most cases, connecting a WAP to your network is as simple as hooking the WAP up to your Ethernet switch. The WAP will usually bridge the wireless network to the main wired network, and computers connected to the wireless network will behave identically to computers connected to a wire. That is, systems on the wireless network will have access to the internal DHCP and DNS daemons, and will be protected by the firewall.

However, there are a few caveats for this case. First, many (if not most) of the inexpensive WAPs on the market require a Windows system for configuration. If your system is strictly Unix or Linux-based, you may have some troubles. Even some WAPs that are advertised as supporting the standard SNMP still do not have enough information available to actually make that possible. This can be either a minor inconvenience or a major headache, depending on your situation.

A larger, and vastly more dangerous problem, is that the WAP's bridging is a two-edged sword. It provides machines on the wireless network transparent access to the internal network, but this can be a huge vulnerability if misconfig-ured. Specifically, the 802.11b standard supports a Wired Equivalent Privacy (WEP) scheme that includes encryption of transmissions between the nodes and the WAP. However, most WAPs are shipped with this functionality disabled; even if it's enabled, it's been cracked rather completely, to the extent where it really has to be regarded as insecure. Additionally, some WAPs themselves are not highly secure beyond WEP, and can easily be hijacked by attackers.

The potential issue here is that after you've gone to all that trouble to secure your private network from the wild, wild Internet, you add a WAP and open it right up again. Maybe your neighbor notices you have a wireless network running and decides to mooch off your bandwidth (which may violate the terms of service with your ISP), or an attacker may notice your unsecured wireless LAN and decide to do some real damage.

Unfortunately, discussing solutions to these issues is beyond the scope of this book. The goal here is simply to make sure you know what you're getting yourself into. The firewall configuration discussed in this chapter will be available to your wireless network, but that can cut both ways. Make sure you do your homework on 802.11b, its WEP security scheme, and the particular WAP hardware you purchase before turning on that switch. Above all, be aware that using a wireless LAN vastly reduces your network's security. Your firewall will still protect you from typical "script kiddie" attacks on the Internet, but adding a wireless LAN will make you easy pickings for anyone who is truly motivated to attack your systems.

Enhancing the DNS Server

One thing that you'll probably very quickly notice is that if you have two machines on the internal network, they can only refer to each other by IP address. For example, if you wish to access the firewall itself, you have to refer to it as 192.168.0.1, as in this example for SSH: `ssh -l root 192.168.0.1`. Depending on how you use your network, this may not be a problem, but then again you might want a better solution.

One alternative is to assign common hostnames in /etc/hosts. (This file works as a sort of "mini-DNS" for the local computer, by mapping IP addresses to names.) Unfortunately, this means you have to maintain the same /etc/hosts entries on multiple machines, and it doesn't work well with dynamic IP addresses used by DHCP. A better option is desirable.

Well, you've already got a DNS server running, so why not extend that? By adding some entries to /etc/named.conf, you can instruct it to create an internal "zone" for your network. The ISC's bind server actually has a degree of integration with the ISC's dhcpd DHCP server, which makes it pretty painless to dynamically update host names when IP addresses change . . . once you've got it running, at least.

The main challenge is that you'll also have to create a zone file for your internal network, which can be a rather arcane process. Your best bet here is to consult the ISC's documentation on bind and dhcpd. This one might be a challenge, and it may not be worth it for a small number of hosts, but if you have more than a few computers on your internal network, you should consider it.

Booting from Read-Only Media

Suppose your firewall is compromised, and an attacker somehow gets inside. The main risk here is that she does something permanent to the system that lets her get back in whenever she wants to. However, what if the firewall's file systems were mounted read-only? In that case, she wouldn't be able to write to disk, and it would be impossible for her to do much to the system.

This involves more than just mounting the hard drive partitions as read-only, of course, because the attacker could always just remount them as read-write. What you *really* need here is read-only media—something that physically can't be written to, such as a CD.

Normally this isn't possible on a typical workstation or even server, because so many files have to change frequently, such as log files, spool files for printers, and so on. However, this system is a firewall, and not much changes at all. The only dynamic thing the firewall does is generate log messages—and if you've implemented the remote logger described earlier, even that doesn't get written to the local disk.

So, it's very possible to boot a firewall from a read-only medium such as a CD, and run it from there. This requires a significant amount of work, of course, and you'll have to chase down a lot of loose ends to make it work. There are tools available that help you do this, such as the Read-Only Linux work at `www.ultimeth.net/RdoLinux/` maintained by UltiMeth Systems.

Booting your firewall from a read-only medium such as a CD or a physically write-protected disk might be a lot of work, but by now you should know the basics of what you need to do it. If nothing else, you can just treat it as an academic exercise: How would *you* go about doing this?

Setting Up a VPN with SSH

If the network you've set up needs to be occasionally connected to another (such as connecting to an employer's network from home), there's a good chance you're familiar with the notion of a virtual private network. A VPN is just two otherwise disconnected networks at separate locations that are connected via some kind of encrypted connection. The most popular method is the "IP Secure" (IPSec) protocol developed for the IP version 6 next-generation Internet project. However, most devices and software that support IPSec tend to be expensive, limited in functionality, or difficult to configure.

However, if you're willing to roll up your sleeves and do it yourself, you can put together a really slick VPN by using PPP across an encrypted SSH connection. Using PPP allows you to create actual network interfaces on your system, so you can do whatever routing you need to do to connect your two computers or networks transparently.

Here it is in a nutshell: You need Linux systems on both ends of the VPN "pipe," and you need root access to both. The destination machine needs to have an SSH server running. Then, you just log in to that machine via the SSH protocol (such as by using OpenSSH), and run the PPP daemon pppd on the remote end. Locally, you also run pppd and connect the two. Voila! An instant VPN. Figure 16-3 depicts this scenario.

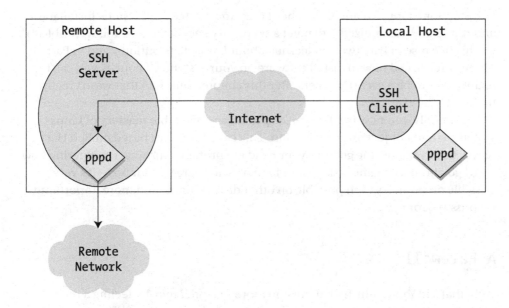

Figure 16-3. A VPN using PPP over SSH

Of course it's not *quite* that simple, but it almost is. The real challenge is to connect the two pppd processes, which are running on different systems; getting them to communicate properly can be a bit tricky. What you have to do is somehow map their standard inputs and standard outputs to each other. If you hunt around on the Internet, you'll find a variety of programs in Perl or C that do this for you. However, even with these tools, you still have to physically establish the connections between the servers, meaning that you also have to automate several things.

Going into this in detail would really be getting off track for this book. However, a complete solution for a VPN using PPP over SSH automated by an expect script is presented on the web site for this book, at www.apress.com. If you're interested, check it out.

Summary

In this chapter, you learned how to construct a firewall. You started with a stock Red Hat Linux installation and customized the package list to exclude anything that's not strictly necessary. Then you installed a script establishing a set of firewall rules that actually set up the protections for the network. Finally, you installed and configured some software that provides important services to your internal, protected machines.

Stop for a moment and think about that. You started with a stock installation, and tuned and customized it to meet a set of very specific needs. You were able to do this because in Part Two you learned about Linux distributions, and in Part Three you learned how to install software on your system. Of course, you can't really claim to be a security expert after this chapter, but then that wasn't really the point.

Hopefully, you now feel like you've gained a respectable mastery of Linux systems—and not just one distribution. This case study was based on Red Hat Linux, but even now the gears in your head are probably turning, considering how you'd go about this same task on a Debian or Slackware system. Yes—it's very possible on both. It's even possible on other distributions, and more importantly it's possible for *you*.

A Farewell

Well, that's it! You've finished; there's no more to read. *I* may be feeling a little sentimental, but if I've accomplished my goal, *you're* not! Hopefully you've had a peek into the world of Linux. Actually, you should have had quite a bit more than a peek; you should have had a guided introduction, and a basic education. If I've accomplished my goal, you should be feeling excited about the possibilities that await you, and the freedom you now have to compute *your way*. Have fun, and happy hacking!

Bibliography

Drake, Joshua. *Linux Networking HOWTO*. CommandPrompt, Inc., 2000.
`www.linuxdoc.org/HOWTO/Net-HOWTO/index.html`.

Russell, Rusty. *Linux 2.4 NAT HOWTO*.
`netfilter.samba.org/documentation/HOWTO/NAT-HOWTO.html`.

Russell, Rusty. *Linux 2.4 Packet Filtering HOWTO*.
`netfilter.samba.org/documentation/HOWTO/packet-filtering-HOWTO.html`.

SecurityFocus. Bugtraq mailing list archive.
`online.securityfocus.com/archive/1`.

Ziegler, Robert L. *Linux Firewalls, Second edition*. New Riders Publishing, 2002. ISBN 0735710996.

Appendix

Pulling It All Together

You've done it! You've reached the end of this book. If you've actually read (or at least reviewed) the entire thing, then hopefully you know a lot more than you did before about the guts of Linux systems. This appendix wraps things up, makes a few suggestions about what to do with your shiny new knowledge, and tries to play psychic a little bit by discussing future trends.

Running with the Ball: Additional Configurations

The case studies in this book introduced you to three common general system configurations. Where can you go from there? Well, with a little creativity, you can build some really interesting things. Here are a few suggestions:

- **Start with the desktop configuration and install the iptables scripts from the firewall configuration**. With a little tweaking, you can set up a desktop system that functions as a simple firewall for a network, which may save you from having to have a separate firewall computer.

- **Start with the firewall configuration and install a web and e-mail (SMTP) server**. (Be security conscious, though!) With a suitable cable modem or DSL connection, this is a great way to run your own Internet domain from your home or office.

- **As a more advanced project, build your own virtual private network (VPN) using *two* Linux systems at different locations**. (Chapter 16 discussed this briefly using the Point-to-Point Protocol over SSH; you can start there or use an actual standard IPSec software package.) This can be as simple or as complicated as you need it to be, and you can do anything from simply connecting your home PC to the office network to permanently linking two different sites as a so-called extruded subnet.

With a little experience and creativity, you'll amaze even yourself with the really cool things you can do with Linux-based operating systems. It's a really great feeling when you tame the Linux wilderness and pull off an elegant hack.

Continuing Education

It's no secret that the Linux world changes quickly. As a result, the level of mastery you reach is directly proportional to the amount of time you spend educating yourself. So, if you're really serious about mastering Linux, you have to be willing to spend the time to stay informed. This section discusses some good resources to that end.

Linux-Kernel List

If you want to hang out with the *real* Linux gurus, you need to follow the kernel hackers' mailing list. Known as the linux-kernel list (sometimes abbreviated as "l-k"), much of the content is very technical in nature. However, it does have a lot of information useful to nondevelopers on issues and trends related to the kernel, so it's worthwhile to follow. Information on subscribing to the linux-kernel list is available at vger.kernel.org/majordomo-info.html. This list is *extremely* high traffic, so you may instead wish to check out some of the excellent summary sites, such as Kernel Traffic at kt.zork.net/kernel-traffic/.

Distribution Mailing Lists

Another invaluable resource is the mailing list for your distribution. Typically, each distribution will have separate lists for the production-quality version and any testing or beta versions that are in development. If you're really interested in staying on top of trends and future developments, follow the beta lists, because that's where the action is. The following links can get you started with the mailing lists for each of the sample distributions discussed in this book:

- **Red Hat Linux**: www.redhat.com/mailing-lists/

- **Slackware Linux**: slackware.com/lists/

- **Debian GNU/Linux**: www.debian.org/MailingLists/

Perhaps most of all, keep an open mind. Many users frequently become familiar with a preferred distribution and tend to ignore or even dismiss (or worse!) the other distributions. This is a mistake for anyone who truly wishes to master a system, since there are *always* compromises in a given distribution, and each is best at something. Whenever you get ready to upgrade, consider checking out another distribution; at best, you may find it superior and switch, and at worst you are reminded how good you've already got it. Most likely you'll just learn something new along the way. After all, I didn't learn enough to write this book by spending all my time on one distribution!

Tracking Ongoing Work and Initiatives

The Linux world is a very active place. Believe it or not, this book really focuses exclusively on *traditional* applications of Linux systems. In fact, there's a great deal of research and engineering going on to push Linux (the kernel) in directions that few—or perhaps even no—operating systems have gone before. Here are a few initiatives, traditional and otherwise, that may impact the future of Linux.

Pursuing Security

The world today is an increasingly complicated and dangerous place, and nowhere is this more evident than in the world of computing. Information security has become the top priority of many major corporations, and undoubtedly interest will only continue to grow.

Linux, of course, gets its share of this attention. The U.S. National Security Agency (NSA), for example, is spearheading an effort to develop a "Security-Enhanced" Linux kernel, SE-Linux. You can find more information at www.nsa.gov/selinux/. The NSA also supports many smaller-scale security-related projects. Private companies and other organizations are also developing technologies such as encrypted filesystems, secure networking and VPN technologies, and kernel-level security features.

As information security becomes increasingly prominent in the industry, watch for similar progress to be made in the Linux arena.

Improving the Kernel

There is much debate today (some objective, much not so objective) about whether Linux (as a kernel) is "ready for the enterprise." The answer to this is probably a matter of professional opinion, and like anything else, there are things Linux is good at and things it is poor at. This situation is also true for whether Linux is "ready for the desktop."

However, it's an indisputable truth that a vast amount of engineering effort is taking place to improve the performance of the Linux kernel in a number of areas. Some of these improvements are to make a good thing better, and others are to address pronounced weaknesses. Effort is ongoing in both server and desktop performance areas.

For example, there are a number of projects to improve the kernel's performance and features as a server. There are several journaling filesystems in development, with status ranging from production-ready to deep academic research. On the desktop side, there are several efforts to improve the responsiveness of the core "virtual machine" to provide for smoother performance on desktop systems.

With companies joining the free and open source software movement (and providing the accompanying financial resources), you should expect to see a lot of progress on Linux and Linux-based operating systems in the coming years. Who knows, maybe someday Linux really *will* achieve world domination.

Stretching and Squeezing the System

Some people claim that there's a sea change underway in the computing industry. The point to rapid growth in the wireless and "embedded systems" markets as proof that the world is migrating away from wired desktop systems toward the somewhat ill-defined notion of "mobile computing." Here again, Linux is being stretched and squeezed to fit into this potential new world order.

Like any new area, this is an extremely nebulous field. It's hard to pin down exactly what "embedded computing" means, for example. However, given current trends, you can be pretty sure that wherever the world goes, Linux will be there, too. There are a number of companies that are working toward scaling Linux to fit into embedded devices, and there are even several companies releasing actual handheld computing devices that run Linux.

NOTE *There's already at least one Linux-based PDA on the market— namely, Sharp's Zaurus SL-5500 product, which you can find today in your local electronics store. You can find information on the Zaurus at Sharp's web site (*`www.sharp-usa.com`*).*

Actually, Linux itself (that is, the kernel) is pretty lean and mean to begin with, so it takes a comparatively small amount of effort to get Linux to run on embedded devices. However, by now you should realize that most of the *real* work gets done not by the kernel, but by the distribution that runs on it. So, the task of developing embedded Linux is less a task of kernel development than it is developing the distribution—the user interface, system libraries, and so on. Expect to see a lot of work in this area in coming years, as well.

Summary

Linux is constantly evolving. Maybe the future computing world will look just like it does today only with faster computers, or maybe it will look radically different. Either way, there's a good chance Linux will be there in some form. Keep on top of things, stay informed, and enjoy the ride!

Welcome to the world of Linux.

Index

Symbols and Numbers

A

B

Printed in the United States
by Baker & Taylor Publisher Services